Accounting and Federal Regulation

Accounting and Federal Regulation

James P. Bedingfield, D.B.A., C.P.A.

Associate Professor of Accounting
University of Maryland

Reston Publishing Company, Inc.
Reston, Virginia
A Prentice-Hall Company

Library of Congress Cataloging in Publication Data

Bedingfield, James P.
    Accounting and federal regulation.

    Bibliography: p. 302
    Includes index.
    1. Accounting—Law and legislation—United States.   I. Title.
KF1357.B4   343.73'034   81-8532
ISBN 0-8359-0052-5   347.30334   AACR2
ISBN 0-8359-0051-7   (pbk.)

10   9   8   7   6   5   4   3   2   1

Printed in the United States of America

To Dr. Howard W. Wright
Teacher, colleague, and friend.

Contents

107255

Preface

This book was occasioned by my perception of a number of factors that are important to accounting and yet undocumented in its literature:

· *Accounting in the United States is usually considered synonomous with generally accepted accounting principles (GAAP).* GAAP is of, by, and for the accounting profession. GAAP is accounting; accounting is GAAP. Very few inroads are permitted in this perceptual set by non-GAAP, or quasi-GAAP, or extra-GAAP material. The most noteworthy inroad is that of accounting for Federal income tax purposes. However, this is usually dismissed as not being "real" (i.e., GAAP) accounting. It is "income tax accounting." Income tax accounting is an area of accounting that traces its development and derives its legitimacy from Federal law, and not from an historical, evolutionary process that has wrought GAAP. Rather, it is regarded as the product of political and bureaucratic considerations.

Legitimacy based on Federal statute is the root for the Securities and Exchange Commission's (SEC) involvement in the area of accounting. It is widely recognized that the SEC has virtual power to dictate the accounting principles for the companies that it regulates (i.e., the largest entities in the U.S.). In the main, however, it has elected not to unleash the full force of its regulation; rather, it attempts to accommodate its legislative mandate within the framework of GAAP.

Many (accountants and others) would stop with these two scions of accounting in enumerating the inroads made by Federal regulation. I do *not* do so here. Rather, I recall a comment (related to me by an employee of a Federal agency) of an executive of American Telephone and Telegraph Company, who said: "To AT&T, depreciation is whatever the Federal Communications Commission says that it is!" I feel that this comment distills the feeling of many businessmen who are faced with regulations that employ accounting as a *tool*.

If one accepts the premise that the Federal regulatory use of accounting is important, the issue of the quantity and quality of this regulation arises. Who regulates via accounting? Who is regulated? How is the basic accounting (GAAP) model modified in fulfilling its regulatory role? This book is intended to answer such questions.

· *Regulators are concerned with regulating, and not with preserving the sanctity of the accounting model.* A staff member of one of the agencies reported upon in this book was defending a proposed accounting regulation of his agency. It was pointed out to him that the regulation contained a technically *incorrect* definition of an accounting term. This staff member's response was that "This is the definition if we say that it is!" So the question arises: How much sacrificing of the GAAP accounting model has been carried out in the name of regulatory imperatives?

· *A broad range of Federal agencies employ accounting as a regulatory tool.* The major users of this tool (as I have identified them) comprise the subset of agencies reported upon in this book. A review of the Table of Contents points out the specific agencies identified. Each agency is responsible for the regulation of one *or more* industry (e.g., the Interstate Commerce Commission regulates railroads, trucking companies, bus lines, and commodity pipelines). The deeper one gets immersed in the clockwork of Federal regulations, the clearer it becomes that all economic entities are indeed regulated by the Federal government.

· *Accounting has a role as a tool of public policy.* When a Federal agency wants to encourage or discourage certain behavior, it can often do so by changes in its accounting regulations. This is often noted in the area of income tax regulations; however, it can be found in virtually all regulated areas.

My consideration of all of these points led me to believe that a broad review of accounting's place in Federal regulation would serve a latent need in the accounting literature.

STRUCTURE OF THE BOOK

I reviewed all Federal agencies and attempted to distill a subset of those for whom accounting is a significant tool in their regulatory repertoire. A review of their regulations comprises the bulk of this text. The first chapter (a) introduces the reader to the clockwork of Federal regulations; (b) reviews the relationship between GAAP and Federal regulation; and, (c) provides a grounding in the basic terminology that will be relied upon in later chapters. The remaining chapters individually review a major area of Federal regulation. Generally, a single agency is covered in a chapter. However, where a number of agencies have virtually identical regulations, they are explored together. Further, where different agencies employ a similar mechanism, it is generally reviewed in depth only once, with appropriate cross-reference. For example, in the regulation of financial institutions, all of the agencies reported upon have computerized models that evaluate the strengths and weaknesses inherent in the basic financial statements of their respective clienteles. Only one such model is reviewed in detail.

Each agency that is reviewed is first introduced to the reader before the accounting regulations are explored. I have attempted to give the reader a feel for the scope of the agency by reviewing such things as who heads the agency; of what department it is a component; what laws it enforces; what and how many entities it controls; and so forth. This provides the contextual background for the exploration of the accounting regulations of the agency.

In reviewing the accounting regulations, I have attempted to do several things. First, departures from GAAP are highlighted. Second, an overview is given of the fabric of the regulation by illustrating account systems, length and content of reports, and the like. Quotations of the actual laws and regulations are used extensively in order to get the reader as close as possible to the regulatory pulse of the agency. I have tended to decide issues of summarization and interpretation versus actual quotation of the regulations in favor of the latter. Regulations are to be applied as written. They often lose something (e.g., intent, strength, thrust, etc.) in summarization. Where the regulations proved to be too lengthy, or did not otherwise lend themselves to quotation, or where I felt that a synthesis was necessary, I have interjected my observation.

I have included descriptions of such things as report length and schedule content in order to illustrate several points. One is that regulators are not above requiring those whom they regulate to go beyond the basic financial statements and to disclose much more detail that usually is not seen outside of the entity. Another is that there is quite often a mixing of financial and operating data in reports. Finally, regulators are not bound by what is possible under GAAP. They can, and do, require sortings of data that are neither contemplated under GAAP nor used for internal purposes by the entity; they only serve the needs of the regulators.

If any reader would like additional information about any of the agencies covered in the book, Appendix A, "Agency Addresses and Telephone Numbers," and Appendix B, "Selected Bibliography," should prove useful.

VALIDATION

Virtually all chapters were reviewed by someone involved with the accounting regulations at the various agencies. The comments of the reviewers were taken into consideration in revising the chapters. (Chapter 19, on the Internal Revenue Service, was reviewed by two of my colleagues at the University of Maryland.) I have thanked the reviewers individually; I now thank them collectively.

I would like to thank all of those other individuals who have facilitated my work on this book: several research assistants and typists at the University of Maryland, Mrs. Dorothy Barney, and a number of my colleagues in academia who, over the years, have encouraged my pursuit of this project.

I would like to single out four specific catalysts for this project. One was the Association of Government Accountants. It was upon appointment as chairman of its Regulatory Accounting Task Force that I put this project in motion. In particular, I would like to thank Mr. William C. Kennedy, chairman of AGA's National Research Board, who offered constant support during this project. The second catalyst was the time afforded me by the University of Maryland in granting me a sabbatical leave during which time this project was launched. The third catalyst was the Reston Publishing Company—in particular, Mr. Frederic K. Easter—who saw merit in the publication of this book. Finally, the fourth catalyst is the one of most lasting influence on this book and my entire career. This has been my association with Dr. Howard W. Wright (to whom this book is dedicated). It has been through my association with Dr. Wright that I have been introduced to and developed a keen interest in the area of accounting and Federal regulation.

Chapter 1

Introduction

The following quotation can be taken as typical of accounting's recognition of its raison d'etre of service to those in need of the information that it (accounting) can provide:

> Accounting is a service activity. Its function is to provide quantitative information, primarily financial in nature, about economic entities that is intended to be useful in making economic decisions—in making reasoned choices among alternative courses of action.[1]

In short, accounting is a tool. Its existence is a function of its usefulness.

Despite accounting's reliance on its utility, very little work has been done to document *who* those users (or consumers) are and *how* their needs vary. Equally important (and equally sparse as to documentation) is how the users apply accounting to their individual areas of interest.

Virtually all lists of accounting data consumers agree that the government, particularly the Federal government, is a major user of accounting data. This book is intended to flesh out the concept of the Federal government as a consumer of accounting data in its regulation of economic entities. In this review, a broad concept of "accounting" will also be used to encompass the kindred area of auditing (i.e., the Federal government's use of and requirements for audits in regulating entities will be explored).

THE FEDERAL GOVERNMENT AND ACCOUNTING

The Federal government is a very special consumer of accounting data. Most of accounting's consumers are either silent or, at best, have only minimal impact on the form and content of the financial reports they receive.

However, the Federal government's requirements are enunciated very clearly through (a) the laws passed by Congress (the legislative branch), (b) the regulations promulgated by the executive branch's agencies, and (c) the court decisions rendered by the judicial branch. In short, the Federal government has a very vocal and proactive relationship with the broad area of accounting.

The concept of the Federal government as a homogeneous entity is only useful to politicians, social commentators, individuals, etc., in need of a term that can be called upon to elicit some expected visceral reaction from an intended audience. Depending upon one's socioeconomic background and immediate role(s), the concept of the Federal government can shade from very positive to very negative. Such a simplistic view of the Federal government is discarded here. Rather, the emphasis is on the individual agencies that fall under the rubric of the "Federal government." There are over 400 individual Federal agencies that publish Federal regulations. It is from these agencies that the subset of those discussed in this book was taken.

Another pitfall to be avoided would arise from the careless reading of the title of this book. The title is "Accounting *and* Federal Regulation," *not* "Federal Regulation *of* Accounting." The agencies discussed in this book are in the business of regulating some form of economic activity. The nature of this regulation varies from that which is very active (as, for example, where companies' entry, rates charged, quality of service rendered, etc., are regulated) to that which is relatively passive (as, for example, where an agency only gathers information from companies which is then made available inside and/or outside of government). Each of the agencies discussed in the following chapters falls at some point on this spectrum of regulation.

Regardless of their degree of activism, these agencies all employ accounting as a tool to accomplish the regulatory mandate placed upon them by Congress. In some cases, Congress has specifically charged the agency with the responsibility to employ accounting as a tool in carrying out the provisions of the law. For example, the Urban Mass Transportation Administration Act of 1974 called for the Urban Mass Transportation Administration (UMTA, Chapter 8) to " . . . develop, test, and prescribe a reporting system to accumulate public mass transportation financial and operating information by uniform categories and a uniform system of accounts and records." In other cases, the agencies resort to accounting as a tool to accomplish a legislatively mandated goal. For example, the Federal Trade Commission's (FTC, Chapter 22) line of business reporting program was begun in 1973. The then-current commissioners decided that the following provision of the Federal Trade Commission Act *permitted* the FTC's initiative to establish such a system:

> . . . [The FTC is authorized] . . . to require, by general or special orders, corporations engaged in commerce . . . to file with the commission in such form as the commission may prescribe annual or special, or both annual and special reports or answers in writing to specific questions . . .

Since this law was passed in *1914,* no one could argue that Congress mandated such a program. Rather, Congress legislated a general requirement which, over a half-century later, gave rise to the FTC's line of business program. Thus, we find that Federal agencies use accounting as a regulatory tool *either* because the law dictates it *or,* as is more common, because the Federal agencies find it useful in carrying out their legal mandate.

Regulation

The concept of regulation is subject to many shades of interpretation. A narrow definition would limit itself to application for only the most tightly controlled entities, such as public utilities, that have a number of facets of their operations monitored by the government. Alternatively, a broad definition would hold that *any* entity that has to follow *any* regulation is indeed regulated.

The subset of Federal agencies reviewed in this book includes those which regulate industries that have traditionally been viewed as public utilities (e.g., electric, telephone, natural gas, transportation). Other major arenas of active Federal regulation include the oversight of financial institutions, security markets, and health care. The Federal government exercises a great deal of control in its roles of raising revenues through taxes and the expending of funds through grant, loan, and procurement programs. Finally, a somewhat unexpected form of regulatory use of accounting was found in the control of Federal elections' financing and reporting.

In the remainder of this chapter, the reader is first introduced to the clockwork of Federal regulation. There is a protocol of authority from the U.S. Constitution down through Congressional legislation and ending with the agency regulation. This protocol prevents any agency from becoming a latter-day Don Quixote and engaging in activity that is either unconstitutional or outside the purview of the law authorizing the agency's regulations. This protocol is closely tied to an indexing and citation system of laws and regulations which assists in comprehending the interplay between laws and regulations. Finally, the relationship between Federal regulation and generally accepted accounting principles is reviewed.

FEDERAL LAWS AND REGULATIONS

The route from the enactment of a law by Congress to the effectuation of that law on the actions of individuals or entities can be long and drawn out, or compressed (as in the case of emergency legislation). Regardless of the time horizon involved, the documentary trail is the same. When the law is passed by the Congress, it is given a "slip law" citation such as *P.L. 87-653.* This is translated as shown in Figure 1-1.

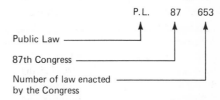

FIGURE 1-1. Format for Slip Law Citation.

The slip laws are accumulated and published annually as sequential additions to the *U.S. Statutes at Large.* For example, the law cited above can be cited as *76 Stat. 528.* This means that it can be found in Volume 76 of the U.S. Statutes at Large beginning at page 528.

All laws are codified (i.e., collated by topic) in the *U.S. Code.* The U.S. Code is arranged by *Title* (i.e., major subject heading). Table 1-1 contains the Titles found in the U.S. Code. For example, Title 10 of the U.S. Code is reserved for the Armed Forces. The law cited above can be found in section 2306(f) of Title 10. This is commonly cited as *10 USC 2306(f).*

Finally, some laws are given a vernacu-

lar title by the Congress, the news media, industry, or the public at large. The law that has been used as an example here in tracing citations is commonly known as the Truth-in-Negotiations Act. (This law is discussed in Chapter 16.)

The Constitution's division of Federal power among the three branches of the Federal government calls for Congress to pass the laws and for the executive branch, headed by the President, to " . . . take care that the laws be faithfully executed. . . . "[2] Over 400 executive agencies are involved in implementing the laws passed by Congress. The executive agencies implement the laws through the promulgation of agency regulations. These regulations appear daily in the *Federal Register,* which is

TABLE 1-1
Titles of United States Code

1. General Provisions	15. Commerce and Trade	29. Labor	Works
2. The Congress	16. Conservation	30. Mineral Lands and Mining	41. Public Contracts
3. The President	17. Copyrights	31. Money and Finance	42. Public Health and Welfare
4. Flag and Seal, Seat of Government, and the States	18. Crimes and Criminal Procedure	32. National Guard	43. Public Lands
	19. Customs Duties	33. Navigation and Navigable Waters	44. Public Printing and Documents
5. Government Organization and Employees	20. Education	34. [Reserved]	45. Railroads
	21. Food and Drugs	35. Patents	46. Shipping
6. Surety Bonds	22. Foreign Relations and Intercourse	36. Patriotic Societies and Observances	47. Telegraphs, Telephones, and Radio-telegraphs
7. Agriculture	23. Highways		
8. Aliens and Nationality	24. Hospitals and Asylums	37. Pay and Allowances of the Uniformed Services	48. Territories and Insular Possessions
9. Arbitration	25. American Indians		
10. Armed Forces	26. Internal Revenue Code	38. Veterans' Benefits	49. Transportation
11. Bankruptcy	27. Intoxicating Liquors		50. War and National Defense; and Appendix
12. Banks and Banking	28. Judiciary and Judicial Procedure	39. Postal Service	
13. Census		40. Public Buildings, Property, and	
14. Coast Guard			

published by the Office of the Federal Register. The *Federal Register* was started in 1936. Each year is given a different volume number (e.g., Volume 46 is for 1981). The *Federal Register* is paged continuously during the year. For example, a *Federal Register* citation might appear as *44 FR 38826*. This would refer to page 38826 of the 1979 volume (i.e., Volume 44) of the *Federal Register*. It is customary to cite the date of the *Federal Register* (for example, 44 FR 38826, July 3, 1979) to facilitate location of the cited regulation.

The regulations of each agency are codified annually in the *Code of Federal Regulations* (CFR). The CFR consists of approximately 150 volumes which contain the regulations of all Federal agencies. It is organized by title. Table 1-2 lists the 50 titles of the CFR. Some of these titles coincide with those of the U.S. Code. Each title of the CFR can be broken down by subtitle, chapter, sub-chapter, part, subpart, section, paragraph, and divisions below paragraphs.

Citations in the CFR take the form *4 CFR Part 410* if an entire part of the CFR is being referenced. For example, *4 CFR Part 410* happens to be an entire standard issued by the Cost Accounting Standards Board. If one were interested in only the "definitions" used in this standard, this would be cited as *4 CFR 410.30*. The ".30" is the section designation. Further designations are available through the use of additional alphanumeric extensions as shown in Figure 1-2.

Some agencies have complete titles

TABLE 1-2
Titles of the Code of Federal Regulations

1. General Provisions	15. Commerce and Foreign Trade	Firearms	38. Pensions, Bonuses, and Veterans' Relief
2. [Reserved]	16. Commercial Practices	28. Judicial Administration	
3. The President		29. Labor	39. Postal Service
4. Accounts	17. Commodity and Securities Exchanges	30. Mineral Resources	40. Protection of Environment
5. Administrative Personnel		31. Money and Finance: Treasury	41. Public Contracts and Property Management
6. Economic Stabilization	18. Conservation of Power and Water Resources		
7. Agriculture		32. National Defense	42. Public Health
8. Aliens and Nationality	19. Customs Duties	32A. National Defense, Appendix	43. Public Lands: Interior
9. Animals and Animal Products	20. Employee Benefits	33. Navigation and Navigable Waters	44. Emergency Management and Assistance
	21. Food and Drugs		
10. Energy	22. Foreign Relations	34. Education	45. Public Welfare
11. Federal Elections	23. Highways	35. Panama Canal	46. Shipping
12. Banks and Banking	24. Housing and Urban Development	36. Parks, Forests, and Public Property	47. Telecommunication
13. Business Credit and Assistance	25. American Indians		48. [Reserved]
	26. Internal Revenue	37. Patents, Trademarks, and Copyrights	49. Transportation
14. Aeronautics and Space	27. Alcohol, Tobacco Products and		50. Wildlife and Fisheries

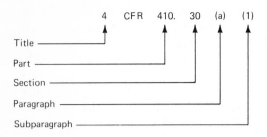

FIGURE 1-2. Format for Code of Federal Regulations Citation

devoted to them. For example, Title 26, Internal Revenue, is exclusively for the Internal Revenue Service. Other titles are shared by a number of agencies. For example, Title 41, Public Contracts and Property Management, is shared by some 36 agencies. Some agencies have regulations in more than one title. For example, the U.S. Coast Guard has regulations in Title 33, Navigation and Navigable Waters; Title 46, Shipping; and, Title 49, Transportation.

If one wants to have up-to-date content of a particular regulation appearing in the CFR, it is necessary to update the most recent annual volume with any regulations that were issued since its publication. This is done by consulting the Office of the Federal Register's monthly "List of CFR Sections Affected." This will update the annual volume of the CFR to the most recently completed month. The most recent daily issues of the *Federal Register* contain a cumulative (for that month) list of CFR parts affected. This will update the regulations to the most recent day on which the *Federal Register* was issued.

While the *Federal Register* recently has been averaging nearly 7,000 pages

per month, this does not translate into a similar increase in the CFR (which is currently approaching 100,000 pages in length). This is because the *Federal Register* publishes more than actual amendments in the CFR. It is also used to publish (a) Presidential documents (e.g., ceremonial proclamations, non-ceremonial proclamations, executive orders), (b) proposed amendments to the CFR, and (c) agency notices and announcements (e.g., of meetings open to the public).

Proposed regulations that are published in the *Federal Register* generally allow at least a 60 day period during which interested parties may submit comments. *Final* regulations (i.e., issued after proposed regulations have been re-evaluated in light of comments received) generally become effective no sooner than 30 days from their publication in the *Federal Register.*

Agency regulations can sometimes be found outside the CFR, as, for example, where the regulations are embodied in instructions on how various forms or reports are to be compiled. Even here, though, it is fairly common to find the forms (and, therefore, instructions) referenced in the CFR.

GENERALLY ACCEPTED ACCOUNTING PRINCIPLES

When a Federal agency initiates a program that entails reliance on accounting data—as the Energy Information Administration (EIA) did recently with its Financial Reporting System for major energy companies (Chapter 14) —it does *not* have to develop from scratch a complete accounting framework for its own unique purposes. At any point in time there exists a body or "code" of accounting which is referred to as *generally accepted accounting principles*. The following description of generally accepted accounting principles underscores their temporal nature:

> Generally accepted accounting principles encompasses the conventions, rules, and procedures necessary to define accepted accounting practice at a particular time. The standard of "generally accepted accounting principles" includes not only broad guidelines of general application, but also detailed practices and procedures.
>
> Generally accepted accounting principles are conventional—that is, they become generally accepted by agreement (often tacit agreement) rather than by formal derivation from a set of postulates or basic concepts. The principles have developed on the basis of experience, reason, custom, usage, and, to a significant extent, practical necessity.[3]

The development of generally accepted accounting principles is best viewed as an evolutionary process, whereby a combination of practice and formal codification by established bodies has molded the existing structure. Over the last 50 years, the established bodies have increased in significance. These bodies are shown in Table 1-3. A Federal agency can tap into this existing body of generally accepted accounting principles *by reference,* and proceed to make whatever modifications it deems appropriate on an *exceptions* basis. This is what most of the agencies reported upon in this book have done.

A question that can be asked is, "Does Federal regulation affect generally accepted accounting principles?" The answer to this question—either affirmative or negative—would not affect the significance of investigating the use of accounting as an important regulatory tool. However, it would be of some interest to note if there is an interactive relationship between Federal regulation and generally accepted accounting principles or, alternatively, if generally accepted accounting principles evolve oblivious to the existence of Federal regulatory interest in accounting.

The answer proposed here is that there is an interaction between Federal regulation and generally accepted accounting principles. A complete litany of all areas of interfacing between that malleable body known as generally accepted accounting principles and Federal regulation is not presented. Rather, some of the more prominent vignettes are cited.

TABLE 1-3

From	To	Body	Pronouncements
1938	1959	Committee on Accounting Procedure	Accounting Research Bulletins
1959	1973	Accounting Principles Board	Opinions
1973	Present	Financial Accounting Standards Board	Statements of Financial Accounting Standards

Securities and Exchange Commission (SEC)

For nearly 50 years, the SEC has had legal primacy for determining the form and content of the financial statements of most large publicly owned companies. The SEC has generally tried to work along with the accounting profession's standard-setting bodies. Only occasionally has the SEC publicly broken ranks with the profession. The reason for this degree of harmony is that the standard-setting bodies have maintained a close working arrangement with the SEC so that most potential areas of dispute are settled before they are aired in public. A recently instigated program requires the SEC to submit an annual report to Congress on the accounting profession and the profession's stewardship over the areas of accounting and auditing standards. Suffice it to say that the SEC has significant formal and informal leverage over the accounting profession.

Internal Revenue Service (IRS)

Most accountants might like to regard income tax accounting as a separate and distinct discipline from the broad, general area of financial accounting (i.e., generally accepted accounting principles). However, the facts indicate otherwise. Professor Eldon Hendriksen concluded as follows:

> In more recent years, the income tax rules have had a considerable adverse effect on accounting theory and principles. The tendency to accept income tax provisions as accepted accounting principles and practices is

unfortunate. The following are examples: (1) Any depreciation method acceptable for tax purposes is acceptable for accounting purposes also, regardless of whether or not it follows good accounting theory in the situation. (2) Lifo must be used for financial reporting purposes if it is used in the tax return. (3) Items that should be capitalized in some cases are charged to expense to obtain the earliest possible tax deduction. (4) Since the tax law does not permit it, no provision is generally made for "accruing" repair and maintenance expenses except indirectly and haphazardly through accelerated depreciation.[4]

Federal Energy Regulatory Commission (FERC)

The FERC, through its predecessor agency, the Federal Power Commission (FPC), established its authority to set the accounting principles for reports filed with it *and* for reports issued to stockholders. Although the law was silent as to the FPC's primacy over reports to stockholders, the U.S. Court of Appeals held that the legislative history of the Federal Power Act indicated that the FPC's power extended control over companies' published financial statements.

Government Contractors

In its 1976 survey of the financial reporting and accounting practices of major companies that engage in extensive contracting with the Federal government, Price Waterhouse & Co. noted:

> Inventory costing concepts used almost solely in government contract accounting are the program method

of accounting for long-term contracts and the inclusion of general and administrative costs in inventory. Under the program method, costs are deferred and amortized over the estimated number of units to be delivered, frequently including anticipated future orders.[5]

Additionally, there are some modifications to methods of revenue recognition under long term contracts that are usually limited to government contractors.

Addendum to APB Opinion No. 2

The Accounting Principles Board attempted to define the nexus between generally accepted accounting principles and the accounting practices of "regulated industries" in an Addendum to its Opinion No. 2:

1. The basic postulates and the broad principles of accounting comprehended in the term "generally accepted accounting principles" pertain to business enterprises in general. These include public utilities, common carriers, insurance companies, financial institutions, and the like that are subject to regulation by government, usually through commissions or other similar agencies.

2. However, differences may arise in the application of generally accepted accounting principles as between regulated and non-regulated businesses, because of the effect in regulated businesses of the rate-making process, a phenomenon not present in non-regulated businesses. Such differences usually concern mainly the time at which various items enter into the determination of net income in accordance with the principle of matching costs and revenues. For example, if a cost incurred by a regulated business during a given period is treated for rate-making purposes by the regulatory authority having jurisdiction as applicable to future revenues, it may be deferred in the balance sheet at the end of the current period and written off in the future period or periods in which the related revenue accrues, even though the cost is of a kind which in a nonregulated business would be written off currently. However, this is appropriate only when it is clear that the cost will be recoverable out of future revenues, and it is not appropriate when there is doubt, because of economic conditions or for other reasons, that the cost will be so recoverable.

3. Accounting requirements not directly related to the rate-making process commonly are imposed on regulated businesses by orders of regulatory authorities, and occasionally by court decisions or statutes. The fact that such accounting requirements are imposed by the government does not necessarily mean that they conform with generally accepted accounting principles. For example, if a cost, of a kind which in a non-regulated business would be charged to income, is charged directly to surplus pursuant to the applicable accounting requirements of the regulatory authority, such cost nevertheless should be included in operating expenses or charged to income, as appropriate in financial statements intended for use by the public.

4. The financial statements of regulated businesses other than those prepared for filing with the government for regulatory purposes preferably should be based on generally accepted accounting principles (with appropriate recognition of rate-making considerations as indicated in paragraph 2) rather than on systems of accounts or other accounting requirements of the government.[6]

Some say that the Addendum raises more issues than it settles. For example, what is a *regulated industry*? The Addendum tells us what the term includes, but not what it excludes. In a sense, all entities are in a "regulated industry." In fact, the Financial Accounting Standards Board has recently recognized that the waters are so unsettled as to warrant further investigation. It currently has a project underway entitled "Effect of Rate Regulation on Accounting for Regulated Enterprises."

Accounting and Deregulation

Currently, there is a move afoot in Washington to eliminate unnecessary Federal regulation. For example, the Motor Carrier Act of 1980 eliminated much of the exclusivity of operating rights (i.e., the right to serve a route) that was previously afforded trucking companies. The Financial Accounting Standards Board immediately reacted to this by enacting rules whereby the carriers (i.e., trucking companies) would have to write off and disclose the unamortized cost of any operating rights that had been purchased or otherwise acquired by the carriers. Thus, even the curtailment of regulation can have accounting ramifications.

Other examples could be cited, but the point has been made: There is an interactive relationship between accounting and Federal regulatory programs.

PUBLIC UTILITIES

Governmental control over economic entities has been greatest for that group

known as public utilities. Public utilities are entities that provide necessary public services (such as electricity, natural gas, telephone, etc., services). In exchange for the right to provide the service under conditions that limit (or eliminate) any competition, the public utility must render adequate service to all customers at reasonable rates. Competition is usually not available to assist in setting a price for the services of the public utility. Therefore, the relevant governmental agency usually intercedes by monitoring the rates and rate structure of the utility. Since several of the Federal agencies covered in this book control industries that are public utilities, a brief review of the meshing of accounting and rate regulation for public utilities is presented. This will serve both to familiarize the reader with certain terms that are germane to accounting for regulated utilities and to eliminate the need to restate these terms for each agency involved in such regulation.

The establishment of rates for a public utility begins with the determination of the *revenue requirement* of the entity. The revenue requirement is the amount of revenue that the utility is expected to need in light of its anticipated demand, costs, etc., in order to cover its operating expenses and provide a return on capital.

Regulatory commissions control the operating expense element, in part, by setting such accounting policies as depreciation, inventory costing, etc. Also, they designate which expenses are unallowable for rate-making purposes (i.e., they cannot enter into the computation of the revenue requirement). Allowable expenses are said to be "above the line" items; unallowable expenses are said to be "below the line" items. The "line" referred to is the net operating income from regulated operations. Thus, above the line expenses are deducted from operating revenues in arriving at the utility's net operating income from its regulated operations. Below the line expenses are deducted from this net operating income from regulated operations in arriving at the utility's net income. Below the line expenses do not enter into the rate-making process. They are not underwritten by the utility's customers. They are borne by the stockholders.

In setting the return on the utility's investment in assets devoted to serving the public, the regulatory commission considers (a) the rate to be allowed and (b) the rate base (i.e., the investment base) to which the rate is to be applied. The rate base is measured by the cost (or other means of valuation such as "fair value") of the assets devoted to public use.

Accounting enters the consideration of the return on investment in two ways. First, the allowable return percentage is usually set, in part, in consideration of the existing debt/equity structure of the utility and its historic (accounting based) cost of capital. Secondly, accounting is integral to the costing (or other valuation) of the rate base. If a utility is not allowed to include an asset in the rate base (e.g., property under construction) it is not allowed a return on that property. Similarly, such practices as depreciation accounting, accounting for repairs and maintenance, accounting for retirements, etc., all affect the rate base and are controlled by pronouncements of the regulatory authority.

ACCOUNTING: A TOOL OF PUBLIC POLICY

Accounting has evolved as a "micro" information system to be applied on an entity by entity basis. Further, accounting has historically been "controlled" by accountants. The idea of accounting as a *tool* of "macro" regulation of entire industries, or the economy taken as a whole, is an outgrowth of the pervasive spread of government regulation. Only rarely are those in *policy-making* positions endowed with an accounting background. This dichotomy was commented upon some years ago by Professor Eli W. Clemens:

> Accounting systems mean many things to many people. To the accountant a system reflects an expression of precise but generalized principles applicable to many business enterprises. To management an accounting system may legitimately reflect an appraisal of business situation peculiar to the enterprise; with less justification it may reflect the special desires of management. To the tax collector and the regulator an accounting system reflects the determinants of the application of public policy. The interest of the accountant lies toward definity, precision, and immutability; in that way his profession is made a science. The interest of the others is practical usefulness. The querulous complaint of the accountant that "it is good regulation but poor accounting" epitomizes the conflict of views. Neither definity nor immediate pragmatic usefulness should be sacrificed too far to gain the other.[7]

It would be advisable to recollect this comment before reading each chapter in this book. Federal agencies exist to regulate. They do so, in part, by making that utilitarian art known as "accounting" serve another master—that of public policy as it is implemented through Federal regulation.

REFERENCE NOTES

1. Accounting Principles Board, *APB Statement No. 4: Basic Concepts and Accounting Principles Underlying Financial Statements of Business Enterprises,* October 1970, paragraph 40.

2. U.S., *Constitution of the United States of America,* Article 2, Section 3.

3. Accounting Principles Board, *op. cit.,* paragraphs 138, 139.

4. Eldon S. Hendriksen, *Accounting Theory* (3d. ed. rev.; Homewood, Ill.: R.D. Irwin Co., 1977), p. 49.

5. Price Waterhouse & Co., *Survey of Financial Reporting and Accounting Practices of Government Contractors* (New York: Price Waterhouse & Co., 1976), p. 21.

6. Accounting Principles Board, *APB Opinion No. 2: Accounting for the Investment Credit,* December 1962, pp. 4-5. (©1962, American Institute of Certified Public Accountants, Inc. Reprinted with permission.)

7. Eli W. Clemens, *Economics and Public Utilities* (New York: Appleton-Century-Crofts, Inc., 1950), p. 463.

Chapter 2

Bank Regulation:
Office of Comptroller of the Currency, Federal Reserve System, Federal Deposit Insurance Corporation

The Federal regulation of banks in the United States is vested in three agencies: the Office of the Comptroller of the Currency (OCC), the Federal Reserve System (FRS), and the Federal Deposit Insurance Corporation (FDIC). Some banks are under the purview of all of these agencies, others are under two agencies, and still others are under the control of only one agency. Finally, there are some banks that are not subject to regulation by these agencies.

There are over 15,000 commercial banks and mutual savings banks (less than 500) in the United States. Their composition by type and regulatory agency is shown in Figure 2-1.

Where the regulatory responsibilities of the Federal agencies overlap, effective control has been delegated to one of the agencies. The effective control—as to accounting and reporting regulation —is as follows:

	Percentage of all banks		Regulated by		
	Number	Assests	FDIC	FRS	OCC
National banks	30%	49%	√	√	√
State banks, members of FRS	7	16	√	√	
State banks, non-members of FRS, insured by FDIC	60	30	√		
State banks, non-members of FRS, not insured by FDIC	3	5			
	100%	100%			

FIGURE 2-1. Composition of Commercial and Mutual Savings Banks (*Source:* FDIC, *Annual Report*, 1978, p. 6).

Category	*Agency*
National banks	Office of Comptroller of the Currency
State banks, members of the Federal Reserve System	Federal Reserve System
State bank, nonmembers of the Federal Reserve System, insured by FDIC	Federal Deposit Insurance Corporation

The accounting and reporting regulations of these agencies are of two types. First, the agencies require that all banks periodically file financial statements with the agency. The form and content of these financial statements, known as *call reports,* is basically the same for all agencies. Each agency conducts periodic examinations of the banks over which it has effective control. Second, the agencies control the financial reporting practices of the banks (over which they have primary control) that are subject to the Federal securities regulations.

In the remainder of this chapter, each of the Federal agencies will be briefly reviewed in the chronological order of their establishment. Then, since the accounting regulations of the agencies are so similar, only those of the FDIC will be reviewed in depth to avoid repetition. Any significant exceptions involving the other agencies will be noted. FDIC was selected since it has primary regulatory control over the largest number of banks—state banks that are not members of the Federal Reserve System, but are insured by FDIC.

In the last section of the chapter, the regulation and reporting of bank holding companies is discussed.

OFFICE OF THE COMPTROLLER OF THE CURRENCY

The Office of the Comptroller of the Currency (OCC) is the oldest of the Federal agencies regulating banks, having been established in 1863 to oversee the newly organized national bank system. The OCC is headed by the Comptroller of the Currency who is appointed by the President, with concurrence of the Senate, to a five year term. The OCC operates through 14 geographical regions and is financed mainly by assessments levied on the national banks.

Prior to the establishment of the OCC, all banks were chartered and regulated at the state level. One characteristic that distinguishes the OCC from the other Federal agencies that regulate banks is that it alone can grant charters for national banks. The OCC also must approve mergers of banks where the resulting entity is to be a national bank. The OCC is very concerned with the competitive environment of banking. On the one hand, it wants enough banks available to provide the volume of banking services needed, at reasonable rates; on the other hand, it does not want so many banks that few of them can maintain a firm financial position during periods of economic recession. Figure 2-2 is an example of a decision by the OCC on a merger. The OCC's concern with both financial strength and competition is evident in its decisions.

In making its merger decisions, the OCC is required to gather the opinions of the other two banking agencies and the U.S. Attorney General's Office. The U.S. Attorney General's Office can go to court to block an OCC (or FDIC and FRS) approved merger.

Examinations

A bank examination is oriented toward reviewing the financial strength

CONCORD NATIONAL BANK,
Concord, N.H., and The Pittsfield National Bank, Pittsfield, N.H.

Names of banks and type of transaction	Total assets	Banking offices	
		In operation	To be operated
The Pittsfield National Bank, Pittsfield, N. H. (1020), with...	$ 4,520,000	1	———
and Concord National Bank, Concord, N. H. (318), which had	70,946,000	4	———
merged June 29, 1978, under charter and title of the latter bank (318). The merged bank at date of merger had	75,430,000	———	5

COMPTROLLER'S DECISION

Application has been made to the Comptroller of the Currency seeking prior permission to effectuate a merger of The Pittsfield National Bank, Pittsfield, N. H. ("Merging Bank"), into Concord National Bank, Concord, N. H. ("Charter Bank"), under the charter and title of Concord National Bank. Under the proposed merger, the sole office of Merging Bank would become a branch office of the resulting bank. The subject application rests upon an agreement executed between the proponent banks, and is incorporated herein by reference, the same as if fully set forth.

Merging Bank has operated as a national banking association since April 17, 1865, when it was granted charter number 1020 by this Office. As of December 31, 1977, Merging Bank had total commercial bank deposits of $4.0 million, and operated its sole banking office in Pittsfield.

Charter Bank was granted national banking association charter number 318 by this Office on March 15, 1864, and had total commercial bank deposits of $58.9 million as of December 31, 1977. A wholly-owned subsidiary of First Bancorp of New Hampshire, Inc., Manchester, N. H., a registered multi-bank holding company, Charter Bank operates a main office and three branch offices within the city of Concord.

The town of Pittsfield is located approximately 19 miles to the northeast of the city of Concord, both localities are in Merrimac County. The closest office of Charter Bank is approximately 16 miles distant from Merging Bank's office. Given the geographic distance separating the proponent banks, and the presence of competing banking alternatives, approval of the instant merger would not have the effect of eliminating any meaningful degree of existing competition between the two banks. Additionally, the potential for increased competition between Merging Bank and Charter Bank appears to be minimal.

Charter Bank proposes to improve and expand the banking services currently provided by Merging Bank, and to offer new banking services such as, trust services, credit cards, automatic savings plans and overdraft checking privileges. Additionally, through an increased legal lending limit, the resulting bank would be able to accommodate larger loan requests of the Pittsfield banking community. Considerations relative to convenience and needs are consistent with, and add weight toward, approval of this application.

The financial and managerial resources of both Charter Bank and Merging Bank are satisfactory, and should favorably enhance the future prospects of the resulting bank. The financial and managerial resources of Charter Bank's parent organization are also satisfactory.

Accordingly, applying the statutory criteria, it is the conclusion of the Office of the Comptroller of the Currency that this application is in the public interest, and should be, and hereby is, approved.

May 4, 1978.

SUMMARY OF REPORT BY ATTORNEY GENERAL

We have reviewed this proposed transaction and conclude that it would not have a substantial competitive impact.

* * *

CENTURY NATIONAL BANK OF BROWARD,
Fort Lauderdale, Fla., and Century National Bank of Coral Ridge, Fort Lauderdale, Fla.

Names of banks and type of transaction	Total assets	Banking offices	
		In operation	To be operated
Century National Bank of Coral Ridge, Fort Lauderdale, Fla. (14848), with	$107,275,000	3	———
and Century National Bank of Broward, Fort Lauderdale, Fla. (14554), which had	301,434,000	4	———
merged June 30, 1978, under charter and title of the latter bank (14554). The merged bank at date of merger had	408,709,000	———	7

COMPTROLLER'S DECISION

Pursuant to the Bank Merger Act (12 USC 1828(c)), an application has been filed with the Office of the Comptroller of the Currency that requests prior written consent to the proposed merger of Century National Bank of Coral Ridge, Fort Lauderdale, Fla. ("Merging Bank"), into Century National Bank of Broward, Fort Lauderdale, Fla. ("Charter Bank"), under the charter and title of Century National Bank of Broward. The subject application rests upon an agreement executed

FIGURE 2-2. Sample OCC Decision on a Merger (*Source:* OCC, *Annual Report,* 1978, p. 87).

and operating efficiency of the bank. (This is contrasted with an annual audit by a certified public accountant [CPA] which is concerned with the *fairness* of the presentation of the financial statements.) Such factors as the bank's capital adequacy, earning capacity, liquidity, and the general quality of its management are considered in the bank examination. Bank examinations also review the bank's compliance with Federal laws such as those pertaining to truth-in-lending and discrimination against minorities.

Until recently, all national banks were to be examined twice each year. One examination could be waived by the OCC during a two-year period. Due to its inability to keep up with this volume of examinations, the OCC modified its policy so that now, the following guidelines are in effect:

All national banks with assets of $100 million or more are examined at least once each year.

All national banks with assets of less than $100 million are examined at least once every 18 months.

All banks that present some supervisory concern to the OCC are examined at least twice each year.

The banks presenting supervisory concern include those designated by the OCC as falling in the following categories:

Explanation of Bank Descriptions Used:
Critical—Banks so characterized exhibit a combination of weaknesses and adverse financial trends which are pronounced to a point where the ultimate liquidity

and solvency of the institution and its continuance as an independent entity are in question. The probability of failure is high for such banks. . . .

The precarious condition of these banks and the attendant uncertainties as to possible contingent losses arising from the threatened or protracted litigation or from the prospects for further financial deterioration, combine to virtually preclude outside support from existing or prospective shareholders. Moreover, the traditional remedy of merger with or sale to a stronger institution is obviated by the same considerations and uncertainties.

Such institutions obviously require the most intense supervision and monitoring by the Comptroller's Office.

Serious—Banks in this category reflect combinations of all or some of the adverse factors noted for critical banks, except that the weaknesses and financial trends are not so severe as to threaten the immediate liquidity and solvency of the institution. The potential for failure is present but not pronounced. In addition to financial and management considerations, banks may also be placed in this category when significant violations of law or regulation are evident, when unsafe and unsound banking practices or policies first become apparent, or when self-dealing practices of officers and directors come to light. This is true even though such violations or practices may not yet be actually threatening the viability of the bank. Such banks also require continuous monitoring, supervision and attention from the OCC.

Close Supervision—The category includes banks that may be experiencing a combination of adverse factors noted for banks rated critical and serious to the same or lesser degree than those banks in the serious category. However, they possess certain characteristics more favorable than banks in the problem bank categories. Those favorable characteristics might include all or a combination of the following: A strong market position with solid fund sources and a diversified asset structure; a strong ownership affiliation; management quality; earnings capacity; and capital protection. These banks are less vulnerable than serious banks and their strength and financial capacity as a whole is such as to make failure a remote possibility. Nevertheless, certain problems remain and require more than ordinary supervisory concern and monitoring. Such banks have typically identified their problems and have implemented remedial action, but because of the nature of some of their problems, such as depressed real estate conditions, a return to a satisfactory condition is primarily dependent upon the rate of economic recovery of other factors beyond the bank's control.[1]

While the OCC's listing of troubled banks has numbered well over 100, few banks actually fail. From 1972–1976, only eight banks failed.[2] In part, the remedial measures required of banks subject to the OCC's special attention accounts for this. Also, many troubled banks elect to merge with "healthy" banks as a means of relieving their problems.

National Bank Surveillance System

The OCC is aided in its monitoring of national banks by an automated information system—the National Bank Surveillance System (NBSS). This system is described by the OCC as follows:

> The NBSS Bank Performance Report (BPR) is a refinement of the bank's official financial reports in a form which can be readily analyzed. The BPR is designed as a bank supervisory, examination, and management tool which shows the effect of management's decisions and economic conditions on the bank's performance and composition.

> The Bank Performance Report is only one portion of The National Bank Surveillance System (NBSS). While the BPR is designed as an analytical tool, the other elements of the NBSS are supervisory and administrative systems of the Office of the Comptroller of the Currency (OCC).

> . . . The bank's performance and composition ratios can be used in making decisions concerning the adequacy of earnings, liquidity, asset and liability management, capital adequacy, and future expansion or contraction. National bank examiners use the BPR in examination planning and control so that the examination will be as effective and efficient as possible. Bankers and examiners can use it in analyzing the earnings performance of the bank. Thus, the BPR is not simply a tool to be used by the OCC and other bank supervisory agencies. It is also a senior bank management tool, displaying data in a form for trend and level analysis of an individual bank and its peers. The BPR is designed for use in improving the performance of individual banks as well as the national banking system.[3]

The NBSS is composed of four basic elements:

The bank performance report (BPR). This is the display of the bank's financial information. The following partial table of contents (for banks with less than $300 million in assets) indicates the extensive nature of the report:

Significant Ratios

Balance Sheet Information

    Trend of Condition—Assets

    Trend of Condition—Liabilities and Capital

    Source and Uses of Funds

    Asset Distribution

    Liability Distribution

    Investment Securities Information

    Loan Mix

    Past Due Loan Analysis

    Uncollected Income Analysis

    Analysis of Allowance for Possible Loan Losses

    Capital Analysis

    Additional Capital Factors

    Dividend Analysis

Income Information

    Income Statement—Tax Equivalent

    Net Income Components

    Supplemental Information—Results from Operations

    Net Interest Earnings Analysis

    Capacity to Hedge Interest Margins

    Seasonal Trend Data

    Other Earnings Components

    Noninterest Expense Components

    Income Taxes and Nonoperating Income

The exact content of a BPR is controlled by a bank's size. The BPRs for large banks would have more detail than that noted above. Likewise, banks with less than $100 million in assets would have less detail in their BPRs.

Much of the BPR's analysis is carried out on a "peer group" basis. Each bank is classified into one peer group. Peer groups are formed on the basis of asset size, rural or urban location, and unit banks versus banks with branches. In analyzing an individual bank, the BPR not only displays the bank's current and comparative (five prior years) data, but the peer group's means are often shown as well as the bank's percentile in relation to the peer group. For example, the BPR might report that Bank A's loan growth rate is 30 percent while its peer group's mean growth rate is 20 percent. Thus, we know that Bank A is above the mean. Further, a percentile rank, of say 95, tells us exactly how far above the mean it is in relation to the total number of banks in the peer group. Here we know that 95 percent of the banks in this peer group have lower loan growth rates than Bank A.

Anomaly seventy rating system (ASRS). The data in the BPR are analyzed by ASRS. This system is described in the NBSS *User's Guide* as follows:

> The ASRS is a computerized scoring system which allocates the highest numerical score to those banks having the most abnormal positions, changes, and trends in performance or composition. The performance ASRS measures the current positions, the short-term changes, and the long-term trends of significant performance ratios. The composition ASRS measures the short-term changes in the components of certain groups of assets and liabilities. Those banks receiving the highest scores are selected for review.[4]

Analysis by an NBSS specialist. This component involves the review of a bank's BPR, ASRS ranking, and other bank-specific information by a national bank examiner who specializes in these reviews. The specialist reports his (or her) results to the relevant regional administrator of national banks.

Action control system (ACS). The ACS insures the follow-up weaknesses identified in the various other stages of the NBSS. It is described in the NBSS *User's Guide* as follows:

> This element is a separate computerized system that records: (a) banks selected for priority review; (b) any conditions of concern observed by the NBSS specialists; (c) the projected date correction is anticipated for each condition; (d) the desired level for each condition; and (e) each condition's current status. Status, progress, and summary reports are rendered at intervals to regional administrators and other senior OCC officials.
>
> Conditions of concern which have been recorded in this monitoring system cannot be removed until correction has been achieved. Conditions of concern which have been corrected are removed from the active file but are retained in an historical record.[5]

Banking Services

In addition to carrying out such traditional commercial banking activities as holding demand deposits, time deposits, and making various types of business and personal loans, the OCC permits national banks to perform such nontraditional services as (a) acting as a loan servicing agent for others (e.g., on mortgages), (b) administering credit card plans, (c) operating a local branch of the Post Office, (d) offering messenger services, (e) offering money orders, and, (f) providing data processing services. These services are generally compatible with those allowed to banks that are regulated by the FRS and FDIC. However, certain states prohibit some activities such as the operation of a Post Office.

FEDERAL RESERVE SYSTEM

The Federal Reserve System (FRS) was established in 1913. Its primary purpose is to control national monetary policy. It exercises this control over all national banks and state-chartered banks that have voluntarily joined the Federal Reserve System. Our concern here is not with its role in monetary policy, but rather with FRS control of the organization, administration, and reporting of its members.

The FRS is headed by a board of governors composed of seven members who serve 14 year terms. The members are appointed by the President, with the concurrence of the Senate. The FRS chairman (one of the seven members) is designated by the President.

The FRS is divided into 12 districts. Each district has a Federal Reserve Bank and, usually, one or more branches. It is through these district banks that most of the dealings with members are carried out. The FRS is funded mainly by interest on loans made to the Federal government and loans to member banks, and by assessments levied on member banks.

The FRS does *not* grant charters to banks. The Office of the Comptroller of the Currency (OCC) charters national banks and the various states (and territories) charter state (and territorial) banks which may subsequently join the FRS. The FRS does have the authority to regulate the merger of banks where the emerging entity is to be a state bank that is a member of the FRS. As is true of the other regulatory agencies, it is concerned with both the competitive effects as well as the financial and operating soundness of the prospective merger.

Examinations

The FRS policy on examination is as follows:

All state member banks are examined at least once each year.

Banks that present no supervisory concern can have every other examination conducted on a modified basis.

Banks that present supervisory concern are generally examined at least twice each year.

The FRS conducts its examinations jointly with state banking agency examinations whenever possible.

The FRS has an automated monitoring system (the Uniform Interagency Bank Rating System, discussed later in this chapter) which it uses in assessing the financial condition of the banks that it examines.

FEDERAL DEPOSIT INSURANCE CORPORATION

The Federal Deposit Insurance Corporation (FDIC) is the newest of the Federal agencies that regulate banks, having been established by the Banking Act of 1933. The FDIC insures over 95 percent of all commercial banks and mutual savings banks in the United States. Specifically, the FDIC insures the following classes of banks: (a) national banks, (b) state banks belonging to the FRS, and (c) state banks not belonging to the FRS that voluntarily insure with the FDIC. It is in regulating this last category—state nonmember (of the FRS) banks—that the FDIC exercises the greatest degree of control since it has no competing Federal regulatory agency. For example, the FDIC has the primary control over approval of mergers where the emerging entity is an insured state nonmember (of the FRS) bank. For mergers of other insured banks, the FDIC renders an advisory opinion to the Federal agencies having primary control—the OCC or the FRS.

The FDIC is headed by a board of directors composed of a chairman, the Comptroller of the Currency (ex officio), and one other director. The non-ex officio members are appointed by the President, with the approval of the Senate, for six year terms. The FDIC is headquartered in Washington, D.C., and operates through 14 regional offices located throughout the country. The FDIC is funded mainly by assessments (based on average deposits) of the insured banks.

Examinations

The FDIC has the following policy in effect for the frequency of examinations of those banks over which it has primary control—insured state banks that are not members of the FRS:

Problem banks (defined below) are subject to a full examination at least annually.

Banks which are of some concern (but not problem banks) are subject to a full examination at least every 18 months.

Other banks are subject to an examination (generally limited in scope) at least every 18 months.

The FDIC relys on examination reports of the OCC and the FRS for those banks over which they have primary control. Further, all banks over which the FDIC has primary control are subject to examinations by state banking agencies. The FDIC attempts to reduce the duplication of examining efforts by conducting examinations jointly with state examiners. In some states, the FDIC and the state agencies conduct alternate examinations and provide the results therefrom to each other. The FDIC maintains a list of "problem banks" which require especially close supervision. These problem banks are placed into one of the following categories:

Problem banks. Problem status generally is accorded after analysis of the most recent examination report of a bank or consideration of other pertinent information . . . :

Serious Problem—Potential Payoff: An advanced serious problem situation with an estimated 50 percent chance or more of requiring financial assistance from the FDIC.

Serious Problem: A situation that threatens ultimately to involve the FDIC in a financial outlay unless drastic changes occur.

Other Problems: A situation wherein a bank contains significant weaknesses, but where the FDIC is less vulnerable. Such banks require more than ordinary concern and aggressive supervision.[6]

Table 2-1 shows the composition of the problem bank list as of December 31, 1977.

The problem bank list maintained by FDIC and that maintained by the OCC include some of the same banks. However, a bank could be on one agency's list and not the other agency's. Further, since FDIC has responsibility for more banks than does the OCC, its list is, as expected, longer. During the 10 year period ending in 1978, an average of about eight banks per year were closed due to financial difficulties.[7] These

TABLE 2-1
Problem Bank List as of December 31, 1977

Category	Total	State Bank, Nonmember of FRS	State Bank, Member of FRS	National Bank
Serious Problem— Potential Payoff	12	10	1	1
Serious Problem	100	82	3	15
Other Problem	256	194	18	44
Total	368	286	22	60

Source: FDIC, *Annual Report,* 1977, p. 11.

failures gave rise to average losses to the FDIC of about $3 million per closed bank.[8]

The FDIC is aided in its monitoring of banks by a computerized analytical system:

> Integrated Monitoring System (IMS). The IMS, a computerized analysis system for monitoring bank performance between examinations, was implemented nationwide on November 1, 1977. The system is based on data submitted by the banks in their Reports of Condition and Income. Although the IMS is not a substitute for the examination process, it enables the Corporation to identify with more accuracy banks, or particular aspects of a bank's operation, that especially merit closer supervisory attention; it promotes more efficient use of limited manpower resources, both in the actual examination itself and in the review process; and it should serve to alert the Corporation to the presence of a deteriorating situation before it assumes serious proportions and thereby facilitate a swifter response by the Corporation. As presently structured, the IMS is limited in its application to insured commercial State non-member banks.

> The IMS utilizes eight basic tests which measure a bank's capital adequacy, liquidity, profitability, and asset and liability mix and growth against a predetermined standard. If a bank fails one or more of the eight basic tests, additional data are provided to facilitate in-depth and detailed analysis of the apparent problem. Where analysis indicates a potential problem or deteriorating conditions, appropriate action is initiated, which could be an early examination, bank visitation, or other follow-up activity. [9]

UNIFORM INTERAGENCY BANK RATING SYSTEM

In 1978, the three agencies (OCC, FRS, and FDIC) adopted the Uniform Interagency Bank Rating System (UIBRS) for assessing the financial and operating condition of banks. UIBRS produces a composite rating of a bank that is based on five factors:

Adequacy of capitalization

Quality of assets

Quality of management

Amount and stability of earnings

Liquidity

These factors are evaluated on a five point scale (the higher the score, the worse the evaluation). The UIBRS composite rating is, again, on a five point scale.

The individual agencies take these ratings and either use them as the primary rating basis of their problem banks (as is the case of the FRS) or use them in conjunction with their existing evaluation systems.

CALL REPORTS

The Federal agencies all have regulations and required forms for submission of financial and operating data. These reports, formally entitled *Reports of Condition and Income*, are more generally known as "call reports." Each agency has a number of different forms of call reports, based on various classifications of banks. Table 2-2 illustrates the degree of coordination in their reporting requirements (i.e., they all have similar strata in their requirements). This degree of coordination is necessary so that banks do not have to complete multiple forms which are, in essence, the same. For example, national banks are regulated by all three agencies —OCC, FRS, and FDIC. The OCC is the agency having primary control. Therefore, a national bank would complete the appropriate OCC form and, generally, only have to send copies to the FRS and FDIC.

TABLE 2-2
Forms for Call Reports, by Agency

Agency	Forms Balance/Income Sheet / Statement	Category of Bank
OCC	8022-01/8022-02	National banks with less than $100 million in assets
	8022-05/8022-14	National banks with only domestic operations
	8022-18/8022-4	National banks with domestic and foreign operations
	Supplement	National banks with assets of $300 million or more
FRS	2103/2104	State member banks (of FRS) having only domestic offices with less than $100 million in assets
	2105/2107	State member banks (of FRS) with only domestic offices
	2106/2107	State member banks (of FRS) with domestic and foreign operations
	Supplement	State member banks (of FRS) having assets of $300 million or more
FDIC	8040/11/8040/01	State nonmember banks (of FRS) with less than $100 million in assets
	8040/12/8040/02	State nonmember banks (of FRS) with only domestic operations
	8040/13/8040/02	State nonmember banks (of FRS) with domestic and foreign operations
	Supplements (8040/14/8040/03)	State nonmember banks (of FRS) with domestic and foreign operations
	Supplement (8040/17)	State nonmember banks (of FRS) with $300 million or more in assets

Each agency has a set of instructions for its call report. Those of FDIC will be reviewed and any significant differences from the other agencies' instructions will be noted. (The agencies are currently preparing uniform call report instructions that will apply to all agencies' call reports.)

Statements and Schedules

The basic components of the call report are the income statement and the report of condition. These are reproduced as Figures 2-3 and 2-4. In addition, the call reports contain a number of other schedules which generally expand on components of these statements. Some of these schedules are:

Changes in equity capital

Analysis of allowance for loan losses

Analyses of other operating income and expenses

Analyses of: securities held, cash, deposits, other assets, and other liabilities

Computation of assessment payable to FDIC

Accounting Basis

There is a certain degree of flexibility in banks' selection of the basis of accounting (cash versus accrual) and in the extent to which the accrual basis must be followed:

All banks must prepare the Report of Income on a fully consolidated domestic and foreign basis and the Report of Condition on a domestic only basis. Every bank with total assets of $25 million or more on June 30 of the previous year must prepare the Report of Income and the Report of Condition on the basis of accrual accounting. Where the results would not be significantly different, a cash basis may be used in reporting for particular accounts except as noted elsewhere in these instructions. The accounting method used for the Report of Income must also be used for the Report of Condition. Accruals shown in the Report of Income must also be reflected in the Report of Condition.

- At the option of bank, trust department accounts may be reported on a cash basis.

- Unearned income on loans must be reported on an accrual basis regardless of size of bank.

- Federal, State, and local income taxes must be reported on an accrual basis and computed on the current period's reported income regardless of size of bank.

- "Investments in unconsolidated subsidiaries and associated companies," Assets, item 13, must be reported on an equity basis of accounting with the investment and individual profits adjusted quarterly for reporting purposes to include the parent bank's share of the subsidiaries' net worth.

- Internal accounting methods are the province and responsibility of the reporting bank; however, the Corporation's examiners may be consulted on specific questions with respect to acceptable accounting techniques.[10]

Generally Accepted Accounting Principles

All of the agencies pay homage to generally accepted accounting principles *but* reserve the right to vary therefrom:

(Domestic and Foreign)
(COMMERCIAL BANK)

CONSOLIDATED REPORT OF INCOME
(Including Domestic and Foreign Subsidiaries
(Dollar amounts in thousands)

RETURN ORIGINAL AND ONE COPY TO
FDIC, BANK REPORTS SECTION,
WASHINGTON, D.C. 20429

PLEASE READ CAREFULLY INSTRUCTIONS
FOR THE PREPARATION OF REPORTS OF
INCOME.

Every item and schedule must be filled in. Printed items must not be amended. Amounts which cannot properly be included in the printed items must be entered under Other income or Other expenses.

NAME AND ADDRESS OF BANK:

SECTION A — SOURCES AND DISPOSITION OF INCOME (Indicate losses in parentheses)

	A. Year-to-date	
	Mil.	Thou.

1. Operating income:
   a. Interest and fees on loans . . . . — 1a
   b. Interest on balances with depository institutions . . . . — 1b
   c. Income on Federal funds sold and securities purchased under agreements to resell in domestic offices of the bank and of its Edge and Agreement subsidiaries 1c
   d. Interest on U. S. Treasury securities 1d
   e. Interest on obligations of other U. S. Government agencies and corporations . . . 1e
   f. Interest on obligations of States and political subdivisions of the U.S. 1f
   g. Interest on other bonds, notes, and debentures 1g
   h. Dividends on stock 1h
   i. Income from lease financing 1i
   j. Income from fiduciary activities 1j
   k. Service charges on deposit accounts in domestic offices 1k
   l. Other service charges, commissions, and fees 1l
   m. Other income . . . . (Section D, item 4) 1m
   n. TOTAL OPERATING INCOME (sum of Items 1a thru 1m) 1n

2. Operating expenses:
   a. Salaries and employee benefits 2a
   b. Interest on time certificates of deposit of $100,000 or more issued by domestic offices . 2b
   c. Interest on deposits in foreign offices 2c
   d. Interest on other deposits 2d
   e. Expense of Federal funds purchased and securities sold under agreements to repurchase in domestic offices of the bank and of its Edge and Agreement subsidiaries 2e
   f. 1. Interest of demand notes (note balances) issued to the U.S. Treasury 2f1
      2. Interest on other borrowed money 2f2
   g. Interest on subordinated notes and debentures 2g
   h. 1. Occupancy expense of bank premises, Gross 2h1
      2. Less: Rental income 2h2
      3. Occupancy expense of bank premises, Net 2h3
   i. Furniture and equipment expense 2i
   j. Provision for possible loan losses . . . . . (Section C, item 4) 2j
   k. Other operating expenses . . . . . . (Section E, item 3) 2k

   l. TOTAL OPERATING EXPENSES . . . . . (sum of items 2a thru 2k) 2l

3. Income before income taxes and securities gains or losses. . (item 1n minus 2l) 3

4. Applicable income taxes 4

5. Income before securities gains or losses. . . . (item 3 minus 4) 5

6. a. Securities gains (losses), Gross 6a
   b. Applicable income taxes 6b
   c. Securities gains (losses), Net 6c

7. Net income . . . . (item 5 plus or minus 6c) 7

OR

7. Income before extraordinary items 7
8. Extraordinary items, Net of tax effect. . . . . (Section F, item 2c) 8
9. Net income . . . . (item 7 plus or minus 8) 9

I/We the undersigned officer(s), hereby certify that this Report of Income (including the information in the supporting schedules) has been prepared in conformance with the instructions issued by the Federal Deposit Insurance Corporation and is true and correct to the best of my knowledge and belief.

NAME AND TITLE OF OFFICER(S) AUTHORIZED TO SIGN REPORT	AREA CODE/TELEPHONE NO.
SIGNATURE OF OFFICER(S) AUTHORIZED TO SIGN REPORT	DATE SIGNED

FIGURE 2-3. Form for Income Statement.

NAME AND ADDRESS OF BANK:

(COMMERCIAL BANK)
CONSOLIDATED REPORT OF CONDITION
(Including Domestic Subsidiaries)
(Dollar amounts in thousands)
RETURN ORIGINAL AND ONE COPY TO
FDIC, BANK REPORTS SECTION,
WASHINGTON, D.C. 20429
PLEASE READ CAREFULLY INSTRUCTIONS
FOR THE PREPARATION OF REPORTS OF
CONDITION.

Every item and schedule must be filled in. Printed
items must not be amended. Amounts which cannot
properly be included in the printed items must be
entered under Other assets or Other liabilities.

CLOSE OF BUSINESS DATE

	Mil.	Thou.	

ASSETS

1. Cash and due from depository institutions *(From Schedule C, item 8)* — 1
2. U.S. Treasury securities *(From Schedule B, item 1, Column E)* — 2
3. Obligations of other U.S. Government agencies and corporations *(From Schedule B, item 2, Column E)* — 3
4. Obligations of States and political subdivisions in the United States *(From Schedule B, item 3, Column E)* — 4
5. Other bonds, notes, and debentures *(From Schedule B, item 4, Column E)* — 5
6. Federal Reserve stock and corporate stock — 6
7. Trading account securities — 7
8. Federal funds sold and securities purchased under agreements to resell — 8
9. a. Loans, Total (excluding unearned income) *(From Schedule A, item 10)* — 9a
   b. Less: allowance for possible loan losses — 9b
   c. Loans, Net — 9c
10. Lease financing receivables — 10
11. Bank premises, furniture and fixtures, and other assets representing bank premises — 11
12. Real estate owned other than bank premises — 12
13. Investments in unconsolidated subsidiaries and associated companies — 13
14. Customers' liability to this bank on acceptances outstanding — 14
15. Other assets *(From Schedule G, item 3)* — 15
16. TOTAL ASSETS (sum of items 1 thru 15) — 16

LIABILITIES

17. Demand deposits of individuals, partnerships, and corporations *(From Schedule F, item 1, Column A)* — 17
18. Time and savings deposits of individuals, partnerships, & corporations *(From Sched. F, item 1, Cols. B&C)* — 18
19. Deposits of United States Government *(From Schedule F, item 2, Columns A & B & C)* — 19
20. Deposits of States and political subdivisions in the United States *(From Sched. F, item 3, Cols. A & B & C)* — 20
21. Deposits of foreign governments and official institutions *(From Schedule F, item 4, Columns A & B & C)* — 21
22. Deposits of commercial banks *(From Schedule F, items 5 & 6, Columns A & B & C)* — 22
23. Certified and officers' checks *(From Schedule F, item 7, Column A)* — 23
24a. Total Deposits (sum of items 17 thru 23) — 24a
   a1. Total demand deposits *(From Schedule F, item 8, Column A)* — 24a1
   a2. Total time and savings deposits *(From Schedule F, item 8, Columns B & C)* — 24a2
25. Federal funds purchased and securities sold under agreements to repurchase — 25
26. a. Interest-bearing demand notes (note balances) issued to the U.S. Treasury — 26a
   b. Other liabilities for borrowed money — 26b
27. Mortgage indebtedness and liability for capitalized leases — 27
28. Bank's liability on acceptances executed and outstanding — 28
29. Other liabilities *(From Schedule H, item 4)* — 29
30. TOTAL LIABILITIES (excluding subordinated notes and debentures) (sum of items 24 thru 29) — 30
31. Subordinated notes and debentures — 31

EQUITY CAPITAL

32. Preferred stock   a. No. shares outstanding _____   (par value) — 32
33. Common stock   a. No. shares authorized _____
                    b. No. shares outstanding _____   (par value) — 33
34. Surplus — 34
35. Undivided profits — 35
36. Reserve for contingencies and other capital reserves — 36
37. TOTAL EQUITY CAPITAL (sum of items 32 thru 36) — 37
38. TOTAL LIABILITIES AND EQUITY CAPITAL (sum of items 30, 31 and 37) — 38

MEMORANDA

Memo

1. Amounts outstanding as of report date: a1. Standby letters of credit, total — 1a1
   a2. Amount of standby letters of credit in Memo item 1a1 conveyed to others through participations — 1a2
   b. Time certificates of deposit in denominations of $100,000 or more — 1b
   c. Other time deposits in amounts of $100,000 or more — 1c
2. Average for 30 calendar days (or calendar month) ending with report date:
   a. Cash and due from depository institutions (corresponds to item 1 above) — 2a
   b. Federal funds sold and securities purchased under agreements to resell (corresponds to item 8 above) — 2b
   c. Total loans (corresponds to item 9a above) — 2c
   d. Time certificates of deposits in denominations of $100,000 or more (corresponds to Memoranda item 1b above) — 2d
   e. Total deposits (corresponds to item 24a above) — 2e
   f. Federal funds purchased and securities sold under agreements to repurchase (corresponds to item 25 above) — 2f
   g. Other liabilities for borrowed money (corresponds to item 26b above) — 2g
   h. Total assets (corresponds to item 16 above) — 2h

NOTE: This report must be signed by an authorized officer and attested by not less than three directors other than the officer signing the report.

I/We the undersigned officer(s), do hereby declare that this Report of Condition (including the supporting schedules) has been prepared in conformance with the instructions issued by the Federal Deposit Insurance Corporation and is true to the best of my knowledge and belief.

SIGNATURE OF OFFICER(S) AUTHORIZED TO SIGN REPORT | DATE SIGNED *(Month, Day, Year)*

NAME AND TITLE OF OFFICER(S) AUTHORIZED TO SIGN REPORT | AREA CODE/PHONE NO.

We, the undersigned directors, attest the correctness of this Report of Condition (including the supporting schedules) and declare that it has been examined by us and to the best of our knowledge and belief has been prepared in conformance with the instruction issued by the FDIC and is true and correct.

SIGNATURE OF DIRECTOR | SIGNATURE OF DIRECTOR | SIGNATURE OF DIRECTOR

SCHEDULE A — LOANS (including rediscounts and overdrafts) | Dollar Amounts in Thousands | Mil. | Thou.

1. Real estate loans (include only loans secured primarily by real estate) a. Construction and land development — 1a
   b. Secured by farmland (including farm residential and other improvements) — 1b
   c. Secured by 1-4 family residential properties: (1) Insured by FHA or guaranteed by VA — 1c1
   (2) Conventional — 1c2
   d. Secured by multifamily (5 or more) residential properties:
   (1) Insured by FHA — 1d1
   (2) Conventional — 1d2
   e. Secured by nonfarm nonresidential properties — 1e

FIGURE 2-4. Form for Report of Condition.

Additional information on technical subjects such as generally accepted accounting practices that include references to Accounting Principles Board (APB) Opinions and Financial Accounting Standards Board (FASB) Statements may be obtained from accountants, trade associations, and regulatory offices. These instructions may depart from stated opinions and statements because of the special supervisory, regulatory, and economic policy needs served by the reports.[11]

There may be areas in which a bank wishes more technical detail on the application of accounting standards and procedures to the requirements of these instructions. Supplementary information on such technical accounting matters, including references to applicable comprehensive Accounting Principles Board ("APB") Opinions and Financial Accounting Standards Board ("FASB") Statements, will be available from the Reserve Banks. It should be noted, however, that these instructions are not always directed entirely by such opinions and statements because of the special supervisory, regulatory, and economic policy needs served by these reports.[12]

Inquiries concerning the reporting of transactions not covered by these instructions should be addressed to the Division of Financial Reports and Statistics, Comptroller of the Currency, Administrator of National Banks, Washington, D.C. 20219, (202-447-1825). In general, response to such inquiries will be guided by generally accepted accounting principles.[13]

Goodwill

One area where the agencies depart from generally accepted accounting principles is in the treatment of goodwill:

> *Business combination, mergers and acquisitions.* A bank or other business acquired in a purchase acquisition is recorded at cost. The cost should be assigned to all identifiable assets acquired and liabilities assumed, normally in amounts equal to their fair values. Any unassigned or excess cost, which is called goodwill, should be written off directly against undivided profits and shown in Section B—Changes in Equity Capital, under item 6, "Changes incident to mergers and absorptions, net."[14]

This treatment is in contrast to generally accepted accounting principles under which goodwill is amortized against income over future periods.

Subsidiaries and Associated Companies

Banks are required to consolidate any subsidiary (i.e., a company in which it owns over 50 percent of the outstanding common stock) if the subsidiary is "significant." The tests of "significance" are:

> "Significant" subsidiary—one meeting any of the following tests:
>
> A subsidiary in which the bank's direct or indirect investment and advances represent 5 percent or more of the equity capital accounts of the parent bank.
>
> Any subsidiary whose gross operating revenues exceed 5 percent of the gross operating revenue of the parent bank.
>
> Any subsidiary whose "Income (Loss) before income taxes" exceeds 5 per-

cent or more of the "Income (Loss) before income taxes" of the parent bank.

The subsidiary is the parent of one or more subsidiaries which, when consolidated, constitute a significant subsidiary.[15]

The rules requiring consolidation do not apply to a bank's holding of a controlling interest in another bank. Each bank files its own call report, with no consolidation of the subsidiary in the parent's call report.

An associated company is one in which the bank owns between 20 and 50 percent of the outstanding common stock. The investment in these companies must be maintained on the equity basis—where the bank's investment is adjusted for its proportionate share of the associated companies' earnings or losses—*unless* the bank can establish that it exercises no significant control over the associated company. In the latter case, the investment can be carried at cost.

Investment

Gains and losses on securities held as investments appear on the income statement. This represents a change in bank practices from the recent past when banks excluded these from the determination of income and carried them directly to undivided profits (retained earnings). In addition, some banks advocated *amortizing* realized gains and losses over *future periods* in order to mitigate their effect on the period of realization. Both of these methods have been replaced by the recognition of realized gains and losses in the income statement.

Loan Losses

Losses on loans is another item that, in the past, has been charged to undivided profits (retained earnings) and, thus, bypassed the income statement. These losses now appear in the income statement.

Banks on the accrual basis (and banks on the cash basis who so elect) must provide for loan losses on an estimated basis. This basically consists of establishing an allowance for *estimated* loan losses (a contra-asset account) and charging the estimated loss to expense. As actual losses are encountered, they are charged to the allowance. This is the same basic procedure that companies use to provide for accounts receivable whose collection is doubtful. However, banks use a somewhat expanded version of this procedure which also accomplishes income tax allocation and appropriations of undivided profits. In reading the FDIC's description of this procedure the following terms have the indicated equivalent meanings outside of banking:

Bank Term	Equivalent
Valuation portion	Contra-asset account
Contingency portion	Appropriated retained earnings
Undivided profits	Retained earnings

The bank's procedure is as follows:

Three-Way Allocation of Loan Loss Reserve

An entry is necessary in the deferred income tax liability and the contingency portion is affected when the gross amount added to the valuation portion during a given year as the provision for possible loan losses is different from the amount reported to the IRS as an expense for bad debt reserves. For example, suppose that during a given year a bank reports provision for possible loan losses of 125 (Report of Income Section A) . . . For the same year, however, the bank reports to the IRS an amount of 225 as the expense for provision for possible loan losses. If this bank had an applicable tax rate of 25 percent, the 100 difference between the amount reported in . . . [the Report of Income] . . . and the amount expensed in the IRS tax return would be allocated to the contingency portion which is included in undivided profits (Report of Condition, Equity Capital) . . . and deferred income taxes . . . The contingency portion would be increased by 75 and deferred income taxes would be increased by 25. The opposite would be the case if the provision for possible loan losses (Report of Income, Section A) . . . which is added to the valuation portion . . . exceeded the amount reported in the IRS statement. For example, if the provision made to the valuation reserve exceeded by 100 the amount expensed for the reserve for possible loan losses in the IRS report, the net effect would be that the contingency portion which is included in undivided profits (Equity Capital) . . . would be reduced by 75 . . . and the ending balance for deferred income tax liabilities . . . would be reduced by 25.[16]

Errors in Prior Reports

The agencies' rules on extraordinary items and prior periods adjustments are generally in accord with Accounting Principle Board and Financial Accounting Standards Board pronouncements.

Under these pronouncements, corrections of errors are treated as prior period adjustments. The agencies agree with this treatment. However, the FDIC and OCC go further and have banks submit revised statements for prior periods for which "significant errors" exist. The FDIC requirement is:

Revisions to prior reports

Significant errors or inconsistencies in prior reports noted by either bank personnel, auditors, or examiners should be brought to the attention of the FDIC by bank management. If the errors or inconsistencies are of such a magnitude that an amended report is necessary, such reports must be clearly and prominently marked "amended" and all subsequent reports, both income and condition, must be prepared or refiled on the basis of the amended figures. For these purposes, a "significant" change is any adjustment that results in a difference in any income or expense item of more than 2 percent provided the change is over $5,000, or a difference in any asset or liability item of more than 5 percent provided the change is over $30,000.[17]

According to the OCC, a "significant error" exists if correction of the error would result in any of the following:

Report of Income:

(a) changing any amount reported in Section A, B or C by:

    (1) more than 1% of Total Operating Income, provided the amount is greater than $5,000,

    (2) more than $1,000,000 or

(b) a material effect on the amount

reported as Income Before Income Taxes and Securities Gains or Losses or on Net Income.

Report of Condition:

Changing any amount reported in the balance sheet by more than 1% of Total Assets, provided the amount is greater than $50,000.[18]

REPORTS UNDER THE SECURITIES ACTS OF 1933 AND 1934

Banks are exempted from most of the provisions of the Securities Act of 1933 (which is enforced by the Securities and Exchange Commission). Section 3 of the Act reads, in part, as follows:

Exempted Securities

Sec. 3. (a) Except as hereinafter expressly provided, *the provisions of this title shall not apply to any of the following classes of securities:*

* * *

. . . *any security issued or guaranteed by any bank;* or any security issued by or representing an interest in or a direct obligation of a Federal Reserve bank or any interest or participation in any common trust fund or similar fund maintained by a bank exclusively for the collective investment and reinvestment of assets contributed thereto by such bank in its capacity as trustee, executor, administrator, or guardian; . . . (Emphasis added)

Banks are *not* exempted from the provisions of this Act prohibiting fraud involving interstate commerce in securities (Section 17 of the Securities Act of 1933). The banking agencies have

their own disclosure requirements for security issues. For example, FDIC's *Statement of Policy* on the content of a security issue's offering circular reads as follows:

FDIC believes that every offering circular prepared by an insured State nonmember bank should, to the extent applicable, include the information listed below:

(1) the name, address, principal place of business and telephone number of the issuing bank;

(2) the amount and title of the securities being offered;

(3) the offering price and proceeds to the bank on a per share and aggregate basis;

(4) the plan and cost of distribution;

(5) the reasons for the offering and the purpose for which the proceeds are to be used, and a brief description of the material risks, if any, involved in the purchase of the securities;

(6) a description of the present and proposed business operations of the bank and its capital structure;

(7) the principal officers, directors and principal security holders and the amount of securities owned by each;

(8) the remuneration and interest in recent or proposed transactions of management and principal security holders and their associates;

(9) the high and low sales prices of the securities within the past two years and the source of the quotations;

(10) a brief description of any material pending legal proceedings;

(11) a summary of any material terms and restrictions applicable to the securities;

(12) Financial Statements: a balance sheet as of the preceding fiscal year end; statements of income for the preceding two fiscal years and interim periods where necessary; notes to financial statements; and schedules of the allowance for possible loan losses.[19]

Under the Securities Exchange Act of 1934, the relevant banking agency (i.e., OCC, FRS, or FDIC) has the authority to administer the financial disclosure practices of the banks that it regulates. (That is, the OCC is responsible for national banks; the FRS is responsible for state banks that are members of the FRS; the FDIC is responsible for state banks which are not members of the FRS but which are insured by FDIC.) These agencies' regulations in carrying out their responsibilities under the Securities Exchange Act of 1934 are contained in the Code of Federal Regulations:

Agency	CFR
OCC	Title 12, Chapter I, Part 11
FRS	Title 12, Chapter II, Part 206
FDIC	Title 12, Chapter III, Part 335

The regulations that the agencies have promulgated are virtually identical with each others' and with those of the SEC. The regulations of FDIC are referenced here.

The regulations call for a series of "forms" (i.e., reports) to be filed by banks that have publicly held securities. These "forms" all have counterparts in the SEC's regulation for other entities. For example, Form F-3, the Current Report, is the equivalent of the SEC's Form 8-K, Current Report. (In general, the financial statements that are filed with the banking agencies are audited by certified public accountants.) The following forms required by FDIC all involve the filing of accounting data by the banks.

Form F-1, Form for Registration of Securities of a Bank. This is the *registration statement* required to be filed by banks whose securities are held by the public (i.e., when the number of shareholders exceeds 500). A comprehensive set of financial statements (see Forms F-9 A, B, C, D, and E below) is required.

Form F-2, Annual Report. This is the required form of the annual report—including the financial statements encompassed in Forms F-9 A, B, C, D, and E—that must be filed by banks that have securities registered under the Securities Exchange Act of 1934.

Form F-3, Current Report. This report is to be filed within 10 days of the close of any month in which certain specified events have occurred. The events are:

Item	Event
1 —	Changes in Control of Bank
2 —	Acquisition or Disposition of Assets (of significant amount)
3 —	Legal Proceedings
4 —	Changes in Securities
5 —	Changes in Security for Registered Securities

6 — Defaults Upon Senior Securities
7 — Increase in Amount of Securities Outstanding
8 — Decrease in Amount of Securities Outstanding
9 — Submission of Matters to a Vote of Security Holders
10 — Changes in Banks Certifying Accountant
11 — Resignation of Bank's Directors
12 — Other Materially Important Events

For example, Item 10 of Form F-3 requires the following [12 CFR 335.43]:

Item 10—Changes in Bank's Certifying Accountant.

If an independent accountant who was previously engaged as the principal accountant to audit the bank's financial statements resigns (or indicates he declines to stand for reelection after the completion of the current audit) or is dismissed as the bank's principal accountant, or another independent accountant is engaged as principal accountant or if an independent accountant on whom the principal accountant expressed reliance in his report regarding a significant subsidiary resigns (or formally indicates he declines to stand for re-election after the completion of the current audit) or is dismissed or another independent accountant is engaged to audit that subsidiary:

(a) State the date of such resignation (or declination to stand for re-election), dismissal or engagement.

(b) State whether in connection with the audits of the two most recent fiscal years and any subsequent interim period preceding such resignation, dismissal or engagement there were any disagreements with the former accountant on any matter of accounting principles or practices, financial statement disclosure, or auditing scope or procedure, which disagreements if not resolved to the satisfaction of the former accountant would have caused him to make reference in connection with his report to the subject matter of the disagreement(s); also, describe each such disagreement. The disagreements required to be reported in response to the preceding sentence include both those resolved to the former accountant's satisfaction and those not resolved to the former accountant's satisfaction. Disagreements contemplated by this role are those which occur at the decision-making level; i.e., between personnel of the bank responsible for the presentation of its financial statements and personnel of the accounting firm responsible for rendering its report.

(c) State whether the principal accountant's report on the financial statements for any of the past two years contained an adverse opinion or a disclaimer of opinion or was qualified as to uncertainty, audit scope, or accounting principles; also describe the nature of each such adverse opinion, disclaimer of opinion, or qualification.

(d) The bank shall request the former accountant to furnish the bank with a letter addressed to the Corporation stating whether he agrees with the statements made by the bank in response to this item and, if not, stating the respects in which he does not agree. The bank shall file a copy of the former accountant's letter as an exhibit with all copies of the Form F-3 required to be filed pursuant to 335.4(s).

(e) State whether the decision to change accountants was recommended or approved by:

(1) Any audit or similar committee of the board of directors, if the bank has such a committee; or

(2) The board of directors if the bank has no such committee.

Form F-4, Quarterly Report. This quarterly report (which includes financial statements) must be filed within 45 days of the end of each of the first three quarters of the fiscal year.

Forms F-9 A, B, C, D, and E: Forms for Financial Statements. These "forms" outline the content of the various financial statements and other schedules of accounting-related information that are called for in the annual report, registration statement, etc. Most of the instructions are to insure adequate disclosure. However, in some instances the application of generally accepted accounting principles to circumstances faced in the banking industry is involved. For example, the statement of financial position is "unclassified" in that there are no segregations of current assets and current liabilities in accordance with reporting practices in the banking industry (and in contrast to the practices in most other industries).

The general content of the various forms is:

Form F-9 A   Balance Sheet

Form F-9 B   Statement of Income

Form F-9 C   Statement of Changes in Equity Capital

Form F-9 D   Statement of Changes in Financial Position

Form F-9 E   Schedules:

I – U.S. Government and State Government Securities Held

II – Loans to Officers, Directors, etc.

III – Loans

IV – Banks Premises and Equipment

V – Investment (and Income therefrom)

VI – Allowance for Possible Loan Losses

BANK HOLDING COMPANIES

A bank holding company is an entity that has a significant and influential investment in one or more banks. There are various criteria for measuring the significance and influence of holdings (e.g., control over 25 percent of the voting power in a bank; ability to elect a majority of the board of directors of a bank). Bank holding companies are regulated by two Federal agencies, the Securities and Exchange Commission (SEC) and the Federal Reserve System (FRS).

Under the Bank Holding Company Act of 1956, the FRS exercises control over the formation and activities of bank holding companies. The FRS regulations for bank holding companies are contained in Part 225 of Chapter II of Title 12 of the Code of Federal Regulations. This Part is also known as Regulation Y.

The FRS exercises the approval function, at the Federal level, over the formation of a bank holding company. In addition, the holding company must comply with regulations of the state(s) in which it operates. State regulations vary widely. Some states prohibit bank holding companies entirely; others only permit single-bank holding companies; and yet others permit multibank holding companies.

The FRS also controls the nonbanking

activities in which bank holding companies may engage. These are outlined in 12 CFR 225.4. They include such activities as investment counseling, credit life insurance underwriting, and bank consulting services.

The FRS requires bank holding companies to file annual reports with it. The FRS also has the right to conduct examinations of the bank holding companies [12 CFR 225.5 (b)] :

> Reports and examinations. Each bank holding company shall furnish to the Board in a form prescribed by the Board a report of the company's operations for the fiscal year in which it becomes a bank holding company, and for each fiscal year thereafter until it ceases to be a bank holding company. Each such annual report shall be filed with the Federal Reserve bank. Each bank holding company shall furnish to the Board additional information at such times as the Board may require. The Board may examine any bank holding company or any of its subsidiaries and the cost of any such examination shall be assessed against and paid by such bank holding company. As far as possible the Board will use reports of examinations made by the Comptroller of the Currency, the Federal Deposit Insurance Corporation, or the appropriate State bank supervisory authority.

Bank holding companies with 500 or more shareholders are regulated by the SEC. The SEC controls the financial reporting practices of the bank holding company (and any individual banks whose financial statements are presented with those of the holding company). The SEC's regulations on financial disclosure relevant to bank holding companies are contained in Parts 210 and 229, Chapter II, Title 17 of the Code of Federal Regulations. "Regulation S-X" is the more commonly recognized term for 17 CFR Part 210. "Regulation S-K" is the more commonly recognized term for 17 CFR Part 229. Regulation S-X contains certain modifications and/or expansions of the SEC's basic disclosure rules. For example, bank holding companies are *not* required to distinguish current from noncurrent assets and liabilities in their balance sheets.

Where the financial statements of individual banks controlled by bank holding companies are filed with the SEC, some additional reporting requirements, over and above those of the banking regulatory agencies (i.e., the FRS, FDIC, and OCC) must be followed. These are found in 17 CFR 210.9-05 of Regulation S-X.

REFERENCE NOTES

1. U.S. Office of the Comptroller of the Currency, *Annual Report, 1977*, pp. 223-224.

2. *Ibid.*, p. 231.

3. U.S., Office of the Comptroller of the Currency, *National Bank Surveillance System User's Guide,* 1979, p. I-1.

4. *Ibid.*, p. I-2.

5. *Ibid.*, p. I-3.

6. U.S., Federal Deposit Insurance Corporation, *Annual Report,* 1978, p. 8.

7. *Ibid.*, p. 183.

8. *Ibid.*, p. 188.

9. U.S., Federal Deposit Insurance Corporation, *Annual Report,* 1977, p. 12.

10. U.S., Federal Deposit Insurance Corporation, *Instructions for Call Reports,* p. G-2.

11. *Ibid.*, p. G-1.

12. U.S., Federal Reserve System, *Instructions for Call Reports,* p. 10.

13. U.S. Office of the Comptroller of the Currency, *Call Report Instructions,* p. 1.

14. U.S., Federal Deposit Insurance Corporation, *Instructions for Call Reports,* p. G-3.

15. *Ibid.*, p. G-3.

16. *Ibid.*, p. R/I-14.

17. *Ibid.*, p. G-2.

18. U.S., Office of the Comptroller of the Currency, *Call Report Instructions,* p. 5.

19. U.S., Federal Deposit Insurance Corporation, *Statement of Policy Regarding Use of Offering Circulars in Connection with Public Distribution of Bank Securities* (July 2, 1979), p. 203.

Chapter 3

Federal Home Loan Bank Board

The Federal Home Loan Bank Board (FHLBB) is an independent agency of the Federal government. It was established by the Federal Home Loan Bank Act of 1932. It regulates both Federal and state chartered Federally insured savings and loan associations. The FHLBB is headed by a bipartisan board of three members, appointed by the President with the approval of the Senate. The FHLBB operates 12 district offices throughout the country: Boston, New York, Atlanta, Cincinnati, Indianapolis, Chicago, Des Moines, Little Rock, Topeka, San Francisco, Pittsburgh, and Seattle. The FHLBB carries out its regulatory functions through four programs:

1. The Federal Home Loan Bank System performs functions for the savings and loan industry similar to that performed for banks by the Federal Reserve System. The Federal Home Loan Bank System, operating through its 12 District Banks, acts as a provider of funds, through loans, to its members. The members of the System are mainly savings and loan associations (over 4,000). However, there are some members, such as mutual savings banks (less than 100), who are heavily involved in the financing of housing.

2. The Federal Home Loan Mortgage Corporation purchases existing residential mortgages from lenders, thus providing funds with which more loans can be made.

3. The Federal Savings and Loan System charters Federal savings and loan associations. There are over 2,000 Federally chartered savings and loans.

4. The Federal Savings and Loan Insurance Corporation (FSLIC) was established by the National Housing Act of 1934. It insures the savings accounts of all Federal savings and

loans, as well as over 2,000 state chartered savings and loans, up to $100,000 per account. It is through the FSLIC and the FHLBB's Office of Examinations and Supervision that the accounting regulation of savings and loan associations is exercised.

The FHLBB is a financially self-sufficient entity and receives no appropriations from Congress. The FHLBB, its District Banks, and the FSLIC are financed out of such sources as assessments for insurance, fees for examinations, interest on investments, etc.

SAVINGS AND LOAN ASSOCIATIONS

The savings and loan industry began about 150 years ago in the United States. The industry evolved out of a need for financing of housing purchases, something in which commercial banks, at that time, did not engage. For the first century, the industry was relatively unregulated. The depression of the late 1920s and the 1930s witnessed the failure of many associations. This gave rise to the establishment of control at the Federal level, described above. In over 40 years of Federal regulation, fewer than 20 associations have failed and been forced into receivership. Most cases of financial difficulty are short-circuited by the FSLIC's vigilance in monitoring the operations of its insured associations. Frequently, the operations of a faltering association can be turned around, if detected early enough. If the deterioration is too severe, the faltering association

is generally merged with a healthy association.

The FSLIC is greatly aided in its monitoring of associations by the examinations of the FHLBB's Office of Examinations and Supervision, independent audits of the associations, and a computerized financial information system.

Form of Organization

Savings and loan associations have historically been mutual associations. That is, they are "owned" by the individuals who have savings accounts with the association. Prior to the mid-1970s, all Federally chartered associations were mutual associations; some states did permit state chartered associations to be stock companies (i.e., whose ownership was vested in stockholders and whose stock could be traded). Public Law 93-495 changed the rules for Federally chartered associations, permitting their conversion from mutual associations to stock associations.

The current acceptance of the stock form of organization is generally viewed as a positive factor in the future growth of the savings and loan industry. It provides a new source of equity funds (i.e., through the issuance of stock). This new source of funds facilitates the associations' tasks of meeting reserve requirements and maintaining a balanced capital structure. Further, it also facilitates expansion via a holding company. One feature that investors should consider is that the stock is *not* insured by FSLIC whereas any savings (or "share") accounts are insured.

FHLBB REGULATIONS

The FHLBB's regulations appear in Chapter V of Title 12 of the Code of Federal Regulations. Subchapter D of Chapter V is devoted to FSLIC. This subchapter is composed of Parts 561 through 571 of Title 12. These parts are collectively known as the "insurance regulations." There are some accounting regulations interspersed throughout the insurance regulations, most notably in 12 CFR Part 563 (Operations) applicable to all insured institutions, and in 12 CFR Part 563C (Accounting Requirements) applicable to all Federally chartered savings and loan associations that have converted from mutual to stock associations. Additionally, the Office of Examinations and Supervision of FHLBB issues a series of bulletins, known as PA (i.e., public accounting) Bulletins that control the required independent audits of insured associations.

Accounting for Savings and Loan Associations

Savings and loan associations basically follow generally accepted accounting principles in the preparation of their financial statements. (This is a significant change from the condition that existed about 20 years ago when most savings and loan associations prepared cash basis financial statements.) With generally accepted accounting principles as the basic frame of reference, exceptions or modifications peculiar to the savings and loan industry are:

1. Savings and loan associations generally prepare "unclassified" statements of financial condition, i.e., they do not distinguish current from noncurrent in their asset or liability sections. The ordering of assets varies. Some associations list their assets from most liquid to least liquid; others list their most material assets (e.g., mortgage loans) first, followed by the less material assets.

2. Savings and loan associations treat some items as liabilities which might more generally be classified as contra-assets. The most notable of these is loans-in-process (i.e., loans that have not been disbursed); they are treated as assets and liabilities, and not offset. Other examples are the discounts on loans and deferred loan fees.

3. Savings and loan associations can amortize premiums or discounts and deferred loan fees over periods that do not coincide with the term of the loans. This results in the recognition of the interest yield on a particular loan which is *not* constant during the term of the loan as is required under generally accepted accounting principles.

4. Savings and loan associations' accounting for investments in securities is somewhat varied. Some of the practices that have been employed which conflict with generally accepted accounting principles include: (a) failure to amortize a premium or discount on the investment; (b) charging a loss (on the disposition of securities) to a reserve (i.e., appropriated retained earnings) account, rather than recognizing it as an operating item; and (c) amortizing gains and losses (on disposition of securities) over future periods.

5. Reserve accounts for prospective losses are often established by charges to retained earnings. These reserve accounts are disposed of in absorbing losses as they are specifically identified. This procedure, again, results in losses not being reported on the income statement.

6. When goodwill is recognized upon the acquisition of an entity by a savings and loan association, the goodwill must be written off over a period not greater than 10 years. This 10-year limit also applies to other categories of intangible assets. This limit is shorter than that permitted under generally accepted accounting principles (i.e., 40 years).

7. The FHLBB permits institutions to recognize as revenue a "loan origination fee" of 2 to 2½ percent of the amount of the loan, immediately upon finalization of the loan. The position under generally accepted accounting principles is that the loan origination fee is a reimbursement for the cost of obtaining the loan and should *not* exceed that cost. To the extent that an individual institution's costs are less than its recognized loan origination fees, there is a disparity between the FHLBB's rules and generally accepted accounting principles.

Savings and loan associations follow these and other reporting practices, as required by the FHLBB. However, in preparing financial statements that purport to be in conformity with generally accepted accounting principles, the statements can be recast to accomplish the conformance. Thus, the savings and loan association would be reporting on one basis to Federal authorities and on another basis to users of the published statements. Where this occurs, the savings and loan association is required to reconcile any resulting difference(s) in net worth in a footnote to the financial statements.[1]

As a final comment on the conformity of the statements with generally accepted accounting principles, the FHLBB does not require savings and loan associations whose total assets do not exceed $10 million to follow the accrual basis of accounting. They are permitted to employ the cash or modified cash basis.

Audits of Savings and Loan Associations

Since 1966, the FHLBB has required all insured institutions to have an annual audit. This audit is required to be conducted by either an independent public accountant (generally a certified public accountant) or a "qualified" internal auditor. The use of an internal auditor to fulfill the audit requirement is closely monitored by the FHLBB.

When a savings and loan institution elects to satisfy the audit requirement by having an internal auditor perform the examination, it must take several actions. First, the board of directors must formally pass a resolution approving the audit program in some detail (e.g., its objectives, minimum audit requirements, the timing of the examination). Second, it must designate, by resolution, a full-time employee of the institution as the internal auditor, accountable directly to the board of directors. Third, it must file a copy of the aforementioned resolution with the FHLBB's district director of examinations. Fourth, the designated internal auditor must have (a) the right to audit any branch or department of the institution, without notice and, (b) unrestricted access to all records, documents, etc., of the institution. Finally, any changes in the implementation of the resolutions filed with the FHLBB must be approved by the institution's board of directors and, again, filed with the FHLBB's district director of examinations.

The FHLBB's district director of examinations has the responsibility of reviewing the resolutions filed by institutions employing internal auditors. In particular, the director must pass judgment on the designated internal auditor's qualifications (e.g., his technical competence, as witnessed by such things as educational background and professional certification). The initial approval by the district director of examinations is subject to change if it is felt that the internal auditor is not performing adequately (e.g., is not carrying out the audit program as approved by the board of directors).

The designation of an independent auditor (i.e., a certified public accountant or licensed public accountant) to conduct the audit is usually subject to less stringent scrutiny by the FHLBB. However, the "independent" auditor's *appearance* of independence is of concern. Certain activities or relationships between the institution and the independent auditor are prohibited (e.g., the ownership of stock in the institution). Any questions about potential violations of the appearance of independence are to be addressed to the FHLBB's district director of examinations.

Internal auditors are generally subject to the same requirements of independence as is a public accountant, given the constraint that the internal auditor is a full-time employee of the institution.

Upon completion of the audit, the savings and loan association is required to file copies of *all* reports rendered by the auditor, including not only the report on the financial statements, but also any " . . . special or supplemental reports, letters or reports to management or any other documents which are related to the audit or the report thereof . . . "[2]

Additionally, the auditor is put on notice that he must follow up on evidence of defalcations:

> The public accountant shall, upon discovering an apparent defalcation or being informed of such a matter, determine that the institution has immediately notified the District Director-Examinations in writing of the apparent defalcation. If the institution does not make such notification, the public accountant shall immediately notify the District Director-Examinations of such defalcation.[3]

This FHLBB requirement is greater than the usual degree of responsibility thrust on the auditor (i.e., that of notifying management and/or the board of directors of his discovery).

Change in Auditors. The FHLBB has a regulation that must be followed by any institution that changes independent auditors. The regulation is very close to that promulgated by the Securities and Exchange Commission (SEC) for publicly held companies subject to its jurisdiction. The FHLBB requires an institution that has terminated the services of an independent auditor to notify (within 15 days) the district director of examinations of:

1. The fact that the termination has been accomplished.
2. The reason for the termination.
3. Any disagreements that took place in the prior 24 months between the institution and the auditor on any matter of: (a) accounting principles, (b) financial statement disclosure, or (c) auditing procedures that would have caused the auditor to qualify his opinion if he did not prevail in the disagreement.

The institution also must request that the terminated auditor review the institution's representations made to the district director and write a letter stating whether he agrees or outlining any areas of disagreement with the institution's letter to the district director.

This requirement is obviously an attempt to discourage institutions from "shopping around" for an auditor in order to achieve a given result (regarding accounting disclosure or auditing procedure).

Securities Regulations

Savings and loan institutions are exempted—by Section 3 (a) (5) of the Securities Act of 1933—from the provisions of that Act (as enforced by the Securities and Exchange Commission) which deal with the original issuance of securities *except for* those provisions dealing with fraud. Institutions that are organized as stock corporations, and whose stock is publicly traded, are subject to the Securities Exchange Act of 1934 which is administered by the SEC. The SEC has delegated primary cognizance over FSLIC insured savings and loans to the FHLBB. As part of its duties, the FHLBB specifies the form and content of the financial statements filed under the Securities Exchange Act of 1934. The FHLBB has control over the public financial disclosure of savings and loan stock corporations in (a) the proxy solicitation for the vote to convert to the stock form, (b) the offering circular or private placement filing for the issuance of securities, and (c) the periodic reporting of the stock corporation. The FHLBB has adopted most of the SEC's disclosure requirements contained in the SEC's Regulation S-X (17 CFR Part 210) by reference. Additionally, the FHLBB has expanded the requirements of Regulation S-X for matters peculiar to the savings and loan industry. The FHLBB's regulations supplementing the SEC's Regulation S-X are found in 12 CFR Part 563C (entitled "Accounting Requirements").

Holding Companies. The FHLBB and the SEC both exercise control over savings and loan holding companies. The SEC administers the securities laws that are applicable to the holding companies. As part of its functions, it prescribes the form and content of these holding companies' financial statements. The FHLBB controls the operating practices of holding companies that have control over one or more FSLIC-insured savings and loan institutions. The FHLBB requires the holding company to register with it, periodically report to it, and to follow the FHLBB's rules controlling holding companies' operating practices (e.g., as in 12 CFR Part 584, Regulated Activities).

FHLBB Examinations

The FHLBB's Office of Examinations and Supervision conducts examinations of all FSLIC-insured savings and loan associations. Approximately 80 to 90 percent of the associations are examined each year by the Office's staff of ex- aminers. Since the imposition of the independent audit requirement in 1966, the Office has been able to spend more time and effort in pursuing issues that are not usually captured on a typical audit, such as compliance with Federal laws dealing with truth-in-lending, civil rights, equal opportunity for credit, etc.

REFERENCE NOTES

1. U.S., Federal Home Loan Bank Board, *Bulletin PA–7a and Related Regulations* (1977), p. 15.

2. *Ibid.,* p. 5.

3. *Ibid.,* p. 11.

National Credit Union Administration

The National Credit Union Administration (NCUA) is an independent Federal agency that regulates and insures the nation's Federal credit unions and provides insurance coverage to some state chartered credit unions. A *credit union* is a nonprofit cooperative of individuals with some common denominator (such as employment, professional association, residence, etc.) organized to promote savings among its members and to provide loans, at low rates, to its members. Credit unions are relatively new institutions in this country. The first one was started in 1908 in New Hampshire. As of 1934, there were about 2,000 credit unions, all state chartered. The Federal Credit Union Act of 1934 started the Federal credit union system. Under this law, as amended, NCUA charters Federal credit unions. NCUA also controls mergers, divisions, and conversions (state to Federal or Federal to state) for credit unions. Currently, there are over 22,000 credit unions; approximately 13,000 are Federal credit unions and the remainder are chartered in 46 of the 50 states.

The NCUA is directed by a three member bipartisan board. The members are appointed by the President, with approval by the Senate, for six year terms. The chairman is named by the President. The NCUA is headquartered in Washington, D.C., and operates out of its six regional offices located in Boston, Harrisburg, Atlanta, Toledo, Austin, and San Francisco. NCUA is financed by fees charged to the individual credit unions for the services that it performs.

The credit union industry is a major source of credit for consumer installment loans, providing between 15 and 20 percent of the amount of such loans in recent years.[1] The growth of Federal credit unions seems assured since they recently (1977) were authorized to engage in real estate lending (e.g., financing home purchases).

The NCUA directly controls the Federal credit union system. In addition, NCUA acts as an insurer of the savings (i.e., shares) of about 4,000 state chartered credit unions, accounting for one half of all savings in all state chartered credit unions. Federal credit unions and these state chartered, Federally insured credit unions have their members (share) accounts individually insured for up to $40,000 through the National Credit Union Share Insurance Fund administered by NCUA.

The credit union industry is quite diverse in size. Some credit unions are quite small, having less than $100,000 in assets. Others are quite large; the largest has over one-half billion dollars in assets. This diversity in size is, in part, reflected in the degree of accounting refinement required by NCUA of its Federally chartered credit unions.

NCUA REGULATIONS

The regulations of the NCUA are published in Title 12 of the Code of Federal Regulations, Parts 700–760. While some agencies incorporate their accounting regulations directly in the Code of Federal Regulations, others, like NCUA, incorporate their accounting regulations by reference. The following publications of NCUA are related to accounting:

Accounting Manual for Federal Credit Unions

Supervisory Committee Manual for Federal Credit Unions

Accounting Guidelines for Real Estate Lending

Data Processing Guidelines for Federal Credit Unions

Accounting Machine Handbook for Federal Credit Unions

Special Accounting and Operating Procedures for Federal Credit Unions Maintaining Overseas Offices

Accounting for the Sale of Food Stamps.

The first two of these documents cover the basic accounting and auditing requirements of NCUA.

ACCOUNTING

The NCUA *Accounting Manual* is a very comprehensive document. It covers everything about credit union accounting from the most elementary (e.g., the purposes of accurate and current records) to the most technical (e.g., disposition of the proceeds of the liquidation of collateral in possession of the credit union). It also allows credit unions to employ *either* the modified cash basis of accounting *or* the accrual basis of accounting. The degree of detail of the instructions and the flexibility in the choice of an accounting system is apparently NCUA's way of accommodating the diverse group that it regulates (i.e., ranging from very small to very large credit unions).

Double Entry System and Basic Data Flows

In Part I of the *Accounting Manual,* the double-entry system is introduced and the basic data flows (e.g., from books of original entry to books of final entry) are explained. Also, the main differences between the accrual basis and modified cash basis are described:

This manual prescribes that the accounting records of Federal credit unions will be maintained on either of two accounting bases; namely, the modified cash basis or the accrual basis.

Modified Cash Basis

Generally under a strictly cash basis of accounting, income is recorded and accounted for when actually collected and expenses are accounted for when paid. Under the modified cash basis prescribed herein, the accounting will be based on the actual receipt and disbursement transactions of the credit union except that provisions will be made to reflect:

- liabilities which are not promptly paid when due.

- dividends and interest refunds applicable to the accounting period but not yet paid.

- deferred income or expenses applicable to future periods.

- estimated losses to be sustained on loans outstanding and other risk assets.

- depreciation on fixed assets.

The foregoing exceptions to maintenance of accounting records on a strictly cash basis are designed to recognize in the accounts certain significant financial transactions not involving the concurrent receipt or disbursement of cash and to show their effect in financial reports prepared from the accounts.

Credit unions for which adoption of the accrual basis of accounting is not practicable will use the modified cash basis of accounting.

Accrual Basis

The accrual basis of accounting refers to that method under which liabilities and expenses are recorded when incurred, whether or not paid, and income is recorded when earned, whether or not received.

It is intended that credit union accounting will be maintained on the accrual basis by all credit unions for which such basis is deemed practicable by them. The adoption of the accrual basis of accounting is particularly recommended for use by large credit unions, e.g., those with assets of more than $1 million, at the option of their boards of directors.[2]

Accounting Principles and Their Application

Part 2 of the *Accounting Manual* entitled "Accounting Principles and Standards for Federal Credit Unions" explains some of the basic concepts underlying the accounting principles and their application to credit unions:

Separate Enterprise

Going Concern

Monetary Basis for Accounting

Consistency

Timely Recognition in Accounting Records

Materiality

Conservative Accounting

Internal Control

For example, the following is the *Accounting Manual's* discussion of materiality and conservatism:

Materiality

Material facts, individually and cumulatively, relating to credit union financial activity must be recognized in the accounts of a credit union and reported on its financial statements. A statement, fact, or item is material if, giving full consideration to the surrounding circumstances as they exist at the time, it is of such a nature that its disclosure, or the method of treating it, would be likely to influence or to "make a difference" in the judgment and conduct of a reasonable person. The accumulation of many small items, each of which in itself would not be "material," would be "material" if the overall effect would tend to influence the judgment and conduct of a reasonable person.

Conservative Accounting

Each credit union will maintain its accounting records on a conservative basis. It will make reasonable provisions in the accounts, based on its best judgment, for potential losses in the realization of recorded assets and in the settlement of actual or contingent liabilities. It will neither overstate nor understate materially its assets, liabilities, revenues or expenses.[3]

The *Accounting Manual* highlights the fact that within accounting principles there often exist a number of alternative practices to accommodate varying circumstances:

Accounting Alternatives Available

Within the accounting principles authorized by the NCUA for the use by credit unions, various alternatives are provided for adoption at the option of any credit union for certain types of transactions. These alternatives are designed to provide the flexibility required for meaningful accounting under a variety of circumstances that may be encountered by credit unions of different size and scope of operations.

Absolute uniformity is neither required nor desirable so long as each credit union conforms its accounting to the authorized generally accepted accounting principles. Credit unions may, at any time, adopt accounting principles promulgated by the Financial Accounting Standards Board which are not inconsistent with principles and standards set forth herein. When a significant change in the accounting method is made, however, the facts concerning the change must be disclosed on financial reports.[4]

The accounting principles applicable to the various categories of financial statement components (i.e., assets, liabilities, equity, revenues, and expenses) are described under both the modified cash basis and the accrual basis. The term *modified cash basis* might better have been labeled "modified accrual basis" since it is really closer to the accrual basis than to the cash basis. For example, after going through an extended discussion of the principles governing liabilities under the modified cash basis, the following are the only differences noted from the accrual basis:

Under the Accrual Basis of Accounting

The principles and standards applicable to the modified cash basis of accounting apply under the accrual basis of accounting, except as follows:

Accrued Interest Payable

Credit unions will record in each month or dividend period the accrued interest payable on notes and mortgages payable, with offsetting charge to interest expense.

Accrued Expenses

Credit unions will accrue expenses to

allocate the costs to the periods benefited, e.g., accrued examination and supervision fees, salaries, etc. The accruals normally will be recorded each month or dividend period so that all significant expenses will be shown on financial reports provided to directors and members.[5]

Under the modified cash basis accounts payable and estimated losses on loans *are* accrued. These are accrual accounting, not cash basis accounting phenomena.

Since a credit union's major activity is loaning funds, the regulations dealing with the recognition of losses on loans are very important. The regulations on loan losses are as follows:

Loan Losses

Losses on loans and related assets will be recorded as described below:

• Loan losses, and losses on property acquired in liquidation of loans, will be charged off with the approval of the board of directors as they occur by charges to the valuation allowance established for losses on loans and other receivables. Recoveries on loans charged off will be recorded as they occur as credits to the valuation allowance.

• The valuation allowance will be established and maintained to reflect the estimated amount of (1) uncollectible loans, (2) losses on assets acquired in liquidation of loans, and (3) losses on loans purchased from other credit unions. The amount of the allowance provision will be adjusted at least at the end of each dividend period. For this purpose, the amount of the adjustment will be determined based on either the "Experience Method" or the "Adjustment Method" as described below.[6]

The *experience method* referred to above bases the current period's expense for loan losses on the credit union's most recent six year period. The actual loan losses divided by the loans granted during this period yields the historical loan loss rate for the credit union. This rate is then applied to the loans granted during the current period to determine the current period's loan loss expense and the accompanying increase in the loan valuation allowance (i.e., contra asset) account. If the credit union feels that the valuation allowance is still not adequate, it may increase it (and the period's loan loss expense) appropriately.

The *adjustment method* referred to above is much more subjective than the *experience method*. The adjustment method entails a review of all outstanding loans, collateral, loan delinquency status, general economic conditions, etc. Based upon this review, the credit union is to determine what valuation allowance is necessary to provide for loan losses. The existing valuation allowance (i.e., any remaining from prior periods) is increased up to the level needed. This establishes the period's loan loss expense.

Financial Reports

Part 3 of the *Accounting Manual* deals with financial reports. The NCUA is very concerned with the internal reporting structure of credit unions. Therefore, it prescribes mandatory reports and the frequency with which they must be produced for the directors and members of the credit union:

In order to provide the directors and members with facts about their credit union, it is required that monthly financial reports be prepared. A copy of the reports must be displayed so that the members may have a picture of the development and financial condition of their credit union. A copy also must be submitted to the directors for consideration at their regular meeting. These reports represent the financial report specified by the bylaws. In addition, each credit union will prepare and display a statement of changes in undivided earnings at the end of each dividend period. Also, as of the calendar year end each credit union following the accrual basis of accounting will prepare and display all five financial reports listed in . . . [Table 4-1].[7]

The NCUA gives credit unions two options in regard to the format of the financial statements that they produce for their directors and members. They can either use forms designed by the NCUA or:

Under the second optional procedure, any credit union may adopt a form of financial report designed to satisfy its particular needs provided it accomplishes a full disclosure of the current financial condition of the credit union and results of its operations for the period covered. Any alternative report format adopted should be substantially similar to the corresponding standard form.[8]

In addition to these reporting requirements, all Federal credit unions are required to file a Year End Report with NCUA. The report includes a statement of financial position, an earnings statement, and a number of detailed schedules of operating information.

NCUA has explicitly stated the *qualitative* disclosure requirements that it expects Federal credit unions to follow:

Full and Fair Disclosure Defined

"Full and fair disclosure" is the level of disclosure which a reasonable person would provide to a member of a credit union, a creditor, or the NCUA in order

TABLE 4-1
Frequency of Report Requirements

Name of Report	Frequency	By Which Credit Union
Statement of Financial Condition	Monthly	All
Statement of Income	Monthly	All
Statement of Changes in Undivided Earnings	End of each dividend period	All
Statement of Changes in Equity	Annually	Those on accrual basis
Statement of Changes in Financial Position	Annually	Those on accrual basis
Statistical Report	Monthly	All

Source: U.S. National Credit Union Administration, *Accounting Manual for Federal Credit Unions* (1975), p. 3-1.

to fairly inform them of the financial condition and the results of operation of the credit union.[9]

General Ledger Accounts. The general ledger accounts to be maintained by Federal credit unions are enumerated in Part 4 of the *Accounting Manual.* The accounts are not only listed, they are also explained for both the accrual basis and modified cash basis of accounting where there are differences in the accounting under each system. The basic structure of the accounts are:

100s — Operating Income

200–300s — Operating Expense

400s — Nonoperating Income and Expense

700s — Assets

800s — Liabilities

900s — Equities

The equity section of the credit union's statement of financial position is composed of three main components: (a) shares, (b) reserves, and (c) undivided earnings.

The *shares* accounts represent the investment (i.e., "savings accounts") of the members of the credit union *plus* any accumulated dividends (i.e., the periodic posting of an interest equivalent based on the member's shares balance) *less* any withdrawals by the member. The shares are accounted for somewhat like a cross between a partnership capital account and a principle-plus-interest liability account.

The *reserves* accounts are the equivalent of appropriations of retained earnings for a stock corporation. Most reserves are voluntary; however, the "Regular Reserve" is a statutory requirement (12 U.S.C. Sec. 1762):

Reserves.—(a) At the end of each accounting period the gross income shall be determined. From this amount, there shall be set aside, as a regular reserve against losses on loans and against such other losses as may be specified in regulations prescribed under this Act, sums in accordance with the following schedule:

(1) A credit union in operation for more than four years and having assets of $500,000 or more shall set aside (A) 10 per centum of gross income until the regular reserve shall equal 4 per centum of the total outstanding loans and risk assets, then (B) 5 per centum of gross income until the regular reserve shall equal 6 per centum of the total of outstanding loans and risk assets.

(2) A credit union in operation less than four years having assets of less than $500,000 shall set aside (A) 10 per centum of gross income until the regular reserve shall equal 7½ per centum of the total of outstanding loans and risk assets, then (B) 5 per centum of gross income until the regular reserve shall equal 10 per centum of the total of outstanding loans and risk assets.

(3) Whenever the regular reserve falls below the stated per centum of the total of outstanding loans and risk assets, it shall be replenished by regular contributions in such amounts as may be needed to maintain the stated reserve goals.

(b) The Board may decrease the reserve requirement set forth in subsection (a) of this section when in its opinion such a decrease is necessary or desirable. The Board may also require special reserves to protect the interests of members either by regulation or for an individual credit union in any special case.

This reserve procedure serves to limit the dividends available to be distributed from the undivided earnings account to the shares account which then could be withdrawn by members.

The *undivided earnings* account is the equivalent of the retained earnings account for a stock corporation. (There is also provision in the equity section for donated equity which is to be amortized to income as the donated asset is amortized to expense.)

Account Forms and Procedures

Part 5 of the *Accounting Manual,* "Account Forms and Procedures," covers a number of procedural issues related to the accounting function (e.g., "Daily Balancing of Postings to Individual Share and Loan Ledgers") as well as recommended components of a good system of internal control.

Charts and Tables

The last Part (6) of the *Accounting Manual* contains frequently needed charts and tables for credit unions.

AUDITS

The NCUA requires that all Federal credit unions be audited at least once each year. The responsibility for the conduct of the examination rests with the credit union's supervisory committee. The supervisory committee's duties are fully explained in the NCUA's *Supervisory Committee Manual for Federal Credit Unions.*

The supervisory committee is appointed by the board of directors of the credit union. It consists of a minimum of three and a maximum of five members. One of the members of the supervisory committee can concurrently serve on the board of directors (other than the treasurer). The *Supervisory Committee Manual* describes the committee's duties and responsibilities as follows:

THE FUNCTIONS OF THE SUPERVISORY COMMITTEE

The primary function of the committee is to make internal audits designed to determine that: (1) accounting records and reports are prepared promptly and accurately reflect operations and their results; (2) established internal controls are effectively maintained and adequately protect the credit union, its members, its management, and its employees; and (3) each unit of the credit union is carrying out the plans, policies, and procedures for which it is responsible.

The supervisory committee also appraises policies and provides safeguards against error, carelessness, and fraud.

Another important objective of the supervisory committee's independent appraisal of operations and policies is to safeguard the reputations of operating officials of the credit union against unfair and unfounded criticism by members and outsiders.

The supervisory committee, as the members' representative, can also exercise various other important functions:

(1) It can suspend directors, executive officers, or members of the credit committee and call a special meeting of the members to act on the suspension. The suspension requires a unanimous vote of the committee. . . .

(2) It can call a special meeting, by a majority vote of the committee members, to consider any violation of the Federal Credit Union Act, rules and regulations, charter or bylaws, or to consider any practice of the credit union which the committee deems to be unsafe or unauthorized. . . .[10]

Thus, the supervisory committee has a much broader slate of duties and responsibilities than does the *audit committee* of the board of directors of publicly held corporations.

In discussing the qualifications of members of the supervisory committee, the *Manual* notes the following:

QUALIFICATIONS OF SUPERVISORY COMMITTEE MEMBERS

The board's appointment of supervisory committee members reflects the fact that the board has confidence in the committee member's integrity and in his ability to assume positions of responsibility in safeguarding the credit union's assets and the interests of the members. Whether the confidence of the board and the members is justified by the subsequent performance of the committee depends to a great extent on the attitude of each committee member. Special knowledge and techniques required to do a creditable job on the supervisory committee can be acquired if the individual committee member has a genuine interest in acquiring them. *However, other qualities being equal, members who have accounting knowledge should be appointed to the committee. Such knowledge will enable them to more readily become competent auditors of credit union activity.*[11] [Emphasis added.]

Use of Independent Accountants

Many Federal agencies require that annual audits of the entities that they regulate be conducted by independent public accountants. NCUA insists that any role played by an independent accountant remain *secondary* to that of the supervisory committee:

SERVICES OF PUBLIC ACCOUNTANTS

In Federal credit unions which have grown in size and complexity, the supervisory committees have found it practical to engage professional accountants to make audits. Payment of the fees charged by the professional accountants must be authorized by the board of directors. The selection of the accountants and the coordination of their work with the work of the supervisory committee, however, are responsibilities of the committee. Since the committee will need to continually evaluate the effectiveness of the work of the accountant or accounting firm, there should be freedom to change the accountant or firm when the committee determines there is need to do so. For this reason, it is recommended that any written contracts with professional accountants be limited to 1 year.

The function and responsibility of a supervisory committee in a Federal credit union is a matter of law. The fact that the determination has been made to engage the services of a professional accountant and that the accountant signs the audit report(s) does not change the requirement of the Federal Credit Union Act in this respect. *The responsibilities of the supervisory committee cannot be delegated to a professional accountant engaged by the credit union.* The professional accountants should be instructed to submit signed audit reports to the supervisory committee and not to the board of directors. The committee will then explain the findings and report of the professional accountants to the officials and members.[12] [Emphasis added.]

There is a class of credit unions, known as "Corporate Central Federal Credit Unions," which has a somewhat different audit requirement than other Federal credit unions. A Corporate Central Federal Credit Union is one whose depositors are *other* credit unions, i.e., it is a credit union for credit unions. The supervisory committees of Corporate Central Federal Credit Unions *must* have their annual audits conducted by independent public accountants. The committee *cannot* perform its own examination to satisfy the audit requirement.

Examination by the Supervisory Committee

The majority of the *Supervisory Committee Manual* is taken up with a detailed discussion of the audit objectives and the audit procedures deemed necessary or advisable in order to achieve those objectives. The major sections are:

Audit Procedures

Verification of Members Accounts

Conducting Audits when an EDP System is used

Preparation of Workpapers and Reports.

The *Manual* recommends that the supervisory committee rely on one of the more traditional audit techniques —the surprise audit:

> Some of the procedures that lead to effective controlled conditions are discussed below. Successful use of the procedures requires careful planning by the committee and effective teamwork and coordination.

> (1) The surprise contact. — The element of surprise has always been considered desirable in connection with audits of financial institutions. A surprise contact has the important advantage of finding operations on a normal, everyday level, since no one has had the opportunity to "clean house" or manipulate records in anticipation of a visit from the supervisory committee.

> (2) Physical control of the records. — In addition to the element of surprise in making the contact for an audit, it is essential that the committee establish and maintain effective control over the liquid assets and key records of the credit union immediately upon entry into the credit union office.[13]

At the completion of its examination, the supervisory committee is to render reports to the board of directors, the members of the credit union, and NCUA. The supervisory committee is responsible for following up on any weaknesses in a credit union's internal controls that were brought to light by an examination:

> Occasionally a supervisory committee finds that the credit union's records are not being kept current or are out of balance. The condition should be reported to the board of directors as soon as discovered with the recommendation that corrective action be instituted at once. Depending on the

circumstances, the board of directors may have to employ temporary help, provide additional assistance on a permanent basis, or replace the person responsible for the unsatisfactory conditions. If the board of directors does not take prompt and effective action, the supervisory committee should communicate with the regional office of the National Credit Union Administration.

Records that are not up to date or that are out of balance sometimes indicate a defalcation. Therefore, it is important for the committee to follow through carefully in such instances to assure itself that any problems in this area are fully resolved.[14]

Similarly, at any time during the year the suspicion or discovery of defalcations may call the committee into action:

SPECIAL AUDITS AND SUPPLEMENTARY PROCEDURES

The completion of an annual audit each year represents only the minimum work of the committee. The committee may expand this program as it sees fit. In special instances, the supervisory committee may find it necessary to perform special audits or supplementary procedures. These special instances would include situations such as when a defalcation or defalcation indicators are encountered or when there is a change of treasurer or other key operating personnel. The time schedule for the performance of the annual audit is flexible so that it may serve the purposes of a special audit, especially in connection with a defalcation. In cases of defalcations suspected or discovered during an audit, the procedures should be expanded to cover at least the minimum procedures of the annual audit. If a defalcation is suspected or discovered

at a time that an audit is not in progress, the committee should promptly commence an annual audit and immediately notify the regional office of the National Credit Union Administration as well as the surety bond company. *Also, where there is evidence of a defalcation, the local office of the FBI should be notified promptly.*[15] [Emphasis added.]

Examinations by NCUA

All Federal credit unions are subject to examination by NCUA's staff of examiners. In recent years, 80 to 90 percent of all Federal credit unions have been examined annually by NCUA. The main objectives of the NCUA examination are: (a) to determine the extent of compliance with applicable laws and regulations, (b) to review the soundness of the management practices of the credit union, (c) to assess the financial condition, in general, and the solvency, in particular, of the credit union, and (d) to review NCUA's exposure through its insurance program.

The NCUA examiners are greatly aided in directing the thrust of their examination for a specific credit union by the supervisory committee's examination and its supporting workpapers (which are accessible to the examiners) and NCUA's own *Early Warning System* (EWS). The EWS is a computerized model that provides early notice of any worrisome trends or deterioration in a credit union's condition. This permits NCUA to conduct a more efficient examination, and to recommend effective remedial measures.

REFERENCE NOTES

1. U.S., National Credit Union Administration, *1978 Annual Report of the National Credit Union Administration,* p. 4.

2. U.S., National Credit Union Administration, *Accounting Manual for Federal Credit Unions* (1975), p. 1-2.

3. *Ibid.,* p. 2-2.

4. *Ibid.,* p. 2-3.

5. *Ibid.,* p. 2-7.

6. *Ibid.,* p. 2-8.

7. *Ibid.,* p. 3-1.

8. *Ibid.,* p. 3-1.

9. *Ibid.,* p. 2-11.

10. U.S., National Credit Union Administration, *Supervisory Committee Manual for Federal Credit Unions* (1978), p. 1.

11. *Ibid.,* p. 2.

12. *Ibid.,* p. 3.

13. *Ibid.,* p. 10.

14. *Ibid.,* p. 11.

15. *Ibid.,* p. 13.

Chapter 5

Interstate Commerce Commission

The Interstate Commerce Commission (ICC) was established in 1887. It was originally charged with the regulation of interstate commerce by railroad. However, amendments to the Interstate Commerce Act and various other laws have extended its authority to most modes and agents of surface transportation in interstate commerce: railroads, trucking companies, bus companies, freight forwarders, water carriers, transportation brokers, and express agencies. Rate bureaus (organizations of carriers that establish rate agreements) are also regulated. Petroleum pipelines were recently transferred to the purview of the Federal Energy Regulatory Commission (Chapter 13); now the ICC only has responsibility for a few commodity pipelines such as those that transport coal slurry.

The ICC is headed by an 11 member bipartisan commission appointed by the President with the approval of the Senate. Commissioners hold seven year terms. The chairman of the Commission is designated annually by the President. The commissioners elect their own vice-chairman. The ICC is headquartered in Washington, D.C. and operates about 80 field offices among its six regions located throughout the country. The regional offices are located in Boston, Philadelphia, Atlanta, Chicago, Fort Worth, and San Francisco.

The ICC controls most of the economic facets of the operations of the entities that it regulates. Some of the specific aspects of its authority are:

1. To control entry of new carriers into the interstate markets.

2. To control rates.

3. To regulate mergers and the formation of holding companies.

4. To administer the bankruptcy laws applicable to railroads.

5. To regulate the issuance of securities by carriers.

6. To approve the extension or termination of services to geographic areas.

The ICC's regulation over interstate commerce could be viewed as mainly economic; the safety practices of the modes are controlled by other Federal entities, generally within the Department of Transportation. The following tabulation gives an approximate number of carriers (and regulated noncarriers) by mode of transportation:

	No. of Firms
Trucking	16,870
Railroads	320
Railroad switching and terminal companies	150
Motor carriers of passengers	1,100
Water carriers	180
Regulated holding companies	90
Freight forwarders	180
Rate bureaus	90
Other noncarrier entities	300[1]

The ICC's control over the various modes is greatest for railroads where 100 percent of intercity traffic is subject to Federal regulation; it drops off to about 45 percent for motor carriers (e.g., trucks and buses); and it is least significant in the case of water carriers —about 7 percent of which are regulated. The unregulated segments of these modes are accounted for by such entities as governmental units, companies transporting their own goods (i.e., private carriers), and exempt carriers (e.g., certain carriers of agricultural goods).

ICC REGULATIONS

The ICC's regulations are contained in Chapter X, Title 49 of the Code of Federal Regulations, Parts 1000 through 1399. The majority of the ICC's accounting regulations are contained in Parts 1200 through 1211 which comprise the uniform systems of accounts for various carriers. Part 1200 covers the general accounting regulations of the ICC. The remaining parts deal with specific categories of regulated entities:

Part	Regulated Entity
1201	Railroad companies
1204	Pipeline companies
1205	Refrigerator car lines
1206	Common and contract motor carriers of passengers
1207	Class I and Class II common and contract motor carriers of property
1208	Maritime carriers
1209	Inland and coastal waterways carriers
1210	Freight forwarders
1211	Rate bureaus

Rather than reviewing each uniform system in detail, the uniform system for railroads [49 CFR 1201] will be the basis for the balance of this chapter. Any variances or unique provisions witnessed in the uniform systems for other carriers will be addressed to counterpoint the railroad system in a separate section following the discussion of railroads.

GENERALLY ACCEPTED ACCOUNTING PRINCIPLES

The ICC prefaces its enumeration of the various uniform systems of accounts with two overall provisions regarding the interface between its regulations and generally accepted accounting principles (GAAP). The first provision [49 CFR 1200.1] notes that carriers can publish financial statements for the use of their stockholders and other interested parties, which statements are in conformity with GAAP " . . . provided that any variance from this Commission's prescribed accounting rules contained in such statements is clearly disclosed in footnotes to the statements."

The second provision [49 CFR 1200.2] explains the ICC's procedure for *either* incorporating a statement of the Financial Accounting Standards Board (FASB) into its regulations *or* for instructing carriers as to its rationale for not incorporating such a statement into its regulations. In either instance, the ICC issues an Accounting Series Circular (ASC), which addresses the FASB statement, for discussion and comment prior to making any change in its regulations.

CLASSIFICATION OF CARRIERS

The ICC has set up classes of its carriers, based on level of operating revenues. The lower carrier classes generally have reduced reporting requirements and do not have to follow the uniform system of accounts for the larger carriers. The limits for the operating revenues of the various classes of carriers are shown in Table 5-1.

Railroads

Account Structure. There is no uniform account numbering system across carriers. However, the various carrier systems tend to share the same account structure (i.e., organization of accounts within statements). The major segments of the account structure for the balance sheet and income statement are shown in Figure 5-1. The financial statement format differs from that employed in many regulated industries that are capital intensive in that the balance sheet is *not* presented in inverted order (i.e., with the property and long-term liability accounts listed first). However, in common with other regulated industries, the income statement format has the carriers distinguish income from their regulated activity from income for unregulated activity (e.g., interest).

The ICC treatment of (a) extraordinary items, (b) effects of disposing of a segment of the entity, (c) changes in accounting principles, and (d) prior period adjustments appear to be in conformity with GAAP. The one additional requirement is ICC concurrence with the carrier's judgment [49 CFR 1201, General Instructions, 1-2(d) (7)]:

> *Commission Approval and Accountant's Letter.* Items shall be included in the accounts provided for extraordinary items, unusual or infrequent items, discontinued operations, prior period adjustments and cumulative effect of changes in accounting principles only upon approval of the Commission. If the carrier retains the service of an independent accountant, a request for using these accounts shall be accompanied by a letter from the independent accountant approving or otherwise commenting on the request.

Further, carriers are expected to submit any questions involving doubtful interpretation of ICC regulations or GAAP to the Commission for resolution.

TABLE 5-1
Operating Revenue Limits for Carriers

Carrier	Class	Operating Revenues— Over	Class	Operating Revenues Over – Under	Class	Operating Revenues— Under
Railroads	I	$50 million	II	$10 million – 50 million	III	$10 million
Motor carriers of passengers	I	3 million	II*	.5 million – 3 million	III*	.5 million
Motor carriers of property	A	5 million	B	1 million – 5 million	C*	1 million
Inland and coastal waterway carriers	I	.5 million	II	.1 million – .5 million	III*	.1 million
Freight forwarders	A	.1 million			B*	.1 million
Rate bureaus	I	.1 million			II*	.1 million

*Do not have to follow uniform system of accounts.

Materiality. Rather than relying on the variability in judgment from carrier to carrier as to the criteria for materiality, the ICC has adopted the following definition of *materiality* [49 CFR 1201, General Instructions, 1–2(d) (6)]:

> *Materiality.* As a general standard an item shall be considered material when it exceeds 10 percent of annual income (loss) before extraordinary items. An item may also be considered in relation to the trend of annual earnings before extraordinary items or other appropriate criteria. Items shall be considered individually and not in the aggregate in determining materiality. However, the effects of a series of related transactions arising from a single specific and identifiable event or plan of action shall be aggregated to determine materiality.

Just and Reasonable Charges. The ICC's regulations include a requirement [49 CFR 1201, General Instructions 1–6] that all transactions affecting regulated activities of the carrier must be just and reasonable, and not in excess of the amounts necessary for the honest and efficient operation and management of the carrier. Any amount of a trans-

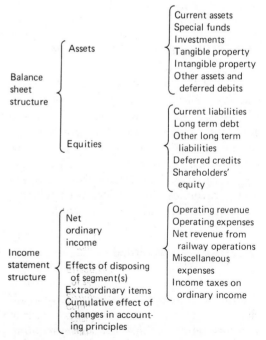

FIGURE 5-1. Account Structure for Balance Sheet and Income Statement.

action that violates this criterion is to be charged off as a nonoperating expense.

Relationship Between Financial Accounting and Managerial Accounting Systems. A recent change in the ICC regulations for railroads put the carriers on notice that, while the regulations are mainly oriented toward the carrier as a unitary entity, it is presumed that the carrier has a managerial accounting system that reflects its unique organizational structure. The ICC expects that the carrier will accumulate cost data by its defined responsibility centers for purposes of cost planning and control. While the ICC does not routinely require data reported at this level of detail, it is expected that " . . . the carrier shall keep the detailed information to provide a ready analysis and verification of the costs collected by cost center" [49 CFR 1201 General Instructions, 1–3 (f)].

Although the ICC's regulations for railroads do not get down to the level of cost centers in their prescriptions, they do give guidance for the accumulation of costs by major functions, classes of customer, and for branch-line accounting. These areas of allocation are discussed later in this chapter.

Currently, a proposed rule is being considered that would require larger railroads to accumulate and report (to the ICC) a great deal of operating data by cost centers and cost categories (i.e., grouping of cost centers). Carriers would be required to routinely (e.g., in their annual report) report cost category data to the ICC *and* to report cost center data when called upon to do so. This "cost center accounting

and reporting system" will move the ICC away from having to rely on system-wide averages. The ICC will be able to relate different levels of operating expenses to such explanatory elements as traffic and/or track-related factors. The carriers will charge operating expenses to specific line segments. Then, these expenses will be accumulated separately, for example for heavily used versus lightly used segments or long haul vs. short haul segments. These types of cost centers will permit more hypotheses to be tested in regard to such factors as the impact of traffic volume on costs.

Income Tax Allocation. The ICC requires carriers to employ the procedure of interperiod income tax allocation where there are timing differences between the carrier's revenues and expenses as recognized according to (a) the ICC's uniform system of accounts and (b) the Internal Revenue Service's (and state and local taxing authorities') regulation. This procedure is in conformity with GAAP. However, while GAAP requires that any accruals be based upon the existing tax rates, the ICC regulations provide that the carrier can petition the Commission to allow the carrier to employ expected future rates (i.e., that are expected to be in effect when the timing differences reverse).

Government Transfer. Many railroads receive payments from governmental units (Federal, state, and local) to help sustain the carriers' operations in general, the operation of a specific line (e.g., a commuter rail line), or to improve or expand the carrier's operating property (fixed assets). The accounting for such payments varies, depending upon the circumstances. In general, the following rules apply:

1. Transfers that are designated for the following factors are recorded as *revenues* of the current period:
   a. Payments to offset operating losses.
   b. Payments to underwrite operating expenses.
   c. Payments that the carrier has the *option* of applying to *either* operating expenses *or* improving or expanding operating property.

2. Transfers that are received for the improvement or expansion of *depreciable* operating property are credited to a *deferred revenue account*. As depreciation accrues on the attendant property, an equal amount is amortized from this deferred revenue account to operating revenues.

3. Transfers that are received for the acquisition of *nondepreciable* operating property are immediately credited to a *stockholders' equity* account (i.e., "Other Capital Surplus").

4. Where the carrier and a government unit jointly participate in a construction project the carrier recognizes only its own actual expenditures (and none of the governmental unit's) as the cost of the resulting operating property.

Accounting for Fixed Assets. A great deal of the ICC's regulations are aimed at the carriers' accounting practices for their fixed assets. The ICC has established a $2,000 materiality criterion

for distinguishing capitalizable expenditures from those that are to be immediately expensed. Carriers are cautioned that they cannot parcel out expenditures under an integrated project in order to circumvent the intent of this rule. However, carriers can adopt a limit lower than $2,000 as long as the ICC is notified and the new limit is consistently applied.

Construction Costs. The regulations enumerate those costs that are to be capitalized as the cost of projects for the construction of fixed assets. Most of the costs (e.g., materials, labor, operating costs of work trains servicing the site, etc.) are as expected. Two somewhat unique items enumerated are (a) "Cost of protection from casualties . . . such as payments for discovery or extinguishment of fires, cost of detecting and prosecuting incendiaries, witness fees in relation thereto . . ." [49 CFR 1201, Instructions for Property Accounts, 2-6 (g)]; and (b) "Cost of injuries [to persons] and damages [to property] when incurred directly as a result of construction projects . . ." [49 CFR 1201, Instructions for Property Accounts, 2-6 (h)].

The ICC permits carriers to capitalize the cost of interest during construction by employing the guidelines found in the Financial Accounting Standard's Board Statement No. 34, Capitalization of Interest Cost.

Property Acquired in Merger or Acquisition. When a carrier acquires property in a transaction accounted for as a *pooling of interest*, the cost of the property to the predecessor entity (adjusted, as necessary, to conform to

ICC regulations) emerges as the cost of the continuing entity. When such a transaction is accounted for as a *purchase,* the assets of the acquired entity are *written up* to cost incurred by the purchasing entity. This latter procedure differs from other regulated industries (and, as shall be seen, other carriers regulated by the ICC) wherein any difference between the cost to the predecessor entity and the cost incurred by the purchasing entity is charged to an *acquisition adjustment account* which does not enter the depreciation expense computation of the surviving entity.

Depreciation. The ICC requires that carriers use straight-line depreciation applied on a group basis. The following fixed asset accounts are *not* subject to depreciation: ties, rails, other track material, ballast, and track laying and surfacing. These major components of fixed assets are subject to what some have termed "replacement and betterment depreciation." The accounting for these assets is as follows:

1. The initial complement of these items are installed in asset accounts, at cost, and not depreciated.

2. As replacement (in kind) occurs, the cost of replacement is charged to expense.

3. When the replacement involves a betterment (e.g., light rails are replaced with heavier rails), the differential cost (i.e., the actual cost incurred less the cost of replacement in kind) is capitalized. The cost of replacement in kind is charged to expense.

Over the years, the asset balance in these accounts becomes an amalgam of costs of various vintages.

In 1966, the American Institute of Certified Public Accountants' Committee on Relations with the ICC reviewed the "replacement and betterment" method and concurred with its use as a generally accepted procedure appropriate for railroads due to its substantial authoritative support.

Retirements. When a fixed asset subject to depreciation is retired, the full cost of the fixed asset is charged to the accumulated depreciation account, with no gain or loss being recognized. This is in conformity with the *group* method of depreciation. When fixed assets *not* subject to depreciation (e.g., rails, ties, ballast, etc.) are retired (as when a rail line is abandoned), the capitalized cost is fully charged to the expense of the period.

When a railroad anticipates retiring a major segment of its line, it can petition the ICC to allow it to accrue a charge currently in anticipation of the expected loss. It would do this if its depreciation policy would not adequately amortize the cost of the property to be retired.

Accounting for Segments of Activity. Railroad operations involve a high degree of joint facilities that benefit multiple segments of the carrier's activities. The ICC requires segment data in carrying out its regulatory functions. A major area of interest is in allocating expenses between freight and passenger service. In order to accommodate its needs, it has set up a detailed account numbering system that accomplishes two things. First, it results in a high degree of direct charging of expenses to the segments of activity that they solely benefit. Second, it sets up the remaining expenses in accounts that are relatively homogeneous so as to permit the specification of reasoned allocation bases. The account structure is based on the following six digit code:

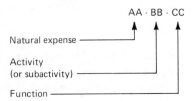

The natural expense field designates the account as being for a generic type of expense (e.g., salaries, materials, purchased services, etc.). The activity (or subactivity) field corresponds to a predefined listing of the segments of the carrier's operations (see Figure 5-2).

Similarly, the function code enumerates over 70 subdivisions (functions) within activities (or subactivities).

Once the expenses are disaggregated by this account coding system, allocations between or among segments of activity can be accomplished. For

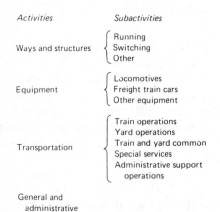

FIGURE 5-2. Segments of Carrier's Operations.

example, in 49 CFR 1242, *Separation of Common Operating Expenses between Freight Service and Passenger Service for Railroads,* the ICC instructs carriers how to determine the cost of these two major segments of their activity. The basic structure followed for the separation is:

1. Direct assignment to one or the other category wherever possible.

2. Allocation of some jointly operating functions on the basis of measures of activity.

3. Allocation of other joint operating functions on the basis of the results of (2) as applied to selected functions. For example, (a) the cost of locomotive repair and maintenance is to be assigned directly to one or the other category wherever possible; (b) the more proximate joint costs that remain are allocated on some basis of activity (e.g., locomotive unit miles, locomotive ton miles); (c) finally, less proximate joint expense accounts related to locomotive repair (e.g., repair of machinery used in the locomotive subactivity) are allocated in the same proportion as the more proximate joint costs of locomotive repair were allocated. In some cases, the less proximate joint cost accounts' allocations are based on several of the more proximate joint cost accounts [49 CFR 1242.34]:

Administrative [costs for locomotives] ...

Separate common expenses according to the distribution of common expenses in the following accounts:

Repairs and Maintenance
Machinery Repair

Equipment Damage
Dismantling Retired Property.

The ICC will permit carriers to vary from the allocation practices contained in this section if the carrier can establish that (a) other methods produce reliable data or (b) the separation procedure is, in any event, too burdensome for it to comply with.

The practical significance of these allocation provisions has been attenuated by the establishment of the National Railroad Passenger Corporation—AMTRAK—in 1970. AMTRAK currently operates over 90 percent of the intercity passenger railroad traffic in the United States. Thus, most railroads are no longer faced with the significant allocation issues that they once had.

Branch Line Accounting System. Railroads that (a) have filed for the abandonment of a rail line, (b) plan to file for such abandonment, (c) are operating a rail line under a directed service order of the ICC, or (d) are operating a rail line under a rail continuation service agreement are required to have a branch-line accounting system for such a line. The purpose of such a system is to " . . . determine accurately the revenues attributable, avoidable costs, and service units of light-density lines scheduled for abandonment. This accurate information is intended to facilitate the determination of the revenues and avoidable costs in abandonment proceedings and in potential offers of subsidy" [49 CFR 1201, Subpart B, § 910 (a)]. The branch-line accounting system matches "attributable" revenue of the line with its "avoidable" costs.

While this process would appear to result in a pure "marginal cost-marginal benefit" analysis of the line, an examination of the enumerated expenses reveals that there are some allocations of expenses. Therefore, the resulting branch-line statement is an approximation of the revenues and expenses attributable to the line. This observation is not a criticism of the branch-line accounting system but rather a recognition of the fact that any accounting system that is based on the full costing concepts inherent in GAAP can generally produce only approximations of marginal or incremental costs without significant modifications.

Refrigerator Car Lines

The uniform system of accounts of 49 CFR 1205 applies to refrigerator car line companies that are owned or controlled by railroads and operate in interstate commerce. Most of the provisions of this uniform system conform to the principles on which the railroad system is grounded. However, certain exceptions are noted in the area of depreciation. First, refrigerator car lines are to use straight-line depreciation applied on a *group* basis for their rolling stock (as is true for railroads) and on a *unit* basis for all other depreciable assets. While most depreciation programs prescribed by the ICC call for depreciation to be accrued monthly in 12 equal amounts, refrigerator car line property that is used seasonally (e.g., ice facilities only in warm months and heater facilities only in cold months) is to have its depreciation accrued over the seasonal period of its use. Finally, the ICC requires refrigerator car lines to record an "acquisition adjustment" for the purchase of used transportation equipment where the consideration paid by the refrigerator car line differs from the seller's book value (original cost less accumulated depreciation). The acquisition adjustment is not subject to amortization as an operating expense. Thus, it does not enter into the determination of income from operations.

Motor Carriers of Passengers

The accounting regulations for motor carriers of passengers have several provisions that differ from the principles applied to railroads. First, the carriers can employ the mileage method of depreciating automotive equipment on either a unit or group basis. This method accrues the depreciation on each unit (or group) of property at a fixed rate per mile run. For those assets that are not depreciated on this basis, the straight-line method is required. The regulations allow carriers that are engaged in seasonal operations to charge their annual depreciation only to those months during which operations are actually conducted.

When a carrier receives a transfer of cash (or other property) from a governmental agency, it follows basically the same procedures as do railroads. The receipt can be recorded either as revenue, deferred revenue, or direct increases in owners' equity (via "unearned surplus"). Payments received from a governmental agency for (a) reimbursement for operating losses (e.g., as is often encountered on a commuter line), (b) subsidies intended to offset operating expenses, and (c) subsidies that are available, at the carrier's discretion, for operating expenses or operating property are to be recorded as *revenue* when received. Payments received that are to be expended by the carrier *only* on operating property are initially recorded as deferred revenue and are amortized to operating revenue in future periods in amounts equal to the depreciation on the attendant assets. Payments received in the form of, or designated for the purchase of, non-depreciable operating property are to be immediately credited to unearned surplus (an owners' equity account). Railroads credit such receipts to an "other capital surplus" account.

Motor Carriers of Property

Motor carriers of property share most of the accounting procedures employed by motor carriers of passengers (e.g., accounting for depreciation). The most unique aspect of the accounting regulations of motor carriers of property is a requirement that the carrier's operating expenses be charged directly to or allocated across functions. The identification of the functions that are required to be costed out is determined by a carrier's operations. Large carriers of *general commodities* have the following array of functions that must be accounted for:

1. Line haul
2. Pickup and delivery
3. Billing and collecting
4. Platform
5. Terminal
6. Maintenance
7. Traffic and sales

8. Insurance and safety

9. General and administrative

Carriers of *household goods* have a different array of functions:

1. Interstate moving

2. Intrastate moving

3. Local moving

4. Indirect operating—carrier only

5. General and administrative—carrier only

6. Packing and crating

7. Warehousing

8. Overseas import and export

9. Indirect operating—noncarrier

The regulations go into some detail in describing the procedures to be employed in allocating expenses to these functions. For example, the following instructions apply to the allocation of property-related expenses [49 CFR 1207, Instruction 28 (A)]:

> (d) (2) . . . carriers shall distribute building- and structure-related expenses to the appropriate activity using one of the following methods (in order of preference):
>
> (i) Carriers may assign the full expense of a particular building or structure to a particular activity based upon the primary purpose of the building or structure, and the activity for which it is used.
>
> (ii) Carriers may assign a proportion of the expense of a building or structure to an activity based upon the square footage used by that particular activity.
>
> (iii) Carriers may use any other reasonable and equitable method they can substantiate.
>
> (iv) Furniture and fixture expenses

> shall be assigned to the building or structure in which it is located.
>
> * * *
>
> (g) All carriers shall be prepared to describe the basis of apportionment used to distribute expenses included in this instruction.
>
> (h) Any carrier which finds it impracticable to distribute expenses as required by this instruction should furnish the Commission with full particulars of the conditions which prevent the proper distribution. Upon receipt of such information carriers will be advised of the procedure to be followed.

If carriers find that the ICC's procedures are impracticable in their circumstances, they can petition the Commission to allow alternative procedures for accumulating expenses by function.

Maritime Carriers

The ICC's regulations for maritime carriers in interstate commerce are interrelated with the regulations of the Maritime Administration (Chapter 11). For example, the ICC's instructions for determining the capitalizable costs and depreciating the maritime vessels incorporate those of the Maritime Administration (MarAd) by reference. Likewise, the ICC regulations include instructions for the proper accounting for operating differential subsidies and capital construction funds, both of which are covered under the Merchant Marine Act and are administered by MarAd. The ICC's account numbering system coincides with that of MarAd. Finally, the annual report filed with the ICC is the same report form required by MarAd.

One aspect of maritime carriers' operations that distinguishes them from other carriers regulated by the ICC is the materiality and duration of individual voyages (vis-á-vis the much shorter and less individually material transports that characterize other modes). Considering this, the ICC has required maritime carriers to (a) treat each voyage as an individual cost objective and (b) defer the recognition of the activity of voyages that are still in progress at the end of an accounting period [40 CFR 1208, General Instruction E] :

> *Voyage accounts.*
>
> (1) The carrier shall keep its records in a manner that will report with respect to operating revenue, operating expense, and other accounts affected, the revenues accrued and the expenses incurred for each terminated voyage of its vessels operated.
>
> (2) The revenues and expenses applicable to unterminated voyages at the end of an accounting period shall be transferred to account 500, "Deferred revenues—unterminated voyages" and account 200, "Deferred expenses—unterminated voyages."

Inland and Coastal Waterway Carriers

Inland and coastal waterway carriers share with maritime carriers the procedure of deferring revenues and expenses on voyages that are incomplete at the end of an accounting period. Unlike most other classes of carriers regulated by the ICC, these carriers *do not* use the group method of depreciation. Depreciation is accrued on a straight-line basis, applied to individual units. When units are retired, a gain or loss is recognized.

These carriers do employ an acquisition adjustment account to record the difference between the consideration paid and the book value (to the seller) on units of property that are acquired. Here again, this results in this portion of the cost of the asset not being amortized as an operating expense through depreciation. This acquisition adjustment account is also used by these carriers to absorb credits on the donation of assets to the carrier [49 CFR 1209, Account 151 (d)] :

> This account shall be credited with donations or contributions in cash or property from governmental agencies, individuals, and others for construction purposes, concurrent charges being made to the appropriate property or other asset accounts.

This procedure differs from other carriers (e.g., motor carriers of persons) wherein an owners' equity account is credited.

Freight Forwarders

Freight forwarders regulated by the ICC are middlemen that arrange for the shipment of goods for the public by one of the classes of carriers regulated by the ICC. One of the services that they perform is the consolidation of smaller shipments which can then be transported more economically. The uniform system of accounts contains no significant exceptions from the basic principles discussed in reference to railroads except that freight forwarders are to use straight-line depreciation applied on a unit basis.

Rate Bureaus

Rate bureaus composed of carriers regulated by the ICC are themselves subject to ICC regulation. In 49 CFR 1211, the ICC has presented a very brief uniform system of accounts that basically (a) sets out the general parameters that bound the presentation of the bureaus' financial statements (e.g., materiality, charges to be just and reasonable, etc.) and (b) lists a very abbreviated chart of accounts that can be further refined by individual bureaus as long as the bureaus can reconcile to the basic system prescribed by the ICC (and, thus, be able to prepare the annual report required of the bureau).

ICC REPORTS

The ICC requires the entities that it regulates to submit periodic reports. The reports vary in terms of their frequency of filing (e.g., quarterly, annually) and in the amount of detail required (e.g., more detail for Class I carriers; less detail for Class III carriers). The annual report required of each carrier is generally the most comprehensive report that it files. For example, the R-1 report is required of all Class I railroads. It is composed of approximately 80 separate schedules. These schedules vary in content from the railroad's basic financial statements, to schedules that enumerate financial statement components (e.g., Schedule 361, Capitalized Capital Leases), to schedules that present railroad operating statistics (e.g., Schedule 750, Consumption of Fuel by Motive-Powered Units). However, Class II railroads file the R-2 report. It is composed of less than 60 schedules. These also vary in content from the basic financial statements to operating statistics.

AUDITS

The ICC conducts audits of those entities that are required to follow a uniform system of accounts. The larger carriers (e.g., Class I railroads) are audited annually. The smaller carriers are audited on a cyclical basis. A significant amount of audit effort is devoted to assisting carriers that have recently become subject to a uniform system of accounts (i.e., because of increased operating revenues) in making the transition to compliance with that system. In addition to auditing for compliance with the uniform system, the audits can also be used to develop data for projects of special interest to the Commission (e.g., reasonableness of depreciable lives of fixed assets).

ICC AND DEREGULATION

Several of the industries controlled by the ICC are currently undergoing a process of deregulation by the Congress. In 1980, a series of laws were passed—the Rail Act of 1980, the Motor Carrier Act of 1980, and the Household Goods Carrier Act of 1980 —which reduced some of the economic controls in the various industries (such as pricing and entry). These laws have not reduced the carriers' financial reporting responsibilities. In fact, some of the financial reporting environment has been bolstered. For example, the Rail Act of 1980 requires the establishment of a Railroad Accounting Principles Board (RAPB). The RAPB is to develop accounting principles that railroads must follow when they report cost accounting data to the government.

REFERENCE NOTE

1. American Trucking Association, *Research Review,* No. 211, June 15, 1979, p. 2.

Chapter 6

Federal Communications Commission

The Federal Communications Commission (FCC) was established by the Federal Communications Act of 1934 to regulate wire and radio communications. The FCC's functions have been expanded (to accommodate technological developments) to include television and satellite communications. The FCC's main functions are to:

Allocate transmission frequencies

Issue transmission licenses

Promulgate and enforce safety regulations

Foster effective and efficient use of communication resources

Regulate common carriers engaged in interstate and foreign operations

The FCC is headed by seven commissioners appointed by the President with concurrence by the Senate. No more than four commissioners can be from the same political party. One commissioner is designated by the President to serve as chairman. Each commissioner is appointed to a seven year term.

The FCC operates out of its headquarters in Washington, D.C., and six regional offices in Atlanta, Boston, Chicago, Kansas City (MO), San Francisco, and Seattle.

The commissioners are supported by a staff which is organized into five functional bureaus:

Broadcast

Cable television

Field operations

Safety and special radio services

Common carrier

While the FCC does accumulate a great deal of economic information about broadcasting entities, it only directly controls the rates, mergers, accounting systems, etc., of the common carriers that it regulates. Communications common carriers provide their services for hire. The main classifications are telephone, telegraph (by wire and radio), satellite communications, and specialized carriers (who provide such services as data, voice, record, and facsimile transmission; remote metering; and control services, all in competition with established carriers). Common carriers regulated by the FCC are required to provide their interstate services (such as message transmission, interconnection of customer-owned equipment, etc.) to all customers at reasonable rates. Their interstate rates (i.e., interstate tariff schedules) must be filed with and approved by the FCC. The FCC has promulgated accounting regulations for the major categories of common carriers.

There are over 1,600 telephone companies in the United States only 62 of which are subject to all of the interstate common carrier provisions administered by the FCC. One domestic telegraph carrier and six international telegraph carriers are subject to FCC regulation.

ACCOUNTING

The system of accounts prescribed by the FCC has been in existence for some time. In its *42nd Annual Report/ Fiscal Year 1976 (Including Transition Quarter),* the FCC noted, "The system of accounts prescribed by the FCC and followed by the States is little changed from the one first developed by AT&T in 1884."[1] The FCC is currently considering revising the system of accounts to accommodate changes in technology and the economic environment, as well as the FCC's and the carriers' data needs.

Code of Federal Regulations

The FCC's regulations are contained in the Code of Federal Regulations, Title 47, Chapter 1, Parts 0-99. Subchapter B (Parts 20-69) contains the regulations for common carriers. The following Parts are most applicable to accounting:

Part	Title
31	Uniform system of accounts for Class A and Class B telephone companies
33	Uniform system of accounts for Class C telephone companies
34	Uniform system of accounts for radio-telegraph carriers
35	Uniform system of accounts for wire-telegraph and ocean cable carriers
42	Preservation of records of communications common carriers
67	Jurisdictional separations

Classifications of Common Carriers

The FCC classifies common carriers based on their volume of business. For telephone companies the classifications are:

Class	Operating Revenues
A	Exceeding $250,000
B	Exceeding $100,000, but not more than $250,000
C	Exceeding $50,000, but not more than $100,000
D	Not exceeding $50,000

Class A and Class B telephone companies, specialized carriers, and domestic satellite carriers are subject to the same basic accounting requirements (contained in Part 31). Class C companies are subject to the accounting requirements of Part 33. Class D companies are requested (but not required) to follow Part 33. A company's classification can be changed over time as it experiences increases or decreases in revenues for a sustained period (3 years).

The classifications for radiotelegraph companies are:

Class	Operating Revenues
A	Exceeding $100,000
B	Exceeding $50,000 but not exceeding $100,000

Class A and Class B radiotelegraph carriers are subject to the same basic system of accounts (Part 34). Class B carriers do not have to keep their operating accounts on as detailed a basis as Class A carriers. No accounting regulations have been specified for carriers having annual operating revenues of $50,000 or less.

Wire-telegraph and ocean-cable carriers have the same Class A and Class B criteria as do radiotelegraph companies. The smaller carriers (Class B) do not have to maintain their operating accounts in as much detail as Class A carriers (as specified in Part 35). No accounting regulations have been promulgated for carriers smaller than the Class B.

Charts of Accounts. Each type (and Class within type) is given guidance as to its chart of accounts. The following generalizations can be made

about the systems of accounts found in all of these Parts (of the CFR).

First, in regard to the balance sheet, the fixed asset accounts are given primacy both in regard to the amount of detail in the regulations and their placement in the statement (i.e., they are listed first, before the current asset accounts). Likewise, on the equity side, long-term debts are listed before current liabilities. For example, the major groupings for telephone companies subject to Part 34 are:

Assets	Liabilities and Owners' Equity
Communications plant	Long term debt
Investments and funds	Current liabilities
Current assets	Provision for future settlements
Prepayments	Deferred credits
Deferred charges	Capital stock
	Capital surplus
	Earned surplus

Second, the amount of detailed instructions given in the regulations tends to vary inversely with the size of the entity. For example, in Part 33 (Class C telephone companies, which are rather small), the regulations actually illustrate the journalization of entries in order to avoid ambiguities [47 CFR 33.65 (e)]:

> For illustration of the application of the straight-line method, assume that depreciable telephone plant costing $100,000 has an estimated service life of 30 years, and an estimated net salvage value of 10 percent, or $10,000, and a service value of 90 percent, or $90,000. The annual depreciation rate would be 3 percent computed by dividing 90 per-

cent by the service life of 30 years. The annual depreciation charge would be $3,000, or 3 percent of $100,000. The monthly charge for depreciation expense would be one-twelfth of the annual charge, or $250.

The journal entries to record the monthly depreciation charge as computed above would be as follows:

	Debit	Credit
Account 5000, "Depreciation expense"	$250	
Account 2600, "Depreciation reserve"		$250

Third, the regulations of all types of carriers attempt to clearly distinguish (a) communications related operations from non-communications related operations and (b) ordinary operating items from extraordinary items. This is illustrated in reviewing the account captions for the various categories of carriers. The following major headings for the income statement outlined in Part 34 (radiotelegraphic carriers) illustrate these distinctions:

Operating revenue
− Operating revenue deductions (e.g., operating expenses)
± Other communication income (losses)
= Operating income
+ Ordinary income—noncommunication (e.g., interest income)
= Gross ordinary income
− Deductions from ordinary income (e.g., interest expense)
= Net ordinary income
+ Extraordinary income—credits
− Extraordinary income—charges
= Net income (before taxes)
− Taxes on net income
= Net income (after taxes)

It should be noted that the regulations' definition of *extraordinary* items does not coincide with that currently employed in generally accepted accounting principles (i.e., APB Opinion No. 30, para. 19-24). For example, the regulations for radiotelegraphic carriers give the following examples of "other extraordinary income credits" [47 CFR 34.6119] and "other extraordinary income charges" [47 CFR 34.6299]:

Other extraordinary income credits . . .

Forfeitures of amounts deposited with the carrier under options for the sale or lease of property.
Profits derived from the sale of property, the cost of which is includible in account 1610, "Miscellaneous physical property."
Profits derived from the sale of reacquired securities other than capital stock.
Profits derived from the sale of securities of other persons.
Profits from the sale of plant . . .
Unclaimed customers' deposits.
Unclaimed wages and dividends written off.

Other extraordinary income charges . . .

Amounts charged to corporate income to provide for the extinguishment of amounts includible in account 81, "Organization."
Amounts charged to income in recognition of decline in value of current

assets and securities owned . . .

Capital stock expenses written off . . .

Forfeitures of amounts deposited by the carrier under options for the purchase or lease of property.

Inventory, appraisal, and other costs incident to the acquisition, sale, or lease of property when the projects are abandoned.

Long-term debt expense written off . . .

Losses of funds due to bank failure.

Losses on the sale of plant.

Losses resulting from the sale, destruction, or retirement of property the cost of which is includible in account 1610, "Miscellaneous physical property."

Losses resulting from the sale of reacquired securities other than capital stock.

Losses resulting from the sale of securities of other persons.

Penalties and fines paid on account of violations of statutes pertaining to regulation.

In the following paragraphs, significant provisions in the accounting regulations of the various types and classes of carriers are reviewed. It should be noted that the same words are not found in all of the sections of the CFR dealing with these carriers. Therefore, the quotations used are intended to be representative.

Accounting for Property and Equipment. Where fixed assets are acquired, their invoice or contract cost (including any peripheral costs such as installation) is to be capitalized. There is an exception when used fixed assets are acquired from a company that is a common carrier. Here the seller's original cost is installed in the buyer's accounts along with the related allowance for depreciation. Any difference between the book value (original cost less allowance for depreciation) of the seller and the amount paid by the buyer is placed in a "Plant acquisition adjustment account." This account is amortized to expense. Depending upon the facts surrounding the acquisition, and FCC approval, it may be treated as an operating item (i.e., considered in setting rates) or as a nonoperating item (i.e., not considered in setting rates). It is more common for it to be considered a nonoperating item.

When assets are constructed, the following costs are to be capitalized [47 CFR 31.2-22]:

Cost of construction

(a) The cost of construction of property chargeable to the telephone plant accounts shall include the cost of labor, material and supplies, transportation, contract work, relief and pensions, protection, injuries and damages, privileges and permits, and rights of way, taxes, special machine services, interests during construction, insurance, construction services, and other analogous elements in connection with said work.

The interest allowed during construction applies *only* to projects whose period of construction is *over* one year. Projects that are constructed in one year or less are not subject to capitalization of interest. The interest allowed during construction is on both the borrowed and/or company provided funds devoted to the construction project. No set formula is given to determine the appropriate rate(s) at which interest is to be accrued. Companies can continue to capitalize interest during a period of suspension of construction (limited to a period of six months unless the FCC approves a longer period).

The insurance allowed as a cost can be either the premium cost of contracted insurance or self-insurance charges estimated (and credited to account 169 "Insurance reserve") by the carrier.

Overhead is to be charged to construction on a fully allocated basis (rather than a marginal or incremental basis) [47 CFR 31–22A (a)] :

Overhead construction costs

All overhead construction costs, such as engineering, supervision, general office salaries and expenses, construction engineering and supervision by others than the accounting company, law expenses, insurance, injuries and damages, relief and pensions, taxes and interest, shall be charged to particular jobs or items on the basis of the amounts of such overheads applicable thereto, to the end that each job or item shall bear its equitable proportion of such costs and that the entire cost of the item, both direct and indirect, shall be deducted from the plant accounts at the time the item of plant is retired.

Minor purchases of fixed assets ($50 or less) need not be capitalized unless the investment being made in such items is relatively large (i.e., the initial complement of low cost equipment used to outfit a plant). Under the latter circumstances, the purchase would have to be capitalized.

Depreciation. The FCC's basic rules on depreciation require companies to employ the straight-line method of depreciation applied on a group basis. (All companies are required to use the straight-line method; larger companies must employ the group basis.) Over the years, companies have proposed variations on the basic straight-line, group basis. Some of these variations have been accepted by the FCC. The general thrust of these variations is to depreciate the fixed assets using subgroup factors (such as asset life or asset life weighted by cost) that can result in a declining pattern of depreciation charges over time. The two most prominent methods are the "straight-line vintage group" and the "straight-line equal life" group.

The service lives to be used for individual assets or groups of assets are to be based upon the carrier's actual experience with the type of equipment in question. If a carrier (with revenues of over $1 million) desires to change any of its depreciation factors (e.g., service life), there is a very extensive process of documentation and approval with which it must comply [47 CFR 43.43].

Over the years, the FCC has frequently had the area of depreciation accounting under study for many reasons, such as its impact on the rate base, operating expenses, flow of funds, and the rapid technological changes witnessed in the communications field in recent years.

Retirements. The FCC's accounting for retirements of fixed assets serves to normalize the effect of retirements on earnings. Fixed assets that are retired in the normal course of business generally have no gain or loss recognized due to the use of the group method of depreciation. The original cost of the retired property is charged to the "depreciation reserve" (i.e., contra-asset) account [47 CFR 31.2-25].

When the retirement is caused by factors that were not anticipated in the asset's pattern of depreciation, the following provision applies [47 CFR 31.02-83]:

> #### Plant retired for causes not factors in depreciation
>
> The service value of depreciable telephone plant retired (note also § 31.2-25) shall be charged in its entirety to account 171, "Depreciation reserve." If the cause of retirement is not a recognized factor in depreciation and the loss is not covered by insurance, the company may upon proof that the charge to the depreciation reserve will result in undue depletion thereof, and with the approval of this Commission, credit account 171 "Depreciation reserve," and charge account 138, "Extraordinary maintenance and retirements," with the unprovided-for loss in service value and distribute it from that account to account 609, "Extraordinary retirements," over such period as this Commission may approve.

The accounting for fixed assets that are *sold* can entail the recognition of the gain or loss currently, or the normalization of the gain or loss through the allowance for depreciation. The following regulation controls the recognition of a gain or loss [47 CFR 31.2-251 (g)]:

> When the telephone plant is sold together with the telephone traffic associated therewith, the original cost of the property shall be credited to the appropriate plant accounts and the estimated amounts carried with respect

thereto in the depreciation and amortization reserve accounts shall be charged to such reserve accounts. The difference, if any, between (1) the net amount of such debit and credit items and (2) the consideration received (less commissions and other expenses of making the sale) for the property shall be included, if a credit, in account 360, "Extraordinary income credits," and if a debit, in account 370, "Extraordinary income charges." The accounting for depreciable telephone plant sold without the traffic associated therewith shall be in accordance with the accounting provided in § 31.171 (b).

The following regulation controls the adjustment of the gain or loss through the "depreciation reserve" (i.e., allowance for depreciation) account [47 CFR 31.171 (b)]:

> At the time of retirement of depreciable telephone plant, this account [i.e., the depreciation reserve] shall be charged with the original cost of the property retired plus the cost of removal and shall be credited with the salvage value and insurance recovered, if any.

Maintenance. The FCC's regulations generally require carriers to expense maintenance costs as they are incurred. However, in the event of "extraordinary" repairs, the carrier can request FCC approval to defer and amortize maintenance costs or to accrue maintenance costs in advance of their incurrence [47 CFR 31.138; 35.2220]:

> #### *Extraordinary maintenance and retirements*
>
> (a) This [asset] account shall include the unprovided-for loss in service value of telephone plant retired in accordance with provisions of § 31.02-83 . . .

(b) This account shall include also the cost of extensive replacements of station apparatus, inside wires, and drop and block wires, in accordance with the provisions of § 31.6-64 . . .

(c) Charges provided in paragraphs (a) and (b) of this section shall be included in this account only after permission of this Commission has been obtained. The company's application to this Commission for such permission shall give full particulars concerning the property retired or of the extensive replacements of apparatus or wires, the amount chargeable to operating expenses, and the period over which in its judgment the amount of such charges should be distributed.

Provisions for equalization of maintenance expenses

(a) This [estimated liability] account shall be credited with such amounts as the Commission may authorize or direct to be charged to account 4180, "Maintenance-expense equalization," under a plan to equalize maintenance expenses.

(b) When maintenance work is performed for which provision has been made in this account, the cost of such work shall be charged to the appropriate maintenance accounts. Concurrently this account shall be charged and account 4180 shall be credited with an amount equal to the provision for the cost of such maintenance work.

(c) The carrier's application to the Commission for permission to institute an equalization program shall show full details as to the plan of administration of the program, the character of the work to which amounts accrued may subsequently be applied, and the amount of the monthly or annual accruals for equalization purposes.

(d) A separate subaccount, with appropriate title, shall be maintained for each project or program for which provision is made in this account.

Insurance. The regulations permit carriers to employ a self-insurance program. The account used to provide for future losses has a dual nature. It can be used as an appropriation of retained earnings (not true self-insurance) or it can be used as an estimated provision for risk not covered by purchased insurance [47 CFR 31.169]:

Insurance reserve

(a) This account shall be credited, with appropriations of retained earnings specifically made to cover self-carried risks for losses through accident, fire, flood, or other causes.

(b) In case the company elects to carry its own risks for losses through accident, fire, flood, or other causes and provides a reserve, other than provision made in the depreciation reserve, to equalize anticipated losses, the charges to account 668, "Insurance," and other appropriate accounts to cover such risks shall be credited to this account. Such charges and credits shall be upon the basis of rates which fairly cover the risks insured. These rates should be determined according to the company's experience and best estimate as to the hazard covered. A schedule of risks covered by this reserve shall be maintained giving a description of the property or the character of the risks covered.

(c) If the company reinsures with insurance companies risks initially covered in this account, the premiums for such reinsurance shall be charged hereto and the amounts recovered under such commercial insurance shall be credited hereto.

(d) To the extent that losses and damages sustained are covered by this account, an amount equal thereto shall be charged to this account and credited to the accounts appropriate for the losses and damages sustained.

NOTE: All losses and damages sustained including those covered by commercial insurance or by this account, shall be charged in the first instance to the depreciation reserve, construction, repair, accidents, and damages, or other appropriate account according to the character of the loss, insurance recoverable or chargeable to this account on account of losses and damages sustained shall be credited to the account to which the losses and damages are chargeable.

Delayed Items. The FCC's regulations include a provision for the disposition of errors and other items arising from prior years' activity [47 CFR 31.01-5].

Delayed items

(a) The term "delayed items" means items which are accounted for in the current accounts with respect to transactions which occurred before the current calendar year. It includes adjustments of errors and additional entries with respect to items in the operating revenue, operating expense and other income accounts of prior years.

(b) Unless the inclusion of a delayed item in the current accounts would seriously distort those accounts, it shall be included in the same account in the current year that would have been credited or charged if the item had not been delayed. If the delayed item would seriously distort the current accounts, it shall be credited to account 365, "Delayed income credits," or charged to account 375, "Delayed income charges," as appropriate.

(c) The company shall keep such records as are necessary in order to show the full particulars with respect to all delayed items included in accounts 365 and 375 and also with respect to such other delayed items included in the ordinary accounts as are required to be reported in its annual report to the Commission.

Accounts 365 and 375 (Delayed income credits; Delayed income charges) are included in the extraordinary items section of the income statement.

Deferred Income Taxes. The FCC requires the interperiod allocation (i.e., the deferral) of income taxes for differences between book income (i.e., per FCC rules) and taxable income (i.e., per the tax return) due to the use of accelerated depreciation for tax purposes (versus straight-line depreciation for FCC purposes). However, a carrier can elect not to defer income taxes if it is subject to regulation by a state law that does not require deferral.

Accelerated depreciation is the only item for which the FCC requires interperiod allocation of income taxes. Any other items for which a carrier desires to employ this procedure must be submitted to the FCC for approval.

AUDITS AND REPORTS

The FCC audits the carriers subject to its regulations in order to verify the reports submitted to it and to study specific topics affecting the financial statements of all carriers (e.g., depreciation). The carriers subject to FCC control must submit periodic reports. All carriers submit annual reports. The larger carriers must submit monthly reports. The annual reports vary in length from approximately 70 schedules (as in Report Form M, for telephone companies) to less than 10 schedules (as in Report Form P, for specialized carriers). All of the reports include the basic financial statements (and detailed supporting schedules in the longer reports) and various operating statistics.

SEPARATIONS

The FCC regulates the interstate operations of communications common carriers. However, a great deal of communications operations involve both interstate and intrastate considerations. In order to separate assets, revenues, and expenses into interstate and intrastate categories, an allocation procedure must be employed. 47 CFR Part 67—Jurisdictional Separations—of the FCC's regulations covers this issue:

JURISDICTIONAL SEPARATIONS

§ 67.1 Separations manual;
incorporation by reference

(a) Jurisdictional separations of telephone companies' property costs, revenues, expenses, taxes, and reserves are determined under principles and procedures set forth in the Separations Manual ("Standard Procedures for Separating Telephone Property Costs, Revenues, Expenses, Taxes, and Reserves"), as amended by the Federal Communications Commission, which is hereby incorporated by reference into this Part 67, pursuant to 5 U.S.C. 552 (a) (1) and 1 CFR Part 20. The contents of the Manual, as incorporated by reference, include the April 1963 edition of the Manual, 1964, 1965, and 1969 Addenda, subsequent amendments of the

Manual adopted by the Federal Communications Commission, and subsequent editions of the Manual authorized by the Federal Communications Commission. The principles and procedures set forth in the Manual are designed primarily for use in the allocation of property costs, revenues, expenses, taxes, and reserves between intrastate and interstate jurisdictions.

(b) The Separations Manual is published by the National Association of Regulatory Utility Commissioners (formerly the National Association of Railroad and Utilities Commissioners). Copies of the current edition of the Manual, with current Addenda and Amendments, may be obtained at a cost of two dollars ($2.00) [now $2.50 plus postage] per copy, by writing to the Association, Post Office Box 684, Washington, D.C. 20044.

The Separations Manual is approximately 100 pages in length. The Foreword presents a very thorough review of the historical development of the separations procedure. The majority of the Manual gives instructions for accomplishing the allocations. Tables 6-1 and 6-2 are reproduced from the Manual in order to give the reader an overall feel for the allocation bases employed. The detailed discussion contained in the Manual amplifies and provides for exceptions to the general rules.

The issue of separations is being closely examined due to the increasing use of customer-owned equipment. Previously, all equipment was owned by the carrier. The trend to the interconnection of customer-owned equipment calls into question the continued acceptability of bases that include equipment.

Table 6-1
Illustrative Apportionment Bases for Major Categories of Plant

Major Categories	Bases of Assignment to Categories	Bases of Apportionment Among the Operations
Land and Buildings		
Operating Room and Central Office Equipment Space	On square feet of space used for each category or by identification from records	Weighted Cost of Central Office Equipment
Operators' Quarters		Traffic Units
Office Space		
(a) General Traffic Supervision		Traffic Expense
(b) Commercial		Commercial Expense
(c) Revenue Accounting		Revenue Accounting Expense
(d) General Office		General Expense
Space used by another company for Interstate Operations		Assigned Interstate
Garages, Storerooms, Warehouses and Pole Yards		Cost of Station Equipment, Outside Plant and Material and Supplies, Combined
Space constructed for another Co. for Interstate Operations		Assigned Interstate
Space Rented to Others		Consistent with the associated Rent Revenues
Antenna Supporting Structures		Costs of Antennae Supported
Outside Plant		
Exchange	By direct assignment or apportionment of plant used jointly for more than one category as follows: cable on conductor cross section; poles on equivalent wire load; conduit on cost of underground cable	
Wideband Exchange Trunk and Loop		Direct Assignment or Relative Minutes-of-Use
Exchange Trunk Excluding Wideband		Direct Assignment or Relative Minutes-of-Use
Subscriber Line Excluding Wideband		Relative TWX Minutes-of-Use, Direct Assignment, or Subscriber Plant Factor
Interexchange		
Plant Furnished to another Co. for Interstate Use		Assigned Interstate
Wideband Services		Direct Assignment or Relative TWX Message Minute Miles
All Other		Direct Assignment, Relative Conversation Minute Miles or Relative TWX Connection Minute Miles
Central Office Equipment		
Manual Switching Equipment	In general, by identification from records	Traffic Units
Dial Tandem Switching Equipment		Minutes-of-Use
Intertoll Dial Switching Equipment		Minutes-of-Use
Automatic Message Recording Equipment		Minutes-of-Use and/or Messages Involved
Other Toll Dial Switching Equipment		Minutes-of-Use
Local Dial Switching Equipment		Weighted Minutes-of-Use or Subscriber Plant Factor
Special Services Switching Equipment		Direct Assignment or Relative TWX Minutes-of-Use, or Traffic Units
Circuit Equipment		Generally Follows Apportionment of Outside Plant as Outlined above
Station Equipment		
TWX Equipment	By identification from records	Relative TWX Minutes-of-Use
Private Line Equipment		Direct Assignment
Station Identification Equipment		Number of Messages Recorded
Wideband		Relative Minutes-of-Use
Other		Subscriber Plant Factor
Furniture and Office Equipment		
Data Processing Equipment	By identification from records	Work Functions Performed
Other		Wage Portion of Maintenance, Traffic, Commercial and Revenue Accounting Expenses
Vehicles and Other Work Equipment		
		Cost of Outside Plant, Station Equipment and Material and Supplies, Combined

Table 6-2
Illustrative Apportionment Bases for Major Items of Revenues and Expenses

Major Items	*Bases of Apportionment Among the Operations*
Revenues	
Local Service	
(a) Wideband	
(1) Local Message	Assigned Exchange
(2) Other Message	Relative Minutes-of-Use
(b) Private Line	
(1) Broadcast	Assigned Interstate
(2) All Other	Assigned Exchange
(c) All Other	Assigned Exchange
Toll Service	
(a) Message Telephone	Direct Assignment Based on Analyses and Settlement Studies
(b) TWX	
(1) Message Revenue	Direct Assignment Based on Analyses and Settlement Studies
(2) Other	Relative TWX Minutes of Use
(c) Wideband	
(1) Message Revenue	Direct Assignment Based on Analyses and Settlement Studies
(2) Other	Relative Minutes-of-Use
(d) WATS	Direct Assignment Based on Analyses and Settlement Studies
(e) Private Line	
(1) Broadcast	Assigned Interstate
(2) Other	Direct Assignment Based on Analyses and Settlement Studies
Miscellaneous	
(a) Telegraph Commissions and Directory	Assigned Exchange
(b) Rent	Analyzed and Treated Consistently with Plant Rented to Others
(c) Other	Analysis of Services Furnished
Uncollectible	Analysis of Uncollectible Accounts
Expenses	
Maintenance and Depreciation	Cost of Related Plant
Traffic	
(a) General Traffic Supervision—Engineering	Cost of Central Office Equipment and Interexchange Outside Plant Combined
(b) Service Inspection and Customer Instruction	
(1) PBX	Current Billing
(2) Customer Instruction and Miscellaneous	Subscriber Line Minutes-of-Use
(c) All Other	Generally Traffic Units
Commercial	
(a) Advertising, Sales and Connecting Company Relations	Analyses of Current Billing and Settlements
(b) Local Operations	Number of Service Users—With Message Toll User Portion on Business Office Contacts
(c) Public Telephone Commissions	Study of Commissions Paid
(d) Directory Expenses	Analysis of Prepaid Directory Expenses
(e) General Administration	Accounts 643, 644 and 645, Combined
(f) Other	All Other Commercial Expenses Combined
Revenue Accounting	Analysis of Work Operations
General Expenses	Separation of Wage Portion of Maintenance, Traffic, Commercial and Revenue Accounting Expenses or Plant in Service
Relief and Pensions and Social Security Taxes	Separation of Wage Portion of Maintenance, Traffic, Commercial and Revenue Accounting Expenses
Property and Miscellaneous Taxes	Separation of Cost of Plant in Service
Gross Earnings Taxes	Separation of Receipts, etc., on Which Levied
Income Taxes	Taxable Income for Each Operation

REFERENCE NOTE

1. U.S., Federal Communications Commission, *42nd Annual Report/ Fiscal Year 1976 (Including Transition Quarter)*, p. 205.

Chapter 7

Civil Aeronautics Board

The Civil Aeronautics Board (CAB) is an independent agency of the Federal government. It is a leader in the Federal "Regulatory Reform" movement. The CAB is currently in the process of deregulating the air transportation industry. While this process progresses in an orderly fashion, the CAB is continuing its monitoring and regulation of the financial reporting of air carriers.

The civil aeronautics industry has been regulated since 1926. At that time, the regulation dealt only with safety factors. Economic regulation—controlling fares, routes, entry into the industry, etc.—came in 1938 with the passage of the Civil Aeronautics Act. The CAB was established in 1940 to administer this act. The CAB's duties were recodified in the Federal Aviation Act of 1958 which, as amended, continues as the basic legislation for the Board. In 1958, the safety regulations were assigned to the Federal Aviation Agency. They are now exercised by the Federal Aviation Administration (FAA), a part of the Department of Transportation. The FAA and the National Transportation Safety Board are the prime movers in air safety regulation and investigation. Thus, today the CAB's concern is, by and large, the *economic* regulation of air carriers engaged in interstate commerce.

The term *air carrier* covers (a) direct air carriers—airlines—whether providing regularly scheduled trunkline, local, or supplemental (e.g., charter) service, and (b) indirect air carriers such as air freight forwarders and travel agents. Most of the direct air carriers are "certificated," i.e., operate under certificates issued by the CAB. The indirect air carriers are noncertificated and are not subject to as close regulation as the certificated carriers.

The CAB is headed by five board members appointed by the President, with consent of the Senate. No more than three members can be from the same political party. The members are appointed to terms of 6 years.

CAB REGULATIONS

In its regulation of certificated carriers, the CAB has control over the carriers' operations, the routes served, the rates charged, and the mail service and mail subsidy rates of the carriers. The Federal government has, from the inception of commercial air service, subsidized the carriers with the mail service. Two rates are paid to the carriers for the mail service: (a) a service rate for actually carrying mail and (b) a subsidy rate for providing air transportation service. The service rate applies to the actual ton-miles of mail carried and is paid to the carrier by the U.S. Postal Service. The subsidy rate is based on the carrier's need to earn a fair return in providing air transportation service. The subsidy rate can be set either for a group of carriers or for individual carriers. Where the subsidy rate is set for individual carriers, the CAB considers the profitability of all operations of the air carrier in determining the need for a subsidy. The subsidy rates are true subsidies based on need and can entail payments for routes on which no mail is transported. The subsidy is paid by the CAB to the carrier. Currently, approximately $80 million in subsidies is paid to the following airlines:

Regional:	Air Midwest, Air New England, Cochise, Skywest
Local Service:	Frontier, Hughes Airwest, Ozark, Piedmont, Republic, Texas International, U.S. Air
Alaskan:	Alaska Airlines, Kodiak-Western, Wien Air Alaska

The CAB also exercises control over the following aspects of air carrier operation:

1. Accounting practices to be followed.

2. Operating statistics to be accumulated.

3. Mergers and acquisitions of carriers.

4. Intercarrier agreements.

5. Methods of competition (e.g., advertising).

6. Government loans and financial aid.

7. Acquisition of controlling interest of carriers.

This list is not all-inclusive but rather illustrative of the extent of CAB involvement and interest in air carrier operations.

Deregulation

The Airline Deregulation Act of 1978 (Public Law 95-504) has greatly affected the role of the CAB. The provisions of the law are quite complex; however, its overall thrust is clear: to end regulatory controls and encourage competitive controls in the airline industry. Airlines will have much greater freedom to open new routes, adjust fares, and terminate service—in general, to compete in the market place. By 1983, most of the

CAB's powers to actively regulate domestic routes and fares expire. On January 1, 1985, its remaining duties (e.g., determining the ability of air carriers to provide quality service) expire and the CAB is scheduled to be terminated.

Even the mail subsidy program was changed by the Act. When fully implemented in 1983, the new subsidy program will no longer preserve the façade of being for the movement of mail. The program is to be run on more of a "procurement" basis, i.e., the CAB will be attempting to provide the necessary air transportation to small communities on a competitive basis. The subsidy will be the amount needed to attract a responsible carrier to come forth and provide the service. The law also orders the CAB to study the feasibility of having the states share in the cost of the new subsidy program.

By January 1, 1984, the CAB must submit to Congress a study detailing the impact of the Airline Deregulation Act on the airline industry. It is presumed that this study will be a key input in Congress' decision regarding the January 1, 1985 "sunset" of the CAB. Presumably, if the airline industry's current financial woes—i.e., low earnings, low coverage of fixed charges, high debt/equity ratios, market value of stock less than book value—have improved, the scales will be weighted in favor of allowing the CAB to expire on schedule. If conditions have worsened, the Board could be continued. In any event, the monitoring of the industry—and intensive analysis of its accounting reports—will be a key input to the report.

Code of Federal Regulations

The CAB's regulations are contained in Title 14, Chapter II, Parts 200-1199 of the Code of Federal Regulations. Subchapter A (Parts 200-299) contains the economic regulations. The following Parts are of particular interest in regard to accounting regulation:

Part	Title
240	Inspection of Accounts and Property
241	Uniform System of Accounts and Reports for Certificated Air Carriers
248	Submission of Audit and Reconciliation Reports
249	Preservation of Air Carrier Accounts, Records and Memoranda

The CAB's authority for (a) issuing accounting regulations, (b) obtaining periodic reports, and (c) auditing the carriers' proceeds form the following provisions of the Federal Aviation Act of 1958 [49 U.S.C. 1301]:

GENERAL POWERS

The Board is empowered to perform such acts, to conduct such investigations, to issue and amend such orders, and amend such general or special rules, regulations, and procedures, pursuant to and consistent with the provisions of this Act, as it shall deem necessary to carry out the provisions of, and to exercise and perform its powers and duties under, this Act.

* * * *

FILING OF REPORTS

(a) The Board is empowered to require annual, monthly, periodical, and special reports from any air carrier; to prescribe the manner and form in which such reports shall be made; and to require from any air carrier specific answers to all questions upon which the Board may deem information to be necessary. Such reports shall be under oath whenever the Board so requires.

* * * *

FORM OF ACCOUNTS

(d) The Board shall prescribe the forms of any and all accounts, records, and memoranda to be kept by air carriers, including the accounts, records, and memoranda of the movement of traffic, as well as of the receipts and expenditures of money, and the length of time such accounts, records, and memoranda shall be preserved; and it shall be unlawful for air carriers to keep any accounts, records, or memoranda other than those prescribed or approved by the Board: *Provided,* That any air carrier may keep additional accounts, records, or memoranda if they do not impair the integrity of the accounts, records, or memoranda prescribed or approved by the Board and do not constitute an undue financial burden on such air carrier.

INSPECTION OF ACCOUNTS AND PROPERTY

(e) The Board shall at all times have access to all lands, buildings, and equipment of any carrier and to all accounts, records, and memoranda, including all documents, papers, and correspondence, now or hereafter existing, and kept or required to be kept by air carriers; and it may employ special agents or auditors, who shall have authority under the orders of the Board to inspect and examine any and all such lands, buildings, equipment, accounts, records, and memoranda.

SYSTEMS OF ACCOUNTS

The CAB has promulgated separate systems of accounts for certificated air carriers and air freight forwarders.

Certificated Air Carriers

The CAB stratifies certificated air carriers into three groups based on operating revenues:

Group	Operating Revenues
I	0 – $25,000,000
II	$25,000,001 – $75,000,000
III	$75,000,001 and over

The following airlines fall in the indicated group:

Group I air carriers:
Air Florida, Inc.
Air Micronesia, Inc.
Air Midwest, Inc.
Air New England, Inc.
Air Wisconsin, Inc.
Altair Airlines, Inc.
Apollo Airways, Inc.
Aspen Airways, Inc.
Chicago Helicopter Airways, Inc.
Cochise Airlines, Inc.
Empire Airlines
Evergreen International Airlines, Inc.
Golden West Airlines
Imperial Airlines
Kodiak-Western Alaska Airlines, Inc.
McCulloch International Airlines, Inc.
Mississippi Valley Airlines, Inc.

Modern Air Transport, Inc.

Munz Northern Airlines, Inc.

New Haven Airways, Inc.

New York Airways, Inc.

Reeve Aleutian Airways, Inc.

Rich International Airways, Inc.

Skywest Aviation, Inc.

Southern Air Transport, Inc.

Swift Aire Lines, Inc.

Wright Air Lines, Inc.

Zantop International Airlines, Inc.

Group II air carriers:

Air California

Alaska Airlines, Inc.

Aloha Airlines, Inc.

Hawaiian Airlines, Inc.

Wien Air Alaska, Inc.

Group III air carriers:

Airlift International, Inc.

American Airlines, Inc.

Braniff Airways, Inc.

Capitol International Airways, Inc.

Continental Air Lines, Inc.

Delta Air Lines, Inc.

Eastern Air Lines, Inc.

The Flying Tiger Line, Inc.

Frontier Airlines, Inc.

Hughes Corp., doing business as Hughes Airwest

National Airlines, Inc.

Northwest Airlines, Inc.

Overseas National Airways, Inc.

Ozark Air Lines, Inc.

Pacific Southwest Airlines, Inc.

Pan American World Airways, Inc.

Piedmont Aviation, Inc.

Republic Airlines

Seaboard World Airliners, Inc.

Texas International Airlines, Inc.

Trans International Airlines, Inc.

Trans World Airlines, Inc.

United Air Lines, Inc.

US Air, Inc.

Western Air Lines, Inc.

World Airways, Inc.

The accounting requirements (e.g., detail of accounts, number and frequency of reports) are generally more demanding for the larger carriers.

Chart of Accounts

The CAB employs a four digit account numbering system. The balance sheet accounts are numbered in the 1000 and 2000 series. The 1000 series is for assets:

Current assets	1000 thru 1400s
Investments and special funds	1500s
Property and equipment— operating	1600s
nonoperating	1700s
Other assets	1800s

The 2000 series is for equities:

Current liabilities	2000 thru 2100s
Noncurrent liabilities	2200s
Defined credits	2300s
Stockholders' equity	2800 thru 2900s

The operating accounts are specified in much greater detail in that each account has both a *functional* and *objective* code. For example, all accounts in the 6700s are *promotion and sales expenses* (function) and they are further identified by various objective codes:

Account	Objective
6721	General management personnel
6737	Communications purchased
6739	Traffic commissions
6747	Rentals
6750	Stationery, printing, and office supplies

The chart of operating accounts is more detailed for the larger carriers than for the smaller carriers.

Accounting for Property and Equipment

A great deal of the CAB's accounting regulations deal with the accounting for property and equipment. In this section, the determination of cost will be covered. In the next two sections, depreciation and repairs and maintenance will be covered.

Fixed assets are generally governed by the rule that " . . . all assets shall be recorded at cost to the air carrier and shall not be adjusted to reflect changes in market value" [14 CFR 241, Sec. 2-12 (a)]. The term *cost* is defined in 14 CFR 241, Sec. 03 in a conventional fashion:

> *Cost*—The amount of cash (or its equivalent) actually paid for property, materials and supplies, and services, including that amount paid to put the property or materials and supplies in readiness for use. It includes such items as transportation charges, installation charges, and customs duties, less any cash or other discounts.

Exchange transactions between carriers are subject to special accounting treatment. As to exchanges, the following provision controls apply [14 CFR 241, sec. 2-12 (b)]:

> Costs of assets charged against income by an air carrier shall not be reinstated through property exchanges, and again charged against income by another air carrier but shall be recorded by each successive user at the unrecovered cost of property given in exchange, adjusted by the amount of any additional cash or other consideration given or received. For purposes of this system of accounts, an exchange is defined as a transaction in which tangible property represents more than 75 percent of the fair market value of the total consideration. Capital gains or losses, as a matter of policy, will not be recognized in property exchanges.

Property acquired through a combination of reorganization of carriers is controlled by the following provisions [14 CFR 241, Sec. 5-3 (e) (4)]:

> If property and equipment is acquired as part of a business from another air carrier through consolidation, merger, or reorganization, pursuant to a plan approved by the Civil Aeronautics Board, the costs and related allowances for depreciation as carried on the books of the predecessor company at the date of transfer shall be entered by the acquiring air carrier in the appropriate accounts prescribed for recording investments in tangible assets. Any difference between the purchase price of the property and equipment acquired and its depreciated cost at date of acquisition shall be recorded in balance sheet account 1870 Property Acquisition Adjustment. Property acquired from

an associated company shall also be accounted for in accordance with this paragraph unless otherwise approved by the Board.

Account 1870 is an "Other Asset" account that is amortized as a non-operating expense.

When used property is exchanged to acquire other property, the recording of the new property can *either* be at its fair market value *or* the book value of the used property plus the cash value of the other consideration given [14 CFR 241, Sec. 5-3 (e) (8)]:

> When property and equipment owned by the air carrier is applied as part payment of the purchase price of new property and equipment, the new property and equipment shall be recorded at its full purchase price provided an excessive allowance is not made for assets traded in, in lieu of price adjustments or discounts on the purchase price of assets acquired. The difference between the depreciated cost of assets applied as payment and the amount allowed therefor shall be treated as retirement gain or loss. When used tangible property is exchanged for other used tangible property and no other form of consideration is involved, the book cost less related allowance for depreciation of the property given in exchange shall be assigned to the property received. When the consideration consists of both cash or its equivalent and tangible property, and the cash or its equivalent is less than 25 cash or its equivalent is less than 25 percent of the fair market value of the total consideration, the entire transaction is to be treated as an exchange of property. The cost of the properties received by each party shall be the book cost less related allowance for depreciation of the properties given

in exchange, plus or minus the cash, or the cash value of any other consideration, paid or received. Capital gain or loss is not to be recorded on the books of either party, except to the extent that the additional cash or other consideration received exceeds the depreciated book cost of the properties given. When the additional cash, or the cash value of other consideration, is at least 25 percent of the fair market value, the transaction shall be treated as a purchase and sale. The property received by each party shall be entered on the books at its fair market value and the net increase or decrease in asset values resulting from the transaction shall be treated as capital gain or loss.

The CAB's regulations permit the capitalization of interest on the funds used to finance the acquisition or construction of property [14 CFR 241, Sec. 2-10]. Interest on such funds is to be computed at the current effective interest rate on the long-term debt of the airline. Interest can be imputed on owner's equity when the amount of funds used for the acquisition or construction exceeds the carrier's long-term debt. When interest is imputed on owner's equity, the impact of the imputation on earnings is deferred and credited to nonoperating income as the capitalized imputed interest is amortized as an operating expense. Interest capitalized on long-term debt is immediately credited to nonoperating income.

Depreciation

The CAB's requirements in regard to depreciation are contained in 14 CFR 241, Sec. 2-14, which reads:

(a) Depreciation shall be calculated by the air carrier in such a manner as will prevent the charging of either excessive or inadequate expense or the accumulation of excessive or inadequate allowances, and shall be based upon a study of the air carrier's history and experience or such engineering or other information as may be available with respect to prospective future conditions and without regard to depreciation accounting practices adopted for tax purposes. Undepreciable residual values shall be established for each class of property and equipment and shall represent the fair and reasonable estimate of the recoverable value as of the end of the service life over which the property is depreciated. Depreciation chargeable against operations shall be limited to the actual costs incurred in the acquisition of the properties to which related. The cost of properties which are generally repaired and reused shall not upon retirement be charged against current operating expenses, but to the extent not written off in the form of depreciation, shall be treated as part of the capital gain or loss. The cost of properties of a type which are recurrently expended and replaced shall be charged to operating expenses as issued for use. However, the net charge to operating expense for any asset used, consumed or abandoned shall be limited to the difference between the cost incurred in acquisition and any related accrued depreciation.

(b) In accordance with the provisions of section 22 (d) each air carrier shall file with the Civil Aeronautics Board a statement which shall clearly and completely describe for each classification of property and equipment the methods, service lives, and residual values used for computing depreciation on the different subcategories of property or equipment included therein.

This statement shall be sufficiently descriptive to permit a pro forma construction of the depreciation calculation of each accounting period and shall include identification of those categories depreciated on a unit basis and those categories depreciated on a group basis, as well as the mathematical bases employed for allocating applicable costs to the different accounting periods.

These are more in the nature of general guidelines and disclosure requirements as opposed to fixed rules on allowable methods, asset lives, etc.

Costs Related to Fixed Assets

The CAB uses the following terms to describe activities that result in improvements in the productive capacity of fixed assets and are to be capitalized [14 CFR 241, Sec. 03]:

Addition, property—Additional equipment, land, structures, and other tangible property; extensions of fuel, water, and oil distribution equipment; additions to buildings and other structures; and additional safety devices applied to equipment not previously thus equipped.

Betterment—Any improvement to property or equipment through the substitution of superior parts for inferior parts retired, the object of which is to make such property more useful or of greater capacity than at the time of acquisition or installation.

Improvement—An addition or alteration to land, a building, or a unit of equipment that results in a better piece of property, in the sense of greater durability, or in increased productivity or efficiency.

Modification—An alteration in a structure or unit of equipment that changes its design and is made to correct an error, increase production, improve efficiency of operation, or for some other reason.

The costs to be capitalized would be the direct cost of the program plus " . . . an allocated portion of overhead costs to the full extent overhead expenses have been responsive to the volume of capitalizable projects currently or periodically in process" [14 CFR 241, Sec. 2-9 (b)].

Generally, costs that do not qualify for capitalization are to be expensed as incurred. However, where the cost of overhauls is sporadic in occurrence such that there would not be an equitable allocation of their cost among accounting periods, the carrier is to allocate the cost among the accounting periods affected in a systematic fashion [14 CFR 241, Sec. 5-4 (f) and (g)]. There is a provision in the regulations that bridges the gap between capital versus period costs for replacements [14 CFR 241, Sec. 2-9 (c)]:

When superior parts are substituted for old parts in existing units of property and equipment as an incident to normal maintenance operations where normal retirement procedures are not practicable, the excess cost of new parts of the kind replaced shall be charged to the related property and equipment account.

Materiality

In discussing the materiality of unusual and infrequently occurring events [14 CFR 241, Sec. 2-7], the regulations state that they should be evaluated in relation to their individual impact on net income (or loss) before extraordinary items or in relation to the trend of earnings. Further, an item is assumed to be material for CAB reports if it would be identified as material in an annual report filed with the Securities and Exchange Commission, or if it is greater than 1/2 percent of the immediately preceding 12 months' operating revenues or expenses. Further, when an unusual and infrequently occurring event is not material (per these tests) but exceeds 1 percent of the functional account to which it belongs, it is to be included in that account and footnoted in a separate schedule (CAB Form 41, Schedule P-2) filed with the CAB.

Restating Prior Periods Financial Statements

A carrier cannot restate the financial statements of prior periods without first obtaining the approval of the CAB.

Allocation

Whenever the carrier is operated as a segment of a larger entity, or the carrier itself operates nonregulated segments, the issue of allocation arises. The CAB's regulations deal separately with the allocation of assets and revenues and expenses. Assets are not allocated; rather, they are charged to a segment on the basis of *predominate usage* [14 CFR 241, Sec. 2-1 (c)]:

For purposes of this section, investments by the air carrier in resources or facilities used in common by the regulated air carrier and those transport-related revenue services defined as separate nontransport ventures under section 1-6 (b) shall not be allocated between such entities but shall be reflected in total in the appropriate accounts of the entity which predominantly uses those investments. Where the entity of predominate use is a non-transport venture, the air carrier shall reflect the investment in account 1520, Advances to Associated Companies.

Revenues and expenses are allocated among entities on the following bases [14 CFR 241, Sec. 2-1 (d)]:

> For purposes of this Uniform System of Accounts and Reports, all revenues shall be assigned to or apportioned between accounting entities on bases which will fully recognize the services provided by each entity, and expenses, or costs, shall be apportioned between accounting entities on such bases as will result: (1) With respect to transport-related services, in the assignment thereto of proportionate direct overheads, as well as direct labor and materials, of the applicable expense functions prescribed by this system of accounts and reports, and (2) with respect to separate ventures in the assignment thereto of proportional general and administrative overheads as well as the direct overheads, labor, and materials.

Income taxes (Federal, foreign, and state, including franchise taxes) determined on a consolidated basis are to be charged to the carrier *as if* the carrier filed a separate return.

Deferred Income Taxes

The CAB requires carriers to employ the interperiod allocation of income taxes for timing differences due to different methods being employed in statements submitted to the CAB and those upon which the income tax liability is based.

Filing of Reports

The CAB has a single report form—CAB Form 41—which services its three classes (I, II, and III, described earlier) of air carriers. This Form is composed of five major sections:

A — Certification

B — Balance Sheet Elements

P — Profit and Loss Elements

T — Traffic and Capacity Elements

G — General Corporate Elements

These sections include over 60 individual schedules. The CAB varies its reporting requirements for the three classes of carriers by (a) requiring a different frequency (annually, quarterly, or monthly) of filing across the classes and (b) not requiring all schedules from all classes of carriers. Over two-thirds of the schedules in Form 41 are balance sheet and income statement (profit and loss statement) schedules.

The Form 41 must contain a certificate signed by an officer of the carrier attesting to the report's accuracy. Additionally, all carriers must either file a copy of their audited financial statements with the CAB or notify the CAB that they have not had an independent audit conducted. If they do issue audited financial statements, they must submit a copy of them to the CAB along with a reconciliation of any differences between the amounts appearing in the various schedules of

Form 41 and the audited financial statements.

Air Freight Forwarders

Until January 1979, air freight forwarders having operating revenues of $10 million or more had to follow a uniform system of accounts contained in 14 CFR Part 244. Smaller freight forwarders did not have to follow the uniform system; however, they did have to submit reports to the CAB. As part of the loosening of the regulatory strings, the uniform system was eliminated. Now, air freight forwarders only have to report certain financial data (basically revenues and expenses associated with their regulated activities) and cerain operating statistics (e.g., number of shipments, number of tons shipped, etc.).

Chapter 8

Urban Mass Transportation Administration

The Urban Mass Transportation Administration (UMTA) is a component of the Department of Transportation. UMTA was established by the Urban Mass Transportation Act of 1964. In 1968 it became a unit of the newly-organized Department of Transportation. UMTA operates out of its Washington headquarters and 10 regional offices located in Cambridge (MA), New York, Philadelphia, Atlanta, Chicago, Fort Worth, Kansas City (MO), Denver, San Francisco, and Seattle.

The UMTA's programs fall into the following categories:

1. Research and development related to the hardware components of urban mass transportation systems.

2. Research and development related to the software components (e.g., managerial techniques, professional training, strategic and tactical plan-ning systems, etc.) of urban mass transportation systems.

3. *Discretionary* capital assistance programs (i.e., where UMTA agrees to voluntarily fund some of the capital —not operating—needs of an urban mass transit system).

4. *Formula* operating and capital assistance whereby UMTA acts as a conduit for funds for operating needs as well as capital projects. These funds are apportioned to the various jurisdictions on the basis of a "formula" that takes into account both population *and* population density, or in the words of the UMT Act as amended [49 USC 1604 (a) (1) (4)]:

Grants for construction or operating assistance; Apportionment of funds; authorization of appropriations

Such sums shall be made available for expenditures in urbanized areas or parts thereof on the basis of a formula under which urbanized areas or parts thereof will be entitled to receive an amount equal to the sum of—

(i) one-half of the total amount so apportioned multiplied by the ratio which the population of such urbanized area or part thereof, as designated by the Bureau of Census, bears to the total population of all the urbanized areas in all the States as shown by the latest available Federal census; and

(ii) one-half of the total amount so apportioned multiplied by a ratio for that urbanized area determined on the basis of population weighted by a factor of density, as determined by the Secretary.

As used in this section, the term "density" means the number of inhabitants per square mile.

UNIFORM SYSTEM OF ACCOUNTS, RECORDS, AND REPORTS

The UMTA's funding of operating costs was authorized by the Mass Transportation Act of 1974, an amendment to the Urban Mass Transportation Act of 1964. The 1974 Act also required the Secretary of Transportation to develop the reporting system described in Section 15 of the Act:

> The Secretary shall by January 10, 1977, develop, test, and prescribe a reporting system to accumulate public mass transportation financial and operating information by uniform categories and a uniform system of accounts and records. Such systems shall be designed to assist in meeting the needs of individual public mass transportation systems, Federal, State, and local governments, and the public for information

on which to base planning for public transportation services, and shall contain information appropriate to assist in the making of public sector investment decisions at all levels of government. . . .

As a condition of receiving funding for operating costs, mass transportation systems must comply with the requirements of the reporting system (known as the *Uniform System* or the *Section 15 Reporting System*) prescribed by UMTA.

UMTA Regulations

UMTA's regulations are published in Parts 600–699 of Title 49 of the Code of Federal Regulations. Part 630, Uniform System of Accounts and Records and Reporting System, contains (in about 12 pages) the summary regulations that control the Uniform System. In 49 CFR 630.6, the UMTA refers to a four volume report entitled *Urban Mass Transportation Industry Uniform System of Accounts and Records and Reporting System.* These four volumes are:

Volume I General Description

Volume II Uniform System of Accounts and Records

Volume III Required Reporting System Forms and Instructions

Volume IV Voluntary Reporting System Forms and Instructions

These volumes comprise more than 500 pages of instructions and forms. They contain all of the detailed components of the Uniform System.

Objectives of the Uniform System

The UMTA had many objectives in mind when it was developing the Uniform System. Some of the overall objectives were (a) the improvement of transportation management at all levels—Federal, state, regional, and local; (b) the encouragement of uniformity in gathering data; and (c) the monitoring of public investment in transportation. These overall objectives had to be reconciled with several pragmatic objectives:

> The consequence of increased governmental participation is a substantial increase in analytical activity at all levels of government. This analytical activity, in turn, has increased the need for uniform, consistent and accurate data to be provided by the respective transit systems (especially financial and operating data). Several types of analyses are being performed that require financial and operating data at various levels of detail. For example, the analysis of the causes of cost increases requires a breakdown of costs by type of expenditure (e.g., labor, materials, etc.). The analysis of operating efficiency requires a breakdown of costs by function (vehicle operations, maintenance, etc.). Both of these forms of analyses require relevant operating data (resources used, service supplied, passengers carried, passenger miles, etc.) in order to place the analyses on a comparable basis and to analyze the physical inputs and outputs relative to costs.[1]

Another objective was to minimize the duplication and contradictions that a mass transit entity might be subject to if the Uniform System were to conflict with the reporting requirements of other agencies (e.g., state, regional, municipal, county) to whom the entity reported.

A final objective was to provide flexibility for wide variances in system size, organizational structures, and existing information systems that were already in place in the various entities throughout the country. Accommodations to these objectives can be found throughout the fabric of the Uniform System.

Uniform System Components

The UMTA distinguishes the components of what is referred to collectively as the Uniform System as follows:

Differentiation of a System of Accounts and Records and a Reporting System

A uniform system of accounts and records consists of (1) various categories of accounts and records for classifying financial and operating data, (2) precise definitions of the data elements to be included in these categories, and (3) definitions of practices for systematic collection and recording of such information. Clearly, all three of the above are necessary to ensure that information is uniformly defined.

On the other hand, a reporting system consists of forms and procedures (1) for transmitting information from the operators to the central processing agency designated to collect data from all operators, (2) for editing and storing information, and (3) for the central processing agency to report the information to various user groups. User reports may consist of basic data summaries and analytical measures of performance indicators which would assist users in their analyses.[2]

Further, it relates the components of the Uniform System to the *internal (accounting and reporting) systems* of mass transit entities.

> *Relationship of Section 15 Systems to Internal Accounting and Reporting Systems*
>
> As stated previously, the Section 15 requirements consist of two systems: a reporting system and a system of accounts and records. The main purpose of the system of accounts and records is to insure that data to be reported is defined uniformly for all transit operators.
>
> Each transit system needs to maintain accounting and reporting systems which meet its own *internal* financial and management information requirements *as well as those* specified in Section 15. In most cases, information needed for internal management purposes will include data elements that are not required to be collected or reported under Section 15. (One such example in larger transit systems would be costs incurred by organizational responsibility centers within a transit system.)
>
> In customizing its internal accounting systems, the transit system must be able to translate its accounts to the prescribed uniform system of accounts and records. The translation to the uniform system of accounts must be auditable.[3]

The point of the above analysis is that while UMTA accounting and reporting requirements must be met, they need not be the basis of the internal accounting and reporting system. The internal accounting and reporting system is designed by the entity to adapt to its size, managerial structure, etc. However, the internal system must be reconcilable with the UMTA system in order to provide an audit trail from the reports submitted to UMTA back to the basic source documents.

Flexibility of the Uniform System

In addition to the flexibility allowed between the internal system and the UMTA Uniform System, the Uniform System has quite a degree of "flex" in and of itself. For example, the Uniform System classifies mass transit entities into three classes or "levels":

Level A   Applies to operations with more than 500 vehicles and all rapid rail operations.

Level B   Applies to operations with 101 to 500 vehicles.

Level C   Applies to operations with 100 vehicles or less.

About 30 Level A systems, 75 Level B systems, and 280 Level C systems report to the UMTA (i.e., they receive funds and are, therefore, obligated to report in conformity with the Uniform System).

An entity's "level" dicates the *minimum* degree of sophistication in its compliance with the Uniform System. For example, the Uniform System requires that expenses be classified by *object* (e.g., labor versus materials versus taxes, etc.) and by *function* (e.g., operations versus maintenance versus administration). Table 8–1 indicates how an entity's level dicates the *minimum* number of functions to be reported. Thus, while a Level C entity need only report expenses of *Vehicle Operations,* a Level B entity must break operations down into three functions (Administration of Transporta-

TABLE 8–1
Aggregation of Functions for Expense Classification

Level A	Level B	Level C Required
011 Transportation Administration		
012 Revenue Vehicle Movement Control	010 Administration of Transportation Operations	
021 Scheduling of Transportation Operations	020 Scheduling of Transportation Operations	010 Vehicle Operations
031 Revenue Vehicle Operation	030 Revenue Vehicle Operation	
041 Maintenance Administration—Vehicles	041 Maintenance Administration—Vehicles	
051 Servicing Revenue Vehicles	050 Servicing Revenue Vehicles	
061 Inspection & Maintenance of Revenue Vehicles	060 Inspection & Maintenance of Revenue Vehicles	
062 Accident Repairs of Revenue Vehicles	062 Accident Repairs of Revenue Vehicles	041 Vehicle Maintenance
071 Vandalism Repairs of Revenue Vehicles	070 Vandalism Repairs of Revenue Vehicles	
081 Servicing & Fuel for Service Vehicles	080 Servicing & Fuel for Service Vehicles	
091 Inspection & Maintenance of Service Vehicles	090 Inspection & Maintenance of Service Vehicles	
042 Maintenance Administration—Nonvehicles	042 Maintenance Administration—Nonvehicles	
101 Maintenance of Vehicle Movement Control Systems	100 Maintenance of Vehicle Movement Control Systems	
111 Maintenance of Fare Collection & Counting Equipment	110 Maintenance of Fare Collection & Counting Equipment	
121 Maintenance of Roadway & Track		
122 Maintenance of Structure, Tunnels, Bridges & Subways		
123 Maintenance of Passenger Stations		
124 Maintenance of Operating Station Buildings, Grounds & Equipment	120 Maintenance of Other Buildings, Grounds & Equipment	042 Nonvehicle Maintenance
125 Maintenance of Garage & Shop Buildings, Grounds & Equipment		
126 Maintenance of Communication System		
127 Maintenance of General Administration Buildings, Grounds & Equipment		

(continued)

TABLE 8-1 *(continued)*

Level A	*Level B*	*Level C Required*
128 Accident Repairs of Buildings, Grounds & Equipment		
131 Vandalism Repairs of Buildings, Grounds & Equipment	130 Vandalism Repairs of Buildings Grounds & Equipment	
141 Operation and Maintenance of Electric Power Facilities	140 Operation & Maintenance of Electric Power Equipment	
145 Preliminary Transit System Development	145 Preliminary Transit System Development	
151 Ticketing & Fare Collection	150 Ticketing & Fare Collection	
161 System Security		
165 Injuries & Damages		
166 Safety		
167 Personnel Administration		
168 General Legal Services		
169 General Insurance		
170 Data Processing	160 General Administration	160 General Administration
171 Finance & Accounting		
172 Purchasing & Stores		
173 General Engineering		
174 Real Estate Management		
175 Office Management & Services		
176 General Management		
162 Customer Services		
163 Promotion		
164 Market Research	179 Marketing	
177 Planning		
181 General Function	180 General Function	

tion Operations, Scheduling of Transportation Operations, and Revenue Vehicle Operations), and a Level A entity breaks operations down into four functions (i.e., the Level B function "Administration of Transportation Operations" is further refined into Transportation Administration and Revenue Vehicle Movement Control). An entity at any level may *voluntarily* report in more detail than is required by its level (i.e., *Volume IV, Voluntary Reporting System Forms and Instructions*). Systems can apply for funding from UMTA for meeting these expanded reporting requirements.

Expense classification by *object* of expenditure requires the following object classes as a *minimum:*

Object Classes:

501. Labor
    01. Operators' Salaries & Wages
    02. Other Salaries & Wages
502. Fringe Benefits
503. Services
504. Materials and Supplies Consumed
    01. Fuel and Lubricants
    02. Tires and Tubes
    99. Other Materials & Supplies
505. Utilities
506. Casualty and Liability Costs
507. Taxes
508. Purchased Transportation Service
509. Miscellaneous Expense
510. Expense Transfers
511. Interest Expense
512. Leases and Rentals
513. Depreciation and Amortization

All levels of entities must report expenses in at least the degree of detail of these object classes. Entities at any level may elect to report more detail. For example, the Uniform System requires Object Class 502—Fringe Benefits, but permits fringe benefits to be reported in the following detail:

502. FRINGE BENEFITS
    01. FICA or Railroad Retirement
    02. Pension Plans (including long-term disability insurance)
    03. Hospital, Medical and Surgical Plans
    04. Dental Plans
    05. Life Insurance Plans
    06. Short-Term Disability Insurance Plans
    07. Unemployment Insurance
    08. Workmen's Compensation Insurance or Federal Employees Liability Act Contributions
    09. Sick Leave
    10. Holiday (including all premiums paid for working on holidays)
    11. Vacation
    12. Other Paid Absence (bereavement pay, military pay, jury duty pay, etc.)
    13. Uniform and Work Clothing Allowances
    14. Other Fringe Benefits
    15. Distribution of Fringe Benefits

Thus, you can regard the Uniform System's expense classification system as an $n \times m$ matrix where n is the object classes and m is the functions. Both n and m have minimums: for object classes, the minimum is the same for all entities; for functions, the minimum is determined by the entity's "level." Entities can voluntarily expand their object classes and/or functions by reporting at a more detailed level. Also, UMTA has the ability to compare all reporting entities (or any subset in which they are interested) regardless of the level of detail by accumulating data in an $n \times m$ matrix where n is the minimum object classes and m is the minimum functions.

The other financial statement elements (revenues, assets, liabilities, and capital accounts) share the same flexibility in their object classes. However, there are no function classes for these elements. For example, the following are the *required* revenue object classes:

Required Revenue Object Classes

401. Passenger Fares for Transit Service
402. Special Transit Fares
403. School Bus Service Revenues
404. Freight Tariffs
405. Charter Service Revenues
406. Auxiliary Transportation Revenues

407. Nontransportation Revenues
408. Taxes Levied Directly by Transit System
409. Local Cash Grants and Reimbursements
410. Local Special Fare Assistance
411. State Cash Grants and Reimbursements
412. State Special Fare Assistance
413. Federal Cash Grants and Reimbursements
430. Contributed Services
440. Subsidy from Other Sectors of Operations

An entity can elect to report in more detail. For example, Object Class 401—Passenger Fares for Transit Service—can be subdivided into:

401. PASSENGER FARES FOR TRANSIT SERVICE
  01. Full Adult Fares
  02. Senior Citizen Fares
  03. Student Fares
  04. Child Fares
  05. Handicapped Rider Fares
  06. Parking Lot Revenue
  99. Other Primary Ride Fares

There are no function classes for revenues, assets, liabilities, and capital because (a) all revenues come from a single function—operations and (b) it would be virtually impossible to come up with a meaningful procedure for allocating these accounts to functions (e.g., such questions as "How much of a cash balance do we carry to support our maintenance program?" would have to be answered).

ACCOUNTING PRINCIPLES

The UMTA's Uniform System has its accounting principles set out in *Volume II—Uniform System of Accounts and Records.* This book contains three basic sections: (a) General Instructions controlling the Uniform System (e.g., where the voluntary and required elements are distinguished); (b) Accounting Practice Instructions which go into the details of acceptable and unacceptable accounting principles and/or practices; and, (c) Definitions covering all of the components of the financial statements broken down by object classes and/or functions (for expenses).

Accrual Basis

The UMTA's Uniform System requires that all entities report on the accrual basis:

Accrual Method of Accounting

The accrual basis of accounting is to be used in the Section 15 uniform system of accounts and records. Using the accrual basis, revenues will be recorded when earned, regardless of whether or not payment of the expenditure is made in the same accounting period.

Those transit systems that use cash-basis or encumbrance-basis accounting, in whole or in part, in their books of account will have to make work sheet adjustments to record the data on the accrual basis in the uniform system of accounts and records.[4]

While the UMTA requires the accrual basis, it does not blindly follow generally accepted accounting principles. For example, the role of depreciation is downplayed:

Property and Depreciation Accounting

At present, the urban transit industry practices a wide variety of depreciation treatments. The treatment practiced by any one transit system is dependent on such factors as public/private ownership of the transit system, bond indenture covenants, the expected means of financing the replacement of fixed assets, etc.

In those situations where the transit property elects to publish financial statements in accordance with generally accepted accounting principles, those statements should reflect the economic and physical expiration of the life of an asset. This calculation should be based on appropriate factors, including wear and tear, deterioration, inadequacy and obsolescence. The system of accounts and records described herein includes accounts for accumulating such depreciation charges.

The reporting system does not include the reporting of depreciation charges by function. Instead, depreciation charges, if any, as reported in the transit system's published financial statements are reported as a reconciling item in the Section 15 reporting system so that the Section 15 reports can be reconciled to the transit system's published financial statements.[5]

Thus, depreciation—"if any"—is not treated as an operating expense but rather as a reconciling item between the entity's statements filed with UMTA and its statements prepared in conformity with generally accepted accounting principles.

Other items that are similarly treated as "reconciling items" as opposed to expenses include interest, rent expense, and the expense associated with capitalized leases.

Another variance between the UMTA Uniform System and generally accepted accounting principles is that the UMTA permits entities to establish provisions for uninsured losses (with concurrent charges to expense). When actual losses are incurred, they are charged to the provision for uninsured losses. Accruals of this sort for "self-insurance" are not permitted under generally accepted accounting principles.

In the area of accounting for leases, the UMTA's provisions are:

Lease Accounting

For the purposes of the Section 15 uniform system of accounts and records, three types of leases are recognized:

— *True leases* are those in which the lessor and lessee are not related parties, the total lease payments cover the lessor's cost of the property for the period of the lease plus interest and the ownership of the property remains with the lessor upon expiration of the lease.

— *Purchase leases* are those in which the arrangement is substantively a financing plan for the purchase of the property by the lessee. The ownership of the property passes to the lessee upon expiration of the lease, sometimes with an additional payment far below the expected market value of the property at lease expiration. The property covered by such leases may or may not have been booked as owned assets, either during or after the period of the lease, in the transit system's internal accounting records.

— *Related-parties leases* are those in which the lease payments required of the lessee differ substantially from those in a true lease arrangement because the lessor and lessee are related organizations.

The treatment to be given these types of leases in the Section 15 uniform system of accounts and records is described below.

For the true lease, the lease payments for the accounting period on true lease property are to be classified in expense object class 512—Leases and Rentals.

Purchase leases are to be reported on the "capitalization" basis, in accordance with the transit system's capitalization cutoff. If the lease has been capitalized in the internal accounting records of the transit system, it is to be accounted for in the Section 15 system as it has been accounted for internally. If it has not been capitalized internally, the following adjustments are to be made in the Section 15 systems:

(1) The lease payments for the accounting period are to be reported as reconciling items in the Section 15 reporting system.

(2) The property covered by the non-capitalized purchase lease is to be recorded as owned property. This treatment is to be given to property on which lease payments are currently being made and property for which all lease commitments have been met (i.e., the purchase has been completed), but the property is carried on the books at nominal ($1) or no value. The capitalized value of the total lease commitment is to be classified as the cost of an asset owned in asset object class 111.01—Tangible Transit Operating Property, Property Cost or 112.01—Tangible Property Other Than for Transit Operations, Property Cost. The remaining lease payments, discounted to the current period ending date to remove the interest component of those payments, are to be recorded as a liability, short-term or long-term debt, as applicable. The difference between the capitalized

value of the lease and the discounted future payments is to be credited to equity object class 305.01—Accumulated Earnings (Losses).

Related-parties leases are to be recorded on a modified capitalization basis in accordance with the transit system's capitalization cutoff. The adjustments necessary to classify this data are the same as items (1) and (2) in the preceding paragraph, except that the lessor's cost of the property is to be classified as the property cost rather than the capitalized value of the lease.[6]

Since these provisions differ from the controlling provisions of the various financial accounting standards, differences in treatment between UMTA and generally accepted accounting principles would appear to be likely to occur.

REPORTING OF FINANCIAL DATA

The UMTA minimum reporting requirements for every level (A, B, or C) include the following:

Balance Sheet

Schedule of Capital Accounts

Revenue Schedules

Expense Schedules

Operator Wage Subsidiary Schedules

Fringe Benefit Subsidiary Schedules

Pension Plan Questionnaire

The UMTA requires that the financial reports submitted by the transit system be "reviewed" (a) by an independent public accountant in conjuction with the system's annual audit or (b) if the system is not subject to an annual audit by an independent public accountant, by an independent governmental agency such as a state audit agency. The transit system must nominate the independent governmental agency. The independent governmental agency must represent itself to UMTA as being independent with regard to the transit system. UMTA has the right to pass judgment on the independence of the agency and either accept the agency or request that a new appointment be made.

The UMTA requires the transit system's auditor to render its opinion on the conformance of the transit system's report with UMTA's Uniform System.

REPORTING OF OPERATING DATA

The UMTA requires eight schedules of operating statistics which are *not* generated by the accounting system. These schedules contain such data as maintenance and energy consumption, mileage and load statistics, safety statistics, etc. For example, Form 405, Transit System Accident Schedule, requires the transit system to classify its accidents into eight categories:

Fatality, Personal Injury and Property Damage

Fatality and Personal Injury

Fatality and Property Damage

Fatality Only

Personal Injury and Property Damage

Personal Injury Only

Property Damage Only

The fatality and injury categories must be further classified as vehicle operators, occupants, pedestrians, etc.

Some of the operating data reported by the transit system are based on statistical sampling. The UMTA provides transit systems with a series of circulars that outline the sampling procedures to be employed in accumulating sample data and projecting the sample results to population totals. The UMTA has set confidence levels of 95 percent and precision levels of 10 percent in its sampling plans.

UMTA REPORTING

The UMTA accumulates and summarizes the reports received from the individual operating systems. In addition to using the data for its own purposes, UMTA provides the operating systems with three reports. One report presents the industry averages; a second report presents the individual operating system's own report analyzed in percentage and ratio format; and the third report groups operating systems into peer groups (i.e., homogeneous groups based upon size) and reports the composite percentages and ratios for the peer groups.

REFERENCE NOTES

1. U.S., Urban Mass Transportation Administration, *Uniform System of Accounts, Records and Reporting System,* Volume I, p. 1-2.

2. *Ibid.,* p. 2-3.

3. *Ibid.,* p. 1-10.

4. *Ibid.,* Volume II, p. 1-4-1.

5. *Ibid.,* p. 2.6-1.

6. *Ibid.,* p. 2.8-1, 2.

Chapter 9

Federal Railroad Administration

The Federal Railroad Administration (FRA) is a unit of the Department of Transportation. The FRA is headquartered in Washington, D.C. and operates from its five regional offices located in Philadelphia, College Park (GA), Chicago, Fort Worth, and San Francisco. The FRA was one of the original units of the Department of Transportation (DOT) when DOT was established in 1966.

FRA PROGRAMS

Safety

The FRA is responsible for the enforcement of the Federal government's safety regulations for the nation's railroads. The safety regulations set minimum standards for rail vehicles and track structures. Its basic authority in this area comes from the Rail Safety Act of 1970. The FRA sets performance standards and carries out programs of inspection of such facets of rail operation as track, railbed, signals, brakes, transportation of dangerous substances, etc. The FRA also investigates railroad accidents.

Research

Both in conjunction with its safety programs and as a means of fostering improvements in railroad technology, the FRA carries on an active program of research and development. A major component of this program is the operation of its Transportation Test Center in Pueblo, Colorado. The Center includes a wide variety of facilities and test tracks on which currently deployed as well as prototype equipment and track structures can be tested.

Program and Policy Formulation

In addition to its "hardware" research, the FRA is involved in strategic and tactical planning for the U.S. railroad industry. In this area, the FRA is interested in making railroads accessible to the greatest number of users. An example of the programs being researched in this area are "intermodal" programs wherein the interface between rail transportation and other modes of transportation is being investigated. An example of an intermodal program is the "piggyback" service wherein a trailer is used to pick up freight at the shipper's location and is placed aboard a train for the major portion of the transit. The trailer is off-loaded and then delivered to the final destination. Such programs as this are, in part, aimed at keeping up with the rapid expansion and significant relocations taking place in many parts of the country.

Financial Assistance

The FRA administers a number of Federal financial aid programs. These programs vary in their intent from FRA's payment of subsidies to insure continuance of service that would otherwise be terminated, to the financing of safety programs, historic preservation of architecturally significant railroad stations, and the support of intercity rail passenger service.

Other Programs

The FRA is responsible for many other programs. Among them are the operation of the Alaska Railroad (now over 50 years old) and, a recent (1976) addition, the administration of the Minority Business Resource Center. This latter program is an effort to encourage the participation by minority businesses in the nation's railroad industry.

ACCOUNTING REGULATION

The FRA does not have to start from "ground zero" in regard to the accounting for railroads since this is, by and large, controlled by the Interstate Commerce Commission (See Chapter 5). Thus, the FRA can call upon railroads to provide data that are structured in accordance with a known set of rules—the uniform system of accounts specified by the ICC. However, the FRA is at liberty to request the data and reports that it feels are needed to administer its programs. To illustrate how the FRA employs accounting data, two of its programs, which are administered under the Railroad Revitalization and Regulatory Reform Act of 1976 (Public Law 94-210), will be reviewed.

Preference Shares Program

Section 505 of the Railroad Revitalization and Regulatory Reform Act authorizes the FRA to make equity investments (through the purchase of redeemable preference shares) in railroads. The purpose of the preference shares program is to provide funds to railroads so that they can refurbish their plant facilities, including catching up on maintenance that has been long deferred.

Loan Guarantee Programs

Section 511 of the Railroad Revitalization and Regulatory Reform Act authorizes the FRA to guarantee the payment of the principal plus interest of borrowings of railroads. The loan guarantee program is mainly intended to improve the railroads' rolling stock (e.g., locomotives, freight cars, etc.) and attendant systems such as those for power, communications, and safety.

FRA REGULATIONS

The FRA's regulations are contained in Chapter II, Title 49 of the Code of Federal Regulations. Part 258 contains the FRA regulations that implement Section 505 (i.e., the preference shares program) of the Railroad Revitalization and Regulatory Reform Act of 1976; Part 260 contains the FRA regulations that implement Section 511 (i.e., the guarantee program) of the Act. Since both Sections of the Act deal with the financing of railroads, the regulations are somewhat similar. However, since Section 505 involves direct investment by the government (whereas Section 511 involves only a guarantee of a loan made by others), the regulations of Part 258 go beyond the regulations of Part 260 to insure that the direct investment by the government is used only as a last resort.

APPLICATION FOR PROGRAMS

The application formats for the preference shares and loan guarantee programs are similar in many respects. For example, the following are required as exhibits to be appended to the main body of the applications under both programs.

Balance Sheets

The railroad must provide (a) the most recent year end audited balance sheet, (b) an unaudited balance sheet that updates the most recent year end audited balance sheet to within three months of filing the application, and (c) forecasted year end balance sheets for a four year period *subsequent* to the year of the filing of the application assuming, first, that the railroad *would not* receive the financial assistance that it sought and then another set of projections assuming that it *would* receive the financial assistance sought.

Income Statement and Statement of Changes in Financial Position

These statements must be arrayed similar to the balance sheets. Additionally, the most recent audited statements must be projected to the end of the year in which the application is filed.

Details of Selected Accounts

The FRA requires the railroad to submit schedules of the detailed composition of the following accounts: loans and notes, both receivable and payable; investments in affiliates; other assets; deferred credits; and capital stock.

PREFERENCE SHARES PROGRAM REQUIREMENTS

The law establishing the preference shares program requires that the FRA (acting in behalf of the Secretary of the

Department of Transportation, who is cited in the law) shall consider the following three factors in deciding on the advisability of purchasing preference shares [Sec. 505 (b) (2), P.L. 94-210]:

> (A) the availability of funds from other sources at a cost which is reasonable under principles of prudent railroad financial management in light of the railroad's projected rate of return for the project to be financed, (B) the interest of the public in supplementing such other funds as may be available in order to increase the total amount of funds available for railroad financing, and (C) the public benefits to be realized from the project to be financed in relation to the public costs of such financing and whether the proposed project will return public benefits sufficient to justify such public costs.

Alternative Sources of Funds

The regulations require that the railroad applying for preference shares financing must upset the FRA's presumption that funds are available to the railroad at a reasonable cost. The FRA sets out criteria that the railroad must meet in order to upset this presumption. The criteria are for the following four types of financing:

Borrowed money

Internal funds

New issues of common stock

New issues of preferred stock

The criteria generally involve the in-depth analysis of the operating performance and cash-flow pattern inherent in the railroad's historic and projected financial statements.

Borrowed Money. Borrowed money is presumed to be available at a reasonable cost to the railroad if the railroad currently has a Moody's bond rating of Baa or higher for any of its existing long-term debts (other than obligations secured by liens on equipment). If the railroad does not have a Moody's rating, then borrowed funds are presumed to be available if [49 CFR 258.23 (b) (1)]:

> . . . the ratio of the applicant's consolidated net operating income before taxes to the sum of its consolidated fixed and contingent charges for the three calendar years preceding the date of submission of the application equals or exceeds the average of such ratios for all Class I railroads with debt securities rated Baa as at the last day of the most recent calendar year for which all such railroads shall have reported their results to the [Interstate Commerce] Commission.

The railroad can rebut the presumption in *either* case if it can document that the potential sources of borrowed funds have been canvassed and that no funds are available.

Even if borrowed funds were found to be available, the railroad can call into question the reasonableness of this potential source of funds if (a) it impairs the railroad's projected cash flow so as to cast doubt on the railroad's ability to service its total debt or (b) the borrowed funds would have a significant adverse effect [as specified in 49 CFR 258.23 (b) (1) (ii)] on the railroad's rate of return.

Internal Funds. Internal funds are assumed to be available to the railroad if, in its most recent balance sheet, it has positive working capital (current assets less current liabilities).

If the railroad does have positive working capital, it can rebut the presumption that these funds are available for investment in the project for which the preference shares financing is being sought if it can establish either that the working capital is needed for the continuing operation of the railroad (e.g., where the funds are only seasonally available), or that there would be a significant adverse effect on the railroad's rate of return if the funds were invested in the project.

New Issues of Common Stock. Funds are presumed to be available from a new issue of common stock if the current market price per share of the railroad's common stock is greater than the current tangible book value per share.

The railroad can discount this as a potential source of funds either by establishing (a) that it has found that there are no viable market prospects for such a new issue or (b) if there is a viable market, that any new issue would result in either a reduction in the railroad's tangible book value per share, a substantial reduction in the railroad's market price per share, or a significant deterioration in the railroad's rate of return.

New Issues of Preferred Stock. Funds are assumed to be available through the issuance of preferred stock unless the railroad can show (a) that there is no viable market for such an issue or (b) if there is a viable market, either that the issuance would result in a significant reduction in the railroad's

rate of return or that the [49 CFR 258.23 (b) (x) (i)] :

> . . . forecasted financial condition and operating results of the applicant (after giving effect to the project's net cash stream) appear inadequate to provide reasonable assurance that the applicant can pay dividends on a current and continuing basis.

It is clear from the legislative mandate and the FRA's regulations that the Federal government *does not* want to be regarded as the "source of first resort" for financing. All other potential sources are to be exhausted before preference shares financing is to be considered.

Public Interest

The FRA is required to consider the public interest in preference shares financing. It has interpreted this to mean that the railroad must establish that the project for which the financing is sought will be an integral part of the nation's long-term rail freight service program. Further, the railroad must establish that the preference shares to be purchased by the government will be "reasonably likely" to be serviced (as to dividends) and redeemed by the railroad.

Public Costs and Benefits

While under these criteria one might expect to find that the FRA requires railroads to identify all of the costs and benefits of a particular project to be financed by preference shares funding, this is not the approach taken. Rather, the FRA has taken a "broadbrush" approach to the evaluation of costs versus benefits [49 CFR 258.27 (b)]:

> *Standards. The public benefits of a proposed project will be deemed to justify the public costs of the project if the project satisfies any of the following standards.*
> (1) *Essential Freight Services.* The proposed project enhances the ability of the applicant or other carriers to provide essential freight services by acquiring by lease, purchase or merger, constructing, rehabilitating, or significantly improving mainlines, including yards or other facilities used primarily to serve traffic moving on such lines. . . .
> (2) *Competitive Freight Services.* The application provides for:
> (i) Rehabilitation or improvement of a line of an applicant who is competitive with one and only one rail carrier in the market served by the line and is shown by applicant to be economic in light of the current or reasonably prospective levels of traffic in the market and the number of alternative rail carriers in the market; or
> (ii) Financial assistance to enable an applicant to withdraw from a market which has more than two competing rail carriers, where the applicant demonstrates that the reasonably prospective levels of traffic in the market are insufficient to enable all of the railroads competing in that market to earn a reasonable rate of return.
> (3) *Special Projects.* The proposed projects will eliminate identifiable and severe public safety hazards.
> (4) *Equipment Rebuilding.* The proposed project provides for rebuilding equipment which the applicant requires in order to serve adequately traffic which originates or terminates on applicant's lines at levels which are consistent with the applicant's average market share in

the commodity hauled for the three calendar years preceeding the filing of the application or are reasonably prospective. . . . [Emphasis added]

Thus, the railroad must qualify the project as being covered by one (or more) of the four categories. The proper balance of costs and benefits is then presumed.

RATE OF RETURN

Both the Part 258 preference shares program and the Part 260 loan guarantee program require railroads to submit detailed computations of the rate of return on the project(s) to be financed by the funds to be acquired. The details of the rate of return submission are set out in 49 CFR Part 260, Subpart C *—Procedures for Computing the Internal Rate of Return on Projects.* The computation of the project's internal rate of return (IRR) can be viewed as consisting of four stages. The *first* stage is the identification of the project to be financed and all of its cash flow ramifications. The *second* stage is the identification of the "base case" and all of its cash flow ramifications. The *base case* is defined as follows [49 CFR 260.35 (a) (2)] :

> The base case is the most favorable alternative action the applicant could take with little or no investment. The description must be comparable in scope to the description of the project. In some cases, the most favorable alternative action may be to do nothing, i.e., making no change in the current situation. In other cases, the applicant

may have other alternative actions such as rerouting traffic, changing operating practices (perhaps with an increase in operating costs), or relying more heavily on facilities or equipment belonging to others. If the applicant has considered more than one alternative action (requiring little or no investment) to the project, the applicant must describe each of the actions considered and give the rationale for the selection of the base case from among those other actions.

The *third* stage of the process is the descriptive documentation of the project *and* the base case (i.e., the first two stages). In the words of the regulations, this stage consists of the following [49 CFR 260.35 (a)]:

A narrative discussion of the IRR computation for the project consisting of the following five parts shall be prepared and provided:

(1) *A detailed description of the project.* This description must present the following: the objectives of the project; what assets will be improved, rehabilitated, acquired or constructed; where they will be located; and how they will be used. It must also describe any other work to be done as a part of the project, and any operating changes, including retirement of assets, which will accompany the investment.

(2) *A detailed description of the base case....*

(3) *A discussion of key assumptions.* All general assumptions and those relating only to a particular cash flow impact which substantially affects the IRR should be explained. Assumptions regarding traffic volumes deserve particular attention. The applicant must specify how much traffic is expected if the project and base case are undertaken, and where the difference, if any, between the project and base case is ex-

pected to come from (e.g., diverted from truck, diverted from other railroads, generated by the project, etc.). Other key assumptions may relate to actions by third parties, such as regulatory agencies and other railroads.

(4) *A discussion of each of the project's and base case's cash flow impacts.* The applicant must identify all the benefits and costs of the project and base case which will affect its cash flow. For each cost and benefit used in the IRR computations, the applicant must explain why the particular cash flow will result from the project or base case, and how the size of the cash flow and the corresponding measure in physical units were estimated. In addition, the applicant must identify and discuss important costs and benefits which it has not been able to quantify. Since the project will be audited to provide a continuing assessment of the IRR computation, applicant must indicate how an audit trail could best be facilitated . . .

(5) *A discussion of the principal areas of uncertainty.* This discussion must indicate why particular values might be different from those used in the computation, and the range into which each uncertain value could be expected to fall. It must also indicate the applicant's subjective level of confidence that the computed IRR is a reasonably close prediction of the project's and base case's financial performance. Such a level of confidence may, for example, indicate that a prospective labor saving, although quantifiable, has little likelihood of realization. In some circumstances, the applicant must point out where the IRR fails to incorporate certain important features of the project or the base case, or both. Applicant may enhance its discussion by presenting examples of its own prior experiences with IRR, stating, perhaps, that an audit of past computations has shown marked

deviations from actual results regardless of the detail of those computations.

The *fourth* stage of the process is the computation of the IRR, which consists of five schedules that analyze the following aspects of the project:

Form I   — Analysis of capitalized investment

Form II   — Analysis of sale or retirement of assets

Form III — Analysis of expenses and contribution to profit

Form IV — Consolidation of cash flows

Form V   — Computation of the IRR

The FRA makes several modifications to the basic IRR computation technique. One is that the IRR is based upon the *difference* between the cash flows of the prospective project and the base case. Thus, it is not the IRR of the project that is computed. Rather, it is the IRR of the marginal investment in the project and marginal returns of the project when compared to the base case.

The FRA also requires all computations to be on a constant-dollar basis (i.e., assuming no inflation). This obviates any possibility of manipulating a project's IRR by assuming some "tailor made" rate of inflation. It also has the advantage of not having the various participants in the projections make their own individual "guess" as to the future rate of inflation.

The FRA does make a concession to inflation in requiring that the figures used in the IRR computation and the pro forma financial statements (submitted as exhibits with the application) be reconciled [49 CFR 260.35 (d)]:

(d) A reconciliation between the cash flows used in the IRR computations and all forecasted data presented in the application, both before (for the base case) and after (for the project) giving effect to Federal assistance. This reconciliation must indicate what inflation factor or factors were used in developing the forecasted financial statements as compared to the constant dollar figures used in the IRR computations. The reconciliation must also show how each of the individual parts and subparts of the project relates to the applicant's forecasted financial statements.

The FRA considers cases where no unique IRR exists (e.g., where, after the project is underway, there are predictions of some years where there are net cash inflows and other years where there are net cash outflows). It requires that " . . . the work done to develop the cash flow stream must be submitted with a note that no IRR could be computed." [49 CFR 260.35 (b) (4)]. The FRA requires that any analysis of projects that the railroad decided not to pursue also be submitted [49 CFR 260.35 (c) (4)].

DIVIDEND PAYMENTS

The loan guarantee program is subject to the following restrictions contained in the Railroad Revitalization and Regulatory Reform Act [Sec. 511 (d), P.L. 94-210]:

> No guarantee of, and no commitment to guarantee, an obligation may be granted, approved, or extended under this section, unless the obligor first agrees in writing that so long as any principal or interest is due and payable on such obligation —

(1) there will be no increase in discretionary dividend payments over the average ratio which such payments bore to earnings for the applicable fiscal period during the 5 years preceding such proposed increase, without prior approval of such increase by the Secretary;

While there are no legal restrictions found in the Sec. 505 (i.e., the preference shares program) the FRA requires that the agreements entered into under both programs include restrictions on the payment of discretionary dividends, as defined above in Sec. 511 (d).

Chapter 10

Federal Maritime Commission

The Federal Maritime Commission (FMC) is an independent agency of the Federal government. It is headed by a bipartisan panel of five commissioners who are appointed to 5 year terms by the President with the approval of the Senate. The FMC was established in 1961. It administers all or parts of the following laws: the Shipping Act of 1916, the Merchant Marine Acts of 1920 and 1936, the Intercoastal Shipping Act, the Federal Water Pollution Control Act, the Clean Water Act, and the Trans-Alaska Pipeline Authorization Act. The FMC operates out of its headquarters in Washington and its five regional offices which are located in New York, New Orleans, San Francisco, Cleveland, and Hato-Rey, Puerto Rico.

Prior to the establishment of the FMC, the Federal Maritime Board had responsibility for both promoting and regulating United States maritime interests. Congress found these two roles to be in conflict. Thus, it established the FMC to administer the regulatory aspects of the laws. The Maritime Administration (MarAd, Chapter 11) was established to foster development and administer subsidization of the maritime industry.

The FMC's functions in administering these laws encompass the following areas:

1. Control over the operating practices and rates (tariffs) of common carriers (by water) engaged in domestic offshore trade and the foreign trade of the United States.

2. Control over the operating practices and rates of terminal operators engaged in domestic offshore trade and in foreign trade.

3. Control over the licensing, operating practices, and rates of ocean freight forwarders.

4. Certification of financial responsibility of operators who elect to self

insure (as opposed to purchasing insurance).

The FMC exercises the greatest degree of economic control over the rates of common carriers engaged in domestic offshore trade (trade between the United States mainland and its non-contiguous states and territories, e.g., Puerto Rico, Guam, Hawaii, Alaska, Virgin Islands, etc.). The FMC's role in the area of domestic offshore trade is proactive in that it can *set* maximum and minimum rates. The FMC's role in the area of foreign trade is essentially reactive in that it does not have authority to set rates in foreign commerce. It can only take action against such rates when they are found to have an adverse effect on the foreign trade of the United States.

FMC REGULATIONS

The regulations of the FMC are contained in Chapter IV of Title 46, of the Code of Federal Regulations. The following parts are of particular interest in regard to accounting and auditing:

Part	
511	Reports by Common Carriers by Water in the Domestic Offshore Trades
512	Financial Reports by Common Carriers by Water in the Domestic Offshore Trades
513	Audits and Auditing Procedures
542	Financial Responsibility for Water Pollution
543	Financial Responsibility for Oil Pollution—Alaska Pipeline
544	Financial Responsibility for Oil Pollution—Outer Continental Shelf
549	Regulations Governing Level of Military Rates

ANNUAL REPORTS

Under 46 CFR Part 511, companies that operate in the domestic offshore trade must file annual reports with the FMC. There are two forms of annual reports. FMC-64 is used by operators of self-propelled vessels and FMC-63 is used by operators of "other than self-propelled vessels" (e.g., barges). Carriers that are required or elect to follow the Maritime Administration's uniform system of accounts, which is found in 46 CFR Part 282, employ this system in filing their annual report with the FMC. (This uniform system is discussed in Chapter 11, The Maritime Administration.) Where this system of accounts is not followed, the carrier must indicate the basis of its accounting system and how it coincides or differs from the Maritime Administration's uniform system of accounts.

Both FMC-63 and FMC-64 are very detailed reports. Since their structure and organization is comparable, only FMC-64 will be described here. FMC-64 is comprised of over 100 pages of text containing nearly 100 separate schedules (or statements). These schedules are numerically broken down into five separate series.

The 100 series includes eight schedules that detail the following:

Schedule Number	Title of Schedule
101	Identity of Respondent
102	Directors
103	Officers
104	Corporations Controlled by Respondent Other than through Title to Securities
105	Corporations Indirectly Controlled by Respondent

106	Corporate Control over Respondent
106A	Stockholders Reports
107	Voting Powers and Elections

The 200 series is led off by the Comparative General Balance Sheet. This is supported by over 50 separate schedules in which most of the components of the balance sheet are detailed.

The 300 series begins with the Comparative Income Statement, which is supported by over 20 separate schedules.

The 400 and 500 series request information that the FMC variously uses in carrying out its regulatory duties. Examples of these schedules are:

Schedule Number	Title of Schedule
400	Gross Income Derived from Transactions with Affiliated Companies
401	Gross Expense Incurred in Transactions with Affiliated Companies
402	Statement of Assets Held as Security for Actual and/or Contingent Receivables
403	Statement of Assets Pledged as Security for Actual and/or Contingent Obligation and Not Available for General Purposes
410	Vessel Statistics
411	Routes or Services
412	Operating-Differential Subsidy
508	Remuneration, Etc., of Directors, Officers, and Others
510	Payments for Services Rendered by Other than Employees
511	Contracts, Agreements, Etc.
512	Important Changes During the Year
515	Competitive Bidding—Clayton Antitrust Act

For example, Schedule 515 (Competitive Bidding—Clayton Antitrust Act) requests information that is used to check on the carrier's compliance with Section 10 of the Clayton Antitrust Act [15 USC 20]. Under this provision, a carrier is prohibited from entering into a contract with another entity that has any interlocking relationship with the carrier (e.g., where an individual holds an influential position with both entities) *unless* strict rules are followed. Basically, these rules require that any contract can be signed only where (a) a process of competitive bidding was undertaken and (b) the firm with the interlocking relationship (with the carrier) submitted the bid that was the most favorable to the carrier. Schedule 515 requires information such as the subject matter of the contract, the number of bidders, the basis of awarding the bid, etc.

STATEMENTS OF RATE BASE AND INCOME

The statements required in 46 CFR Part 511 are for the company taken as a whole. 46 CFR Part 512 requires the allocation of an entity's assets and operating accounts between its regulated operations—i.e., domestic offshore operations, commonly called "the trade"—and its other business. The statements required by 46 CFR Part 512 are required annually and whenever the carrier is filing for approval of a significant change in rates (i.e., a change in the rates of 50 percent or more of its tariff items; or, a projected change of 3 percent or more in the gross revenue of an affected "trade"—i.e., any route served in the domestic offshore trade). These statements—formally known as Exhibit A (for the rate base), Exhibit B (for income), and Exhibit C (for the rate of return)—must be filed for each trade (i.e., route served in the domestic offshore trade). The statements that are to be filed are usually on an historic basis. However, when a change in rates is being requested, certain statements, mainly the income statement and the rate of return, must be filed on a projected basis.

In essence, Exhibits A, B, and C result from the allocation of balance sheet and income statement components (as disclosed in the statements required by Part 511) among the various trades and nontrade operations. The basic principle of allocation is expressed in 46 CFR 512.2 (h), (i), and (j):

> (h) Where it is necessary to allocate property, revenue . . . , costs or expenses, the allocation shall be on a direct basis; if this is not practicable, allocation shall be made in the manner prescribed in §512.6 of this part. . . .

> (i) All carriers subject to these reporting requirements must comply fully with the instructions outlined herein, both as to the submission of specified reports and as to compliance with the methods prescribed for their preparation. A carrier may request relief from full compliance in accordance with the provisions of subparagraph §512.2 (e). . . .

> (j) . . . the Commission reserves to itself the right to employ other bases for allocation and calculation in any instance where, in its opinion, the application of the rules and regulations prescribed herein create unreasonable results.

Exhibit A—Rate Base

Exhibit A requires the allocation of four categories of accounts in accumulating the rate base:

Schedule I   — Investments in Vessels

Schedule II   — Reserve for Depreciation—Vessels

Schedule III — Other Property and Equipment—Net

Schedule IV — Working Capital

Investment in Vessels. The allocation of the investment in vessels proceeds in three steps. First, any vessel that is used solely "in the trade" has its costs assigned directly to the rate base. Second, any vessel that is used partially on routes involving the trade (collectively called "the service") and partially on routes not involving the trade (called "other services") has its costs allocated between the service and other services (i.e., nontrade routes) on the basis of the number of days spent in each category of service. If a vessel was used 110 days in the service and 220 days in other services (the remaining days of the year being spent out of service, as for example, for repairs and maintenance), one-third of the cost of the vessel would be assigned to the service.

Third, the service can include some nontrade (i.e., other than domestic offshore) traffic, as for example, when a route includes both domestic offshore ports and foreign ports. In such a case, the cost allocated to the service must be further allocated between the trade and nontrade categories. This is done on the basis of the cargo-cube-miles in the trade compared to the total cargo-cube-miles in the service. (Cargo-cube-miles is the product of the number of cubic feet of cargo and the number of nautical miles between the port of origin and the port(s) of destination.)

The "cost" of the vessel referred to above is the original cost adjusted by any additions or deductions. The additions or deductions occurring during the current period are included on a prorated basis " . . . reflecting the number of days they were actually in use during the period" [46 CFR 512.6 (b) (1)].

Reserve for Depreciation—Vessels. The allocation of this contra-asset account mirrors that of the asset account [46 CFR 512.6 (b) (2) (i)]:

> Each cargo vessel (excluding chartered vessels) employed in the Service shall be listed separately, showing for each its depreciable life and residual value. For vessels owned the entire year, the accumulated reserve for depreciation as of the beginning and the end of the year shall be reported and the arithmetic average thereof computed. This amount shall be allocated . . . in the same proportions as the cost of the vessel was allocated. . . . When any of the amounts required herein are different from those reported in . . . the annual financial statements (Forms FMC–63 or FMC–64) or from those reported for Federal income tax purposes, the differences shall be set forth and fully explained.

Other Property and Equipment—Net. This category includes the asset and contra-asset accounts (i.e., "reserve" for depreciation) for all fixed assets other than vessels. The base for allocating these assets differs from that used for vessels [46 CFR 512.7 (b) (3) (i)]:

> Actual investment, representing original cost to the carrier or to any related company, in other fixed assets employed in the Service shall be reported as of the

beginning of the year. Accumulated reserves for depreciation for these assets shall be reported both as at the beginning and end of the year. The arithmetic average of the reserves shall also be shown and shall be the amount deducted from original cost in determining rate base. . . .

> Allocation to the Trade shall be based upon the actual use of the specific asset or group of assets within the Trade. For those assets employed in a general capacity such as office furniture and fixtures, the vessel operating expense relationship shall be employed for allocation purposes. The basis of allocation to the Trade shall be set forth and fully explained.

The "vessel operating expense relationship" referred to above is defined [in 46 CFR 512.5 (p)] as the "ratio of total Trade Vessel Operating Expense to total Company Vessel Operating Expense."

Working Capital. The amount of working capital to be included in the rate base is the *lower* of two computed amounts. The first amount involves a computation of the *average voyage expense.* This is basically the carrier's vessel operating expense divided by the average number of voyages. The second amount involves an allocation of the carrier's average working capital between the trade and nontrade activity on the basis of the carrier's vessel operating expense relationship. The *lower* of these two amounts is included in the carrier's rate base.

Other Assets. Other assets of the carrier can be included in the rate base. They must be separately scheduled and the "basis of allocation to the Trade and computations of percentages employed shall be set forth and fully explained" [46 CFR 512.7 (b) (6)].

Property and Equipment of Related Companies. If carriers use property and equipment of related companies in the trade, they can allocate a portion of the net depreciated cost of these assets to the rate base of the trade. They are to follow the same rules as are applicable to the allocation of their own property and equipment.

Exhibit B—Income

The various operating accounts (or groupings thereof) that are involved in the determination of income are to be allocated to the trade in accordance with 46 CFR 512.7 (c). The following illustrates the bases to be used:

Account(s)	*Base(s) for Allocation*
Revenue	Directly assigned.
Vessel Operating Expenses	Directly assigned where possible; otherwise allocated on the basis of cargo-cube-miles or, for certain expenses such as port fees, cargo cubes loaded or unloaded.
Administrative and General Expenses	Directly assigned where possible; otherwise allocated on the basis of vessel operating expenses.
Other Shipping Operations (e.g., cargo handling)	Tonnage or volume.

Inactive Vessel Expense	Directly assigned or on same basis as vessel is allocated in the rate base.
Depreciation and Amortization	Same basis as asset is allocated in the rate base.

Exhibit C—Rate of Return

Carriers must compute *three* different measures of their rate of return. The first measure is the *return on equity,* which is described in 46 CFR 512.7 (d) (2). Basically, it is computed by dividing the carrier's net income attributable to trade by the owner's equity share of trade assets (i.e., trade assets × owner equity percentage). This rate of return measure is to be evaluated (by the FMC) in comparison to the carrier's cost of capital computed on a number of different bases (e.g., discounted future cash flows).

The second measure of the rate of return is the *fixed coverage ratio.* This is computed by dividing net income plus interest expense *plus* depreciation and amortization *plus* income taxes (all as allocated to the trade) by the trade-fixed charges (defined as interest expense plus principal payments plus capitalized lease obligations). The FMC compares the carrier's fixed coverage ratio to those experienced by "(1) public utilities; (2) government-owned corporations; (3) rural electric cooperatives; (4) various municipal enterprises such as airports and hospitals; and (5) various sectors of the transportation industry including subsidized and unsubsidized ocean carriers" [46 CFR 512.7 (d) (3)].

The third measure of the rate of return is the *operating ratio.* This is computed by dividing trade expenses by trade revenues. This ratio is compared to the operating ratios of public utilities, publicly-held corporations, and other transportation entities. The FMC's regulations dictate that, while all three measures will be reviewed, the following will be given primacy in its evaluation: [46 CFR 512.7 (d) (1)]:

(i) For those carriers who have 20 percent or more equity in total company assets, and whose Trade rate base is more than 30 percent of Trade revenue, the return on equity method will be employed;

(ii) For those carriers who have less than 20 percent equity in total company assets, and whose Trade rate base is more than 30 percent of Trade revenue, the fixed coverage ratio will be employed;

(iii) For those carriers whose Trade rate base is less than 30 percent of Trade revenue, the operating ratio will be employed.

Non-vessel Operating Common Carriers

In 46 CFR Part 512, the FMC sets out its reporting requirements for non-vessel operating common carriers (e.g., operators of terminal facilities). The requirements are similar to those for vessel operators. Basically, the carriers are required to file annually a balance sheet, income statement, and, in separate schedules, assets devoted to FMC-regulated trade and operating results from FMC-regulated trade. These schedules also have to be filed on an historic basis *and* an income statement on a projected basis whenever the carrier is filing for a significant change in its rates.

Audit

In 46 CFR Part 513, the FMC's regulations in regard to its audit rights are set forth. The basic provision is contained in 46 CFR 513.2 and 513.3:

§ 513.2 Access to records.

The Commission itself, or through duly accredited special agents or auditors, shall at all times have access to all documents, accounts, records, rates, charges, or correspondence used in the preparation of or pertaining to reports filed with the Commission and all underlying working papers (irrespective of by whom prepared) in support of all exhibits and schedules submitted to the Commission, and the Commission or its accredited special agents or auditors shall be permitted to make copies of such records to the extent they deem necessary.

§ 513.3 Notice of audit.

Notice that inspection of a carrier's books and records as desired for the purpose of audit shall be given by the Commission or its duly accredited special agents or auditors, and such inspection shall be at a place and time convenient to the carrier, but such inspection shall not be unduly delayed after reasonable notice is given to the carrier.

In addition, under 46 CFR 512, filings of financial reports must include an opinion by the carrier's independent auditors regarding the statements' and schedules' conformance with the FMC's rules.

FINANCIAL RESPONSIBILITY FOR ENVIRONMENTAL HAZARDS

Various Federal laws charge the FMC with the task of ascertaining that carriers subject to its control have the financial resources to pay for designated categories of environmental hazards. The FMC generally allows carriers to establish their ability to pay for environmental damages in various ways: purchasing insurance, posting a bond, filing a guaranty by a responsible third party, or establishing the ability to "self-insure." If the latter option is chosen, the carrier must provide accounting data. As an illustration of the FMC's regulations, 46 CFR Part 543, which applies to carriers transporting oil that passed through the trans-Alaska pipeline, will be reviewed.

Each United States maritime carrier involved in transporting the oil must establish its financial ability to pay $14 million to meet its prospective liability for oil pollution. It can establish its financial ability by one or a combination of the following: purchasing insurance, purchasing a surety bond, eliciting a guarantee from an entity approved by the FMC, or "self-insuring." If a carrier wants to self insure, it must meet certain conditions.

It must maintain a designated amount of working capital (current assets less current liabilities) and net worth (total assets less total liabilities) in the United States. The amount depends on the number of vessels operated in the Alaska pipeline service [46 CFR 543.6 (a) (3)]:

Number of Vessels	Amount of Working Capital and Net Worth
1	$14,000,000
2	24,000,000
3	28,000,000
4	31,000,000
5	33,000,000
6 or more	34,000,000

Initially, the carrier must establish its compliance with the appropriate limit by filing financial statements certified by an independent certified public accountant. The CPA must specifically attest as to the amount of current assets and total assets that are located in the United States. The CPA must update his representation every 6 months. Audited financial statements must be submitted yearly with accompanying certification as to the location of the current assets and total assets. All persons involved in establishing the carrier's financial ability to self insure are required to notify the FMC within 5 days of their obtaining the knowledge that the carrier is not in compliance with these financial requirements.

MILITARY CARGO RATES

When the United States military employs negotiated procurement (see Chapter 16) to acquire marine transportation services from carriers regulated by the FMC, the FMC is charged with the responsibility for ascertaining that the proposed rates are not below the carrier's fully distributed costs. *Fully distributed costs* refers to all direct costs plus an allocated portion of the carrier's indirect costs (i.e., overhead).

In order to carry out its responsibilities in this area, the FMC has promulgated regulations in 46 CFR Part 549 which (a) control the determination of the carrier's total operating cost and (b) control the allocation of total operating cost to its military cargo.

For purposes of measuring costs related to military cargo, the FMC requires the following: (a) depreciation must be computed on the straight-line basis, (b) depreciable lives are set for major categories of fixed assets (e.g., 25 years for new vessels; 15 years for rebuilt vessels), and (c) any cost declared unallowable by the Defense Acquisition Regulation which controls military procurement (see Chapter 16) is similarly unallowable for determining cost for the FMC's review of rates.

The FMC's principles of allocation of total cost to carrier's military cargo operations rely heavily on the allocation principles it set out in 46 CFR Part 512 (discussed earlier in this chapter) which were promulgated to assist the FMC in evaluating carriers' rates of return.

Chapter 11

Maritime Administration

The Maritime Administration (MarAd) is a component of the United States Department of Commerce. MarAd is headed by the Assistant Secretary of Commerce for Maritime Affairs. It operates four regional offices in New York, New Orleans, Cleveland, and San Francisco. The agency is involved in a number of programs related to the U.S. merchant marine industry.

MarAd PROGRAMS

Ship Construction Subsidies

MarAd administers several programs that are beneficial to the domestic ship-building industry. The most important is the construction differential subsidy program (CDS) under which MarAd underwrites the cost differential between having merchant ships constructed in the United States or having them constructed abroad. A major purpose of this program is to ensure that a viable ship construction industry exists for rapid conversion to military production in the event of a national emergency. Since 1970, annual outlays for the CDS program have been approximately $175 million.[1] A corollary of this program is the National Defense Features (NDF) program under which modifications are incorporated in the merchant vessels which would permit conversion to defense purposes, if needed. These modifications are paid for by the government.

Ship Operating Subsidies

MarAd administers the operating differential subsidy (ODS) program. Under this program, MarAd is authorized to subsidize the differential between foreign operators' costs and the higher costs faced by United States operators in order to establish a parity for domestic shipping companies. This subsidy enables the companies to charge rates that are competitive with those charged by foreign shipping companies whose operating costs are lower than domestic shipping companies. Since 1970, the annual outlays under the ODS program have been approximately $280 million.[2]

Construction Funds

MarAd administers a program that is intended to facilitate the private financing of ship construction and refurbishing. Under the Capital Construction Fund (CCF) program, designated categories of shipping companies can defer Federal income taxes on earnings that are deposited in the CCF for future use in ship construction (or reconstruction). Since 1971, when the program began, nearly $1½ billion has been deposited in the CCF; over $1 billion was subsequently invested in shipbuilding.[3]

Loan Guarantees

In administering the Federal Ship Financing Program, MarAd is authorized to act as guarantor of loans that are made to finance (or refinance) United States merchant marine vessels. Currently, MarAd is guarantor of over $6 billion in loans.[4]

International Trade

MarAd attempts to ensure that the U.S. merchant marine has equitable access to foreign markets.

Research and Development

MarAd engages in a diversified program of research and development that includes such areas as cargo handling, communications, ship design, etc.

National Security

In addition to the national security aspects already mentioned, MarAd also works jointly with the U.S. Navy in maintaining a reserve fleet and a ready reserve fleet (ready in 10 days or less for use) of merchant vessels.

U.S. Merchant Marine Academy

MarAd is in charge of the U.S. Merchant Marine Academy located in Kings Point, New York.

MarAd REGULATIONS

MarAd's regulations are contained in Chapter II of Title 46 of the Code of Federal Regulations. The following Parts contain accounting regulations:

Part	
202	Procedures Relating to Review by Secretary of Commerce of Accounts by Maritime Subsidy Board
205	Audit Appeals; Policy and Procedure
207	Statistical Data for Use in Operating Differential Subsidy Application Hearings
222	Statements, Reports, and Agreements Required to be Filed
282	Uniform System of Accounts for Maritime Carriers
283	Conservative Dividend Policy
285	Determination of Profit in Contracts and Subcontracts for Construction, Reconditioning, or Reconstruction of Ships
293	Inventories of Vessels Covered by Operating Differential Subsidy Agreements

ODS PROGRAM

Uniform System of Accounts

In Part 282, MarAd has promulgated a uniform system of accounts for maritime carriers operating vessels that receive an operating differential subsidy. The system of accounts contains the following major account groupings:

Accounts	Description
100–199	Current assets
200–399	Noncurrent assets
400–495	Current liabilities
500–579	Noncurrent liabilities
580–599	Owners' equity
600–699	Revenue
700–990	Expenses
995	Extraordinary items

While the uniform system of accounts is very detailed, MarAd's requirements are basically in conformity with generally accepted accounting principles. Many of the regulations are devoted to giving additional guidance on various points. For example, in discussing prior period adjustments and extraordinary items, the regulations limit them to material items and provide the following guidance for materiality [46 CFR 282.1 (k) (1) (iii)]:

> *Material items.* Material items are those which, unless excluded from

ordinary income, would distort the accounts and impair the significance of ordinary income for the year. In determining materiality, the effects of related transactions arising from a single specific identifiable event or plan of action that meet the criteria for an extraordinary item should be aggregated; otherwise an extraordinary item should be considered individually. As a general standard, an item to qualify for inclusion as an extraordinary or prior period item, shall exceed 1 percent of total waterline operating revenues and 10 percent of ordinary income for the year.

MarAd also requires carriers to maintain "voyage accounts"; that is, revenues and expenses must be recorded in such a manner as to permit their attribution to individual "voyages." When financial statements are prepared, any revenues or expenses that are traceable to uncompleted voyages are to be deferred in the balance sheet. The net difference between uncompleted voyage revenue and expense is to be carried as a current asset (where expense exceeds revenue) or current liability (where revenue exceeds expense).

Dividend Limitations

46 CFR Part 283 of MarAd's regulations sets out the rules of its "conservative dividend policy." This policy is intended to assure that operators receiving operating differential subsidies maintain (a) an adequate working capital position, (b) a balanced debt/equity structure, and (c) " . . . the financial ability to assure adequate and timely reinvestment in the merchant marine" [46 CFR 283.2].

MarAd's dividend policy is stated on an exception basis. That is, if an operator can meet the MarAd dividend tests, a dividend can be declared without MarAd's approval. However, if the operator fails under *both* of the MarAd tests and still wants to declare a dividend, it must submit its proposal to MarAd for approval.

MarAd has promulgated two dividend tests: the Retained Earnings Dividend test and the Forty Percent Dividend test. An operator can elect to comply with either.

Retained Earnings Dividend Test. This test is composed of five separate limits:

Earnings Record

Working Capital

Floor Net Worth

Debt/Equity Ratio

Funds Available Limit

The operator may declare a dividend up to the amount of its retained earnings so long as the following limits would be met *after* payment of the dividend.

Earnings record. An operator is precluded from declaring *any* dividend if there is an operating loss in the current fiscal year (that in which the proposed dividend is being considered) *and* there were operating losses in the *two* preceding fiscal years.

Working capital. After payment of the dividend, the operator must have a positive amount of working capital (i.e., current assets must exceed current liabilities). In 46 CFR 283.2 (b) (5) MarAd modifies this basic computation in light of factors peculiar to the operators' financial statements. For example, any net uncompleted voyage accounts (either deferred costs in excess of deferred revenues or vice versa) are ex-cluded from consideration as current assets or current liabilities.

Floor net worth. After payment of the dividend, the operator must have a specified amount of net worth, called the "floor net worth." The amount of floor net worth is initially the greater of 90 percent of an operator's net worth or 50 percent of long-term debt. Once this amount is determined, it is [46 CFR 283.2 (b) (4) (iii)] :

> . . . adjusted from time to time as follows: (A) increased by an amount equal to 50% of the original long-term debt issued with respect to new vessel construction. . . . ; and (B) decreased by an amount equal to 50% of the original long-term debt issued with respect to vessels which are removed from service or otherwise transferred or sold.

The floor net worth limitation is Mar-Ad's attempt to ensure that operators are maintaining their financial ability to reinvest in the merchant marine industry [46 CFR 283.3 (b) (4)].

Debt/equity ratio. After payment of a dividend, an operator's ratio of long-term debt to equity must not be greater than one-to-one.

Funds available limit. An operator is deemed to have adequate "funds" available if it either limits its dividends to 40 percent of prior years' earnings or maintains an excess of funds available [defined in 46 CFR 283.3 (b) (2) (i)] over funds required [defined in 46 CFR 283.3 (b) (2) (iii)]. The concepts of *funds available* and *funds required* are quite complex. In general, they are approaches to determining (a) the obligations that operators will face in maintaining and expanding their vessel holdings and servicing their long-term debts (funds required) and (b) the resources that will be available to meet those commitments (funds available).

Forty Percent Dividend Test. This test includes the same first three limits found in the Retained Earnings Dividend Test (i.e., earnings record, working capital, and floor net worth). The debt/equity ratio under this test must not be greater than two-to-one. Finally, in lieu of the funds available limit, the operator need only establish that the current dividend being considered plus any dividends that were paid in prior years will not exceed 40 percent of prior years' earnings.

Other Requirements of ODS Recipients

There are many other accounting requirements placed on companies receiving operating differential subsidies. Some of the more noteworthy are:

1. Companies receiving operating differential subsidies must file periodic reports with MarAd (Parts 252, 292, and 293). Included in these reports is the Annual Report Form MA-172. This report is the same as the Federal Maritime Commissions's Form FMC-64; it is reviewed in some detail in Chapter 10 on the Federal Maritime Commission.

2. In calculating the operating differential subsidy rates, a great deal of weight is given to the individual shipping companies' costs [46 CFR Part 252]. This data is used in determining the cost differential between United States and foreign operators.

3. Companies receiving operating differential subsidies are required to be audited annually by independent licensed or certified public accountants.

4. Companies engaged in carrying bulk raw and processed agricultural commodities from the United States to the Soviet Union are subject to special operating differential subsidy provisions [46 CFR Part 294]. If this is the only operating differential subsidy program in which they participate, they are not bound to follow MarAd's uniform system of accounts.

CDS PROGRAM

Under the construction differential subsidy program, vessels to be constructed in U.S. shipyards, owned by U.S. companies, staffed by U.S. crews, and operated in foreign commerce are eligible for subsidy payments of up to 50 percent of their shipbuilding costs. MarAd accounting regulations enter into the administration of this program at two stages: during construction of the vessel and during operation of the vessel when it is not used in foreign commerce.

Cost and Profit Determination on Ship Contracts

Whenever MarAd enters into negotiated flexibly-priced contracts (i.e., other than firm fixed-price contracts) for the construction, reconditioning, or reconstruction of ships, 46 CFR Part 285 controls the determination of cost (and profit) under such contracts. This

Part is applicable not only to contracts entered into under the CDS program, but also applies to contracts which MarAd executes on its own account.

Part 285 sets out three types of requirements that are applicable to contractors: audit requirements, reporting requirements, and cost principles. The cost principles comprise the majority of the Part.

The cost principles discuss separately the *allowability* and *allocability* of costs. First, as to *allowability,* the cost principles enumerate individual items of costs within three categories:

1. Items ordinarily allowable
2. Items subject to qualification or disallowance
3. Unallowable items

Categories 1 and 3 generally include items that are either clearly valid contract costs (Category 1) or clearly unacceptable contract costs (Category 3). Examples of Category 1 costs are direct material, direct labor, and overhead; examples of Category 3 costs are fines and penalties, nonoperating expenses, and losses on other contracts. Category 2 involves a gray area; these costs are sometimes allowable, qualified (in amount), or unallowable. Examples are advertising, interest, and intracompany charges. Costs in this category are generally allowed, qualified, or disallowed based upon their reasonableness and/or their allocability to the contract as determined by the specific circumstances faced by the contractor.

The cost principles also discuss the *allocation* of costs to contracts as direct or indirect charges. Direct costs are discussed in relation to three categories of charges: direct material, direct labor, and other direct charges "which are incurred on account of a contract or subcontract may be charged directly thereto: Provided, that such method is consistently followed and that no similar charges on account of other work are made through overhead in such manner as to prorate any part thereof inequitably or to a contract or subcontract" [46 CFR 285.52 (a) (3) (iii)].

The cost principles discussion of overhead [46 CFR 285.52 (a) (4)] is rather brief. It attempts to establish such general guidelines as:

— The distribution of overhead should conform to generally accepted accounting practice to ensure an accurate determination of cost.

— Each "class of work" should bear its proper share of indirect cost.

— Departmental (versus blanket plantwide or shipyardwide) overhead rates will generally be required unless the latter result in "accurate" determination of cost.

— Direct labor is acceptable as an allocation base; other bases must be more closely scrutinized for their equitable distribution of overhead.

— Predetermined overhead rates are acceptable as long as there is a year end adjustment to arrive at actual cost being allocated.

— No change in the overhead practices of the contractor can be made during the progress of the work without the prior approval of MarAd.

CDS Repayment

The CDS program is intended to subsidize United States built, owned, and operated vessels in foreign trade. MarAd requires owners of vessels that were financed in part by a construction differential subsidy to file periodic reports in which the owner discloses the use of the vessel for the period. Use of the vessel in *other than* foreign commerce results in the owner being required to refund a portion of the subsidy. MarAd's regulations on the refund of the CDS are contained in 46 CFR Part 276.

CAPITAL CONSTRUCTION FUND

Shipping companies can avail themselves of the tax advantages of a capital construction fund. By signing an agreement that sets up such a fund, companies can defer income taxes on earnings by making deposits to the fund. The regulations for administering such funds are contained in subchapter K of MarAd's regulations. This subchapter is composed of two parts: Part 390—Capital Construction Fund—is MarAd's regulations for such funds; Part 391—Federal Income Tax Aspects of the Capital Construction Fund—is a reprint of 26 CFR Part 3 which is a component of the Internal Revenue Service's regulations.

These regulations are laden with accounting-based requirements for setting up, administering, and disposing of the fund (e.g., by investing in new vessels) and include a requirement that the annual report of the fund " . . . shall be accompanied by an opinion of an independent certified public accountant to the effect that the exhibits . . . composing the accounting have been prepared in accordance with all published

orders, rules, regulations and instructions issued or adopted . . . " [46 CFR 390.6 (a) (4)] .

LOAN GUARANTEE PROGRAM

MarAd's loan guarantee program for financing vessel construction, reconstruction, or reconditioning employs a number of accounting-based controls in (a) determining eligibility for the guarantee, (b) monitoring financial condition during the guarantee period, and (c) determining the guarantee fee.

Eligibility—Financial Requirements

In order to be eligible for a loan guarantee, a company must establish that with the loan to be guaranteed on its financial statements, it will meet one of two sets of financial requirements: the primary financial requirements or the alternative financial requirements at the time of closing on the vessel.

Primary Financial Requirements. If the owner of the vessel is also to be the operator of the vessel, the owner must (a) have positive working capital [current assets less current liabilities, with certain MarAd modifications in 46 CFR 298.13 (b) (2)] and (b) have owners' equity at closing that is equal to the *greater* of 50 percent of its long-term debt or 90 percent of its owners' equity, both as measured in its most recent audited balance sheet.

If the owner of the vessel is going to lease it to another to operate (i.e., the operator), the primary financial requirements are more complex, covering both the owner and operator. The *operator* must (a) have positive working capital,

(b) have a long-term debt/equity ratio of no more than two-to-one, and (c) have owners' equity that is equal to the greater of 50 percent of its long-term debt or 90 percent of its owners' equity, both as measured in its most recent audited balance sheet. The *owner* must have an owners' equity that is at least equal to the difference between the cost of the vessel and the amount of the MarAd guarantee.

Alternative Financial Requirements. If the primary financial requirements cannot be met, the owner (or owner and operator) can resort to the alternative financial requirements.

For an owner who will also operate the vessel the requirements are: (a) working capital that is equal to 8 percent of the cost of the vessel to be financed *plus* one year's premium for insurance on the vessel *plus* one year's loan guarantee fee and (b) owners' equity that is at least equal to 90 percent of the difference between cost of the vessel to be financed and the MarAd guarantee *plus* its working capital requirement.

For an owner who will *not* act as operator of the vessel, the *operator* must have (a) working capital equal to that which was imposed on the owner acting as operator discussed in the preceding paragraph and (b) owners' equity at least equal to 90 percent of the owners' equity in its last audited balance sheet. The *owner* must meet the same owners' equity requirement that was discussed in the preceding paragraph.

Further, the regulations allow MarAd some flexibility in applying the regulations to different owner-operator circumstances [46 CFR 298.13 (f)]:

> If the owner, although not operating a Vessel, assumes any of the operating

responsibilities, the Secretary may adjust the Working Capital and Equity requirements of the owner and operator, otherwise applicable under paragraphs (d) [Primary Financial Requirements] and (e) [Alternative Financial Requirements] of this section, by increasing the requirements of the owner and decreasing those of the operator by the same amount.

Financial Agreement

When MarAd approves a loan guarantee, the company (owner) must sign a financial agreement that places restrictions on its actions during the term of the guarantee. Some of the possible restrictions are limitations on (a) dividends (similar to those on companies receiving operating differential subsidies), (b) sales of fixed assets, (c) new borrowings, etc. When a guarantee was negotiated by a company that met the primary financial requirements (discussed above), fewer and less restrictive covenants are imposed than if only the alternative financial requirements had been met.

One of the more restrictive provisions for companies that qualify under the alternative financial requirements is the establishment of a *reserve fund.* Such companies are required to deposit the earnings from the vessels that were financed by loans guaranteed by MarAd into a joint account with MarAd. The earnings attributable to the vessels are computed on more of a cash flow basis rather than an accrual basis. The computation is [46 CFR 298.35 (d)] :

$$A = \frac{B}{C} (E + D - P)$$

where

A = earnings attributed to vessels financed with MarAd guarantees

B = cost of vessels financed with MarAd guarantees

C = total cost of fixed assets

E = earnings after taxes per generally accepted accounting principles

D = depreciation expense

P = principal amount of debt paid off during the year

In order to get out from under this and the other more restrictive provisions affecting companies qualifying under the alternative financial requirements, MarAd can be requested to review the financial position of such companies during the period of the guarantee. If they can then qualify under the primary financial requirements, this and the other more restrictive covenants are lifted.

Guarantee Fee

MarAd charges companies a fee for the loan guarantee. The fee is based upon the amount of risk MarAd perceives it is exposed to by the financial position of the company that is primarily liable under the loan. The loan fee is determined annually according to the following schedule:

	Owners' Equity as % of Long-Term Debt	Guarantee Fee as % of Loan Outstanding
Prior to Delivery of Vessel:	Less than 15%	.5%
	15 to 99%	.375%
	100% and over	.25%
After Delivery of Vessel:	Less than 15%	1.%
	15–59%	.75%
	60–99%	.625%
	100% and over	.5%

Financial Statements

During the period that a guarantee is in effect, the company must be audited annually by licensed certified public accountants (or licensed public accountants). The audited financial statements must be submitted to MarAd. They form the basis for the accounting computations referred to above (e.g., guarantee fee, tests of financial requirements). Licensed certified public accountants (or licensed public accountants) can also be requested by MarAd to substantiate the actual cost of the vessel [46 CFR 298.21 (d)]. MarAd is limited to guaranteeing loans only up to a maximum of 87½ percent of the cost of the vessel determined in accordance with its rules on "actual cost" [46 CFR 298.21 (a) through (c)]. MarAd can either accept the company's representation as to actual cost or call for a review by the company's auditors.

OTHER MarAd PROGRAMS

MarAd employs accounting regulations in various other programs that it administers. For example, MarAd administers programs involving the leasing (to private operators) of vessels owned by the U.S. government. MarAd has the following accounting-based requirements [49 CFR 299.31 (a) (2)]:

The applicant must possess the following minimum financial requisites:

(i) Sufficent working capital, as defined in 299.1 (n), to cover preoperating and operating expenses, as defined in 299.1 (p), of the vessel (in addition to basic charter hire) for a period of 60 days and prepaid insurance for one year. In determining the amount of such working capital the amount of any securities pledged or to be pledged with the Administration in lieu of a surety bond, as prescribed in paragraph (g) (7) of this section, shall be excluded.

(ii) Net worth, as defined in 299.1 (o), at least equal to the amount of the annual basic charter hire payable with respect to the war-built vessel. Such minimum financial requirements shall be applicable with respect to each vessel applied for. In instances where the applicant is engaged in the operation of other vessels or in activities other than the operation of vessels, the amount of working capital and net worth required for such purposes will be taken into account in addition to such minimum financial requirements in determining whether the applicant possesses the required financial resources.

These requirements are bolstered by extensive audit rights that are granted to MarAd to validate the application and to protect the government's interest during the term of any resulting lease.

REFERENCE NOTES

1. U.S., Maritime Administration, *Annual Report for Fiscal Year 1978,* p. 97.

2. *Ibid.*

3. *Ibid.,* p. 16.

4. *Ibid.,* p. 10.

Chapter 12

United States Coast Guard: Great Lakes Pilotage

The United States Coast Guard is one of the Armed Forces of the United States. During peacetime it is a component of a civilian agency. Since 1967, that agency has been the Department of Transportation. Prior to that time, it was under the Department of the Treasury. In time of war, or when directed by the President, the Coast Guard operates as part of the U.S. Navy. The Coast Guard classifies its programs as follows:

1. Search and Rescue
2. Maritime Law Enforcement
3. Commercial Vessel Safety
4. Great Lakes Pilotage
5. Marine Environmental Protection
6. Port Safety and Security
7. Aid to Navigation
8. Bridge Administration
9. Ice Operations
10. Deepwater Ports
11. Boating Safety
12. Coast Guard Auxiliary
13. Marine Science Activities
14. Military Readiness
15. Reserve Training
16. Marine Safety Council[1]

Under its responsibility for administering Great Lakes Pilotage (4 above), the Coast Guard is involved in accounting regulations.

The Coast Guard is assigned control over United States pilots who operate the navigational system on the Great Lakes (including the Saint Lawrence Seaway contiguous to the United States). This control comes from the Great Lakes Pilotage Act of 1960.

U.S. COAST GUARD REGULATIONS

The Coast Guard has promulgated its regulations under this Act in Chapter III of Title 46 of the Code of Federal Regulations. There are three Parts to this Chapter:

Part	
401	Great Lakes Pilotage Regulations
402	Great Lakes Pilotage Rules and Orders
403	Great Lakes Pilotage Uniform Accounting System

The Coast Guard has broad authority over Great Lakes pilots. The most important authority is to register (i.e., license) individuals to operate as pilots on the Great Lakes. The regulations attempt to ascertain and, over time, ensure the technical competence and physical fitness of individuals who operate as pilots.

The Coast Guard also exerts significant economic control over the pilots. In 46 CFR 401.400 through 46 CFR 401.440, the Coast Guard has promulgated regulations on:

1. Basic rates for pilotage.
2. Charges for canceling, delaying, or interrupting pilotage.
3. Charges for additional pilots.
4. Carrying charges on past due accounts.
5. Adjudication of disputed charges.

While the Coast Guard registers individual pilots, much of its regulations are directed at *voluntary associations of pilots.* These voluntary associations form pools which serve as distributors of pilotage services.

The Coast Guard (through its Great Lake Pilotage Staff, headed by a Director and based in Cleveland) controls the formation of voluntary associations by its issuance (or withholding) of a Certificate of Authorization. The first condition necessary for the issuance of a certificate is that the Director must determine that a voluntary association is necessary in order to efficiently manage the pool of pilotage services [46 CFR 401.320 (a)].

The voluntary association that is applying for the certificate must meet certain other conditions. It must be exclusively controlled by (i.e., all voting interest must be held by) the member registered pilots of the association. Thus, the voluntary association is to be shielded from the influence of its clients, the shipping or industrial companies. Next, the voluntary association must establish that it has the necessary financial and managerial base to " . . . operate and maintain an efficient and effective pilotage service." [46 CFR 401.320 (c)].

Once in operation, the voluntary association must adhere to certain operating rules prescribed by the Coast Guard. For example, it is to assign pilots to vessels awaiting pilotage service on a first-come, first-served basis unless there are extenuating circumstances (e.g., hazardous cargoes may be given preference). Also, the association must establish reciprocal arrangements with the Great Lakes pilotage associations established under the auspices of the Canadian government.

The voluntary association must also agree to certain financial reporting controls. It must maintain its books in accordance with the uniform system of accounts [46 CFR Part 403] prescribed by the Coast Guard, periodically submit financial reports to the Coast Guard, and agree to permit audits by the Coast Guard. Annually, the association must engage an independent certified public accountant to conduct an examination of its financial statements and render an opinion thereon.

The accounting and auditing requirements assist the Coast Guard in evaluating the financial soundness of the associations and monitoring the impact that the rate structure has on the operating results of the pilots (through their associations).

UNIFORM ACCOUNTING SYSTEM

The uniform accounting system for voluntary associations is structured around the following four-digit account sequence:

Account Number(s)	Accounts
1000–1400s	Current assets
1500s	Investments and special funds
1600s	Property and equipment
1800s	Deferred charges
2000–2100s	Current liabilities
2200s	Noncurrent liabilities
2300s	Deferred credits
2800s	Stockholders' equity
4000s	Revenues
5000s	Expenses

This basic account structure is expanded upon in the regulations. For example, the current asset grouping is broken down into 13 individual accounts, each of which is explained in terms of its content. For example, the following discussion is devoted to prepaid expenses [46 CFR 403.6]:

Short-Term Prepayments

Record here prepayments of obligations which if not paid in advance would require the expenditure of working capital within one year, such as prepaid rent, insurance, taxes, interest, etc. Unexpired insurance and miscellaneous prepayments applicable to periods extending beyond one year where significant in amount shall be charged to balance sheet account 1820 Long-term prepayments.

The accounting system is "open-ended" in an attempt to provide associations with the needed flexibility to expand the accounting system to serve their needs [46 CFR 403.1.3]:

General Description of System of Accounts and Reports

(a) This system of accounts and reports is designed to permit limited contraction or expansion to reflect the varying needs and capabilities of different Associations without impairing basic accounting comparability as between Associations.

(b) Under the system of accounts prescribed, both balance sheet and profit and loss accounts and account groupings are designed, in general, to embrace all activities, both pool and nonpool, in which the Association engages. Except for transactions which are of sufficient magnitude to distort current year operating results, prior year transactions are recorded in the same accounts as current year transactions of a like nature.

(c) In order to afford Associations as much flexibility and freedom as possible in establishing ledger and subsidiary accounts to meet their individual needs, a minimum number of account subdivisions have been prescribed in this

Uniform System of Accounts. It is intended, however, that each Association, in maintaining its accounting records will provide subaccount and subsidiary account segregations which are consistent with the prescribed accounts.

The most striking feature of the accounting system promulgated by the Coast Guard is its close conformance with generally accepted accounting principles. One clear example of this conformance is found in the rules governing "reserves" of retained earnings [46 CFR 403.2.10]:

Establishment of Reserves

(a) Provisions for reserves covering transactions or conditions which do not diminish assets or result in demonstrable liability to the Association, with corresponding diminution in stockholder equity during the period over which accrued, shall not be charged against income but shall be charged directly against balance sheet account 2940, Unappropriated retained earnings.

Another example is the rules governing footnote disclosure [46 CFR 403.2.13]:

Notes to Financial Statements

All matters which are not clearly identified in the body of the financial statements but which may influence materially interpretations or conclusions which may reasonably be drawn in regard to financial condition or earnings position shall be clearly and completely stated as footnotes to the financial statements.

One variance from generally accepted accounting principles is the degree to which interperiod allocation of income taxes is required [46 CFR 403.2.4]:

Federal Income Tax Accruals

(a) All income taxes shall be accrued by proportionate charges or credits to income each accounting period in such manner as will allocate the charges for taxes, or the tax credits for losses, to the periods in which the related profits or losses respectively, are reflected.

(b) The general policy in respect to the accrual of income taxes for each accounting period will require that the Association take up in its accounts an amount equivalent to the actual tax liability applicable to the period as computed or estimated on the basis of income tax laws and regulations then in effect, except where Associations compute depreciation for tax purposes as rates in excess of those which are used for regular accounting purposes. In such cases the deferred income taxes shall be accrued for regular accounting purposes in order to apportion the total income tax cost among the various accounting periods on a basis which will fairly represent the actual tax burden in terms of actual income taken up by the Association in each of the various accounting periods.

This provision requires interperiod allocation *only* for differences between income on a tax basis and income on a "regular accounting" basis due to differences in the depreciation methods employed on each basis. While it is likely that this is the only major timing difference between the two bases, the lack of provision for accommodating other timing differences is noteworthy.

FINANCIAL REPORTING

The Coast Guard requires the voluntary associations to submit budgeted as well as historical financial statements. Each association must submit an operating budget (i.e., budgeted income statement on an itemized basis) to the Coast Guard by the end of the first month of its fiscal year. The operating budget must be approved by the association's board of directors.

As the year progresses, the association must submit quarterly financial statements to the Coast Guard within 30 days of the end of each quarter. The association's annual financial statement must be audited by an independent certified public accountant and the audit report must be submitted to the Coast Guard.

REFERENCE NOTE

1. U.S., Office of the Federal Register, *United States Government Manual,* 1978/79, pp. 434–437.

Chapter 13

Federal Energy Regulatory Commission

The Federal Energy Regulatory Commission (FERC) is an independent regulatory body that is a unit of the Department of Energy (DOE). FERC is the successor agency to the Federal Power Commission (FPC). The FPC was established in 1920 with the original charge of regulating the country's water power resources. This was later expanded to include regulatory responsibility for interstate transmission and sales of electricity and natural gas. In 1977, when the FERC succeeded the FPC, it assumed most of the FPC's regulatory functions *plus* control over oil pipelines which had previously been under the jurisdiction of the Interstate Commerce Commission (ICC). Also, the DOE Organization Act (which established FERC) called for all of DOE's significant energy policies to be submitted to FERC for review and comment. The most recent significant addition to its agenda is the regulation of the *intrastate* sales by producers of natural gas. Prior to the passage of the National Energy Act of 1978, this energy market was not directly regulated at the Federal level.

FERC is headed by a bipartisan Commission of five members. The Commissioners are appointed to 4-year terms by the President, with the approval of the Senate. The President designates one of the Commissioners to serve as chairman. The Commission is headquartered in Washington, D.C., and has five regional offices located in Atlanta, Chicago, Fort Worth, New York, and San Francisco.

There are certain common threads that run throughout the FERC's regulation of electric utilities and natural gas companies. One such thread is that their financial statements employ formats common to many regulated industries. The balance sheet is presented in inverse order of that found in non-regulated entities. That is, the fixed assets (property, plant, and equipment) and long-term equities are presented first, followed by the current assets and current liabilities. This can be justified by the materiality and degree of regulatory interest (particularly as to the fixed asset accounts) in the non-current accounts. Likewise, the income statement is divided into the following sections:

Operating Revenues
− Operating Expenses

= Operating Income

Nonoperating Revenues
− Nonoperating Expenses

= Nonoperating Income

= Income before interest
− Interest

= Net Income

This format is important to remember in reviewing the uniform systems of accounts since an expense which is not a determinant of operating income (e.g., interest) is not considered a part of the utility's cost of service. This concept is often referred to as "above the line" versus "below the line," with the "line" being operating income. "Below the line" items are not considered part of the utility's operations.

Another point in common is that electric utilities and natural gas companies are generally required to employ straight-line depreciation (either for individual assets or on a group basis) in amortizing their fixed assets. (The unit-of-production method may be used for certain gas property.)

Another characteristic shared by both natural gas companies and electric utilities regulated by FERC is that the current portion of long-term debt is *excluded* from treatment as a current liability. This and other modifications of the current liability components are detailed by FERC as follows [18 CFR Part 101 for electric utilities and 18 CFR Part 201 for natural gas companies, Balance Sheet Instruction 7]:

Current and Accrued Liabilities

Current and accrued liabilities are those obligations which have either matured or which become due within one year from the date thereof; except, *however, bonds, receivers' certificates and similar obligations which shall be classified as long-term debt until date of maturity;* accrued taxes, such as income taxes, which shall be classified as accrued liabilities even though payable more than one year from date; compensation awards, which shall be classified as current liabilities regardless of date due; and minor amounts payable in installments which may be classified as current liabilities. If a liability is due more than one year from date of issuance or assumption by the utility, it shall be credited to a long-term debt account appropriate for the transaction, except, however, the current liabilities previously mentioned. [Emphasis added]

The FERC conducts periodic audits of the entities that it regulates. In addition, it requires annual audits by certified public accountants of the large entities (i.e., Class A and Class B, which are defined later). There is a grandfather provision that permits the use of certain licensed public accountants (non-CPAs) for these audits. FERC requires the auditor to represent whether, in his opinion, the financial statements filed with FERC conform to the Commission's uniform system of accounts. Further, FERC requires the companies that it regulates to have their published financial statements conform to the uniform system of accounts. Any variances from the uniform system must be fully described in footnotes to the financial statements.

FERC's uniform systems of accounts will be discussed under the headings of its three main areas of regulation: electric power, natural gas, and oil pipelines.

ELECTRIC POWER REGULATION

FERC exercises rather broad control over the electric power industry (particularly the interstate portion thereof) in the United States. The specific responsibilities of FERC are:

1. Approval of rates for the transmission and sale of electric power in interstate commerce.
2. Regulation of the interconnection of electric utilities engaged in interstate commerce.
3. Approval of certain actions of the electric utilities it regulates (e.g., mergers, abandonment or disposition of property, issuance of securities where not regulated by states, interlocking directorates).
4. Licensing of non-Federally operated hydroelectric projects.

In carrying out its economic regulation of public utilities (subject to its control in their interstate operations) and licensees (of non-Federal hydroelectric projects), FERC has promul-

gated uniform systems of accounts. FERC's uniform systems of accounts are contained in Title 18 of the Code of Federal Regulations. Part 101 contains the uniform system of accounts for Class A and Class B public utilities and licensees. Part 104 contains the uniform system of accounts for Class C and Class D public utilities and licensees. These classes are based on the following breakdowns of operating revenues:

Class	Operating Revenues
A	$2,500,000 or more
B	$1,000,000 to $2,499,999
C	$150,000 to $999,999
D	$25,000 to $149,999

This chapter's discussion will be based on the uniform system of accounts for Class A and Class B utilities (which number about 210) since they are obviously the most significant entities regulated by FERC. The provisions for Class C and Class D are substantially the same as for Class A and Class B.

Accounts

The FERC's system of accounts for electric utilities is structured around the following numbering system:

Series	Accounts
100s and 300s	Assets (with the 300s being only for plant accounts, i.e., fixed assets)
200s	Liability and owners' equity
433, 436–439	Retained earnings
440–459	Revenue

500–599	Expenses of production, transmission, and distribution
900–949	Administrative, sales, and customer service expenses.
400–432, 434–435	Income statement control accounts.

This last group of accounts serves to bridge the gap between line item operating accounts and the summary amounts appearing in the income statement. For example, account 400—Operating revenues, is the summation of all operating revenue accounts:

440 Residential sales

442 Commercial and industrial sales

444 Public street and highway lighting

445 Other sales to public authorities

446 Sales to railroads and railways

447 Sales for resale

448 Interdepartmental sales

There are other similar accounts in the above structure. For example, account 101—Electric plant in service, summarizes approximately 70 of the 300 series accounts for plant in service. These control accounts facilitate the accumulation of the individual component accounts for preparation of summary statements.

Accounting Regulations

FERC's accounting regulations for electric utilities conform, for the most part, with generally accepted accounting principles (GAAP). However, there are certain areas of divergence.

Extraordinary Items. FERC's criteria for extraordinary items are not as stringent as GAAP regarding the probability of occurrence and include an absolute test of materiality [18 CFR 101, Paragraph 7, General Instructions]:

Those items related to the effects of events and transactions which have occurred during the current period and which are not typical or customary business activities of the company shall be considered extraordinary items. Accordingly, they will be events and transactions of significant effect which would not be expected to recur frequently and which would not be considered as recurring factors in any evaluation of the ordinary operating processes of business. (In determining significance, items of a similar nature should be considered in the aggregate. Dissimilar items should be considered individually; however, if they are few in number, they may be considered in aggregate.) To be considered as extraordinary under the above guidelines, an item should be more than approximately 5 percent of income, computed before extraordinary items. Commission approval must be obtained to treat an item of less than 5 percent, as extraordinary.

Prior Period Items. The accounting regulations closely restrict the use of prior period adjustments as a means of bypassing the income statement [18 CFR 101, Paragraph 7.1, General Instructions]:

As a general rule, items relating to transactions which occurred prior to the current calendar year but were not recorded in the books of account shall be included in the same accounts in which they would have been recorded had the item been recorded in the proper period. Such items relate to events or transactions which occurred in a prior period or periods, the accounting effects of which could not be determined with reasonable assurance at the time, usually because of major uncertainty then existing. When the amount of a prior period item is relatively so large its inclusion for a single month would distort the accounts for that month, the amount may be distributed in equal amounts to the accounts for the current and remaining months of the calendar year. However, if the amount of any prior period item is so large that the company believes its inclusion in the income statement would seriously distort the net income for the year, the company may request Commission approval to record the amount in account 439, Adjustments to Retained Earnings. Such a request must be accompanied by adequate justification.

FERC requires that any such adjustments (a) have arisen out of business activities of prior period(s) and were not due to subsequent events, (b) were dependent on determination by persons other than management, and (c) were not subject to estimation prior to their eventual determination. A claimed prior period item must meet these criteria before being afforded treatment by FERC as an adjustment of retained earnings.

Gain or Loss on Reacquisition of Debt. When a utility reacquires its own long-term debt (e.g., a bond issue) without issuing a new long-term debt in its place (i.e., without refunding), any gain or loss is to be *amortized* over the remaining life of the reacquired debt. When a utility reacquires its own long-term debt *with refunding*, any gain or loss on the reacquired debt can be accounted for in any one of three ways (at the option of the utility): (a) recognized immediately, if insignificant; (b) amortized over the remaining life of the reacquired debt; or (c) amortized over the life of the newly issued debt.

The FERC's requirements can be modified to accommodate the accounting provisions of state and/or local regulatory authorities who have cognizance over a particular utility [18 CFR 101 Paragraph 17J, General Instructions]:

> *Alternate method.* Where a regulatory authority or a group of regulatory authorities having prime rate jurisdiction over the utility specifically disallows the rate principle of amortizing gains or losses on reacquisition of long-term debt without refunding, and does not apply the gain or loss to reduce interest charges in computing the allowed rate of return for rate purposes, then the following alternate method may be used to account for gains or losses relating to reacquisition of long-term debt, with or without refunding.
>
> (1) The difference between the amount paid upon reacquisition of any long-term debt and the face value, adjusted for unamortized discount, expenses or premium, as the case may be, applicable to the debt redeemed shall be recognized currently in income and recorded in account 421, Miscellaneous Nonoperating Income, or account 426.5, Other Deductions.
>
> (2) When this alternate method of accounting is used, the utility shall include a footnote to each financial statement, prepared for public use, explaining why this method is being used along with the treatment given for ratemaking purposes.

Income Tax Allocation. Whenever a utility encounters differences in the timing of revenue and/or expense recognition between its reporting for tax purposes and its financial reporting, FERC generally requires the utility to employ *comprehensive interperiod tax allocation.* In short, this means that, for financial reporting purposes, the utility will report an income tax expense based upon its financial statement net income, not its taxable net income (per its tax return). Any difference between this income tax expense and income taxes actually paid is deferred until future periods when the timing difference (and the income tax expense versus income taxes paid) reverses. However, FERC permits utilities to employ other than comprehensive interperiod tax allocation when it is not used for rate-making by a controlling regulatory authority (e.g., state commission) [18 CFR 101 Paragraph 18, General Instruction]:

> Utilities are not required to utilize comprehensive interperiod income tax allocation until the deferred income taxes are included as an expense in the rate level by the regulatory authority having rate jurisdiction over the utility. Where comprehensive interperiod tax allocation accounting is not practiced the utility shall include as a note to each financial statement, prepared for public use, a footnote explanation setting forth the utility's accounting policies with respect to interperiod tax allocation and describing the treatment for rate-making purposes of the tax timing differences by regulatory authorities having rate jurisdiction.

Fixed Assets Purchased from Others. When a utility purchases fixed assets (e.g., an electric plant) from another utility, the cost to the purchasing utility

is allocated between two types of accounts: (a) a fixed-asset account and (b) an "acquisition adjustment" account. The procedure is for the purchaser to record the original cost of the property (i.e., its cost when it was first devoted to serving the public) and the accumulated depreciation thereon, in fixed-asset (property) accounts. The difference between the price paid by the purchaser and the property's book value (i.e., its original cost less accumulated depreciation) is charged to an "Electric plant acquisition adjustments" account. This account is amortized (as the fixed-asset account is depreciated). However, the amortization is generally to a non-operating (i.e., "below the line") expense account. Thus, it does not enter into the determination of operating income. The utility can petition the FERC to have it reclassified as an operating expense.

This procedure originated in utility accounting to avoid what was regarded as a form of "double dipping." That is, an asset that had been included in the operating assets of one utility (and had its depreciation included in operating expense) would, after sale, be written up by a second utility (and again depreciated). It was felt that the public was, in effect, paying twice (through the utility rates) for the utilities' assets (through depreciation) and their return on investment. The procedure that FERC employs requires the segregation of the "acquisition adjustment" and amortization thereof from operating categories.

Cost of Funds Used During Construction. Historically, utilities have *not* been allowed to treat interest charges as operating expenses (and, thus, directly affect the determination of rates). Further, fixed assets under construction are generally *excluded* from the "rate base" (i.e., the assets on which the utility is allowed to claim a rate of return when the revenue requirement of the utility is determined). In order to offset these apparent disincentives to undertaking construction projects, utilities have generally been allowed to capitalize "interest" (either interest paid on borrowed funds, or in some cases, imputed on nonborrowed funds).

FERC's policy on funds during construction is to allow the capitalization of "interest" on borrowed as well as nonborrowed funds. The capitalized amount for the cost of funds used during construction is computed as follows:

$$A_T = A_I + A_E$$

where

A_T = Total allowance for funds during construction

A_I = Allowance for borrowed funds during construction

A_E = Allowance for nonborrowed funds during construction

$$A_I = s \left(\frac{S}{W}\right) + d \left[\left(\frac{D}{D + P + C}\right) \left(1 - \frac{S}{W}\right)\right]$$

where

s = Short-term debt interest rate
S = Average short-term debt
W = Average balance of funds used in construction
d = Weighted average of actual long-term interest rates
D = Long-term debt
P = Preferred stock
C = Common equity

$$A_E = \left[1 - \frac{S}{W}\right] \left[p \left(\frac{P}{D + P + C}\right) + c \left(\frac{C}{D + P + C}\right)\right]$$

where

p = Weighted average of preferred dividend rates

c = Rate allowed utility's common equity in its most recent rate proceeding.

The charges to the fixed asset account are offset by credits to interest expense (for A_I) and to other income (for A_E).

Gain or Loss on Fixed Assets. FERC rules regarding the disposition (retirement, sale, or casualty loss) of fixed assets are quite extensive. The following is an overview.

FERC distinguishes major items (known as retirement units, which are enumerated in 18 CFR 116) from minor items. No gains or losses are recognized on the disposition (with or without replacement) of minor items. They are generally accounted for by charges or credits (e.g., for salvage value) to the accumulated depreciation or maintenance expense accounts. The disposition of retirement units can result in the gain or loss (i.e., the difference between the book value and the proceeds, if any, received) being credited or charged to (a) the accumulated depreciation account, (b) a gain or loss account, or (c) a *deferred* gain or loss account. For example:

—The book cost less net salvage of depreciable electric plant retired shall be charged in its entirety to account 108, Accumulated Provision for Depreciation of Electric Plant in Service. Any amounts which, by approval or order of the Commission, are charged to account 182, Extraordinary Property Losses, shall be credited to account 108. [18 CFR 101, Electric Plant Instructions, Paragraph 11F]

—Deferred losses from disposition of utility plant.

This account shall include losses from the sale or other disposition of property previously recorded in account 105, Electric Plant Held for Future Use, under the provisions of paragraphs B, C, and D thereof, where such losses are significant and are to be amortized over a period of 5 years, unless otherwise authorized by the Commission. The amortization of the amounts in this account shall be made by debits to account 411.7, Losses from Disposition of Utility Plant. (See account 105, Electric Plant Held for Future Use.) [18 CFR 101, Account 187]

—Deferred gains from disposition of utility plant.

This account shall include gains from the sale or other disposition of property previously recorded in account 105, Electric Plant Held for Future Use, under the provisions of paragraphs B, C, and D thereof, where such gains are significant and are to be amortized over a period of 5 years, unless otherwise authorized by the Commission. The amortization of the amounts in this account shall be made by credits to account 411.6, Gains from Disposition of Utility Plant. (See account 105, Electric Plant Held for Future Use.) [18 CFR 101, Account 256]

Research and Development Costs. FERC generally treats "Research, Development and Demonstration" (RD&D) expenditures as expenses of the period of incurrence. However, there is a provision for deferring certain RD&D costs [18 CFR 101, Account 188]:

In certain instances a company may incur large and significant research, development, and demonstration expenditures which are nonrecurring and which would distort the annual research, development, and demonstration charges for the period. In such a case the portion of such amounts that cause the distortion may be amortized to the appropriate operating expense account over a period not to exceed 5 years unless otherwise authorized by the Commission.

Self-Insurance. FERC allows utilities to employ self-insurance procedures for specified categories of losses for which it elects not to contract for insurance (or is unable to contract for insurance) [18 CFR 101, Accounts 261 and 262]:

261. *Property insurance reserve.*

A. This account shall include amounts reserved by the utility for self-insurance against losses through accident, fire, flood, or other hazards to its own property leased from others. The amounts charged to account 924, Property Insurance, or other appropriate accounts to cover such risks shall be credited to this account. A schedule of risks covered by this reserve shall be maintained, giving a description of the property involved, the character of the risks covered and the rates used.

B. Charges shall be made to this account for losses covered by self-insurance. Details of these charges shall be maintained according to the year the casualty occurred which gave rise to the loss.

262. *Injuries and damages reserve.*

A. This account shall be credited with amounts charged to account 925, Injuries and Damages, or other appropriate accounts, to meet the probable liability, not covered by insurance, for deaths or injuries to employees and others, and for damages to property neither owned nor held under lease by the utility.

B. When liability for any injury or damage is admitted by the utility either voluntarily or because of the decision of a court or other lawful authority, such as a workmen's compensation board, the admitted liability shall be charged to this account and credited to the appropriate liability account. Details of these charges shall be maintained according to the year the casualty occurred which gave rise to the loss.

These "operating reserve" accounts appear as a separate category of accounts, not included in either liabilities or owner's equity. However, they are employed, in effect, as estimated liability accounts (a) being credited for charges to expense for estimated losses and (b) being charged for actual losses as they are incurred.

Other FERC Duties

The FERC also has responsibility for approving the merger (or the purchase of one utility's controlling interest by another utility) and the issuance of securities (in certain circumstances) by electric utilities. The regulations controlling these activities are contained in Parts 33 and 34, respectively, of Title 18 of the Code of Federal Regulations. While the FERC's regulations in these areas generally require the filing (with the FERC) of financial statements, no separate accounting rules or procedures are promulgated in these sections.

Report Forms

Part 141 of Title 18 of the Code of Federal Regulations contains the various forms that electric utilities must file with the FERC. Form No. 1 is the annual report for Class A and Class B utilities; Form 1-F is the annual report for Class C and Class D utilities. These forms involve the preparation of the basic financial statements plus numerous additional schedules (over 100 for Form No. 1). In addition to its use as an annual report, Form 1 is also the basis for financial statement filings for mergers and the issuance of securities by utilities.

NATURAL GAS REGULATION

The natural gas industry in the United States is regulated by FERC under two basic laws: the Natural Gas Act of 1938 and the Natural Gas Policy Act of 1978. Under the Natural Gas Act, the Federal government (through FERC, and its predecessor, the FPC) has regulated the sale and transmission of natural gas in *interstate* commerce for over 40 years. Under the Natural Gas Policy Act, its purview was extended to the *intrastate* sale of natural gas. FERC's responsibilities include the approval of (a) producer and pipeline tariffs (rates); (b) construction, maintenance, modification, and abandonment of facilities; and (c) curtailment of service to customers (implemented when demand exceeds supply).

The FERC maintains uniform systems of accounts which must be followed by companies subject to the Natural Gas Act. These uniform systems of accounts are contained in Title 18 of the Code of Federal Regulations. Part 201 contains the uniform system for Class A and Class B natural gas companies. Part 204 contains the uniform system for Class C and Class D natural gas companies. The classes are based on operating revenues, which correspond to the same stratification that was enumerated earlier in the chapter for electric utilities.

Here again, our discussion will be based on the regulations for the larger strata (Classes A and B). The regulations for the smaller strata (Classes C and D) are substantially the same. There are over 80 Class A and B natural gas companies. They account for over 99 percent of interstate sales of natural gas.

Accounts

The uniform system of accounts for gas companies is based on the following account structure:

Series	Accounts
100s and 300s	Assets (with the 300s being only for fixed assets)
200s	Liabilities
433, 436–439	Retained earnings
480–499	Revenue
700–899	Expenses of production, transmission, and distribution
900–949	Administrative, sales, and customer service expenses
400–432, 434–435	Income statement control accounts

A feature of the FERC systems of accounts is the interface provided in the numbering system for "gas and electric" companies. CFR Parts 101 and 201 provide for account numbering systems that eliminate overlap for companies providing both gas and electric service:

	Part 101 Accounts (Electric)	Part 201 Accounts (Gas)
Revenue accounts	440–459	480–499
Production, transmission, and distribution expenses	500–599	700–899

Accounting Regulations

All of the accounting regulations discussed above for electric utilities are found in the regulations for natural gas companies. In addition, natural gas companies are subject to some additional provisions due to the nature of their product (vis-á-vis electricity). The provisions are mainly related to the gas reserves or inventories awaiting sale.

Net Realizable Value of Reserves. The FERC's instructions for natural gas production and gathering plant accounts (fixed assets) are introduced by the following requirement [18 CFR 201, Natural Gas Production Plant]:

> *Special Instructions—Costs Related to Leases Acquired After October 7, 1969.* The net book value of amounts recorded in the natural gas production accounts incurred on or related to leases acquired after October 7, 1969, shall, in general, not exceed the net realizable value (estimated selling price less estimated costs of extraction, completion, and

disposal) of recoverable hydrocarbon reserves discovered on such leases. After initiation of exploration and development on leases acquired after October 7, 1969, the utility must determine after a reasonable period of time, and annually thereafter, whether the net realizable value of such recoverable reserves will be sufficient to absorb the net book value of amounts recorded in the accounts. The recoverable reserves shall be determined and attested to by independent appraisers no less frequently than every 3 years. If the net realizable value of recoverable reserve is not sufficient to absorb the net book value of amounts in the production accounts, the utility shall reduce the net book value of the amounts in the accounts to net realizable value of recoverable reserves. The reduction shall be done by first reducing the unamortized amounts recorded in Account 338, Unsuccessful Exploration and Development Costs, by debiting Account 404.1, Amortization and Depletion of Producing Natural Gas Land and Land Rights. Next, if the net book value related to successful costs exceeds the net realizable value of the recoverable reserves, the production plant accounts shall be written down to such net realizable value by appropriate charges and credits to the expense and valuation accounts.

Account 338—Unsuccessful Exploration and Development Costs—is a logical place to start the writedown to net realizable value since it is composed of the cost of unsuccessful efforts encountered in natural gas exploration and development [18 CFR 201, Account 338]:

Unsuccessful exploration and development costs.

A. This account shall include unsuccessful exploration and development

costs incurred on or related to hydrocarbon leases, on properties in the contiguous 48 States and the State of Alaska, acquired after October 7, 1969. It shall also include costs of a preliminary nature incurred in the search for natural gas in such areas after October 7, 1969.

B. The costs recorded in this account shall be amortized by debiting account 404.1, Amortization and Depletion of Producing Natural Gas Land and Land Rights, and crediting this account using the unit-of-production or other acceptable method of amortization as hydrocarbons are extracted from producing wells.

C. In general, the unamortized costs recorded in this account shall not exceed the net realizable value (estimated selling price less estimated costs of extraction, completion and disposal) of proven hydrocarbon reserves on leases acquired after October 7, 1969. (See "Special Instructions—Costs Related to Leases Acquired After October 7, 1969," above.)

Inventories of Natural Gas. Natural gas inventories can be found in three places in a company's financial statements: as a current asset, as a noncurrent asset, or as a component of the company's underground storage plant.

Gas Stored Underground—Current. This account contains the cost of natural gas (stored underground) that is awaiting resale [18 CFR 201, Account 164.1]:

Gas stored underground—current.

This account shall be debited with such amounts as are credited to account 117, Gas Stored Underground—Noncurrent, to reflect classification for balance sheet purposes of such portion of the inventory of gas stored underground as represents a current asset according to conventional rules for classification of current assets.

NOTE: It shall not be considered conformity to conventional rules of current asset classification if the amount included in this account exceeds an amount equal to the cost of estimated withdrawals of gas from storage for purposes of sale within the 24-month period from date of the balance sheet, or if the amount represents a volume of gas which, in fact, could not be withdrawn from storage without impairing the pressure level of any project for normal operating purposes.

Gas Stored Underground—Noncurrent. This account contains the cost of natural gas held for resale that does not qualify for treatment as a current asset. The account instructions are noteworthy in two respects: (a) the allowable methods of inventory costing are enumerated and (b) the "base stock" method of inventory valuation is held to be allowable [18 CFR 201, Account 117]:

Gas stored underground—noncurrent.

A. This account shall include the cost of recoverable gas purchased or produced by the utility which is stored in depleted or partially depleted gas or oil fields, or other underground reservoirs, and held for use in meeting service requirements of the utility's customers.

B. Gas stored during the year shall be priced at cost according to generally accepted methods of cost determination consistently applied from year to year. Transmission expenses for facilities of the utility used in moving the gas to the storage area and expenses of storage facilities shall not be included in the inventory of gas except as may be authorized or directed by the Commission.

C. Withdrawals of gas may be priced according to the first-in-first-out, last-in-first-out, or weighted average cost method, in connection with which a "base stock" may be employed provided the method adopted by the utility is used consistently from year to year and the inventory records are maintained in accordance therewith. Approval of the Commission must be obtained for any other pricing method, or change in the pricing method adopted by the utility.

D. If the gas of any storage project is withdrawn below the amount established as "base stock" or encroaches upon native gas of a storage reservoir, and such gas is to be replaced within 12 months, it shall be permissible to price such gas at the estimated cost of replacement with purchased gas and to record a deferred credit therefor. For the purpose of this instruction, account 808, Gas Withdrawn from Storage—Debit, shall be charged with the estimated cost of such replacement gas and account 253, Other Deferred Credits, credited. When replacement of the gas is made the amount in account 253 shall be cleared and this account credited. This accounting will not affect normal accounting for inputs and withdrawals from storage.

Nonrecoverable Natural Gas. Finally, a certain amount of natural gas placed in storage will not be available for sale. The cost of this volume of gas is transferred from inventory to a *fixed-asset* account, Account 352.3—Nonrecoverable Natural Gas, a component of the company's underground storage plant [18 CFR 201, Account 352.3]:

Nonrecoverable natural gas.

A. This account shall include the cost of gas in underground reservoirs, including depleted gas or oil fields and other underground caverns or reservoirs used for the storage of gas which will not be recoverable.

B. Such nonrecoverable gas shall be priced at the acquisition cost of native gas or, when acquired for storage by purchase or presumed to be supplied from the utility's own production, priced as outlined in Paragraph B of account 117, Gas Stored Underground—Noncurrent. After devotion to storage, the cost of the gas shall not be restated to effect subsequent price changes in purchased gas or changes in the cost of gas produced by the utility. When the utility has followed the practice of adjusting nonrecoverable gas to the weighted-average cost of gas purchased or supplied from its own production, cost shall be the weighted-average cost of such gas at the effective date of this account.

Deferred Cost of Natural Gas. Due to the lag between a company's experiencing a significant increase in cost of gas and its filing for and receiving permission to pass this on to its customers through higher rates, the company is permitted to defer these costs pending an action by the Commission. The account used for this deferral is classified as a noncurrent asset—a "deferred-debit" account [18 CFR 201, Account 191]:

Unrecovered purchased gas costs.

A. This account shall include purchased gas costs related to Commission approved purchased gas adjustment clauses when such costs are not included in the utility's rate schedules on file with the Commission.

B. This account shall be debited or credited, as appropriate, each month for increases or decreases in purchased gas costs with contra entries to Account 805.1, Purchased Gas Cost Adjustments.

C. After a change in a rate schedule recognizing the increases or decreases in purchased gas costs recorded in this account is approved by the Commission, this account shall be debited or credited, as appropriate, with contra entries to expense Account 805.1, Purchased Gas Cost Adjustments, so that the balance accumulated in this account will be amortized on an appropriate basis over a succeeding 6-month period or over such other periods that the Commission may have authorized. Any over or under applied debits or credits to this account shall be carried forward to the succeeding period of amortization.

Report Forms

Part 260 of Title 18 of the Code of Federal Regulations contains the various statements and reports that natural gas companies must file with FERC. Form No. 2 is the annual report for Class A and Class B companies; Form 2-A is the annual report for Classes C and D. These reports involve the preparation of the basic financial statements plus numerous additional schedules (over 100 for Classes A and B; less than 20 for Classes C and D).

OIL PIPELINE REGULATION

Since the regulation of oil pipelines was transferred from the ICC, FERC has continued to rely upon the uniform system of accounts promulgated by the ICC. This uniform system comprises

Part 1204 of Title 49 of the Code of Federal Regulations. While the accounting regulations in this uniform system were not established by FERC, they are generally consistent with those of FERC (for electric utilities and natural gas companies). Some of the noteworthy features of the uniform system will be discussed in the following paragraphs. Over 150 oil pipelines are regulated by FERC.

Accounts

The system of accounts for oil pipelines is similar in structure to those for electric utilities and natural gas companies. The numbering system for oil pipelines is:

Series	Accounts
10s, 20s, 30s, 40s, 100s	Assets (with the 100s only for property accounts, i.e., fixed assets)
50s	Current liabilities
60s	Noncurrent liabilities
70s	Owner's equity
200s	Revenues
300s, 400s	Expenses of operation and maintenance
500s	General expenses
600s	Income statement control accounts
700s	Retained earnings

Accounting Regulations

The system of accounts insures rather tight control by the government since Commission (once the ICC, now FERC) approval is required for any changes in accounting principles as well as any item being treated as an extraordinary item or as a prior period adjustment. Extraordinary items and prior period adjustments must meet the following test of materiality before they will be considered by the Commission [49 CFR 1204, General Instructions, 1-6 (f)]:

> *Materiality.* As a general standard an item shall be considered material when it exceeds 10 percent of annual income (loss) before extraordinary items. An item may also be considered in relation to the trend of annual earnings before extraordinary items or other appropriate criteria. Items shall be considered individually and not in the aggregate in determining materiality. However, the effects of a series of related transactions arising from a single specific and identifiable event or plan of action shall be aggregated to determine materiality.

In evaluating these items, the Commission is interested in the views of the carrier's (i.e., the oil pipeline company's) independent accountant and requires that its request for accounting changes, extraordinary items, and prior period adjustments " . . . be accompanied by a letter from the independent accountant [if any] approving or otherwise commenting on the request" [49 CFR 1204, General Instructions. 1-6 (g)].

Depreciation. Carriers are generally required to use straight-line, group depreciation. Under a group depreciation system, gains or losses are not recognized upon the retirement of individual units. Rather, the cost of the asset is charged to the accumulated depreciation account. Carriers can request that the Commission authorize it to use other than group depreciation for a particular asset. Whenever a carrier feels that either the economic life of its fixed assets will be significantly shorter than expected or that the retirement or sale of assets will not be properly accommodated by use of the group method, it can request the Commission to grant it permission to change its accounting (e.g., to a shorter depreciable life; to recognizing a gain or loss on retirement or sale).

Capitalization of Interest. Carriers are permitted to capitalize interest during construction. However, the interest is limited to that " . . . on bonds, notes and other interest bearing debt . . . " [49 CFR 1204, Instructions for Carrier Property Accounts, 3-3 (11) (i)]. This contrasts with electric utilities and natural gas companies where interest imputed on owners' equity is allowed.

Reasonableness of Capitalized Amounts. Carriers' property accounts—indeed, all of their accounts—are governed by the following test of reasonableness (49 CFR 1204, General Instructions 1-14):

> Charges to be just and reasonable. All charges to the accounts prescribed in this system of accounts for carrier property, operating revenues, operating and maintenance expenses, and other carrier expenses, shall be just, reasonable and not exceed amounts necessary to the honest and efficient operations and management of carrier business. Payments shall not exceed the fair market value of goods and services acquired in an arm's-length transaction. Any payments in excess of such just and reasonable charges shall be included in account 660, Miscellaneous Income Charges.

A specific illustration of the concept of reasonableness is found when a carrier acquires property in a *non-arm's length* transaction [49 CFR 1204, Instructions for Carrier Property Accounts, 3-1 (c)]:

> Property acquired from an affiliated company through purchase of transfer shall be recorded together with the related accrued depreciation and liabilities assumed, if any, in the appropriate property accounts at the same amount that it was recorded on the books of the affiliate. When the purchase price exceeds the net book value of the property acquired, the difference shall be charged to retained income. When the purchase price is less than the net book value, the difference shall be credited to account 73, Additional Paid-in Capital. This does not apply to small miscellaneous purchases or transfers.

When property is acquired from a nonaffiliated company, it is generally recorded at the actual cost (again, assuming its reasonableness), to the carrier. Thus, no "acquisition adjustment" is required (as for electric utilities and gas companies) to account for the difference between its book value to the seller (i.e., original cost less accumulated depreciation).

Materiality. Another basic concept of the system of accounts is found in establishing a materiality threshhold for sorting capital expenditures from operating expenditures: [49 CFR 1204, Instructions for Carrier Property Accounts 3-2 (a)]:

> *Minimum rule.* To avoid undue refinement in accounting, carriers shall charge to operating expenses acquisitions of property (other than land) including additions and improvements costing less than $500. Expenditures made under a general plan shall not be

parceled to meet the minimum nor shall unrelated items be combined to avoid the minimum.

Income Tax Allocation. Carriers are required to employ *comprehensive interperiod tax allocation* for timing differences between determinants of income for income tax purposes, and determinants of income according to the uniform system of accounts. (This concept was discussed in some detail for electric utilities.) Rather than enumerate the entire framework for income tax allocation, the uniform system calls for the carrier to " . . . follow generally accepted accounting principles where an interpretation of the accounting rules for income taxes is needed or obtain an interpretation from its public accountant or the Commission." [49 CFR 1204, General Instructions, 1–12 (e)].

Oil Inventories. Similar to natural gas companies, carriers have two types of oil inventories among their assets. Account 16—Oil Inventory—is a current asset. It is charged with the cost of oil that has been acquired and is being held for resale. Account 33—Operating Oil Supply—is a property (fixed-asset) account. It is charged with the cost of oil that must be held in the reservoirs, lines, and tanks to permit the transportation of oil for sale. This oil must remain in the line to permit it to maintain a readiness to serve as a conduit for oil for shipment. Thus, it is properly treated as a noncurrent asset.

Report Form

The annual report (Form P) required to be filed by carriers includes the basic financial statements plus additional schedules (e.g., detailing the property accounts). One feature of the balance sheet of oil pipeline companies (vis-à-vis electric utilities and natural gas companies) is that they are prepared in the conventional format of current accounts (assets and liabilities) being followed by noncurrent accounts.

Chapter 14

Energy Information Administration

The Energy Information Administration (EIA) is a unit within the Department of Energy (DOE). In 1977, when Congress passed the Department of Energy Organization Act, it provided for the creation of the EIA as the central information gathering, processing, and dissemination unit within DOE. The EIA took over the information functions of the units that were merged into DOE by Congress. Specifically, the Office of Energy Information and Analysis of the former Federal Energy Administration, and the information units of the Federal Power Commission (now Federal Energy Regulatory Commission—FERC) and the Bureau of Mines (formerly within the Department of Interior) provided the base for EIA.

EIA UNITS

The main units within EIA that are involved in the acquisition, processing, and publication of energy data are the Office of Energy Data (OED), the Office of Financial Reporting System, and the Office of Oil and Gas Information System. OED is by far the largest of these units. It maintains approximately 50 energy data gathering systems; some were carried forward from predecessor agencies and others were initiated within EIA. Examples of the former are 10 data gathering systems that originated in the former Federal Power Commission (now FERC). The annual reports of electric utilities and natural gas companies, which are discussed in conjunction with the FERC (Chapter 13), are processed by the OED.

The Oil and Gas Information System (OGIS) is a new effort initiated by EIA to provide operating data on oil and gas production and reserves. OGIS is intended to extend the data base on oil and gas and to eliminate the duplications and omissions that were present in prior disparate efforts to gather this information.

FINANCIAL REPORTING SYSTEM

From an accounting standpoint, the most significant EIA-initiated project would appear to be the Financial Reporting System (FRS). The DOE Organization Act directed the EIA to gather financial and operating data on major energy producing companies in order to facilitate the following [DOE Organization Act, Sect. 205 (h)]:

(l) (A) In addition to the acquisition, collection, analysis, and dissemination of energy information pursuant to this section, the Administrator shall identify and designate "major energy-producing companies" which alone or with their affiliates are involved in one or more lines of commerces in the energy industry so that the energy information collected from such major energy-producing companies shall provide a statistically accurate profile of each line of commerce in the energy industry in the United States.

(B) In fulfilling the requirements of this subsection the Administrator shall—

(i) utilize to the maximum extent practicable, consistent with the faithful execution of his responsibilities under this chapter, reliable statistical sampling techniques; and

(ii) otherwise give priority to the minimization of the reporting of energy information by small business.

(2) The Administrator shall develop and make effective for use during the second full calendar year following August 4, 1977, the format for an energy-producing company financial report. Such report shall be designed to allow comparison on a uniform and standardized basis among energy producing companies and shall permit for the energy-related activities of such companies—

(A) an evaluation of company revenues, profits, cash flow and investments in total, for the energy-related lines of commerce in which such company is engaged and for all significant energy-related functions within such company,

(B) an analysis of the competitive structure of sectors and functional groupings within the energy industry;

(C) the segregation of energy information, including financial information, describing company operations by energy source and geographic area;

(D) the determination of costs associated with exploration, development, production, processing, transportation, and marketing and other significant energy-related functions within such company; and

(E) such other analyses or evaluations as the Administrator finds is necessary to achieve the purposes of this chapter.

(3) The Administrator shall consult with the Chairman of the Securities and Exchange Commission with respect to the development of accounting practices required by the Energy Policy and Conservation Act to be followed by persons engaged in whole or in part in the production of crude oil and natural gas and shall endeavor to assure that the energy-producing company financial report described in paragraph (2) of the subsection, to the extent practicable and consistent with the purposes and provisions of this chapter, is consistent with such accounting practices where applicable.

The DOE Organization Act (Public Law 95-91) rather broadly defined an *energy-producing company* to include any entity that meets *any* of the following criteria:

l. Owns or exercises control over any

mineral fuel resources or nonmineral energy resources.

2. Engages in the exploration or development of mineral fuel resources.

3. Extracts mineral or nonmineral energy resources.

4. Refines mineral or nonmineral energy resources.

5. Stores mineral or nonmineral energy resources.

6. Generates, transmits, or stores electrical energy.

7. Transports mineral or nonmineral energy resources.

8. Distributes (wholesale or retail) mineral or nonmineral energy resources, or electrical energy.

The law was broadly written in order to minimize the possibility of an entity claiming that it was not the intent of Congress that its category of entity was to be subject to the FRS requirement.

The Office of Financial Reporting System was established within the EIA to develop the FRS. In early 1979, the FRS (formally referred to as EIA-28) was administered to the first group of companies in the energy industry. A group of 27 companies, selected on the basis that they had either 1 percent of domestic production or reserves of oil, gas, coal, or uranium, or 1 percent of domestic refining capacity or petroleum product sales. The companies that qualified were:

Armerada Hess Corp.

American Petrofina

Ashland Oil, Inc.

Atlantic Richfield Co.

Burlington Northern, Inc.

Cities Service Co.

Coastal States Gas Corp.

Continental Oil Co.

Exxon Corp.

General Electric Co.

Getty Oil Co.

Gulf Oil Corp.

Kerr-McGee Corp.

Marathon Oil Co.

Mobil Corp.

Occidental Petroleum Corp.

Phillips Petroleum Co.

Shell Oil Co.

Standard Oil Co. of California

Standard Oil Co. (Indiana)

Standard Oil Co. (Ohio)

Sun Co.

Superior Oil Co.

Tenneco, Inc.

Texaco, Inc.

Union Oil Co. of California

Union Pacific Corp.

EIA eventually plans to broaden this list of companies in the energy industry to include all major firms (over 100) and a sample of smaller firms. While the FRS was not implemented until 1979, the EIA hopes to extend the data base back to 1974 by having firms file reports on a retroactive basis. Reports filed on such a retroactive basis will generally be more condensed than the full FRS discussed below (i.e., certain schedules will be either modified or deleted).

Glossary

While for much of the vocabulary used in the FRS, the EIA could rely on accounting terminology, it found it necessary to include a glossary of several hundred terms. While most of the terms are energy-related, quite a few accounting terms are specifically defined for their role in the FRS (e.g., by-product, transfer price, acquisition costs).

FRS Accounting Procedures

The FRS is intended to be reconcilable with the reporting company's published financial statements. In fact, a copy of the reporting company's SEC form 10-K (annual report) or, if not subject to SEC regulations, a copy of its audited financial statements are required as Exhibit E to the FRS. The summary financial schedules of the FRS are required to agree with or be reconciled to these financial statements:

RELATION TO REPORTING COMPANY'S ACCOUNTING PRINCIPLES

In completing the FRS schedules, reporting companies should follow the accounting principles they currently use to prepare their annual certified financial statements. All of the detailed FRS financial schedules aggregate up into Schedules 5110 [income statement] and 5120 [balance sheet].

Specifically, schedules 5110 and 5120 contain a "Consolidated" column, representing the reporting company's certified consolidated financial statements. However, there may be some differences between the FRS line items in this column and the classifications in the reporting company's published financial statements. Such differences must be explained and reconciled on a separate sheet of paper attached as part of Exhibit B.[1]

While the company's financial statements contain a review of its significant accounting practices, the FRS requires separate representations on certain accounting practices, for example:

1. The manner in which income under the equity method of accounting for investments in affiliated companies is accrued.
2. The method(s) of inventory valuation for all segments.
3. The accounting treatment afforded exchanges of product (e.g., crude oil for refined product).

Segmentation: FRS and FAS No. 14. The EIA recognized that the responding companies were subject to the Financial Accounting Standards Board's *Statement of Financial Accounting Standards No. 14: Financial Reporting for Segments of a Business Enterprise.* The following instructions are given to utilize this:

FRS SEGMENTS AND FASB 14

The FRS is designed to present a company's operations as separate functional lines of business (referred to as "segments"), as though each were a separate entity, entering into transactions with other segments and third parties. In FRS, the reporting company's consolidated financial statements are disaggregated to separate financial statements for each applicable "functional line of business" (i.e., each applicable FRS segment). These disaggregations are generally made in accordance with Financial Accounting Standards Board (FASB) Statement No. 14.

However, the FRS goes beyond FASB 14 in that the FRS segments are often further disaggregations of a line of business than those defined by FASB 14. In addition, while the FRS attributes certain items to specific segments (such as income taxes), FASB 14 treats them as corporate items. In all other respects, the principles outlined in FASB 14 should be followed for FRS purposes.

The reporting company may not have a separate entity for consolidation purposes corresponding to each of the FRS segments. Therefore, to complete the FRS schedules, it may be necessary to disaggregate information from specific operations within the reporting company's consolidation into the FRS segments (functional lines of business) and then perform a new consolidation based on the FRS segments, including appropriate eliminations at each level of subconsolidation as required.[2]

The additional disaggregation required by the FRS necessitates additional allocations to more discrete segments (i.e., compared to FASB 14). Due to this, FRS provides for a "nontraceable" segment in its schedules:

FRS SEGMENT ALLOCATIONS AND NONTRACEABLE COLUMNS

In disaggregating consolidated financial statements for FRS, most items of revenue and expense can be readily assigned to a particular functional line of business, i.e., FRS segment. However, there will be some items (such as general corporate items) which may be more difficult to assign to a particular FRS segment.

If, on the basis of operating realities, these items cannot be assigned to a segment, they should be reported as nontraceable. It is the function of an item and not its geographic location that determines how it should be reported (i.e., within an FRS segment or as nontraceable). That is, some expenses occurring at the corporate office location may in fact be assignable to a particular FRS segment and therefore should not be reported as nontraceable.[3]

Disaggregation. The FRS also requires the disaggregation of a company's operations in ways that may not coincide with their normal operating and/or reporting format. For example, if a company that produced and refined crude oil and sold the refined products were to treat all of its operating units as *cost* centers, only recognizing income for the company taken as a whole, its income statement might appear as follows with no attempt being made to allocate profits:

Sales		$200
Operating expenses:		
Production	$50	
Refining	25	
Marketing	25	$100
Administrative expenses		20
Operating income		$ 80
Interest expense		20
Net income before taxes		$ 60
Income taxes (60%)		36
Net income after taxes		$ 24

The FRS requires the following modifications in its reporting:

1. The recognition of two profit centers: (a) production and (b) refining/marketing.

2. The recognition of a transfer between the profit centers (here of the crude oil produced by production) at going market prices.

3. The allocation of all expenses, *except for interest*, either to the FRS profit centers or to a nontraceable category.

TABLE 14-1
Disaggregated Income Statement

	TOTAL	*Eliminations*	*Non-traceable*	*Refining/ Marketing*	*Production*
Sales	$200	<$100>		$200	$100
Operating expenses:					
Production	$ 50				$ 50
Refining	25			$ 25	
Marketing	25			25	
Purchase of crude	– 0 –	<100>		100	
Administrative expenses	20		5	10	5
Operating income	$ 80		<$5>	$ 40	$ 45
Interest	20		20		
Net income before taxes	$ 60		<$25>	$ 40	$ 45
Income taxes (60%)	36		<15>	24	27
Net income after taxes	$ 24		<$10>	$ 16	$ 18

The income statement presented above would be disaggregated as shown in Table 14-1, assuming (a) that the transfer between production and refining/marketing had a market value of $100, and (b) $5 of the administrative costs were not traceable to either production or refining/marketing.

The FRS disaggregation has accomplished the following:

1. Refining/marketing and production are now set out as freestanding profit centers whose performance can be compared to and aggregated with similar profit centers of other companies by the EIA.

2. The tax benefit—i.e., the <15>—of the nontraceable administrative expense and interest is isolated from the profit centers.

3. The elimination of the FRS-imposed transfer at market between segments permits the FRS to be reconciled with the company's financial statements.

Materiality. Disaggregation compounds the problem of deciding materiality on a subjective basis. Thus, the FRS has opted for a quantitative test of materiality:

SIGNIFICANCE STANDARDS (MATERIALITY)

Significance standards are needed to avoid undue respondent burden. Such standards must be established with the ultimate use of the data in mind, but since it is not possible to describe in advance all the possible uses of each piece of FRS data or all the possible combinations in which they might be used with other data, only general guidelines can be given.

A definition of "material" is contained in Rule 1-02 of Securities and Exchange Commission Regulation S–X (and in Rule 405 under the Securities Act and Rule 12b-2 under the Exchange Act). However, this definition is based on a "prudent man" principle, which is of limited practical help in deciding many questions of materiality for FRS purposes.

To provide more explicit guidance, a 5% significance standard has been established for FRS reporting. This standard should be used to test the materiality of any item within its immediate category. The test should be made on both a vertical (line) and horizontal (row) basis.

* * *

The 5% significance standard must be applied both on a separate and a cumulative basis (i.e., separate reporting is required, for example, when three items each of which causes a 4% overstatement of some expense account, would cause a 12% overstatement in the aggregate).[4]

FRS Framework

The FRS is composed of approximately 40 separate schedules which accumulate to over 120 pages. Many of the schedules require a disaggregation of the reporting company's basic financial statements. For example, the first schedule (number 5110) is the "Reporting Company Consolidating Statement of Income," and five other supporting schedules disaggregate the reporting company's operations into as many of the segments contained in Figure 14-1 as are applicable.

The reporting company's balance sheet is subject to a similar process of disaggregation into these segments. However, only *selected assets* have to be disaggregated. The following asset categories are allocated across FRS segments:

I. Selected Current Assets:
    Trade Accounts and Notes Receivable
    Inventories:
    Raw Materials and Products

Materials and Supplies
II. Noncurrent Assets:
    Property, Plant, and Equipment (Gross) Accumulated Depreciation, Depletion, and Amortization
    Investments and Advances to Unconsolidated Affiliates
    Other Noncurrent Assets

Liabilities are *only* reported at the level of the reporting company. The statement of sources and uses of funds is only disaggregated as to *uses* (with *sources only* being reported at the level of the reporting company). The uses of funds are to be disaggregated into the following segments:

I. Domestic
II. Foreign
    1. Canada
    2. OECD Europe
    3. Africa
    4. Middle East
    5. Other eastern hemisphere
    6. Other western hemisphere

The FRS also requires a separate schedule of funds invested in or advanced to unconsolidated affiliates.

Taxes. The FRS goes into particularly great detail in the disclosure of income taxes. Income taxes are classified into the categories employed for the income statement *and* separate disclosure for these categories is required for current taxes (per the tax return), deferred taxes (due to income tax allocation for timing differences between income tax accounting and financial accounting), and the investment tax credit. Deferred taxes are disaggregated by type of timing difference. For example, the

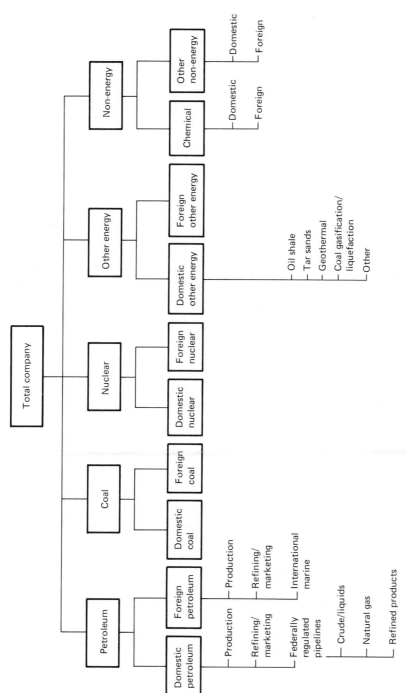

FIGURE 14-1. Schematic Overview of Financial Reporting System (*Source: Performance Profiles of Major Energy Producers*, 1977, p. 128).

following are some of the specific sources of deferred income taxes that are provided for in the FRS:

1. Accelerated depreciation.
2. Exploration and development costs.
3. Production payments.
4. Loss reserves.

These are major sources of timing differences between financial accounting and accounting for income taxes.

Other Disclosures. Many of the FRS's schedules tie directly into the basic financial statements. For example, Schedule 5111—Research and Development Funding and Expenditures—presents a disaggregation of the reporting company's R&D expense by type of R&D effort (e.g., basic research, applied research, etc.) and by energy source (e.g., petroleum, coal, nuclear, etc.). The schedule's total agrees with the reported R&D expense per the reporting company's income statement (Schedule 5110).

Other schedules present operating statistics regarding energy sources. For example, Schedule 5246—Proved Petroleum Reserves—reports the following statistics:

Crude Reserves (thousands of barrels):
A. Net working interest
   1. Beginning of period changes due to:
      a. Revisions of estimates
      b. Improved recovery
      c. Purchases of minerals-in-place
      d. Extensions, discovery, other additions
      e. Production
      f. Sales of minerals-in-place

2. End of period
B. Gross working interest reserves
C. Nonworking royalty interest reserves
D. Proportional interest in investee reserves

These statistics are reported as shown in Figure 14-2.

FRS Data Confidentiality. The data generated by the FRS are not generally available to the public except as they may be used in aggregated reports produced by EIA. Individual companies can request that their FRS response be exempted from any public disclosure that would permit the specific identification of that company's figures. The EIA has set up a procedure for making the FRS data available to other Federal agencies which preserves its (EIA's) and individual responding companies' security interest.

In its first published summary of

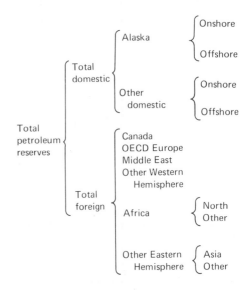

FIGURE 14-2. Disaggregation of Petroleum Reserves.

FRS data, for the year 1977, the EIA included the following assurance of data protection:

Statistical Disclosure
Avoidance Procedures

During the development of this report, the FRS staff has applied a systematic set of procedures that are intended to prevent the disclosure of "individually identifiable energy information." Tables that appear in this report provide summary, rather than company, level information. In most cases, the level of summarization is for all FRS companies. In certain cases, sub-categories have been, or will be, established that break the reporters into size or other descriptive classes that are based on total assets, energy assets, or level of diversification. Each table has been screened to ensure that at least four reporters are represented in a given cell.

A large number of summary computer reports generated from a single selected data base provide the basis for the tables that are published in this report. In conjunction with the summary reports, a parallel set of cell count reports were produced that tabulate for each report cell the number of non-zero values that were aggregated to produce the summary value. The cell count reports were then reviewed to identify whether potential disclosure problems would result from having *three or fewer* reporters or from having values that primarily represent dominant companies in a particular energy sector or activity.

If potential disclosure problems were identified, the tables were restructured to combine values or groups of individual cells in the tables so that the resultant table was essentially disclosure free.[5]

REFERENCE NOTES

1. U.S., Energy Information Administration, Department of Energy, *Instructions for Form EIA–28, Financial Reporting System*, p. 7.

2. *Ibid.*

3. *Ibid.*, p. 8.

4. *Ibid.*, p. 19.

5. U.S., Energy Information Administration, Department of Energy, *Performance Profiles of Major Energy Producers*, 1977, p. 169.

Chapter 15

Rural Electrification Administration

The Rural Electrification Administration (REA) was set up as an emergency relief program by an executive order of the President on May 11, 1935. The Rural Electrification Act of 1936 established the REA as a permanent agency (within the Department of Agriculture) with the responsibility of fostering the establishment and extension of electricity service to rural areas. An amendment to the Act in 1949 charged REA with similar responsibility in regard to telephone service in rural areas. Recently, the REA began preparing a loan program under which it will assist in the establishment of CATV (community antenna television or cable television) systems in rural areas. The REA is headed by an administrator who is appointed by the President, with the approval of the Senate.

The REA provides a myriad of services and assistance to the rural electric and telephone industries. These include advice and counsel on energy conservation engineering problems, environmental concerns, labor relations, safety, consumer education, etc. However, the main service rendered by the REA is its loan programs.

REA LOAN PROGRAMS

The REA is involved in several loan programs in which it either participates in direct loans, or acts as a guarantor of loans, for rural electric and telephone utilities. Virtually all of the nearly 1,000 electric systems participating in REA loan programs are cooperatives, owned and operated by their customers. About one-third of the nearly 1,000 telephone systems participating in REA loan programs are cooperatives. Commercial telephone companies account for about two-thirds of the telephone systems involved in REA financed programs.

Loans made by REA entail low interest rates (specified by law). The majority of REA loans bear interest at the rate of 5 percent. However, a 2 percent rate is available to electric and telephone companies that meet certain criteria specified by Congress (e.g., serving very low customer density areas). Loans that are not directly made by REA (e.g., where REA acts as a guarantor) entail higher rates, consistent with loan market conditions prevailing at the time of the loan.

Since its inception, REA has approved over $15 billion in loans to over 2,000 borrowers. Its program of loan approval and monitoring of the financial condition and operations of the borrowers has produced a low percentage of losses on loans.

ACCOUNTING

The REA relies heavily on the accounting regulations of other agencies —primarily the Federal Energy Regulatory Commission (FERC) for electric utilities and the Federal Communications Commission (FCC) for telephone companies.

Code of Federal Regulations

REA's regulations are contained in Title 7, Chapter XVII, Parts 1700-1799 of the Code of Federal Regulations. These regulations are quite brief and incorporate by reference the *REA Bulletins* that contain the implementing regulations of the agency. A number of the REA Bulletins deal with accounting and auditing. Some of these are enumerated later in this chapter.

Electric Borrowers. The electric companies who borrow from REA are generally required to follow the *Uniform System of Accounts for Class A and B Electric Utilities* as promulgated by the Federal Energy Regulatory Commission (FERC). Chapter 13 on the FERC covers these rules. Certain borrowers, which are not subject to FERC's regulations, are not required by REA to follow FERC's uniform system of accounts and, instead, are allowed to follow the rules and regulations of their jurisdiction's regulatory agency. The REA amplifies on FERC's uniform system of accounts through a series of bulletins, for example:

Bulletin

181-1	Uniform System of Accounts
181-2	Standard List of Retirement Units
181-3	Accounting Interpretations for Rural Electric Borrowers
183-1	Depreciation Rates and Procedures
184-3	Guides for Establishing Continuing Property Records

Bulletin 181-1, *Uniform System of Accounts,* contains REA's basic regulations. It is composed of two parts: (a) the uniform system of accounts prescribed by FERC and (b) REA's expansion on the FERC system. Generally, REA's modifications to the FERC system can be regarded as one of the following:

Substitution of terms. For example,

FERC Term	REA Equivalent
Commission	REA
Utility	REA Borrower
Retained Earnings	Margins
Customer	Consumer or Patron

Definitions added. For example:

> *Patronage Capital.* Amounts paid or payable by patrons in connection with the furnishing of electric energy which are in excess of the cost of service and all other amounts which the cooperative is obligated to credit to the patrons as patronage capital.[1]

Modification of account titles and/or expansion of account structure. For example, FERC provides for Account 224 —Other Long-term Debt. The REA has specified 15 subaccounts to accommodate the likely needs of electric cooperatives financed by REA.

Most of the modifications made by REA to the FERC system are due to the form of organization of most electric borrowers, which are, in the main, cooperatives. The cooperative form of organization is based on a different theory of operation and, in some cases, rate setting, than are investor-owned entities. There is a merging of the owner and customer roles in the cooperative. The cooperative's "patrons" (i.e., owners-customers) are entitled to electric service at cost. This concept is so inherent in the cooperative form that some jurisdictions do not regulate cooperatives' rates. They allow the patrons to set the rates (through their elected representatives on the cooperative's board of directors).

The concept of providing service to each period's patrons at the cost for that specific period causes cooperatives to be very concerned with an exact matching of revenues and expenses. Thus, while current generally accepted accounting principles are very restrictive when it comes to classifying an item as a prior period adjustment (which will, therefore, bypass the current period's income statement), REA feels that more latitude should be given to regulated entities that are organized as cooperatives. This sentiment was expressed by REA in commenting on *Financial Accounting Standard No. 16: Prior Period Adjustments* which virtually sealed off the use of prior period adjustments, save for errors in financial statements:

Matching of Revenue and Cost

One of the very basic accounting principles is that, in the determination of periodic net income, it is imperative that revenues and related expenses be reported in the same period. This principle is essential in the determination of margins for electric cooperatives. Cooperatives are owned by the people they serve. Any amounts received from a patron that are in excess of the cost of service are to be allocated to him. If the cooperative is to treat the patrons of different periods fairly, it must adhere to the matching concept.

The standard setting bodies, including the APB in APB Opinion #9, Reporting the Results of Operations, and the FASB in FAS #16, Prior Period Adjustments, have increasingly restricted the use of prior period adjustments. We infer that a main reason for this has been to remove from the power of management the ability to manipulate current period earnings by arbitrarily transferring costs to prior periods.

The purpose of prior period adjustments by electric cooperatives is not manipulation of margins, but treatment of patrons on an equitable basis.

What apparently exists here is a conflict between the matching concept and the concept of an all-inclusive income statement. To disallow the proper matching of costs and revenues of a cooperative can result in penalizing the patrons of the present or prior years. This is another area we hope the FASB Task Force will explore, giving special consideration to the problems of the cooperative type organization.[2]

Telephone Borrowers. The telephone borrowers of REA are generally required to follow the uniform system of accounts prescribed by the Federal Communications Commission (FCC) for Class A and Class B telephone companies (14 CFR Part 31) or Class C telephone companies (14 CFR Part 33). These are discussed in Chapter 6 on the FCC. These accounting requirements are supplemented by a series of *REA Bulletins* and various sections of the REA's *Telephone Operations Manual.* Some of the more pertinent documents are:

REA Bulletins

461-1	Accounting System Requirements for Telephone Borrowers
462-1	Evaluation and Enforcement of Internal Control of Borrowers' Enterprises
463-1	Depreciation Rates for Telephone Borrowers

Telephone Operations Manual Sections

1855	Material and Supplies Accounting
1865	Station Accounting
1870	Continuing Property Records
1990	Accounting Guidelines for Telephone Borrowers

The REA (in its Bulletin 461-1) has provided for subdivisions of some of the accounts called for in the FCC's systems of accounts. This Bulletin also provides for additional accounts to accommodate nonprofit (i.e., cooperative) telephone companies.

AUDITS OF REA BORROWERS

The REA requires its borrowers to be audited annually. The agency has issued a bulletin entitled *Audit of REA Borrowers Accounting Records* with the dual numbers of Bulletin 185-1 (Electric) and Bulletin 465-1 (Telephone). There is a companion Bulletin 185-2 (Electric) and 465-2 (Telephone) entitled *Audit Working Paper Guide.* REA requires that a CPA firm be appointed by the borrower's board of directors *and* that the appointment be approved by REA. The REA has the right to deny the appointment by the company's board of directors in which case another CPA firm must be selected.

The REA has a suggested "audit agreement" which is to be signed by the CPA and the borrower. The agreement is comparable to the engagement letter, generally transacted between a CPA firm and its client, which indicates what the CPA is responsible to accomplish in auditing the client. However, there are several exceptions to the typical engagement letter's content. One exception is that the CPA firm must agree to notify REA "promptly" upon the discovery of any irregularity (i.e., defalcation, fraud, false report, or false claim) that would affect REA's interest in the borrower.

Another exception is that the CPA must agree to make available to the REA the working papers that are accumulated on the audit. The REA takes advantage of this concession by the CPA and annually reviews the working papers of a number of its borrowers' audits.

CPAs typically transmit a letter to an audit client in which the weaknesses in the client's system of internal control and recommendations for improvements are enumerated. The REA requires that a "supplemental letter" be furnished to the REA borrower *and* to the REA. The CPA *must* make comments on the following matters:

1. Internal control (in general).
2. Condition of accounting records.
3. Inventory control.
4. Compliance with loan covenants.
5. Conformance of annual reports submitted to REA (Forms 7 or 12 for electric companies; Form 479 for telephone companies) to the borrower's records.
6. Service contract provisions being met.
7. Deposits being maintained at insured institutions.
8. Insurance coverage being maintained.
9. Requirements being met for the maintenance of tax exempt income status for cooperative borrowers.[3]

In addition, if any other matters arise that would be of interest to REA, the auditor is to include them in the supplementary letter. The auditor must also include a copy of all adjusting and reclassification entries that were prepared during the audit.

In its Bulletin 185-1 (Electric); 465-1 (Telephone), *Audit of Borrowers' Ac-*counting Records, the REA enumerates the required outputs of the audit that are to be forwarded to the REA. Additionally, the Bulletin contains an enumeration of *minimum* audit procedures that must be performed on audits of REA borrowers. These minimum procedures are supplemented by REA Bulletin 185-2 (Electric); 465-2 (Telephone), *Audit Working Paper Guide.* This guide sets out the organization and documentation standards that REA requires of auditors of its borrowers.

REA's ongoing program of reviewing the audit working papers of the CPAs that audit its borrowers contrasts with most agencies reported upon in this book. Most agencies' concern with independent audits ends with the receipt of the audited statements and accompanying opinion of the auditor on the statements. REA has found that there are gradients of quality in audits as evidenced by the documentation accumulated in the audit working papers. REA has gathered this evidence through its program of visiting CPA firms' offices, reviewing the working papers, discussing the audit with the CPA firm, and, where considered necessary, rendering a written evaluation to the firm. Through its experience in this program, REA has documented a number of common deficiencies found in working papers. These are enumerated in Bulletin 185-2; 465-2.

REA's audit review program has had the backing of the auditing profession (represented by the American Institute of Certified Public Accountants) for over 20 years. REA's experience is that the program has been beneficial to all parties concerned—REA, the borrower, and the CPA firm.

In addition to audits by CPA firms, REA maintains a staff of auditors which conducts special examinations and audits of REA borrowers.

REFERENCE NOTES

1. U.S., Rural Electrification Administration, *REA Bulletin 181-1: Uniform System of Accounts Prescribed for Electric Borrowers,* p. REA-2.

2. U.S., Rural Electrification Administration, *REA Position Paper on Applicability of FAS #16, Prior Period Adjustments to Rural Electric Cooperatives,* 1978, pp. 4-5

3. U.S., Rural Electrification Administration, *REA Bulletin (185-1; 465-1): Audit of REA Borrowers' Accounting Records,* pp. 22-23.

Chapter 16

Procurement Agencies

The Federal government is the single largest purchaser of goods and services in the country. Currently, Federal procurement of goods and services is on the order of $95 billion (about $65 billion is by defense agencies[1]; the remainder—about $30 billion—is by civilian agencies.[2] The government purchases items that we all purchase—soap, paper towels, automobiles, etc. It also purchases items that we would never dream of purchasing—nuclear reactors, lunar rover vehicles, hydroelectric dams. In order to effectively carry out its procurement program, the government has promulgated its own regulations: the Defense Acquisition Regulation (DAR) for military procurement and the Federal Procurement Regulation (FPR) for civilian procurement. (Currently, a project is underway to develop a single government-wide procurement regulation, the Federal Acquisition Regulation —FAR.)

Both the DAR and the FPR appear in the Code of Federal Regulations. The FPR appears in Part 1 of Title 41 (i.e., 41 CFR Part 1). The DAR appears as Parts 1 through 39 of Title 32. The DAR is reproduced in the CFR as a single document (encompassing some 3,000 pages) *without* being renumbered in the CFR format. In citing the DAR in this chapter, the following citation form is used:

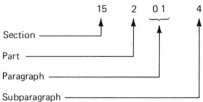

The cited material can be located in Title 32 of the CFR.

PROCUREMENT REGULATIONS

The procurement regulations identify two distinct forms of procurement processes: formal advertising and negotiation.

Formal Advertising

Formal advertising is the preferred method of procurement. Under formal advertising, the government issues an *Invitation for Bids* (IFB). The IFB describes what the government is contemplating purchasing and sets a deadline for the submission of bids. Any interested party can submit a bid. Assuming that the bids are *responsive* to the invitation (i.e., they are bids for exactly what was advertised) and the bidders are *responsible* (e.g., bidders with whom the government has had poor experience may be disqualified), the government, through its contracting officer, will award the contract to the lowest bidder.

Formal advertising is the preferred method of procurement because it allows the forces of supply and demand to control the final price. A study by the Department of Defense outlined the necessary conditions for formal advertising:

> There is no disagreement on what the basic prerequisites for formal advertising are. These criteria are:
>
> 1. A complete, adequate, and realistic specification or purchase description must be available.
>
> 2. There must be two or more suppliers available, willing, and able to compete effectively for the Government's business.
>
> 3. The selection of the successful bidder can be made on the basis of price alone, the evaluation of which we have just described.

> 4. There must be sufficient time to prepare a complete statement of the Government's needs and the terms upon which it will do business, and to carry out the administrative procedures which we described earlier.

Formal advertising is an excellent method of procurement when these criteria are met. When any one of these essentials cannot be satisfied, it is a completely ineffective method of procurement. Someone once likened these criteria to a four-legged stool. Remove one leg and the stool is ineffective.

* * *

When the criteria for effective use of formal advertising are present, this method of procurement is an excellent means of attaining our objective; when they are not present, however, the means of achieving that end are to be found in negotiation. In sum, the goal can be achieved in any procurement only by an intelligent and discriminating selection of that method of procurement which the particular circumstances at hand dictate.[3]

Negotiation

Negotiated procurement proceeds in a much less structured—and less competitive—fashion than formal advertising. In negotiation, the government distributes a *Request for Proposal* (RFP). RFPs can vary in specificity. An RFP for hardware can be quite specific, including engineering drawings, and heat, pressure, and atmospheric tolerances, etc.; an RFP for research and development effort can be rather general, including only rather sketchy details of the area to be investigated. Generally, the RFP is less widely distributed than an IFB for several reasons. First, the technology required to respond is only possessed by a limited number of companies (e.g., not many companies are capable of producing nuclear submarines). Second, many RFPs involve the exchange of classified data that can only be divulged to contractors and their personnel having the appropriate security clearance.

Potential contractors submit their proposals in response to the RFP. The proposals are generally composed of two parts: (a) a technical section where the substance of the contractor's response to the RFP is disclosed, and (b) a cost or pricing section. Generally, all proposals submitted are evaluated by a team of contract specialists. After evaluating the technical and economic aspects of the proposals, the field is usually narrowed to a small number of potential contractors. Negotiations are held with the remaining field and further narrowing results until the contractor is finally chosen.

As contrasted with formal advertising, where only a firm fixed-price contract can result, the contract type arising from negotiation is itself subject to negotiation. The following types of contracts can result from negotiated procurement.

Fixed-Price Contracts. There are five types of fixed-price contracts. Fixed-price contracts are designed to meet the needs of the government and the contractor under varying conditions. In general, fixed-price contracts specify a firm price to the government, with the contractor responsible for the risks of cost control. However, certain fixed-price contracts do provide for some adjustment in price under specified circumstances.

Firm fixed-price contract. A firm fixed-price (FFP) contract contains a set price that is not subject to subsequent adjustment for any changes in the contractor's cost of performance.

Fixed-price contract with economic price adjustment. This type of contract is basically a firm fixed-price contract with the exception that provision is made for changing the price (up or down) if a contingency, specified in the contract, occurs. For example, if a contract were to involve extensive use of a precious metal whose price was very unstable, the contract could call for performance at a fixed price with adjustment (up or down) for the actual price paid by the contractor for the precious metal. The government does not allow these types of contracts to be used where the contingency is under the contractor's control (i.e., they would *not* be used to accommodate potential labor inefficiencies).

Fixed-price with redetermination contract. This type of contract provides for a fixed price with potential adjustments (up or down) for contingencies not provided for in a fixed-price contract with economic price adjustment (e.g., where a contractor's labor efficiency is unknown due to the contract requiring use of a material or technology that has not been previously employed).

Fixed-price incentive contract. A fixed price incentive (FPI) contract provides for upward or downward adjustments in the contract's expected profit based on a set adjustment factor. For example, the incentive provision may provide for the contractor's anticipated profit to be adjusted by 25 percent of the difference between actual costs and target costs (cost underruns resulting in increases in profit; cost overruns resulting in decreases in profit).

Fixed-price level of effort contract. This type of contract commits the contractor to devote a specified "level of effort" (e.g., 20,000 labor hours) to the contract task for a fixed price. This contract is only used where a specific end-product cannot be specified (e.g., for basic research work).

Cost-Type Contracts. There are five forms of cost-type contracts. Basically, they involve payment to the contractor of the costs of contract performance plus a pre- or post-negotiated amount for profit—the "fee."

Cost contract. A cost contract is performed at cost and the contractor receives no fee. Cost contracts are used frequently for research and development contracts with universities.

Cost-sharing contracts. A cost-sharing contract provides for the government's reimbursement of only a percentage of the contractor's cost. The remaining costs are absorbed by the contractor. Cost-sharing contracts are used for research and development work performed by private companies where it is anticipated that the contractor will reap commercial advantages from working on the contract.

Cost plus fixed fee. A cost plus fixed fee (CPFF) contract reimburses the contractor for his cost plus a set fee that is negotiated in advance of performance.

Cost plus incentive fee. A cost plus incentive fee (CPIF) contract is similar to a CPFF contract except for the subsequent (after performance) adjustment

of the fee. The fee is adjusted up or down by a percentage of the difference between the contract's *expected* cost and its *actual* cost. In effect, the contractor's incentive is for cost control since he shares the burden of cost overruns (or reaps some benefit from bringing the contract in below expected cost). This incentive is intended to compensate for the basic lack of incentive in cost-type contracts.

Cost plus award fee. A cost plus award fee (CPAF) contract reimburses the contractor for his costs of performance plus a fee that is composed of two parts: (a) a fixed component that does not change and (b) an "award" component based on the "quality" of the contractor's performance. The government, through its contract administration personnel, evaluates the contractor's performance and rewards exceptional performance by increasing the total fee through the "award" component.

These are the main contract types used in negotiated procurement. One should not get the impression that selecting a contract type is a matter of personal choice by the contracting parties. The parties must conform to the government's guidelines. For example, the following hierarchy is used in defense contracts [DAR 3-808.6]:

The generally accepted progression of the procurement spectrum ranging from Basic Research through Supply procurements and from cost to firm fixed-price contracts, is shown below:

Type of Effort	Type of Contract
(1) Basic Research	Cost, CPFF
(2) Applied Research	Cost, CPFF

Type of Effort	Type of Contract
(3) Exploratory Development	Cost, CPFF
(4) Advanced Development	CPFF, CPAF
(5) Engineering Development	CPFF, CPAF, CPIF
(6) Operational System Development	CPIF, CPAF, FPI
(7) First Production	FPI
(8) Follow-on Production	FPI, FFP
(9) Supply	FFP

It is clear that the various contract types entail varying degrees of risk for the contractor. The most risky, the firm fixed-price contract, also entails the greatest *potential* for profit since all cost savings flow to the contractor. The least risky, the cost plus fixed fee contract, suffers, from the contractor's standpoint, from the fact that the profit formula used by the government in negotiating contracts gives no reward for risk-free or little reward for low-risk contracts [DAR 3–808.6 (d) (5)]:

> Contractors are likely to assume greater cost risk only if contracting officers objectively analyze the risk incident to proposed contracts and are willing to compensate contractors for it. Generally, a cost-plus-fixed-fee contract would not justify a reward for risk in excess of 1%, nor would a firm fixed-price contract justify a reward of less than 6%. Where proper contract type selection has been made the reward for risk by contract type would usually fall into the following percentage ranges:

Type of Contract and Percentage Ranges

Cost-Plus-Fixed Fee . .	0 to 1%
Cost-Plus-Incentive-Fee	1 to 3%
Fixed-Price-Incentive.	3 to 6%
Firm Fixed-Price. . . .	6 to 8%

SIGNIFICANCE OF COST DATA

It is important to recognize the significance of *cost* data in contract formation, performance, and settlement of negotiated contracts. First, Public Law (P.L.) 87–653, the Truth-in-Negotiations Act, *requires* contractors to submit "cost or pricing data" to the government in negotiating contracts that are expected to exceed $100,000. As a practical matter, this generally translates into the submission of cost data since arm's length selling prices (i.e., pricing data) are generally not present for negotiated procurement; if it were, the procurement would likely be formally advertised. Thus, cost data is significant to the negotiation of contracts.

Second, under the cost-type contracts (and the contingent portion of certain fixed-price contracts—e.g., incentive fee) contractors' receipts are a direct result of the cost determination under the contract.

Third, virtually all major government contracts incorporate a "changes" clause that permits the government to make changes in the contract's terms. These changes can vary from major items, such as changing performance specifications for an aircraft, to relatively minor items, such as changing the point of delivery of the aircraft. In any event, the changes are usually to be paid for by an "equitable adjustment" in the contract price. A major consideration in negotiating the equitable adjustment is the contractor's cost in accomplishing the change.

Fourth, most government contracts incorporate a "termination" clause that permits the government to unilaterally elect to terminate the contract. When a contract is terminated, a termination settlement must be made between the government and the contractor. Cost data are often used in the negotiation of termination settlements.

Fifth, progress payments made by the government to the contractor during performance of the contract are often based on the cost incurrence under the contract. In these times of high interest rates, the progress payment provision can mean the difference between a profitable contract or, if the contractor were to have to borrow funds to finance the contract, an unprofitable contract.

Sixth, many contracts with the Federal government are subject to some form of post-performance profit limitation laws. Up until recently (1976), this was the Renegotiation Act. With the failure of Congress to renew the Renegotiation Act, the Vinson-Trammell Act (of 1934) was reactivated. While the provisions of these laws are quite different in their approach to profit limitation, suffice it to say that both require the use of cost data in administering their provisions.

DAR COST PRINCIPLES

With so much riding on the determination of cost, it is not surprising to find that the procurement regulations contain a set of cost principles. There is a set of cost principles in both the Defense Acquisition Regulation and the Federal Procurement Regulation. These cost principles are substantially identical. To avoid duplication in the discussion, the DAR cost principles will be reviewed. (The proposed Federal Acquisition Regulation is to contain a single set of cost principles for both military and civilian agencies.) There are also cost accounting standards that are applicable to some procurements by the Federal government. These are discussed in the next chapter.

History

The DAR cost principles can be looked upon as the latest step in an evolutionary process wherein government agencies have attempted to control their exposure to the vagaries of interpretations of the term *cost*. Codification of cost principles can be traced back to World War I. The significant increase in negotiated procurement occasioned by the war caused the government to adopt Section 302 of the Revenue Act of 1916 as a set of cost principles. This section was never intended to be used as a body of contract cost principles. The inherent weakness is immediately evident: There are no guidelines for allocating cost among cost objectives (e.g., contracts). Section 302 was merely intended to set out deductible expenses for computing taxable income by munitions manufacturers. Be that as it may, Section 302 became the first set of cost principles. Section 302, in its *entirety*, reads as follows:

> In computing net profits under the provisions of this title, for the purpose

of the tax there shall be allowed as deductions from the gross amount received or accrued for the taxable year from the sale or disposition of such articles manufactured within the United States, the following items:

(a) The cost of raw materials entering into the manufacture;

(b) Running expenses, including rentals, cost of repairs and maintenance, heat, power, insurance, management, salaries, and wages;

(c) Interest paid within the taxable year on debts or loans contracted to meet the needs of the business, and the proceeds of which have been actually used to meet such needs;

(d) Taxes of all kinds paid during the taxable year with respect to the business or property relating to the manufacture;

(e) Losses actually sustained within the taxable year in connection with the business of manufacturing such articles, including losses from fire, flood, storm, or other casualty, and not compensated for by insurance or otherwise; and

(f) A reasonable allowance according to the conditions peculiar to each concern, for amortization of the values of buildings and machinery, account being taken of the exceptional depreciation of special plants.

After World War I, tales of profiteering on military contracts caused continued concern. This led to the passage of the Vinson-Trammell Act in 1934 which, as amended, limited the allowable profit on contracts for naval vessels (to 10 percent of contract price) and for military aircraft (to 12 percent of contract price). The Department of the Treasury promulgated a set of cost principles to be used in determining the cost (and thus the profits) on contracts covered by the Vinson-Trammell Act. This set of cost principles comprised Treasury Decison 5000 (TD 5000). TD 5000 was about six pages in length and, while being mainly concerned with the allowability of costs, it contained some guidelines for the allocation of costs among cost objectives (e.g., contracts).

World War II witnessed the application of a series of sets of cost principles to military contracts:

1. The War Department (Army) employed TD 5000 [and supplemented it with an audit manual, Technical Manual (TM) 14-1000] as the principles to be used in its cost-type contracts.

2. The Navy Department promulgated a new set of cost principles—*Explanation of Principles for Determination of Costs under Government Contracts* (commonly referred to as the "Green Book")—for use in its cost-type contracts. The Green Book was, for the most part, in conformity with TD 5000.

3. In 1945, a set of cost principles was promulgated by the Joint Contract Termination Board in anticipation of the large number of contract terminations (i.e., cancellations by the government) at the end of the war. These cost principles, known as the *Joint Termination Accounting Manual,* were to be used in settling terminated fixed-price contracts. Cost-type contracts were settled upon termination by applying the cost principles used in their negotiations (e.g., TD 5000 or the Green Book).

4. At the end of the War, another set of cost principles appeared. These cost principles, entitled *An Explanation of Principles for Determination of Costs under Government Research and Development Contracts with Education Institutions* (more commonly known as the "Blue Book"), were used by the military departments in contracting with colleges, universities, and professional schools.

After the War, military procurement was centralized by the creation of the Armed Services Procurement Regulation (ASPR) in 1948. ASPR included cost principles for the negotiation and settlement of cost-type contracts (in Sec. XV) and cost principles for the settlement of terminated fixed-price contracts (in Sec. VIII). In the intervening years, the cost principles of ASPR (renamed the Defense Acquisition Regulation—DAR—in 1978) have undergone some major changes. A total revision was issued in 1959. This revision, as amended, continues in effect today as the DAR cost principles.

The DAR cost principles are contained in DAR Section XV. This section is composed of the following parts:

Part	Title
1	Applicability
2	Contracts with Commercial Organizations
3	Grants and Contracts with Educational Institutions
4	Construction and Architect-Engineer Contracts
5	Contracts for Industrial Facilities
6	(Reserved)
7	Grants and Contracts with State and Local Governments
8	Training and Other Services-Educational Institutions

Applicability

The DAR cost principles are applicable whenever a company's cost is the basis of the price paid by the government. Thus, the cost principles affect:

1. The *negotiation* of all types of contracts (i.e., the estimated price of cost-type contracts; the final price of fixed-price contracts; the setting of targets under incentive contracts).

2. The reimbursement of allowable costs under cost-type contracts and the price revision of *fixed-price* incentive contracts.

3. The basis of progress payments.

4. The settlement of claims for terminations of contracts by the government.

5. The settlement of claims for changes made in the contract.

Part 2 is the core of the Section XV cost principles. First, it is applicable to a majority of contracts. Second, it is incorporated by reference in other parts. Third, it sets out the basic theoretical structure for the entire Section XV. Due to these reasons, Part 2 will be the basis for the discussion in this chapter.

Part 2 of Section XV can be viewed as containing two distinct divisions. The first, encompassing about five pages, deals with the general factors of cost determination. The second, encompassing about 50 pages, deals with specific costs such as depreciation, interest, lease payments, etc. Generally, this portion of the cost principles either expands on the overall factors of cost determination as they relate to specific costs, or sets out the policy of not allowing or limiting the allowable amount of certain costs in the pricing or reporting under Federal contracts.

Total Cost

The basic DAR provision for determining the cost of a contract is [DAR 15-201]:

> *Composition of Total Cost.* The total cost of a contract is the sum of the allowable direct and indirect costs allocable to the contract, incurred or to be incurred, less any allocable credits. In ascertaining what constitutes costs, any generally accepted method of determining or estimating costs that is equitable under the circumstances may be used, including standard costs properly adjusted for applicable variances.

The heart of this provision is that the cost of a contract is composed of its *allowable* and *allocable direct* and *indirect* costs. The italicized terms are expanded upon in the regulations.

Cost Allowability

DAR 15-201.2 identifies four factors that are to be considered when evaluating a cost's allowability:

> *Factors Affecting Allowability of Costs.* Factors to be considered in determining the allowability of individual items of cost include (i) reasonableness, (ii) allocability, (iii) standards promulgated by the Cost Accounting Standards Board, if applicable, otherwise, generally accepted accounting principles and practices appropriate to the particular circum-

stances, and (iv) any limitations or exclusions set forth in this Part 2, or otherwise included in the contract as to types or amounts of cost items.

These four factors are each the subject of further clarification in the regulations.

Reasonableness. The DAR 15-201.3 (a) explanation of the concept of reasonableness is:

> A cost is reasonable, if in its nature of amount, it does not exceed that which would be incurred by an ordinarily prudent person in the conduct of competitive business. The question of the reasonableness of specific costs must be scrutinized with particular care in connection with firms or separate divisions thereof which may not be subject to effective competitive restraints. What is reasonable depends upon a variety of considerations and circumstances involving both the nature and amount of the cost in question. In determining the reasonableness of a given cost, consideration shall be given to:
>
> (i) whether the cost is of a type generally recognized as ordinary and necessary for the conduct of the contractor's business or the performance of the contract;
>
> (ii) the restraints or requirements imposed by such factors as generally accepted sound business practices, arm's length bargaining, Federal and State laws and regulations, and contract terms and specifications;
>
> (iii) the action that a prudent business man would take in the circumstances, considering his responsibilities to the owners of the business, his employees, his customers, the

Government and the public at large; and

(iv) significant deviations from the established practices of the contractor which may unjustifiably increase the contract costs.

It is clear from the terms used in the definition—such as "ordinarily prudent," "ordinary and necessary," "generally accepted sound business practices, arm's length bargaining," "the action that a prudent business man would take in the circumstances, considering his responsibilities . . . ," "established practices of the contractor"—that what is being sought is a cost determination that is fair and equitable to both parties to the contract.

When disputes have arisen involving interpretations of reasonableness the courts have exhibited a definite affinity for seeking a result that is fair and equitable. For example, in one case, a company claimed, as a cost, a fee that it had paid to one of its subsidiaries for the subsidiary's work on a government contract. The fee was more than the subsidiary's cost of performance on the contract. The court only allowed the subsidiary's cost. In rendering its decision, the court commented as follows:

> When a contractor has such services performed for it by another person or firm under an arrangement which is claimed to preclude scrutiny of allowability propriety, flags must necessarily dot the playing field. This is true regardless of the relationship between the contractor and the person or firm performing these services. The burden of showing the reasonableness of selling expenses incurred in this indirect way

is much heavier than the normal burden, which must always be shouldered ultimately by the contractor when a cost is questioned.[4]

On the other side of the scale, the courts have held that reasonableness does not imply perfection by the company. This was clearly noted in another decision:

> The Government's contention that appellant should have acted earlier to cancel the third contract, thus preventing (the subcontractor) from incurring preparatory costs, is based on hindsight. Perhaps appellant could have reduced such costs by moving earlier. But perfection in contract administration is not one of the tests of reasonableness. . . .[5]

Certain contractors are excluded from any detailed test of reasonableness by establishing that 75 percent or more of their sales are (a) to commercial (nongovernment) customers or (b) to the government under competitively awarded firm fixed-price contracts. This procedure, known as the Contractor's Weighted Average Share in Cost Risk program (CWAS) relies on the inherent incentive of commercial and competitive fixed-price government contracts—under which all cost savings flow to the contractor—to ensure the propriety of the contractor's actions in regard to reasonableness.

Allocability. The second factor determining a cost's allowability is allocability. DAR 15-201.4 defines this factor:

> A cost is allocable if it is assignable or chargeable to one or more cost objectives . . . in accordance with the rela-

tive benefits received or other equitable relationship. Subject to the foregoing, a cost is allocable to a Government contract if it:

(i) is incurred specifically for the contract;

(ii) benefits both the contract and other work, or both Government work and other work, and can be distributed to them in reasonable proportion to the benefits received; or

(iii) is necessary to overall operation of the business, although a direct relationship to any particular cost objective cannot be shown.

A *cost objective*—per DAR 15-109 (e) —is any " . . . . function, organizational subdivision, contract, or other work unit for which cost data are desired. . . ."

This factor delineates the relationships that must exist between a cost and the cost objectives (e.g., contracts) to which it is potentially "assignable or chargeable." The overall relationship specified is *equity* (i.e., as in " . . . benefits received or other equitable relationship"). This is given some substance in the specification of circumstances in which the equitable relationship of the cost to the cost objectives are more traceable (e.g., "[the cost] is incurred specifically for the contract [cost objective]") or less traceable (e.g., "[the cost] is necessary to the overall operation of the business, although a direct relationship to any particular cost objective cannot be shown"). This scaling in the rationale of allocability established the propriety of apportioning to individual contracts costs whose benefits can only be traced to the company taken as a whole (e.g., the cost of a corporate headquarters' staff).

Generally Accepted Accounting Principles. The next factor refers to both Cost Accounting Standards (CAS) and generally accepted accounting principles (GAAP). The CASB and its standards are covered in the next chapter. As to GAAP, it is clear that no set of cost principles could be free-standing (that is, not relying on the broader area of financial accounting) without being extremely lengthy. The DAR cost principles overcome this problem by incorporating GAAP by reference, unless overridden by an explicit provision of the DAR cost principles.

Specific Limitations or Exclusions. The DAR cost principles (in DAR 15-205.1 through 15-205.50) place restrictions on or outright disallow certain costs (e.g., contributions). Additionally, the parties to a specific contract can agree to other exclusions or limitation of cost.

Direct Costs

The DAR provision discussing total cost refers to the ". . . direct and indirect costs. . . ." DAR 15-202 contains the regulations on *direct costs:*

(a) A direct cost is any cost which can be identified specifically with a particular final cost objective . . . . No final cost objective shall have allocated to it as a direct cost any cost, if other costs incurred for the same purpose, in like circumstances, have been included in any indirect cost pool to be allocated to that or any other final cost objective. Costs identified specifically with the contract are direct costs of the contract and are to be charged directly thereto. Costs identified specifically with other final cost objectives of the contractor are direct costs of those cost objectives and are not to be charged to the contract directly or indirectly.

(b) Any direct cost of minor dollar amount may be treated as an indirect cost for reasons of practicality where the accounting treatment for such cost is consistently applied to all final cost objectives, provided that such treatment produces results which are substantially the same as the results which would have been obtained if such costs have been treated as a direct cost.

This discussion of a direct cost pegs its determination to only one level of cost objectives—that of final cost objectives. Per DAR 15-109 (h), a *final cost objective* is one which " . . . has allocated to it both direct and indirect costs, and, in the contractor's accumulation system, is one of the final accumulation points." Generally, individual contracts coincide with the term *final cost objective*.

Many commentators have noted that the DAR definition of *direct cost* (which pegs itself to the lowest level of cost objective) is not compatible with the broader area of cost accounting where any level of cost objective can be the focal point for the determination of direct cost. For example, in cost accounting in general, it would be recognized that not only are certain costs direct to government contract A versus government contract B, but there are other costs which are direct costs of all government contracts (versus nongovernment contracts) though they are indirect to individual government contracts. Finally, there are other costs that benefit the company when taken as a whole and that are indirect to all contracts taken individually or

taken in major groupings (e.g., government versus nongovernment contracts).

Indirect Cost

The basic DAR provision on indirect cost is contained in DAR 15-203 (a):

(a) An indirect cost . . . is one which, because of its incurrence for common or joint objectives, is not readily subject to treatment as a direct cost. Any direct cost of minor dollar amount may be treated as an indirect cost for reasons of practicality under the circumstances set forth in 15-202 (b). After direct costs have been determined and charged directly to the contract or other work as appropriate, indirect costs are those remaining to be allocated to the several cost objectives. No final cost objective shall have allocated to it as an indirect cost any cost, if other costs incurred for the same purpose, in like circumstances, have been included as a direct cost of that or any other final cost objective.

The definition of *indirect cost* [DAR 15-109 (i)] is: "any cost not directly identified with a single final cost objective, but identified with two or more final cost objectives, or with at least one intermediate cost objective." This definition, and the accompanying discussion of indirect cost quoted above, suffers from the same flaw as the treatment of direct cost in that its determination of direct versus indirect is pitched to only one level, that of final cost objectives. The point was discussed above for direct cost and it will not be belabored here.

The remaining discussion of indirect cost is composed of four factors: (a) pool composition, (b) allocation base,

(c) accommodating aberrations, and (d) base period.

Pool Composition. The DAR guidelines for the formation of indirect cost pools are contained in DAR 15-203 (b):

> Indirect costs shall be accumulated by logical cost grouping with due consideration of the reasons of incurring the costs. Each grouping should be determined so as to permit distribution of the grouping on the basis of the benefits accruing to the several cost objectives. Commonly, manufacturing overhead, selling expenses, and general and administrative expenses are separately grouped. Similarly, the particular case may require subdivision of these groupings, e.g., building occupancy costs might be separable from those of personnel administration within the manufacturing overhead group. The number and composition of the groupings should be governed by practical considerations and should be such as not to complicate unduly the allocation where substantially the same results are achieved through less precise methods.

The principles espoused in this paragraph are in conformity with the broader area of cost accounting, in that they call for (a) homogeneous cost pools, (b) consideration of separately pooling major functional groupings, and (c) an evaluation of the materiality of any prospective proliferation of cost pools.

Allocation Base. DAR 15-203 (c) contains the principles governing the selection of an allocation base:

> Each cost grouping shall be distributed to the appropriate cost objectives. This necessitates the selection of a distribution base common to all cost objectives to which the grouping is to be allocated. The base should be selected so as to permit allocation of the grouping on the basis of the benefits accruing to the several cost objectives. This principle for selection is not to be applied so rigidly as to complicate unduly the allocation where substantially the same results are achieved through less precise methods. Once an appropriate base for the distribution of indirect costs has been accepted, such base shall not be fragmented by the removal of individual elements. Consequently, all items properly includable in an indirect cost base should bear a pro-rata share of indirect costs irrespective of their acceptance as Government contract costs. For example, when a cost input base is used for the distribution of G&A, all items that would properly be part of the cost input base, whether allowable or unallowable, shall be included in the base and bear their pro-rata share of G&A costs.

The first portion of this paragraph is conceptually sound. The second portion, dealing with the fragmentation of a base and unallowable costs, needs some explanation. Before this provision was part of the cost principles, the government and its contractors were forever locking horns over this question: When unallowable costs are a part of an allocation base, does a proportional amount of the pool also become unallowable? The government's answer was "yes"; the contractors' answers were "no". The significance of the answer can be illustrated by a brief example. For example, let's take a company that sells exclusively to the government. In negotiating a contract, the following figures were used:

Estimated pool $1,000,000

Estimated base composed of

Allowable
cost   \$4,000,000 ⎫
                    ⎬ \$5,000,000
Unallow-
able cost   1,000,000 ⎭

Under the government's contention, the overhead rate would be 20 percent (\$1,000,000 ÷ \$5,000,000); under the contractor's contention, the overhead rate would be 25 percent (\$1,000,000 ÷ \$4,000,000). Under the former, \$800,000 of the pool (\$4,000,000 × 20 percent) would be included in a contract price; under the latter \$1,000,000 (\$4,000,000 × 25 percent) would be included in the contract price. With the addition of the last portion of the above quoted paragraph, the government attempted to settle the issue in its favor.

Aberrations. The DAR cost principles coverage of indirect cost includes a subparagraph dealing with aberrations [DAR 15-203 (d)]:

> The method of allocation of indirect costs must be based on the particular circumstances involved. The method shall be in accordance with Standards promulgated by the Cost Accounting Standards Board, if applicable to the contract. Otherwise, the method shall be in accordance with generally accepted accounting principles. When Cost Accounting Standards Board Standards are not applicable to the contract, the contractor's established practices, if in accordance with generally acceptable accounting principles, shall generally be acceptable. However, the method used by the contractor may require examination when:
>
> (i) any substantial difference occurs between the cost patterns of work

> under the contract and other work of the contractor;
>
> (ii) any significant change occurs in the nature of the business, the extent of subcontracting, fixed asset improvement programs, the inventories, the volume of sales and production, manufacturing processes, the contractor's products, or other relevant circumstances; or
>
> (iii) indirect cost groupings developed for a contractor's primary location are applied to off-site locations. Separate cost groupings for costs allocable to off-site locations may be necessary to permit equitable distribution of costs on the basis of the benefits accruing to the several cost objectives.

These provisions (a) establish the basis of evaluating allocation practices (i.e., Cost Accounting Standards, generally accepted accounting principles, and the contractor's established practices) and (b) recognize that the government contracting environment can involve many variances in operating circumstances when compared to operations in commercial markets. Many of the circumstances mentioned (e.g., offsite versus onsite operations; pattern of subcontracting) were distilled from experiences where disputes arose in administering contracts.

Base Period

Basically, DAR 15-203 (e) requires contractors to compute overhead rates on the basis of a full year's activity in both the pool and the base in order to insure a true annualized rate. Exceptions to this rule are quite restricted:

> A base period for allocation of indirect costs is the cost accounting period during

which such costs are incurred and accumulated for distribution to work performed in that period. The criteria and guidance set forth in . . . Cost Accounting Standard 406, Cost Accounting Period . . . for selection of the cost accounting periods to be used in allocation of indirect costs, are incorporated in their entirety for application to CAS covered contracts. For contractors not having contracts subject to the Cost Accounting Standards, however, use of a period shorter than the contractor's fiscal year may be appropriate (i) for contracts for which performance involves only a minor portion of the fiscal year, or (ii) where it is general practice in the industry to use a shorter period. In any event, the base period or periods used shall avoid creating inequities in the allocation of indirect costs. When a contract is performed over an extended period, as many base periods will be used as are required to represent the period of contract performance.

MONITORS OF COST PRINCIPLES

The government monitors the implementation of the cost principles through the joint efforts of its contracting officers (official agency representatives who administer contracts) and agency auditors. The contracting officers have varied backgrounds, typically not in accounting. They tend to take their cue on accounting issues from the agency auditors. The largest audit agency is the Defense Contract Agency (DCAA). DCAA, through its 3,000 auditors, conducts audits for the Department of Defense and also services the audit needs of a number of civilian agencies.

When the contracting officer (generally working from the conclusion of an audit report) feels that a contractor is not complying with the cost principles, he can issue a "final decision" to that effect and withhold payment from (or insist on repayment by) the contractor. To recoup these funds, the contractor must file an appeal with the procuring agency's *board of contract appeals* (BCA). There are over a dozen boards of contract appeals. (Some agencies with relatively little procurement activity assign their cases to other, larger agencies' boards.)

The largest board of contract appeals is the Armed Services Board of Contract Appeals. It has nearly 40 administrative judges who hear cases and issue decisons. BCA decisons can be appealed to the U.S. Court of Claims. From the Court of Claims, the appeal can be pursued in the U.S. Supreme Court.

REFERENCE NOTES

1. U.S. Department of Defense, *Prime Contract Awards—Fiscal Year 1979*, p. 1.

2. U.S., General Services Administration, *Procurement by Civilian Executive Agencies for the Period October 1, 1979–September 30, 1980*, p. 1.

3. U.S., Department of Defense, *Historical Development of Procurement Methods,* 1969, pp. 32–34.

4. U.S., Armed Services Board of Contract Appeals, Garrett Corp. ASBCA 13024, 69–2BCA ¶ 7797.

5. U.S., Armed Services Board of Contract Appeals, Teledyne Industries, ASBCA 18049, 73–2BCA ¶ 10088.

Chapter 17

Cost Accounting Standards Board

The preceding chapter reviewed the accounting controls that are applicable to *all* negotiated contracts of the Federal government. This chapter reviews an additional layer of accounting controls— Cost Accounting Standards—that is applicable to *most major* negotiated contracts of the Federal government.

BACKGROUND

During the late 1960s there was some dissatisfaction expressed in the ability of the Federal government to ensure that its interests were being protected in negotiating and expending funds under national defense (i.e., military and certain civilian agency) contracts. The prime spokesman for this cause was Admiral Hyman G. Rickover, the architect of the U.S. nuclear naval fleet. What was needed, he said, was *uniform cost accounting standards.*

Rather than forging ahead with a law requiring the promulgation of uniform cost accounting standards, Congress passed a law in June 1968 requiring the Comptroller General, the head of the General Accounting Office (GAO), to conduct a study that would investigate the need for and feasibility of promulgating a new body of rules that would control the accounting for national defense contracts.

The Comptroller General, through the GAO, and with the advice and assistance of various Federal agencies, outside consultants, and professional associations, carried out the study and transmitted his findings to Congress in January 1970. Basically, the *Feasibility Study* concluded and/or recommended the following:

1. There was a need for additional cost accounting rules in national defense contracts.

2. It was feasible to establish such rules which would be known as *cost accounting standards.*

3. An underlying theme of such standards should be the disclosure and consistent application of cost accounting practices by contractors.
4. A new organization should be established for the promulgation of the standards.[1]

Within six months from the receipt of the *Feasibility Study,* Congress passed Public Law (P.L.) 91-379, which established the Cost Accounting Standards Board (CASB).

The CASB was in operation during the 1970s. This period saw the CASB address what the *Feasibility Study* outlined as the major deficiencies in accounting for government contracts. By 1980, Congress felt that the CASB had accomplished the bulk of the workload assigned to it in 1970. Thus, Congress allowed the CASB to expire on September 30, 1980. The standards that it promulgated remain in effect. Currently, there is some consideration being given to transferring responsibility for modifying and maintaining the timeliness of the existing standards to an executive branch agency. However, this would take an act of Congress.

The CASB is unique among the agencies reported on in this book in that its sole function was to promulgate accounting regulations. The other agencies utilize accounting as a tool to achieve some objective (e.g., rate regulation, public disclosure, etc.). The CASB's objective was to promulgate cost accounting standards.

ORGANIZATION OF THE CASB

The CASB was a component of the *legislative* branch of the Federal government. (This is the same status as that of the General Accounting Office, Chapter 24.) It reported directly to Congress, not to the President (as do executive agencies). The CASB was a five member board and the chairman was the Comptroller General, *ex officio.* He appointed the other members in accordance with the following provisions of Sec. 719 (a) of P.L. 91-379:

> Of the members appointed to the Board, two, of whom one shall be particularly knowledgeable about the cost accounting problems of small business, shall be from the accounting profession, one shall be representative of industry, and one shall be from a department or agency of the Federal Government who shall be appointed with the consent of the head of the department or agency concerned. The term of office of each of the appointed members of the Board shall be four years, except that any member appointed to fill a vacancy in the Board shall serve for the remainder of the term for which his predecessor was appointed.

The CASB met monthly. In the interim, its work was carried on by a full-time staff. The specific charge given the CASB by Congress is contained in the following paragraphs of P.L. 91-379:

> (g) The Board shall from time to time promulgate cost-accounting standards designed to achieve uniformity and consistency in the cost-accounting principles followed by defense contractors and subcontractors under Federal contracts. Such promulgated standards shall be used by all relevant Federal agencies and by defense contractors and subcontractors in estimating, accumulating, and reporting costs in connection with the pricing, administration and settlement of all negotiated prime contract and subcontract national defense procurements

with the United States in excess of $100,000, other than contracts or subcontracts where the price negotiated is based on (1) established catalog or market prices of commercial items sold in substantial quantities to the general public, or (2) prices set by law or regulation. In promulgating such standards the Board shall take into account the probable costs of implementation compared to the probable benefits.

(h) (1) The Board is authorized to make, promulgate, amend, and rescind rules and regulations for the implementation of cost-accounting standards promulgated under subsection (g). Such regulations shall require defense contractors and subcontractors as a condition of contracting to disclose in writing their cost-accounting principles, including methods of distinguishing direct costs from indirect costs and the basis used for allocating indirect costs, and to agree to a contract price adjustment, with interest, for any increased costs paid to the defense contractor by the United States because of the defense contractor's failure to comply with duly promulgated cost-accounting standards or to follow consistently his disclosed cost-accounting practices in pricing contract proposals and in accumulating and reporting contract performance cost data. Such interest shall not exceed 7 per centum per annum measured from the time such payments were made to the contractor or subcontractor to the time such price adjustment is effected. If the parties fail to agree as to whether the defense contractor or subcontractor has complied with cost-accounting standards, the rules and regulations relating thereto, and cost adjustments demanded by the United States, such disagreement will constitute a dispute under the contract dispute clause.

(2) The Board is authorized, as soon as practicable after the date of enactment of this section, to prescribe rules and regulations exempting from the requirements of this section such classes or categories of defense contractors or subcontractors under contracts negotiated in connection with national defense procurements as it determines, on the basis of the size of the contracts involved or otherwise, are appropriate and consistent with the purposes sought to be achieved by this section.

CASB REGULATIONS

The CASB's regulations appear in Title 4 of the Code of Federal Regulations, Parts 300–499. The 4 CFR 300s contain the CASB's regulations pertaining to its administration, its contract clauses (to be included in CAS-covered contracts), and its disclosure statement (discussed later). The 4 CFR 400s contain the CASB's standards. The standards that were promulgated are listed in Table 17–1. Each of them will be briefly reviewed later in this chapter.

CAS COVERAGE

The determination of what contracts are covered by CAS is somewhat complex. There is also the consideration of whether full or modified (i.e., where only certain standards apply) CAS coverage is applicable. The best place to start in sorting out this puzzle is that, in general, all negotiated national defense prime contracts and subcontracts in excess of $100,000 are subject to CAS.

CAS Exemptions

The CASB regulations exempt certain *classes of contracts*. In general, the fol-

TABLE 17-1
Promulgated Cost Accounting Standards

CAS 401*	Consistency in Estimating, Accumulating, and Reporting Costs
CAS 402	Consistency in Allocating Costs Incurred for the Same Purpose
CAS 403	Allocation of Home Office Expenses to Segments
CAS 404	Capitalization of Tangible Capital Assets
CAS 405	Accounting for Unallowable Costs
CAS 406	Cost Accounting Period
CAS 407	Use of Standard Costs for Direct Material and Direct Labor
CAS 408	Accounting for Costs of Compensated Personal Absence
CAS 409	Depreciation of Tangible Capital Assets
CAS 410	Allocation of Business Unit General and Administrative Expense to Final Cost Objectives
CAS 411	Accounting for Acquisition Costs of Material
CAS 412	Composition and Measurement of Pension Costs
CAS 413	Adjustment and Allocation of Pension Costs
CAS 414	Cost of Money as an Element of the Cost of Facilities Capital
CAS 415	Accounting for the Cost of Deferred Compensation
CAS 416	Accounting for Insurance Costs
CAS 417	Cost of Money as an Element of the Cost of Capital Assets Under Construction
CAS 418	Allocation of Direct and Indirect Costs
CAS 420	Accounting for Independent Research and Development and Bid and Proposal Costs

*While officially designated as 4 CFR 401, 4 CFR 402, etc., the standards are commonly referred to as CAS 401, 402, etc.

lowing contracts (prime contracts and subcontracts) are exempt from CAS coverage:

1. Contracts with "small business concerns" as defined by the Small Business Administration.

2. Subcontracts that are subject to adequate price competition (defined in the regulations).

3. Contracts with foreign governments.

4. Contracts made under special government set-aside programs.

5. Contracts with educational institutions except those operating Federally Funded Research and Development Centers.

6. Contracts with foreign companies are generally subject to *some* modified coverage.

7. Until a company receives its first CAS covered contract over $500,000, all contracts of $500,000 or less are exempt; after receiving a CAS covered contract over $500,000, all negotiated national defense contracts over $100,000 are covered by CAS.

8. Certain NATO contracts.

Waivers

The CASB could grant a waiver *for a particular contract* from coverage by its standards. The usual route taken for a waiver was for a potential contractor to request that the procuring (government) agency request a waiver from the CASB for the contract under negotiation. The CASB was very reluctant to grant such waivers; most requests for waivers were rejected.

Modified Coverage

If a company had less than $10 million in CAS covered contracts *and* this was also less than 10 percent of its sales in its prior year, the company can elect to be subject to *modified* CAS coverage. This means that the company would be subject to only two standards: CAS 401 and CAS 402. Further, if a company were to receive a *single* CAS-covered contract of $10 million or more, it would be immediately subject to full CAS coverage regardless of its CAS activity in the preceding year.

Civilian Agency Contracts

The CASB was given purview over national defense contracts. Other contracts (i.e., most civilian agency contracts) were not mentioned in P.L. 91–379. However, civilian agencies have voluntarily brought their contracts under CAS, with certain modifications. First, they added the following exemptions to those of the CASB:

1. Contracts with state and local governments.
2. All contracts with educational institutions.
3. Negotiated firm fixed-price contracts that result from procurements that were competitive and were awarded to the lowest priced offeror.

Further, the civilian agencies have hinged full CAS coverage of civilian contracts (i.e., being subject to all CAS) to full CAS coverage under a company's national defense contracts. That is, until a company either (a) receives over $10 million in national defense contracts or has over 10 percent of its sales in the prior year under CAS-covered national defense contracts, or (b) receives a single CAS-covered national defense contract of $10 million or more, it will only have to comply with modified CAS coverage (i.e., CAS 401 and CAS 402).

CAS DISCLOSURE STATEMENT

One of the first things that the CASB did after it began its operations was to comply with that portion of P.L. 91–379 (quoted, in part, earlier) that required its regulations to " . . . require defense contractors and subcontractors as a condition of contracting to disclose in writing their cost accounting principles, including methods of distinguishing direct costs from indirect costs and the basis used for allocating indirect costs. . . . " It did this by the development of the CASB disclosure statement.

The CASB disclosure statement (officially known as Form CASB–DS–1) appears in Part 351 of the CASB's regulations (4 CFR Part 351).

The disclosure statement is over 40 pages in length (with additional space generally needed to answer questions contained therein in depth). The disclosure statement is composed of the following major sections:

Part I — General Information

Part II — Direct Costs

Part III — Direct versus Indirect

Part IV — Indirect Costs

Part V — Depreciation and Capitalization Practices

Part VI — Other Costs and Credits

Part VII — Deferred Compensation and Insurance Costs

Part VIII — Corporate or Group Expenses

The disclosure statement commits a company to a complete documentation of its cost accounting system so as to permit the monitoring of its consistency within a period, among contracts, and over time. Figure 17-1 is a sample of one page of the disclosure statement.

A contractor must file a disclosure statement for itself and for each of its organizational units (e.g., subsidiaries, divisions, etc.) that has different cost accounting practices from its own if (a) its CAS-covered contracts in its prior year were $10 million or more, or (b) it receives a single CAS-covered contract of $10 million or more in the current year. In matching this requirement with that for CAS coverage, it will be noted that a company can be subject to CAS but not be required to file a disclosure statement.

PROCESS OF ESTABLISHING STANDARDS

The CASB went through a relatively structured series of steps in developing its standards. The steps were:

1. *Identification of Topics.* The CASB distilled those topics or problem areas that were brought to its attention (by its staff, other government agencies, industry, etc.).

2. *Staff Research.* The CASB staff conducted a thorough research study of the topics approved by the CASB.

3. *Issues Paper.* The staff prepared an issues paper that was descriptive of the topic (rather than prescriptive of a solution). The issues paper was distributed throughout government and industry for comments.

4. *Preparation of a Draft Standard.* The staff prepared a draft standard for consideration by the CASB.

5. *Publication in the Federal Register.* The CASB reviewed the draft standard, made changes that it deemed appropriate, and proceeded with its publication in the *Federal Register* for comment.

6. *Evaluation of Comments.* Interested parties were encouraged to submit written comments on the proposed standard. The CASB was particularly interested in the balance between the benefits and costs of the proposed standard.

7. *Promulgation.* After gathering and reviewing the comments the CASB generally proceeded either to redraft the standard (i.e., go back to Step 5) or to finally promulgate the standard.

8. *Congressional Review.* By law (P.L. 91-379) any standard promulgated by the CASB had to lie dormant for a period of 60 days of continuous session of Congress before becoming effective. If, during this period, no concurrent resolution that opposed the standard was passed by Congress, the standard became effective.

A potential standard could be either aborted at any step in the process or sent back to an earlier stage for reworking.

Cost Accounting Standards Board

COST ACCOUNTING STANDARDS BOARD DISCLOSURE STATEMENT REQUIRED BY PUBLIC LAW 91-379	PART IV - INDIRECT COSTS

Item No.	ITEM DESCRIPTION

4.7.0 Continued

    (g) Labor on installation of assets   [   ]

    (h) Off-site work   [   ]

    (i) Other transactions or costs (Enter Code A   [   ]
on this line if there are other transactions
or costs to which less than full rate is
applied. List such transactions or costs on
a continuation sheet, and for each describe
the major types of expenses covered by such
a rate. If there are no other such transactions or costs, enter Code Z.)

4.8.0 Independent Research and Development (IR&D) and Bidding and Proposal (B&P) Costs.

4.8.1 Independent Research and Development. IR&D costs are defined in ASPR 15-205.35 or other pertinent procurement regulations, as revised. The full rate of all allocable manufacturing, engineering, and/or other overhead is applied to IR&D costs as if IR&D projects were under contract, and the "burdened" IR&D costs are: (Check one.)

    A. [   ] Allocated to Government contracts or similar cost objectives as part of the G&A rate

    B. [   ] Allocated as a separate IR&D rate

    C. [   ] Transferred to the corporate or home office level. The corporate or home office level IR&D costs are subsequently allocated back to the reporting unit for allocation as part of the unit's G&A rate

    D. [   ] Treated the same as C above, except that the IR&D costs are allocated as a separate IR&D rate

    Y. [   ] Other (Describe on a continuation sheet.)

    Z. [   ] Not applicable

4.8.2 Bidding and Proposal. B&P costs as defined in ASPR 15-205.3 or other pertinent procurement regulations, as revised, are treated as follows: (Check one.)

    A. [   ] Same as IR&D costs as checked above

    Y. [   ] Other (Describe on a continuation sheet.)

FORM CASB-DS-1   - 20 -

FIGURE 17-1. Cost Accounting Standards Board Form CASB–DS–1.

Objectives, Policies, and Concepts

Before reviewing the individual standards that were issued, it should be noted that the CASB set out the equivalent of its "conceptual framework" in a pamphlet-sized document entitled *Restatement of Objectives, Policies, and Concepts.* This work was originally issued in 1973 and restated in 1977. The conceptual accounting topics covered by the *Restatement* are:

Objectives

  Uniformity

  Consistency

  Allowability and Allocability

  Fairness

  Verifiability

Cost Allocation Concepts

  Hierarchy for Allocating Costs

  Accounting Standards and the Flow of Costs

While small in size, the *Restatement* is an important (and often overlooked) document for anyone seeking an integrated view of CAS. This is particularly true of the "Objectives" and "Cost Allocation Concepts" sections. For example, the *Restatement* sets out the CASB's framework for allocating direct and indirect costs to cost objectives in 2½ pages under the topic "Hierarchy for Allocating Costs." This section of the *Restatement* serves as the "golden thread" that runs through all standards that deal with the allocation of costs to cost objectives (e.g., contracts).

Format

Each individual standard makes up a separate Part in the Code of Federal Regulations, beginning with 4 CFR Part 401 (i.e., commonly referred to as CAS 401). Part 400, entitled *Definitions,* is the repository for all definitions of terms (appearing in the standards) that either have specialized meanings distinct from the broader area of accounting or, while not purely accounting terms, need a precise meaning in their role as key terms in the standards.

Each standard has the following sections:

.10 General applicability. This brief section describes the contracts to which the standard is applicable. It is basically uniform for all standards.

.20 Purpose. This section describes the aim of the standard.

.30 Definitions. This section reproduces definitions that are particularly germane to this standard.

.40 Fundamental requirement. The general thrust of the principles or practices espoused by the standard are contained in this section.

.50 Techniques for application. This section provides the implementing instructions and guidance for the immediately preceding *Fundamental requirement* section.

.60 Illustrations. This section sets out hypothetical examples that illustrate conformance with and violations of the standard.

.70 Exemptions. Any exemptions peculiar to this standard (as opposed to exemptions from all standards) are set out here. Most standards have no exemptions.

.80 Effective date. This determines when companies must follow the standard.

COST ACCOUNTING STANDARDS

In the remainder of this chapter, the standards that were promulgated by the CASB will be reviewed. In reviewing the standards, the *Purpose* section of the standard (e.g., CAS 401.20, CAS 402.20, etc.) will be quoted (in whole or in part) to give an overview. Then a brief analysis of the standard will be presented. The standards will be reviewed in their numerical order, which approximates their order of issuance. However, it might be useful to have an overview of the *major topics* that various standards address:

Topic	Standards
Consistency	CAS 401, 402
Allocation of cost to cost objectives	CAS 403, 410, 418
Employee compensation	CAS 408, 412, 413, 415
Fixed assets	CAS 404, 409, 414, 417
Measurement and allocation of specific types of cost	CAS 414 and 417 (cost of money), 416 (insurance), 420 (independent R&D), 407 and 411 (cost of material)

CAS 401–Consistency in Estimating, Accumulating, and Reporting Costs

The stated purpose of CAS 401 is [4 CFR 401.20]:

> . . . to insure that each contractor's practices used in estimating costs for a proposal are consistent with cost accounting practices used by him in accumulating and reporting costs. Consistency in the application of cost accounting practices is necessary to enhance the likelihood that comparable transactions are treated alike. With respect to individual contracts, the consistent application of cost accounting practices will facilitate the preparation of reliable cost estimates used in pricing a proposal and their comparison with the costs of performance of the resulting contract. Such comparisons provide one important basis for financial control over costs during contract performance and aid in establishing accountability for costs in the manner agreed to by both parties at the time of contracting. The comparisons also provide an improved basis for evaluating estimating capabilities.

This standard is a direct response to the legislative mandate to insure consistency of accounting practices from the proposal (i.e., estimating) stage through the performance (i.e., accumulating and reporting) stage of a contract. In general, this standard is quite compatible with sound accounting practices which pay a good deal of homage to consistency. However, it can work a hardship where *circumstances* change from the proposal to the performance stage. In such circumstances, the contractor would be precluded from allowing its accounting to follow the facts encountered. For example, assume that an allowance for scrap was initially proposed as an indirect cost in an advanced research and development contract. However, in performing the contract, excessive scrap is encountered. The excessive scrap would *not* be allowed to be charged as a direct cost of this contract due to this standard.

CAS 402–Consistency in Allocating Costs Incurred for the Same Purpose

The purpose of this standard is [4 CFR 402.20] :

> . . . to require that each type of cost is allocated only once and on only one basis to any contract or other cost objective. The criteria for determining the allocation of costs to a product, contract, or other cost objective should be the same for all similar objectives. Adherence to these cost accounting concepts is necessary to guard against the overcharging of some cost objectives and to prevent double counting. Double counting occurs most commonly when cost items are allocated directly to a cost objective without eliminating like cost items from indirect cost pools which are allocated to that cost objective.

This standard was in direct response to legislative mandate and a number of "horror cases" that were highlighted in the *Feasibility Study*. The following are examples of these cases:

> In its fixed-price contract proposals, the contractor treated packaging material costs and such hardware items as nuts, bolts and screws as direct costs. Since these costs had been included in the material-related overhead rates which were applied separately to the direct material costs proposed, the proposals were overstated by $27,000.[2]

> The contractor departed from its normal practices or changed its procedures. As a result, travel costs of $390,000 were charged to overhead which should have been charged directly to fixed-price contracts. This resulted in excess costs being allocated to Government cost-type contracts.[3]

The spirit of this standard is well grounded on the accounting concept of consistency. The implementation problems can arise in determining what are "like cost items." That is, where does one draw the line between (a) double counting of costs (by charging "like cost items" to a contract both as direct and indirect costs) and (b) charging two somewhat similar types of cost items to the same contract, one as a direct cost and the other as an indirect cost. The balance of the standard attempts to sort out this issue. The problem is so pervasive that the CASB issued an Interpretation. The Interpretation noted that the cost of preparing a proposal, which proposal was *required* by the terms of an existing contract, could be considered different enough in circumstances from the contractor's normal voluntary submission of proposals (to acquire new business) to warrant the treatment of the former as a direct cost and the latter as an indirect cost allocable to the same contract(s).

CAS 403—Allocation of Home Office Expenses to Segments

Before viewing the purpose of this standard, let us review the CASB's definitions of two key terms:

> *Home Office.* An office responsible for directing or managing two or more but not necessarily all segments of an organization. It typically establishes policy for, and provides guidance to the segments in their operations. It usually performs management, supervisory, or administrative functions, and may also perform service functions in support of the operations of the various segments. An organization which has intermediate levels, such as groups, may have several home offices which report to a common home office. An intermediate organiza-

tion may be both a segment and a home office. [4 CFR 403.30 (a) (2)].

Segment. One of two or more divisions, product departments, plants, or other subdivisions of an organization reporting directly to a home office, usually identified with responsibility for profit and or producing a product or service. The term includes Government-owned contractor-operated (GOCO) facilities, and joint ventures and subsidiaries (domestic and foreign) in which the organization has a majority ownership. The term also includes those joint ventures and subsidiaries (domestic and foreign) in which the organization has less than a majority of ownership, but over which it exercises control. [4 CFR 403.30 (a) (4)]

To illustrate these terms, assume a company has the following organizational structure:

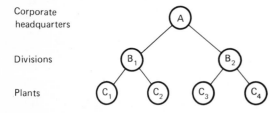

There would be *three* channels of home office-branch office relations. Thus, this standard would be applied three times:

Home Office	Segments
A	B_1, B_2
B_1	C_1, C_2
B_2	C_3, C_4

The purpose of this standard is [4 CFR 403.20]:

. . . to establish criteria for allocation of the expenses of a home office to the segments of the organization based on the beneficial or causal relationship between such expenses and the receiving segments. It provides for (1) identification of expenses for direct allocation to segments to the maximum extent practical; (2) accumulation of significant nondirectly allocated expenses into logical and relatively homogeneous pools to be allocated on bases reflecting the relationship of the expenses to the segments concerned; and (3) allocation of any remaining or residual home office expenses to all segments. Appropriate implementation of this Standard will limit the amount of home office expenses classified as residual to the expenses of managing the organization as a whole.

The standard identifies broad categories of home office expenses:

1. Centralized service functions.
2. Staff management.
3. Line management.
4. Central payments or accruals.
5. Residual expenses (all costs not covered in 1 through 4).

It identifies suggested bases for these categories, which are rather specific where the benefits are traceable (e.g., allocating personnel administration on the basis of the number of employees, labor hours, payroll, or the number of newly hired employees). The bases are rather general where the benefits are not traceable (e.g., where residual expenses are to be allocated using a base "representative of the total activity of such segments").

CAS 404—Capitalization of Tangible Assets

The purpose of this standard is as follows [4 CFR 404.20]:

This Standard requires that, for purposes of cost measurement, contractors establish and adhere to policies with respect to capitalization of tangible assets which satisfy criteria set forth herein. Normally, cost measurements are based on the concept of enterprise continuity; this concept implies that major asset acquisitions will be capitalized, so that the cost applicable to current and future accounting periods can be allocated to cost objectives of those periods. A capitalization policy in accordance with this Standard will facilitate measurement of costs consistently over time.

This standard, again, was in response to issues raised in the *Feasibility Study:*

A survey of 20 contractors on the East Coast disclosed variances in the capitalization policies of these contractors, the low dollar value limit for capitalizing ranging from $0 to $1,000, with 18 contractors at $250 or less. One problem is the expensing of quantity purchases of low value assets. At one plant with a $200 minimum capitalization policy, about $3.3 million in low value items were expensed in two years. Our tests showed that roughly two-thirds of the low cost items expensed were for purchases in quantity. The variation in practices, and the substantial values involved, indicate a need for consideration of capitalization policies in the formulation of cost standards.[4]

This standard is, for the most part, in accord with the broader area of generally accepted accounting principles. Among other things, it (a) sets limits on minimum service life (2 years) and minimum acquisition cost ($1,000) for contractors' capitalization policies; (b) guides the contractor's policies

for betterments, improvements, initial complement of low cost equipment, etc.; and (c) establishes rules for capitalization of tangible assets that are either donated to the contractor, self-constructed by the contractor, or result from "purchase" or "pooling" business combinations.

CAS 405—Accounting for Unallowable Costs

The purpose of this standard is [4 CFR 405.20]:

> . . . to facilitate the negotiation, audit, administration and settlement of contracts by establishing guidelines covering: (1) Identification of costs specifically described as unallowable, at the time such costs first become defined or authoritatively designated as unallowable; and (2) the cost accounting treatment to be accorded such identified unallowable costs in order to promote the consistent application of sound cost accounting principles covering all incurred costs. The Standard is predicated on the proposition that costs incurred in carrying on the activities of an enterprise—regardless of the allowability of such costs under Government contracts—are allocable to the cost objectives with which they are identified on the basis of their beneficial or causal relationships.

The concept of cost allowability (versus unallowability) was discussed in conjunction with the procurement agencies' cost principles (Chapter 16). In this standard, the CASB takes the position that the designation of unallowable costs is a matter for procurement agencies. The CASB is only concerned with what it regards as proper accounting for all costs, including unallowable costs. This standard requires that contractors (a) identify all unallowable costs and (b) have all unallowable costs participate in indirect cost allocation just as they would if they were allowable.

CAS 406—Cost Accounting Period

The intent of the standard is [4 CFR 406.20]:

> . . . to provide criteria for the selection of the time periods to be used as cost accounting periods for contract cost estimating, accumulating, and reporting. This Standard will reduce the effects of variations in the flow of costs within each cost accounting period. It will also enhance objectivity, consistency, and verifiability, and promote uniformity and comparability in contract cost measurements.

This standard requires that the contractor use his fiscal year (i.e., the period used for the preparation of his annual financial statements) for cost accounting purposes. This standard guards against "gaming" a cost accounting period in order to artificially inflate costs allocated to certain cost objectives (e.g., government contracts). For example, if a company had a seasonal pattern of production (heavy in the first half of the year; light in the second half of the year), the use of two six month cost accounting periods

could result in significantly different overhead rates rather than the use of an annual rate. (See Table 17-2, for example.) Depending upon when a contract was produced, its overhead would be either overstated or understated using semiannual rates rather than an annual rate.

CAS 407—Use of Standard Cost for Direct Material and Direct Labor

The aim of the standard is [4 CFR 407.20]:

> . . . to provide criteria under which standard costs may be used for estimating, accumulating, and reporting costs of direct material and direct labor, and to provide criteria relating to the establishment of standards, accumulation of standard costs, and accumulation and disposition of variances from standard costs. Consistent application of these criteria where standard costs are in use will improve cost measurement and cost assignment.

This standard permits the use of standard costs for direct materials and direct labor. However, the contractor must document his practices with regard to setting standards, revising standards, and integrating his standard cost system into his financial accounting system. In particular, the standard requires that material variances (i.e.,

TABLE 17-2
Overhead Rates Based on Two Six-Month Cost Accounting Periods

	First Half Year	Second Half Year	Total Year
A. Overhead pool	$1,000,000	$600,000	$1,600,000
B. Base (e.g., direct labor dollars)	$500,000	$200,000	$700,000
C. Overhead rate (A ÷ B)	200%	300%	229%

differences between actual and standard costs) be allocated to production at least annually. This, of course, results in production being restated on an actual cost basis. Immaterial variances can be disposed of by being charged (or credited) to indirect cost pools. The variances are then allocated to production with the other costs in the pool.

CAS 408—Accounting for Costs of Compensated Personal Absence

The goal of this standard is quite succinct [4 CFR 408.20]:

> The purpose of this Standard is to improve, and provide uniformity in, the measurement of costs of vacation, sick leave, holiday, and other compensated personal absence for a cost accounting period, and thereby increase the probability that the measured costs are allocated to the proper cost objectives.

Many companies have employee leave (personal absence) plans that are structured similar to this scenario: A worker's service (e.g., defined as number of full weeks worked) in 1981 determines her leave entitlements (vacation and sick leave) in 1982. Any unused leave entitlements in 1982 can be carried forward to 1983 and beyond. What period (and its production) should bear the cost of the leave—1981, when entitlement was earned; 1982, when entitlement was granted; or 1982, 1983, and beyond when the leave is used?

The CASB found all three methods in operation. In the standard, only the first, that is, recognizing the expense in the period that entitlement is earned, is permitted. Further, since many companies had previously employed methods

that are now unacceptable, the standard contains a procedure that permits a transition to the standard without an inequitable result being levied on either the government (by having to pay too much) or the contractor (by not being allowed to recover costs arising from entitlements earned prior to becoming subject to CAS 408).

CAS 409—Depreciation of Tangible Capital Assets

The purpose of this standard is [4 CFR 409.20]:

> . . . to provide criteria and guidance for assigning costs of tangible capital assets to cost accounting periods and for allocating such costs to cost objectives within such periods in an objective and consistent manner. The Standard is based on the concept that depreciation costs identified with cost accounting periods and benefiting cost objectives within periods should be a reasonable measure of the expiration of service potential of the tangible assets subject to depreciation. Adherence to this Standard should provide a systematic and rational flow of the costs of tangible capital assets to benefited cost objectives over the expected service lives of the assets. This Standard does not cover nonwasting assets or natural resources which are subject to depletion.

CAS 404—Capitalization of Tangible Assets—controls the determination of the cost of depreciable assets. This standard—CAS 409—controls the assignment of that cost to the periods benefited by the assets' use, i.e., depreciation. The standard sets out the rules controlling the following factors that affect the computation of depreciation:

Useful life

Residual value

Depreciation method

Accounting for gain or loss upon disposition

This standard raised quite a furor when it was proposed; in fact, it resulted in Congressional hearings. Industry claimed that the standard—which it viewed as leaning more on the physical life rather than the economic life of an asset and as favoring straight-line depreciation unless an accelerated method could be clearly supported—would result in cost recovery on depreciable assets being lengthened. Thus, there would be a reduced incentive to invest in such assets, in particular, and in national defense business, in general. Despite these claims, the standard was promulgated without a Congressional override.

CAS 410—Allocation of Business Unit General and Administrative Expenses to Final Cost Objectives

In order to understand the thrust of this standard, the following CASB definitions are needed [4 CFR 410.30]:

> *Segment.* One of two or more divisions, product departments, plants, or other subdivisions of an organization reporting directly to a home office, usually identified with responsibility for profit and/or producing a product or service. . . .
>
> *Business unit.* Any segment of an organization, or an entire business organization, which is not divided into segments.
>
> *Final cost objective.* A cost objective which has allocated to it both direct and indirect costs, and, in the contractor's accumulation systems, is one of the final accumulation points.

General and administrative (G&A) expense. Any management, financial, and other expense which is incurred by or allocated to a business unit and which is for the general management and administration of the business unit as a whole. G&A expense does not include those management expenses whose beneficial or causal relationship to cost objectives can be more directly measured by a base other than a cost input base representing the total activity of a business unit during a cost accounting period.

Thus, we can view business units as the lowest level segments of an entity (i.e., they are not divided into further segments). Final cost objectives, also known outside of the CAS area as "output cost objectives," can be viewed as the individual production cost objectives—such as job orders or contracts —produced by the business unit. Finally, G&A expenses are the most "untraceable" of the indirect costs.

The goal of CAS 410 is [4 CFR 410.20]:

> . . . to provide criteria for the allocation of business unit general and administrative (G&A) expenses to business unit final cost objectives based on their beneficial or causal relationship. These expenses represent the cost of the management and administration of the business unit as a whole. The Standard also provides criteria for the allocation of home office expenses received by a segment to the cost objectives of that segment. This Standard will increase the likelihood of achieving objectivity in the allocation of expenses to final cost objectives and comparability of cost data among contractors in similar circumstances.

The standard requires that G&A expenses be allocated on a "cost input base representing the total activity of the business unit." The standard identifies three such cost input bases:

1. *Total cost input*—i.e., all costs of the business unit other than the G&A expenses.

2. *Value-added cost input*—i.e., total cost input less direct material costs and subcontract costs.

3. *Single element cost input*—e.g., direct labor cost; direct labor hours.

The standard leaves the selection of which base best fits a particular circumstance up to the contracting parties.

There has been much heated debate among contracting offices, auditors, and contractors as to the appropriate base in given circumstances. Generally, the government insists on total cost input, while contractors insist that value-added is often more realistic.

To illustrate this point, let us assume that Company A has two *identical* contracts—one with the government, the other with Company B. The contracts call for the production of identical items, the only difference being that

the government will furnish all of the material needed to produce its contract (a common practice) to Company A. Company A will buy all of the material for its contract with Company B. With the assumed figures shown, the allocations in Table 17-3 will result. Contractors claim that such a difference in allocation is spurious and biased on behalf of the government.

CAS 411—Accounting for Acquisition Cost of Material

The purpose of this standard is [4 CFR 411.20]:

> . . . to provide criteria for the accounting for acquisition costs of material. The Standard includes provisions on the use of inventory costing methods. Consistent application of this Standard will improve the measurement and assignment of costs to cost objectives.

This standard affirms a contractor's right to use any of the common inventory costing methods (specific identification, LIFO, FIFO, average cost, standard cost) in determining costs under government

TABLE 17-3

	Government Contract	Company B Contract	Total
1. Direct Materials	—0—	$400,000	$400,000
2. Direct Labor	400,000	400,000	800,000
3. Factory Overhead	400,000	400,000	800,000
4. Total Cost Input	$800,000	$1,200,000	$2,000,000
5. G&A Expense			320,000
6. G&A Total Costs Input (TCI) Rate [5 ÷ 4]			16%
7. G&A Value Added (VA) Cost Input Rate [5 ÷ (4-1)]			20%
8. Allocation with TCI rate	$128,000	$192,000	$320,000
9. Allocation with VA rate	$160,000	$160,000	$320,000
10. Difference	$<32,000>	$32,000	

contracts. It requires contractors to have written policies and to follow these policies consistently.

CAS 412—Composition and Measurement of Pension Cost and

CAS 413—Adjustment and Allocation of Pension Cost

The rationale for these two standards dealing with pension costs is:

> *412.20 Purpose.* The purpose of this Standard is to provide guidance for determining and measuring the components of pension cost. The Standard establishes the basis on which pension costs shall be assigned to cost accounting periods. The provisions of this Cost Accounting Standard should enhance uniformity and consistency in accounting for pension costs and thereby increase the probability that those costs are properly allocated to cost objectives.

> *413.20 Purpose.* A purpose of this Standard is to provide guidance for adjusting pension cost by measuring actuarial gains and losses and assigning such gains and losses to cost accounting periods. The Standard also provides the bases on which penison cost shall be allocated to segments of an organization. The provisions of this Cost Accounting Standard should enhance uniformity and consistency in accounting for pension costs.

The provisions of these two standards are quite complex. As an overview, it is adequate to note that these standards seek to establish an equitable procedure for insuring (a) that companies are entitled to allocate to government work the costs of initiating, modifying, and maintaining pension plans for their employees and (b) that the government is not obliged to underwrite contractors'

pension plans that are suddenly initiated or upgraded in terms of benefits as a result of an increase in government business. These standards measure cost on a present value basis with such components as any unfunded actuarial liability, actuarial gains and losses, etc., being amortized over specified periods.

CAS 414—Cost of Money as an Element of the Cost of Facilities Capital

The purpose of this standard is [4 CFR 414.20]:

> . . . to establish criteria for the measurement and allocation of the cost of capital committed to facilities as an element of contract cost. Consistent application of these criteria will improve cost measurement by providing for allocation of cost of contractor investment in facilities capital to negotiated contracts.

This standard permits contractors to claim an *imputed interest cost* based on their investment in fixed assets. This "cost" is not a cost under generally accepted accounting principles (GAAP). All other costs that we have reviewed up to this point are recognized under GAAP.

The rationale for the CASB's "invention" of this cost varied: (a) compensation for inflation; (b) recognition of cost of carrying existing fixed assets; and (c) encouragement of investment in new fixed assets. The CASB's efforts in this area were virtually offset by procurement agencies' actions which either (a) refused to recognize this imputed cost (e.g., civilian agencies not subject to P.L. 91-379) or (b) reduced the profit negotiating formulae to offset the CAS 414 cost.

CAS 415—Accounting for the Cost of Deferred Compensation

This standard is another of the "fringe benefit" standards [4 CFR 415.20]:

> The purpose of this Standard is to provide criteria for the measurement of the cost of deferred compensation and the assignment of such cost to cost accounting periods. The application of these criteria should increase the probability that the cost of deferred compensation is allocated to cost objectives in a uniform and consistent manner.

The specifics of this standard are quite complex. However, the essence is to provide a systematic procedure for accruing the cost of deferred benefits earned by employees.

CAS 416—Accounting for Insurance Costs

The main thrust of this standard is [4 CFR 416.20]:

> . . . to provide criteria for the measurement of insurance costs, the assignment of such costs to cost accounting periods, and their allocation to cost objectives. The application of these criteria should increase the probability that insurance costs are allocated to cost objectives in a uniform and consistent manner.

This standard controls contractors' computations of insurance costs, whether contractural insurance or self-insurance. Here, again, we have a cost—self-insurance—that is not recognized under GAAP but is recognized for contract costing purposes. The government recognizes that contractors should be allowed the cost of providing for operating risks (e.g., casualty losses). The government is not concerned with how this risk is underwritten, whether by purchased insurance or by self-insurance.

CAS 417—Cost of Money as an Element of the Cost of Capital Assets Under Construction

The purpose of this standard is to [4 CFR 417.20]:

> . . . establish criteria for the measurement of the cost of money attributable to capital assets under construction, fabrication or development as an element of the cost of those assets. Consistent application of these criteria will improve cost measurement by providing for recognition of cost of contractor investment in assets under construction, and will provide greater uniformity in accounting for asset acquisitions.

This standard allows contractors to capitalize a cost of money factor (i.e., include it in the cost of the asset) for those capital assets that require a period of time (for construction, fabrication, or development) to be brought on line as productive assets. Prior to this standard, there was no recognition of such a cost.

The amount to be capitalized is based upon the other costs of the capital asset (i.e., the investment), the cost of money rate (the same as that used in CAS 414), and the period of time the asset is under construction. The contractor includes the cost of money in the cost of the asset and it increases the depreciation accrued on the asset during its useful life.

Contemporary with the CASB's consideration of this standard, the Financial Accounting Standards Board (FASB) considered and promulgated FAS No. 34, *Capitalization of Interest Cost*. The

CASB modified the acceptable method for computing the cost of money factor under CAS 417 to permit a company to employ its financial accounting method (i.e., under FAS No. 34) as long as it did not result in a materially different amount than would otherwise be determined under CAS 417.

CAS 418—Allocation of Direct and Indirect Cost

The purpose of this standard is [4 CFR 418.20]:

> . . . (a) to provide for consistent determination of direct and indirect costs, (b) to provide criteria for the accumulation of indirect costs, including service center and overhead costs, in indirect cost pools, and (c) to provide guidance relating to the selection of allocation measures based on the beneficial or causal relationship between an indirect cost pool and cost objectives.

This standard has an interesting pedigree. It was originally published as a series of *five* proposed standards. After evaluating the comments on these standards, the CASB republished it as a series of *three* proposed standards. Again, after evaluating the comments, this single standard finally emerged.

This standard requires the following:

1. A written statement of accounting policies for distinguishing direct and indirect costs.

2. The formulation of homogeneous pools of indirect costs (i.e., pools whose components have similar beneficial or causal relationships to cost objectives).

3. The allocation of indirect cost pools involving management of direct costs

on a base representative of the activity being managed.

4. The allocation of other indirect cost pools on the basis of (a) a measure of resources consumed in the pooled activity, (b) a measure of the output of the pooled activity, or (c) a surrogate that is representative of the resources consumed in the pooled activity.

CAS 420—Accounting for Independent Research and Development and Bid and Proposal Costs

The purpose of this standard is [4 CFR 420.20]:

> . . . to provide criteria for the accumulation of independent research and development costs and bid and proposal costs and for the allocation of such costs to cost objectives based on the beneficial or causal relationship between such costs and cost objectives.

The areas of independent research and development (IR&D) costs and bid and proposal (B&P) costs have been the subject of a great deal of interest in the government contracting area for a long time. They have been the subject of Congressional inquiry, extensive treatment in the procurement regulation, and some concern in the *Feasibility Study*.

In brief, this standard requires the following:

1. The accounting for IR&D and B&P costs at the level of individual projects.

2. The charging of all direct and indirect costs to IR&D and B&P projects except for general and administrative (G&A) expenses.

3. The allocation of IR&D and B&P costs accumulated at a home office on the same base as that used for the home office's residual expenses (per CAS 403).

4. The allocation of IR&D and B&P costs from a business unit on the same base as that used for the business unit's G&A expenses (per CAS 410).

CONTRACT ADJUSTMENTS

Under the CAS contract clause, CAS contracts are subject to three types of adjustments in contract price: (a) new standards, (b) voluntary changes, and (c) noncompliance.

New Standards

When a new standard is issued and a company signs one contract that is subject to it, all of the existing contracts that were entered into prior to the new standard are also subject to it. The transition to the new standard is made by equitably adjusting the existing contracts. The concept of *equitable adjustment* permits both upward and downward adjustments. Thus, the contractor may witness either an increase or decrease in revenue.

Voluntary Changes

When a contractor makes a change in his cost accounting practices that is *not* caused by a new standard, his is said to have made a voluntary change. Unless the government *agrees* to allow an equitable adjustment, the contractor will, most likely, end up with a downward adjustment in contract prices (revenue).

Noncompliance

When a contractor is found to have either (a) not followed a standard or (b) not followed his disclosed or established cost accounting practices, he is subject to downward-only adjustment in his contract prices.

REFERENCE NOTES

1. U.S., Comptroller General of the United States, *Report on the Feasibility of Applying Uniform Cost Accounting Standards to Negotiated Defense Contracts*, 1970, pp. 20–23.

2. *Ibid.*, p. 72.

3. *Ibid.*, p. 78.

4. *Ibid.*, p. 95.

Chapter 18

Securities and Exchange Commission

The Securities and Exchange Commission (SEC) is an independent agency of the Federal government. It is headed by a bipartisan commission of five members. Each commissioner is appointed by the President, with the approval of the Senate, to a five year term. The chairman is designated by the President. The SEC is headquartered in Washington, D.C., and operates nine regional offices located in New York, Boston, Atlanta, Chicago, Fort Worth, Denver, Los Angeles, Seattle, and Washington. The SEC was established by the Securities Exchange Act of 1934. The SEC currently carries out its duties under the following laws.

SEC DUTIES

Securities Act of 1933

This law (the "1933 Act") was passed prior to the establishment of the SEC. The SEC took over its administration. This Act primarily controls the initial offering and sale of a security to the public. Before securities can be offered for sale, they must be registered with the SEC. There are certain exemptions from this provision: (a) private offerings (i.e., to parties who are already familiar with the issuer and are not going to resell the securities), (b) offerings limited to residents of the state in which the issuer does business, (c) offerings of governmental units, charitable organizations, certain financial institutions, and carriers regulated by the Interstate Commerce Commission, and (d) offerings of small business investment companies (SBICs) that are regulated by the Small Business Administration (see Chapter 20). Further, certain small issues of securities (not exceeding $1,500,000) are subject to an abbreviated registration procedure.

The registration requirement is intended to provide information to prospective investors that will allow them to make their decisions in light of full disclosure of the significant facts related to the company in question. The SEC does *not* evaluate the prospects of the company. Its role is one of administering rules designed to require the registrants to disclose sufficient information so as to permit each prospective investor individually, and the market, collectively, to evaluate the prospects of the company.

The registration statement that must be filed with the SEC contains four major types of information: (a) a narrative description of the registrant's business, (b) a comprehensive review of the security to be issued, (c) detailed information on the registrant's management, and (d) detailed financial information including audited financial statements. The accounting and auditing provisions surrounding this last element will be reviewed later in this chapter. In recent years, approximately 3,000 registration statements per year have been filed with the SEC[1].

Securities Exchange Act of 1934

The Securities Exchange Act of 1934 (the "1934 Act"), as amended, greatly affects the operations of the securities markets, companies whose securities are traded, and the middlemen (brokers and dealers) in securities transactions. The Act established the SEC as administrator of both it (i.e., the 1934 Act) and the 1933 Act. (Originally, enforcement of the 1933 Act had been assigned to the Federal Trade Commission.)

Under the 1934 Act, all companies that have securities traded on national exchanges or have securities traded "over-the-counter" (i.e., traded publicly other than on national exchanges), *and* have over $1 million in assets and 500 or more stockholders, must file a registration statement with the SEC. Currently, this applies to about 9,000 companies. This required registration is *in addition to* any requirements that arise under the 1933 Act (i.e., for a particular issue of securities). The registration statements promulgated under both Acts are similar but not identical. Both registration forms require audited financial statements. The registration proceeding under the 1933 Act is required for each issue of securities. Registration under the 1934 Act is continuous as long as the entity's securities are publicly traded. The registration statements must be periodically updated by annual and quarterly reports (including financial statements) and by intermittent reports pursuant to the occurrence of specific events (e.g., change in the registrant's auditor) unless the registrant has fewer than 300 shareholders.

The 1934 Act also authorizes the SEC to regulate the following activities of entities registered under the 1934 Act:

1. *Proxy solicitations.* The SEC controls the means by which stockholders can be approached by management (or other groups) to solicit permission to cast the stockholders' votes in their absence.

2. *Tender offer solicitations and takeovers.* The SEC has established rules by which stockholders are ensured of adequate informative disclosure of pertinent facts involved in an attempt by an outside party to acquire a significant interest in their company either by (a) tender offer (i.e., an of-

fer to purchase stock at a stated price) or (b) purchase on the market at the going price.

3. *Insider trading.* The trading activity of officers, directors, and major stockholders (i.e., owners of more than 10 percent of the registered securities) are subject to stringent provisions regulating their trading in the securities of the registered company.

In addition to these provisions of the 1934 Act, which affect registered companies, there are a number of provisions that require registration and adherence to approved operating policies and practices by the "middlemen" in the securities markets — that is, the securities exchanges (e.g., the New York Stock Exchange) and securities brokers and dealers. An example of an operating practice over which the SEC exercises joint control with the Federal Reserve System is the margin trading in securities. The Federal Reserve sets the margin requirement (i.e., specifies the amount of credit that can be offered on securities transactions). The SEC monitors the registered "middlemen" for adherence to the margin requirement. Currently, there are approximately 6,000 brokers and dealers registered under the 1934 Act.[2]

Public Utility Holding Company Act of 1935

This Act empowered the SEC to oversee the restructuring of the interstate electric and natural gas industries. When this Act was passed, these industries were dominated by multitiered holding company systems. Through their intercorporate holdings, a handful of companies were able to exercise nearly complete control over these industries. The Act required holding companies to register with the SEC. Further, the SEC was required to oversee a simplification of the existing holding company structure (e.g., requiring that holding company components be physically integrated). Under the SEC's auspices, most of the operating components of holding companies are now organized as independent utilities. Currently, there are less than 20 holding company systems registered with the SEC.[3] The SEC oversees the organizational structure of these systems, and is actively involved in reviewing the issuance of securities by the holding companies and their subsidiaries.

The SEC has promulgated a uniform system of accounts for mutual service companies and subsidiary service companies that are part of holding company systems. The SEC had promulgated a uniform system of accounts for holding companies; however, this has been replaced by the SEC's general rules for disclosure.

Trust Indenture Act of 1939

This Act empowers the SEC to enforce standards pertaining to the trust indenture provisions of securities. For example, it sets financial responsibility criteria that a corporation must meet in order to be named as trustee for an issue of securities.

Investment Company Act of 1940

This Act gave the SEC control over investment companies (i.e., companies whose main business is the trading in securities of other companies). The Act requires these companies to register and file periodic reports with the SEC. The SEC is given broad authority to regulate the operating practices of these companies. Currently, there are approximately 1,500 companies registered under this Act.[4]

Investment Advisers Act of 1940

This Act empowers the SEC to oversee the individuals and firms that hold themselves out to the public as advisers on security transactions. The SEC reviews the backgrounds of these advisers for any prior behavior that would disqualify them (e.g., prior conviction for securities fraud). It also controls many of the advisers' operating practices (e.g., setting requirements for the maintenance of books and records).

Bankruptcy Act

Under Chapter X of this Act, the SEC is designated as adviser to Federal courts in the prospective reorganization of financially troubled corporations. The SEC applies its expertise in reviewing suggested plans of reorganization as well as actively participating in the formulation of recommended or alternative plans for reorganization.

Foreign Corrupt Practices Act of 1977

This is the most recent addition to the SEC's slate of legal mandates. In addition to banning payments by U.S. companies (or their subsidiaries) in foreign countries, which would be illegal under U.S. laws, this Act has other significant accounting provisions. These provisions apply to the foreign *and* domestic operations of companies.

The accounting provisions of this Act require companies that file reports under the 1934 Act to (a) maintain books, records, and accounts that accurately and fairly reflect (in reasonable detail) their transactions and dispositions of assets and (b) devise and maintain a system of internal accounting control sufficient to provide reasonable assurance that assets are safeguarded and that transactions are executed in accordance with management's authorization and are recorded properly to permit the preparation of financial statements in accordance with generally accepted accounting principles.

SEC ORGANIZATION

The SEC is organized into five divisions:

Division of Corporation Finance

Division of Corporate Regulation

Division of Investment Management

Division of Market Regulation

Division of Enforcement

In addition, there are a number of offices, including an Office of the Chief Accountant. Most of the SEC's accounting activity centers on the Office of the Chief Accountant and the Division of Corporation Finance (which administers most of the disclosure requirements under the various laws). However, other divisions do get involved in accounting matters. For example, the Division of Investment Management reviews the filings of registrants under the Investment Company Act and the Investment Advisers Act, which include financial statements and other financial information. Therefore, in addition to having a staff of accounting experts in the Office of Chief Accountant and the Division of Corporate Finance, each of the other divisions has its own accounting staff.

SEC REGULATIONS

The SEC's regulations are contained in Title 17, Chapter II, Parts 200–299 of the Code of Federal Regulations. The preponderance of accounting regulations are contained in the following parts:

Part	Title
210	Form and Content of Financial Statements, Securities Act of 1933, Securities Exchange Act of 1934, Public Utility Holding Company Act of 1935 and Investment Company Act of 1940.
211	Interpretative Releases Related to Accounting Matters.
229	Standard Instructions for Filing Forms under Securities Act of 1933 and Securities Exchange Act of 1934— Regulation S-K

Part 210—commonly known as Regulation S-X—is the most comprehensive codification of SEC accounting regulations. Part 211 incorporates in the CFR, by reference, two separately issued sets of documents: Accounting Series Releases and Staff Accounting Bulletins. Accounting Series Releases (ASRs)

are the SEC's official pronouncements. They generally deal with a single topic or issue related either to accounting practice, financial statement disclosure, or standards of conduct for independent auditors. Since their inception in 1937, nearly 300 ASRs have been issued. However, many have been withdrawn (e.g., due to obsolescence or being superseded by other ASRs). The Staff Accounting Bulletins (SABs) are not formal Commission rules. Rather, they are issued by the staff of the SEC to clarify positions on various accounting and financial reporting matters. The series began in 1975 and approximately 40 SABs have been issued to date.

In addition to these parts of the CFR, each of the major Acts administered by the SEC is afforded its own parts for (a) general rules and regulations, (b) interpretative releases, and (c) prescribed forms (i.e., statements). The parts devoted to the major Acts are:

Act	17 CFR Parts
Securities Act of 1933	230, 231, 239
Securities Exchange Act of 1934	240, 241, 249
Public Utility Holding Company Act of 1935	250, 251, 259
Investment Company Act of 1940	270, 271, 274

Part 256 of the CFR contains the uniform systems of accounts for service company subsidiaries of public utility holding companies. Part 257 of the CFR contains the vestiges of a uniform system of accounts for public utility holding companies. Both of these uniform systems were promulgated under the Public Utility Holding Company Act of 1935.

Regulation S-X

Regulation S-X (17 CFR Part 210) contains the basic accounting regulations that implement the Securities Act of 1933, the Securities Exchange Act of 1934, the Public Utility Holding Company Act of 1935, and the Investment Company Act of 1940. Regulation S-X can be viewed as dealing with three basic topics: (a) rules controlling audits of registrants, (b) rules controlling the form and content of the basic financial statements and supporting schedules of registrants, and (c) specialized rules for specific types of registrants.

Audits. The SEC's basic rules relating to audits are contained in 17 CFR 210.2:

§210.2	— 01	Qualification of Accountants
	— 02	Accountants Reports
	— 03	Examinations of Financial Statements by Foreign Government Auditors
	— 04	Examinations of Financial Statement of Persons Other than the Registrant
	— 05	Examination of Financial Statements by More than One Accountant

In these sections, the SEC addresses such issues as the independence of auditors [17 CFR 210.2-01], the format requirements of the auditors' reports [17 CFR 210.2-02 (a)] (for example, they must be manually signed), and the content requirements of the auditors' reports [17 CFR 210.2-02 (b) through (d)] wherein the representations to be made by the auditors and the basis for their opinions are discussed. The rather

brief discussion of these and other audit-related topics at this point in the CFR is complemented by many Accounting Series Releases (ASRs). For example, over 20 individual ASRs deal with topics related to auditing standards, practices, and requirements and auditor independence.

Form and Content of Financial Statements and Schedules. The most frequently referenced sections of Regulation S-X are those that deal with the form and content of the basic financial statements and their supporting schedules. These major sections of Regulation S-X are:

§210.3	General Instructions as to Financial Statements
.3A	Consolidated and Combined Financial Statements
.4	Rules of General Application
.11	Contents of Statements of Other Stockholders' Equity
.11A	Statement of Source and Application of Funds
.12	Form and Content of Schedules

In these sections, the rules of disclosure that are generally applicable to all types of registrants are enumerated. The accounting provisions enunciated in these sections are very much in conformity with generally accepted accounting principles (GAAP). This is not accidental. Both the SEC and the accounting profession (most notably the American Institute of Certified Public Accountants, its Accounting Principles Board—from 1959 until 1973 —and the Financial Accounting Standards Board—since 1973) have attempted to work together in developing generally accepted accounting principles (GAAP). While legally the SEC has the right to mandate any individual disclosure rules or the complete set of accounting principles for its registrants to follow, it has historically looked to the private sector's standard-setting bodies for the initiative in improving accounting standards, subject to SEC oversight and concurrence.

Up until recently, there was a certain amount of diversity found between the financial statement disclosures required under the 1933 Act and the 1934 Act, and the annual report issued to shareholders. The SEC initiated its "Integration Project" to simplify and make consistent its basic disclosure requirements. One result of this effort has been the identification of a *minimum disclosure package* which is to be contained in filings under the 1933 Act and the 1934 Act, and in the annual report to shareholders. Further, it has eliminated many of its requirements that were duplicative of GAAP.

Over time the SEC has tended to accomplish its goal of full and fair disclosure through *more extensive disclosure* requirements (than GAAP) or *supplementary disclosure* requirements. An example of the former (i.e., more extensive disclosure) is the extensive set of schedules that must be filed giving the details of individual components of the basic financial statements. An example of the latter (i.e., supplementary disclosure) was the SEC's requirement that certain replacement cost information (not then required under GAAP) be disclosed as a part of or following the footnotes to the financial statements. The SEC has liberally employed procedures such

as these to accomplish its legislative mandate while, at the same time, not upsetting the evolutionary development of GAAP. Those few instances where the SEC and the accounting profession have collided on issues of accounting principles (e.g., accounting for the investment credit; accounting for oil and gas reserves) have not ruptured their longstanding mode of co-operation.

Specialized Requirements. The SEC has accommodated the problem of the heterogeneous operating circumstances of its registrants by promulgating separate disclosure requirements for various categories of registrants:

§210.5	Commercial and Industrial Companies
.5A	Companies in the Promotional, Exploratory, or Development Stage
.6	Investment Companies (including Employee Stock Option Purchase Plans)
.7	Insurance Companies
.8	Committees Issuing Certificates of Deposit
.9	Banks and Bank Holding Companies
.10	Natural Persons

Any registrant not falling under one of the specialized categories follows the regulations of 17 CFR 210.5 for commercial and industrial companies.

The SEC tailors the accounting disclosure of the various categories of registrants by (a) varying the number of schedules that must be filed, (b) varying the disclosure within individual statements, and (c) requiring additional financial statements. An example of

(a) is the disclosure of commercial and industrial companies that are required to file as many as 13 schedules compared to that of management investment companies that are required to file a maximum of 8 schedules. An example of (b) is the following disclosure required of development stage companies [17 CFR 210.5A-02]:

> Additional information required to be included in financial statements filed by companies in the development stage.
>
> (a) Financial statements included in a registration statement or periodic report filed by a company in the development stage shall include additional information, as follows:
>
> (1) In a balance sheet, include any cumulative net losses reported with a descriptive caption such as "deficit accumulated during the development stage" in the stockholders' equity section.
>
> (2) In an income statement, show amounts of revenue and expenses for each period covered by the income statement and, in addition, cumulative amounts from the company's inception.
>
> (3) In a statement of source and application of funds or changes in financial position, show the sources and uses of financial resources for each period for which an income statement is presented and, in addition, cumulative amounts from the company's inception.
>
> (4) In a statement of stockholders' equity, show from the company's inception:
>
> (i) For each issuance, the date and number of shares of stock, warrants, rights, or other equity securities issued for cash and for other consideration.
>
> (ii) For each issuance, the dollar amounts (per share or other equity unit and in total) assigned to the consideration received for shares of stock, warrants, rights, or other equity securities. Dollar amounts shall be assigned to any non-cash consideration received.
>
> (iii) For each issuance involving non-cash consideration, the nature of the non-cash consideration and the basis for assigning amounts.
>
> (b) The financial statements shall be identified as those of a development stage company and shall include a description of the nature of the development stage activities in which the company is engaged.
>
> (c) The financial statements for the first fiscal year in which a company is no longer considered to be in the development stage shall disclose that in prior years it had been in the development stage. If financial statements for prior years are presented for comparative purposes, the cumulative amounts and other disclosures required by paragraphs (a) and (b) of this section need not be shown.

Finally, an example of (c) are management investment companies that must file the following statements (in addition to those generally required of all entities):

Statement of Realized Gain or Loss on Investments

Statement of Unrealized Appreciation or Depreciation of Investments

Statement of Changes in Net Assets

Statement of Sources of Net Assets

Regulation S-K

Regulation S-K (17 CFR Part 229) contains the requirements for the nonfinancial statement sections of registration statements and periodic reports (e.g., annual reports) under the 1933 and 1934 Acts.

Regulation S-K enumerates the following "items" and gives the form and content requirements for their presentation when they are called for in a particular report:

Item	Title
1	Description of Business
2	Description of Property
3	Directors and Executive Officers
4	Management Remuneration
5	Legal Proceedings
6	Security Ownership of Certain Beneficial Owners
7	Exhibits
8	(Reserved)
9	Market Price of Registered Common Stock and Related Security Holder Matters
10	Selected Financial Data
11	Management's Discussion and Analysis of Financial Condition and Results of Operation
12	Supplementary Financial Information

While most of Regulation S-K dwells on the registrant's narrative presentation, there are items that call for the disclosure of certain financial information. For example, in the *description of business* (item 1) the registrant is required to present industry segment information that discloses, among other things, operating profit (or loss) and identifiable assets by segments. Additionally, items 10, 11, and 12 are particularly important for accountants. They require the disclosure and/or discussion of:

Item 10: Extensive financial data for last five years (e.g., net sales, income from continuing operations, in total and per common share), total assets, long-term obligations, etc.

Item 11: Discussion of liquidity, capital resources, and results of operations.

Item 12: Selected quarterly financial data; disagreements (with auditors) on accounting and financial disclosure matters.

SEC FORMS

The SEC requirements as to what forms must be filed vary from act to act. Further, within the individual acts, there is usually a myriad of forms that potentially apply to registrants (e.g., under the 1933 Act, there are over 20 types of registration statements.) The SEC is currently proposing three new registration forms under the 1933 Act which would significantly affect the reporting of companies who are issuing securities. This is another initiative under the SEC's "Integration Project" for simplifying the reporting burden of registrants. The following discussion is intended to summarize the interplay of the current reporting requirements.

Registration under the 1933 Act is required each and every time a registrant wants to issue securities (most commonly on Form S-1). Registration under the 1934 Act (most commonly on Form 10) is required whenever a company is to have its securities traded on a national exchange or on over-the-counter markets. Registration under each Act (while the forms are similar) is a discrete undertaking. Meeting the registration requirements under one Act does not satisfy the registration requirements under the other. The registration statements are periodically updated by annual, quarterly, or intermittent reports unless the company has less than 300 shareholders. For example, most registrants under the 1934 Act file an annual report, Form 10-K; a quarterly report, Form 10-Q; and, are required to file a current report, Form 8-K, when one or more of the following events occur: (a) a change in the registrant's auditor, (b) filing or settlement of material litigation, (c) acquisition or disposition of a material subsidiary, (d) default on a security, etc.

There is a similar meshing of most of the other "registration" acts administered by the SEC; that is, (a) registration under one act does not preclude having to register under another act; and (b) registration statements for the entity (as well as those for a single issue of securities) must be updated over time by the filing of annual, quarterly, etc., reports.

ANNUAL REPORT TO SHAREHOLDERS

Under its control over proxy solicitation, the SEC has effective control over form and content of the annual reports (including audited financial statements) registrants send to their shareholders. Under the 1934 Act, the SEC is empowered to control disclosures that must be made by registrants when they (e.g., the management) are going to solicit shareholders' proxies (i.e., the right to cast the shareholders' vote on an issue or issues to be placed before

shareholders, generally at the annual shareholders' meeting). These requirements are contained in 17 CFR 240.14 a, b, and c. The rules require that the audited financial statements included in the annual report be the same as to form and content as those included in the annual report to the SEC (i.e., Form 10-K).

LEGAL LIABILITY UNDER THE SECURITIES LAW

One of the things that SEC work is most noted for among accountants is the differences that it occasions in the auditor's legal exposure. For non-SEC work, the auditor's basic legal exposure can be summarized as follows: First, the auditor is legally liable for negligence only to the client and third parties who were known by the auditor to be intended users of the financial statements; however, in the case of gross negligence (or fraud) the auditor would be held liable to all parties who suffered damages. Second, all parties who claimed damages resulting from the misleading fianancial statements must establish (a) that they were damaged, (b) that their damages resulted from reliance on the financial statements, and (c) that financial statements were misleading due to the fact that the auditor was negligent (or committed a fraudulent act).

The auditor's legal liability under the 1934 Act is very similar to that summarized above. However, under the 1933 Act, the conditions are different: First, the auditor is liable to *all* damaged parties for any form of negligence (or fraud). Second, the damaged party need *only* establish damages and allege that the financial statements were deficient; he need not prove that he relied on the financial statements. Third, the burden of proof is on the auditor to establish either (a) that the financial statements were *not* deficient or, alternatively, (b) that the auditor was *not* negligent in the conduct of the examination, or (c) that the damaged party's loss was due to matters unrelated to the deficient statements, or (d) that the damaged party knew of the deficient financial statements. Thus, under the 1933 Act, the preponderance of the burden of proof falls on the auditor to establish his innocence.

FOREIGN CORRUPT PRACTICES ACT

The Foreign Corrupt Practices Act of 1977 (FCPA) was an out-growth of Congress's public ire at the widespread disclosures of unethical and illegal corporate activity, particularly in the foreign arena. Specifically, the FCPA prohibits the payment of funds (or anything of value) by U.S. companies to foreign political and government officials where the aim is to influence the officials' decisions to divert business to the U.S. companies. The FCPA was limited to payments to foreign officials since the equivalent domestic behavior was already illegal under various state and Federal statutes.

The Department of Justice administers the antibribery provisions of the FCPA. The accounting provisions of the Act (discussed in the next paragraph) are administered jointly by the SEC (for companies registered under the 1934 Act) and the Department of Justice (for all other companies).

The FCPA contains accounting provisions that require companies to devise and maintain a system of internal accounting control that provides reasonable assurance that transactions are properly authorized and recorded, and that the assets of the company are properly controlled. The internal accounting control features of the FCPA are applicable to companies' *foreign and domestic* operations. Violation of the FCPA carries the potential for criminal and civil actions (e.g., by stockholders' suing management for loss of funds—such as foregone profits—occasioned by weak controls).

While there is a clear onus on the management of a company subject to the FCPA, the water is a bit muddy when the position of the company's independent auditor under the FCPA is reviewed. While the independent auditor is *not* held responsible by the FCPA, the issue of management's reliance on the independent auditor's review of the company's internal controls does raise some new issues. For example, under generally accepted auditing standards the independent auditor is required to report (to the client) on material weaknesses found in its internal control system. What will be the evidential impact of a favorable report from the independent auditor when a violation of the FCPA is alleged? Can a management that has been found guilty of violating the FCPA's internal control provisions have recourse against an independent auditor claiming reliance on the auditor's review of the internal control system that was not informative as to the violations filed under the

FCPA? Since the FCPA has not been fleshed out by extensive agency regulations and interpretations, and litigated in criminal and civil cases, its operational parameters are unclear. However, the law was intended by Congress to strictly limit undesirable practices by registrants. It is very likely to be strictly construed against all parties involved in any eventual litigation.

PUBLIC UTILITY HOLDING COMPANY ACT

Under the Public Utility Holding Company Act, there are some accounting provisions not found under the other laws that the SEC administers. The SEC's regulations envision three types of entities in a holding company's structure: (a) the holding company itself, (b) mutual service or subsidiary service companies, and (c) operating gas and/or electric utilities. The financial statement requirements of the holding company are controlled by the accounting requirements of Regulation S-X (17 CFR Part 210). This is stated in 17 CFR 250.26 (a) (1). There is a part of the CFR (17 CFR Part 257) entitled "Uniform System of Accounts for Public Utility Holding Companies." Currently, this consists only of an appendix that enumerates the record retention rules under the Act. At one time was a uniform system of accounts in this part of the CRF. However, as holding company systems were simplified by divestiture and as Regulation S-X was expanded, it was felt that the rules contained in Regulation S-X were adequate to control holding companies' disclosures.

At the other end of the spectrum, the individual operating utilities are bound by the following provision [17 CFR 250.27 (a)]:

> Classification of accounts prescribed for utility companies not already subject thereto.
>
> (a) Every registered holding company and subsidiary thereof, which is a public utility company and which is not required by either the Federal Power Commission or a State commission to conform to a classification of accounts, shall keep its accounts, insofar as it is an electric utility company, in the manner currently prescribed for similar companies by the Federal Power Commission or, and insofar as it is a gas utility company, in the manner currently recommended by the National Association of Railroad and Utilities Commissioners, except any company whose public utility activities are so limited that the application to it of such system of accounts is clearly inappropriate. A company claiming that its activities are thus limited, shall apply to the Commission for written instructions to that effect.

Thus, operating utilities are required to follow an established uniform system of accounts promulgated by a regulatory agency such as the Federal Energy Regulatory Commission (formerly the Federal Power Commission) or one promulgated by the National Association of Regulatory Utility Commissioners (which many state commissions employ).

The SEC has promulgated a "Uniform System of Accounts for Mutual Service Companies and Subsidiary Service Companies" [17 CFR Part 256]. The role of mutual and subsidiary service companies within the context of a public utility holding company is to " . . . insure the efficient and economical performance of services or construction or sale of goods . . . at the cost fairly and equitably allocated . . . and at a reasonable saving over the cost of comparable services or construction performed or goods sold by independent persons." [17 CFR 250.86 (a)].

The SEC looks very skeptically at intra-holding company transactions since such transactions are not the result of arm's length bargaining. In 17 CFR 250.90 (a) (1), the holding company is virtually prohibited from making any sale of any goods, services, or construction to a member of the holding company. In 17 CFR 250.90 (a) (2), service companies within the holding company are permitted to make such sales *at cost* determined in accordance with the following provisions [17 CFR 250.91]:

Determination of cost.

(a) Subject to the provisions of this section and of any other applicable rule, regulation, or order of the Commission, a transaction shall be deemed to be performed at not more than cost if the price (taking into account all charges) does not exceed a fair and equitable allocation of expenses (including the price paid for goods) plus reasonable compensation for necessary capital procured through the issuance of capital stock (or similar securities of an unincorporated company).

(b) Direct charges shall be made so far as costs can be identified and related to the particular transactions involved without excessive effort or expense. Other elements of cost, including taxes, interest, other overhead, and compensation for the use of capital procured by the issu-

ance of capital stock (or similar securities of an unincorporated company) shall be fairly and equitably allocated. Interest on borrowed capital and compensation for the use of capital shall represent a reasonable return on only the amount of capital reasonably necessary for the performance of services or construction for, or the selling of goods to, customers for whom transactions are required by the rules of the Commission to be performed at cost. Such amount shall not include the cost of assignment of, or any capitalization of, any service, sales, or construction contract.

(c) Any expense (including the price paid for goods) incurred in a transaction with an associated company of the performing or selling company (directly or through one or more other associate companies thereof), to the extent that it exceeds the cost of such transaction to such associate company, shall not be included in determining cost to such performing or selling company.

(d) Any expense (including the price paid for goods) incurred in a transaction with a person other than an associate company but not at arm's-length, to the extent that it exceeds the expense at which the performing or selling company might reasonably be expected to obtain elsewhere, or to furnish itself, comparable performance, goods, capital, or other items of expense involved (giving due regard to quality, quantity, regularity of supply, and other factors entering into the calculation of a fair price), shall not be included in determining cost to such performing or selling company.

Thus, while closely monitoring the reasonableness of overall cost, the service company is allowed a return on capital.

The uniform system of accounts for service companies (found in 17 CFR Part 256) was originally issued in 1936 and completely revised in 1979. The uniform system provides a standardized account numbering structure:

100s and 300s for Assets

200s for Liabilities and Owners' Equity

400s and 900s for Revenues and Expenses

This numbering structure was patterned after that prescribed by the FERC for electric utilities. The uniform system contains a brief discussion of the content of the major accounts and notes that, in lieu of specific coverage in 17 CFR Part 256, service companies are to follow the accounting provisions of Regulation S-X. The uniform system does contain some cost accounting provisions that apply to such facets of service companies' operations as the determination of the cost of services rendered to associated or nonassociated companies.

REFERENCE NOTES

1. U.S., Securities and Exchange Commission, *Annual Report 1979*, p. 113.

2. *Ibid.,* p. 86.

3. *Ibid.,* p. 125.

4. *Ibid.,* p. 103.

Chapter 19

Internal Revenue Service

The Internal Revenue Service (IRS) is a component of the Department of the Treasury. The IRS is headed by the Commissioner of Internal Revenue, who is appointed by the President, with the approval of the Senate. The Commissioner operates out of the IRS National Office in Washington, D.C. He is assisted by a Deputy Commissioner, the Chief Counsel (the IRS's highest legal official), and eight Assistant Commissioners, each dealing with one of the following functional areas:

Taxpayer Service and Return Processing

Compliance

Inspection

Administration

Planning and Research

Technical

Economic Stabilization

Employee Plans and Exempt Organizations

There are seven Regional Commissioners, each of which heads one of the following regions:

Region	Headquarters
Central	Cincinnati
Mid-Atlantic	Philadelphia
Mid-West	Chicago
North Atlantic	New York
Southeast	Atlanta
Southwest	Dallas
Western	San Francisco

The organizational structure of the regional offices mirrors that of the national office (i.e., Assistant Regional Commissioners and Regional Counsel).

The regions are further divided into districts. There are 58 districts, each under the auspices of a District Director. The district offices are generally the point of initial contact between the IRS and taxpayers on such matters as audits, conferences on items of disagreement, fraud investigations, etc.

Each region also has at least one IRS service center (three regions—the North Atlantic, the Southeast, and the Western—have two each). These service centers perform the bulk of the data accumulation and processing function for the regions. For example, all tax returns are mailed by the taxpayers directly to the regional service centers.

IRS FUNCTIONS

The basic function of the IRS is to enforce the Federal internal revenue laws (including income taxes, estate and gift taxes, employment taxes, and excise taxes) except for those sections dealing with alcohol, tobacco, firearms, and explosives, which are administered by other units within the Department of the Treasury (i.e., the Bureau of Alcohol, Tobacco, and Firearms Control). Up until 1972, even these areas were under the purview of the IRS. The specific approaches that the IRS takes in enforcing the revenue laws can be classified as follows:

1. *Dissemination of information.* A great deal of IRS effort goes into providing material (forms, instructions, etc.) to taxpayers and tax return preparers to enable them to determine the proper amount of tax that is due.

2. *Status approval.* The IRS is delegated the authority to approve the tax status of certain entities. For example, entities that are organized to be tax exempt (e.g., charitable associations) must have their status affirmed by the IRS.

3. *Review of tax returns.* The IRS's role in the enforcement of the tax laws is most visible in the review of tax returns that have been filed (or alternatively, in pursuit of those who do not file). Ideally, this process is objective, with the IRS being concerned with both over- and under-payments by taxpayers.

4. *Pursuit of underpayment (or non-payment) of taxes.* Based upon the review, if the IRS finds the taxpayer to be in noncompliance with the law it pursues the government's rights under the law.

THE CODE

The IRS is officially charged with the enforcement of a section of the U.S. Code—specifically, Title 26. This section of the U.S. Code is often referred to as the Internal Revenue Code of 1954. This is because the last comprehensive consolidation of the Code took place in 1954. Since that time, all tax legislation has resulted in amendments to the basic 1954 framework. (Prior to the 1954 consolidation, the last comprehensive codification was that of the Internal Revenue Code of 1939.) The current configuration of the major parts of the Code is:

Title 26	–	*Internal Revenue Code*
Subtitle A	–	Income Taxes
Subtitle B	–	Estate and Gift Taxes
Subtitle C	–	Employment Taxes
Subtitle D	–	Miscellaneous Excise Taxes

Interpretation of the Code—
Regulations, Rulings,
Procedures

The Code is the law that the IRS administers. The IRS is empowered to issue such pronouncements as it deems necessary in administering the code. The main pronouncements issued by the IRS are IRS regulations, revenue rulings, and revenue procedures.

IRS Regulations. Title 26 of the Code of Federal Regulations contains the IRS's regulations. These regulations contain the IRS's most comprehensive and authoritative interpretation of the Federal tax law (i.e., the Code). The following listing of the major sections of Title 26, when compared with the previous listing of sections of the Code, illustrates the correspondence in structure:

Title 26	—	*Internal Revenue Service*
Subchapter A	—	Income Taxes
Subchapter B	—	Estate and Gift Taxes
Subchapter C	—	Employment Taxes
Subchapter D	—	Miscellaneous Excise Taxes

In citing the IRS's regulations, either of the following forms is acceptable: 26 CFR 1.31 or Section 1.31 (with Title 26 of the CFR being implicit). The latter form is used almost exclusively in the area of income tax accounting. It will be followed in this chapter.

Revenue Rulings. Revenue rulings are official pronouncements of the IRS. However, they are not comprehensive in that they deal only with a *specific* set of facts. Thus, their nature is more restricted than that of regulations. While they are followed by the IRS itself, they are not accepted by the courts as having the same legal standing as is accorded the regulations.

The IRS also issues *individual rulings* that are even more restricted than revenue rulings. They are issued to a specific taxpayer and only bind the IRS for a specific transaction. At one time, these rulings were not disclosed to the general public. Now, the IRS makes public the essence of the factual situation and its position on most private rulings. The IRS is selective in agreeing to issue such rulings.

Revenue rulings and individual rulings are issued by the National Office of the IRS. District Directors can issue *determination letters* at the request of individual taxpayers. These are generally used for *completed* (as opposed to prospective) transactions. A determination letter gives the District Director's interpretation of how the law is to be applied to the transaction(s) in question. Determination letters are *not* published. A determination letter is only divulged to the taxpayer who requested it.

Revenue Procedures. Revenue procedures are generally issued by the IRS to facilitate the administration of the tax laws. They typically deal with procedural matters such as how taxpayers can file for extensions, request permission to change either their taxable year or specific accounting procedures (e.g., inventory costing methods), etc.

Judicial Precedents. There is another authoritative source of "regulations" that is distilled from court decisions in tax cases. In order to appreciate this source, it is necessary to understand how tax cases arise and get into the court system. Figure 19-1 illustrates the flow of a tax case within the IRS appeals system. Basically, the flow of the appeals process is as follows:

1. All returns are filed with the IRS.
2. Some returns are selected for examination.
3. Of those examined, some are found (by the IRS) to warrant an adjustment. If the taxpayer does not agree to the adjustment, he (or she) can pursue his rights in court.
4. At the "Choice of Action," the taxpayer decides the route of appeal. If the taxpayer elects *not* to pay the tax due per the IRS, the case must be taken to the Tax Court.
5. If the taxpayer elects to pay the tax due per the IRS, the case can be taken to *either* the Court of Claims or the U.S. District Court after the taxpayer files for a refund.
6. If the taxpayer (or the IRS) loses in the court of original jurisdiction, an appeal can be taken to the U.S. Court of Appeals and/or the U.S. Supreme Court.

The outcomes of cases that enter the court system create a body of case law. This case law serves as an additional source of authoritative interpretation of the law and the IRS regulations.

Taxpayer

Up to this point, the term *taxpayer* has been used to cover all entities (e.g., individuals, corporations). The remainder of the chapter will concentrate on the income tax regulations as they affect entities engaged in a trade or business. This would include sole proprietorships, partnerships, and corporations. Sole proprietorship and partnership are *not* taxed per se. Rather, the earnings therefrom are attributable (and subject to tax) as earnings of the individual proprietor or partners. Further, certain corporations (under Subchapter S of the Code) can elect to have their earnings or losses passed through to their stockholders and enter into the determination of their tax as individuals.

Tax Rates

The Federal tax system is generally considered to be "progressive" (i.e., as taxable income increases, successively higher marginal tax rates apply). The rate structure for corporations is generally regarded as less progressive than that for individuals. The 1980 rate structure for corporations [26 USC 1.11] is shown in Table 19-1. This structure compares with a tax rate of 70 percent for individuals in the highest tax bracket.

Reasonableness

One concept that runs throughout the entire Code and regulations is that of reasonableness. For example, the Code provides that businesses are allowed to deduct from revenues those expenses that are " . . . ordinary and necessary . . . in carrying on any trade or business . . . " [26 USC 162 (a)].

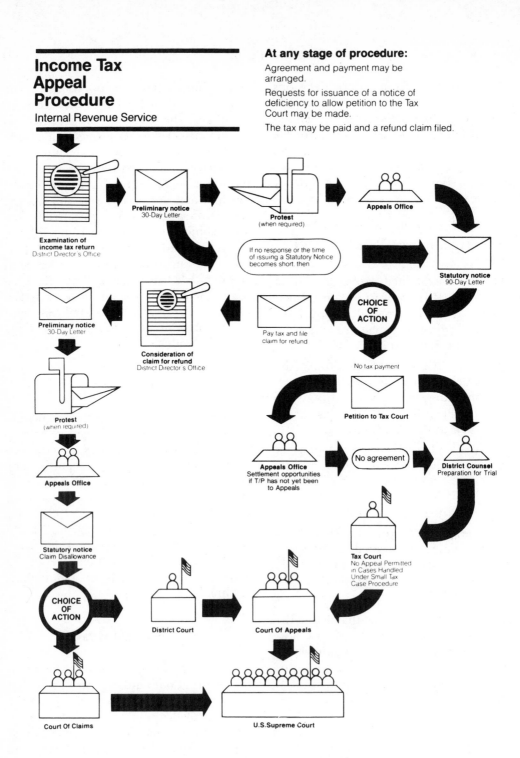

FIGURE 19-1. Income Tax Appeal Procedure (*Source:* IRS Publication 556).

TABLE 19-1
1980 Rate Structure for Corporations

For a corporation with taxable income	The income tax is
Under $25,001	17% of taxable income
From $25,001 to $50,000	$4,250 plus 20% of taxable income over $25,000
From $50,001 to $75,000	$9,250 plus 30% of taxable income over $50,000
From $75,001 to $100,000	$16,750 plus 40% of taxable income over $75,000
Over $100,000	$26,750 plus 46% of taxable income over $100,000

Later, the code permits taxpayers to use their established method of accounting for tax purposes unless it " . . . does not clearly reflect income . . ." [26 USC 446 (b)].

A specific illustration of the overall test of reasonableness is the requirement that compensation paid to employees be reasonable in light of the services rendered. Where there are individuals who are both shareholders *and* employees of closely held corporations, the IRS is particularly concerned about the level of salaries paid to these individuals. That is, these individuals could avoid the "double taxation" of dividends by paying excess salaries to themselves, which salaries would be deductible by the corporation and only taxable to the individual; any dividends of the corporation would be paid out of *after tax* net income (and *not* deductible as expenses by the corporation), and still taxable to the individual. The IRS uses such factors as the nature of services rendered, the salary level of comparable positions in other companies, the existence of a reasonable dividend payment by the company to its shareholders, etc., to establish (or, alternatively refute) a presumption of reasonableness.

Taxable Year

26 USC 441 and Section 1.441-1 of the IRS regulations control the determination of a taxpayer's taxable year. A taxpayer's taxable year is either (a) its annual accounting period (if it is a calendar year or a fiscal year) or (b) the calendar year if the taxpayer has no established annual accounting period (as is generally true for individuals).

If a taxpayer wishes to change his taxable year, he must obtain prior approval from the IRS. When a change in the taxable year is granted, special provisions are applied to any shortened period arising from the transition to the new taxable year (e.g., so that the taxpayer cannot take undue advantage of the low tax rates on the initial brackets of income in *both* the shortened period *and* its full taxable year).

Method of Accounting

The regulations (Section 1.446) provide that a taxpayer is to compute his taxable income on the basis regularly used in keeping his books. Specifically mentioned as acceptable are (a) the accrual method (governed by generally accepted accounting principles), (b) the cash receipts and disbursements method, and (c) combinations of (a) and (b), i.e., so-called "modified cash basis" systems. This overall permissiveness of methods is modified by several considerations:

1. The IRS can disallow *any* method in total or a specific accounting procedure if, in its opinion, the method or procedure does not clearly reflect income.

2. For all entities engaged in a trade or business where inventory is material in amount, it (the inventory) must be properly accounted for in computing income (e.g., cash basis entities cannot charge purchases to expense when paid for; they must await actual sale or disposition of the inventory).

3. Where the IRS Code and regulations differ from the taxpayer's established accounting procedures, the Code and regulations must be followed.

4. Taxpayers can elect to employ different accounting procedures (e.g., methods of depreciation such as straight-line versus an accelerated method) for financial statement purposes versus taxable income determination. The only exception to this is the use of the LIFO inventory method. If the taxpayer uses LIFO for tax purposes, it must also be used for financial statement purposes.[1] This is required by the Code [26 USC 472 (c)]:

> Subsection (a) shall apply only if the taxpayer establishes to the satisfaction of the Secretary that the taxpayer has used no procedure other than that specified in paragraphs (1) and (3) of subsection (b) in inventorying such goods

to ascertain the income, profit, or loss of the first taxable year for which the method described in subsection (b) is to be used, for the purpose of a report or statement covering such taxable year—
> (1) to shareholders, partners, or other proprietors, or to beneficiaries, or
> (2) for credit purposes.

The IRS regulations enforce this provision of the law [Section 1.472-2 (e)]:

> The taxpayer shall establish to the satisfaction of the commissioner that the taxpayer, in ascertaining income, profit, or loss of the taxable year for which the LIFO inventory method is first used or for any subsequent taxable year, for credit purposes or for the purpose of reports to shareholders, partners, or other proprietors, or to beneficiaries, has not used an inventory method other than that referred to in §1.472-1 or at variance with the requirement referred to in paragraph (c) of this section. The taxpayer's use of market value in lieu of cost or his issuance of reports or credit statements covering a period of operations less than the whole of the taxable year is not considered at variance with this requirement.

ACCOUNTING

The more than 6,000 pages of the Code and regulations are a blend of legal, accounting, and economic concepts. In the following paragraphs, an attempt will be made to characterize some of the basic differences between the Internal Revenue Code's approach for determinning taxable income vis-á-vis the more familiar approach of generally accepted accounting principles' determination of income for financial reporting purposes.

Revenue Recognition

A taxpayer's basis of revenue recognition is generally determined by his accounting method (e.g., cash basis, accrual basis). However, taxpayers on the accrual basis are generally required to report revenue received in advance (of its being earned) as income in the year of receipt. There are certain exceptions to this. For example, publishers of periodicals (which typically have subscription revenue collected in advance) and certain membership organizations (which collect dues on a prepaid basis) are allowed to report their revenue as it is *earned* rather than when it is *received.*

Inventory and Cost of Sales

Taxpayers are allowed to use most of the conventional methods of accounting for inventories (and thus determining cost of goods sold) that are allowed under generally accepted accounting principles. For example, specific identification, first-in, first-out (FIFO) and last-in, first-out (LIFO) are allowable methods of *costing* inventories. Further, the lower-of-cost-or-market procedure of inventory valuation can be applied (but not in the case of LIFO) to write down inventories to their market value where it is less than their cost.

Recently, a case involving inventories was appealed all the way to the U.S. Supreme Court. It illustrates a number of the points previously discussed in this chapter (e.g., the relationship between the IRS Code and regulations and generally accepted accounting principles; the IRS concept of "clearly reflecting income"; the use of Revenue Rulings and Revenue Procedures). In this case, the taxpayer (Thor Power Tool Company) followed a procedure of writing its excess inventory (inventory not currently needed in the course of business) down to an extremely low scrap value (below normal market value) at the same time that the items written down were being sold at current market prices. This write-down resulted in higher expense and, thus, lower taxes. The taxpayer claimed that the procedure was generally accepted. However, the IRS claimed that it did not reflect the taxpayer's true income. The taxpayer appealed the IRS's disallowance of its method all the way to the U.S. Supreme Court. The Supreme Court decision was to uphold the IRS's position. Subsequently, the IRS issued a Revenue Ruling (No. 80-60) that informed other taxpayers that this decision was to be the basis for disallowing similar write-downs. The IRS also issued a Revenue Procedure (No. 80-5) that informed taxpayers (and tax return preparers) how they could file for permission to change their accounting procedures to conform to the IRS's interpretation of the decision.

Depreciation

The IRS's rules on depreciation are based on depreciation practices acceptable under generally accepted accounting principles. Generally, the cost or "basis" of assets eligible for depreciation coincides with that determined for financial reporting purposes. The following methods of depreciation are allowed by the IRS: straight-line, declining balance, and sum-of-the-years' digits. The declining balance method can only be used with an effective rate that is, at most, twice the straight-line rate. That is, if an asset has a 10 year life, the straight-line rate is 10 percent. If the declining balance method were used, the maximum rate yielded by the method would be limited to 20 percent. There are other limitations on the declining balance method when applied to specific types of property.

In establishing the useful life and residual value (salvage value) of depreciable property, the taxpayer can either establish his own estimates based on unique operating circumstances (e.g., as supported by experience) or use the factors provided by the IRS in its *Class Life Asset Depreciation Range* (CLADR) system.

To encourage businesses to invest in long-lived assets, the Code allows the deduction of 20 percent of the cost of tangible personal property (used in the business) if the property has a life of six years or more. This is in addition to the normal first year depreciation taken on the asset. This "bonus" depreciation is limited to $2,000 per taxpayer per year.

Depletion and Amortization

Taxpayers are generally allowed amortized (on intangible assets) and depletion (on natural resources). The IRS's rules on amortization generally limit its recognition to the straight-line method. Further, certain intangible assets that are subject to amortization for financial statement purposes are not amortizable for tax purposes (e.g., goodwill recognized in purchasing an entity).

The depletion expense for most natural resources (e.g., oil) can be computed on *either* a cost basis (as is the case under generally accepted accounting principles) *or* percentage basis. Cost-based depletion is generally accrued on a unit of production basis (i.e., each unit extracted is assigned a uniform per unit charge for the total cost of the resource deposit being worked). Percentage depletion permits taxpayers to deduct a percentage of the gross revenue received. This percentage depletion is peculiar to the tax Code and has no counterpart in generally accepted accounting principles. It is an imputed cost that derives its acceptance as a deduction only from the fact that it was included in the Code by Congress.

Sale of Depreciable Assets

When assets are disposed of, taxpayers typically recognize a gain or loss that affects the amount of taxes. An exception is where taxpayers exchange "like" property. For example, not long ago it was reported that the owner of pro football Team A sold the team to a new owner and then the original owner purchased pro football Team B, in another city. If this had occurred, the gain on the sale of Team A would have been taxable. What actually did occur was that the new owner purchased Team B and then the owners *exchanged* teams (i.e., like assets used in a business). This resulted in no tax being due by the original owner. When (and if) he were to sell Team B, the tax at that time will effectively be for the gain resulting from the period that *both* teams were held.

In the case of business assets that are *sold,* the rules on the tax effect of the gain or loss are quite complex. In general, the rules center on the allocation of any gains or losses on the sale of such assets between that portion that affects ordinary income and that portion, if any, that would receive a more preferential tax treatment.

Sale of Capital Assets

Assets that are *not* used in a trade or business generally qualify as *capital assets.* When these assets are held for a specified period (currently, over one year) and are sold at a gain, the gain generally results in less of a tax burden than an equivalent amount of ordinary income. First, losses on the sale of capital assets go to offset any gains on the sale of other capital assets. Any excess of losses over gains can be offset against ordinary income (but not for corporations) up to a limit of $3,000. Any remaining excess can be offset against the capital gains or ordinary income of other years.

Investment Credit

The tax code allows taxpayers a direct *credit* against their taxes due for certain investments in assets used in a trade or business. Most tangible business assets qualify except for buildings or their structural components. The asset must have a useful life of at least three years. The following percentage of cost of the asset qualifies, depending on the life of the asset:

Life	*% of Cost Qualified for Credit*
3–4 years	33 1/3%
5–6 years	66 2/3%
7 and over	100 %

The amount of the credit is 10 percent of the qualified cost. Only $100,000 of the cost of used assets can qualify in any year. There is a maximum credit that can be taken each year. Currently, it is $25,000 *plus* 70 percent of any tax in excess of $25,000. In 1982, this will increase to 90 percent. There is also an *additional* credit (another 10 percent) that is available on certain qualified energy property.

When property on which an investment credit has been taken is sold, some of the credit may be "recaptured" by the government. If it was not held for the length of time intended when the investment credit was taken, the taxpayer must recalculate the credit for the period actually held and pay any excess credit to the government. For example, if an asset was originally intended to be used for eight years, 100 percent of its cost would qualify for the credit. If it were actually held four years, only 33 1/3 percent would qualify. The credit taken on the excess would be repaid to the government.

Contributions

Taxpayers are allowed a deduction for contributions made to approved organizations (e.g., charitable and educational foundations). Corporations are limited to a maximum deduction of 5 percent of taxable income (before considering the deduction for contributions). The organizations that qualify are described, in general, in the Code and regulations. The IRS also publishes a detailed list of such organizations. Individuals are also subject to percentage limitations based upon income and the type of property contributed.

Carrybacks and Carryforwards

Accounting for income taxes attempts to divide the economic affairs of an entity into very finite periods (i.e., accounting periods). In the process, the entity is potentially subject to a rather myopic view of the transactions that affect the tax liability. For example, a new entity that has suffered operating losses of $10,000 in each of its first two years of existence earns a profit of $20,000 in its third year. Thus, the profit for the three year period is zero. Without some provision to overcome the problem of divorcing the single year's profit from the lack of profit for the three year period, an inequitable result (the year by year taxing of that profit) would be experienced by the taxpayer.

To overcome this problem, the Code provides for various "carryforward/carryback" opportunities. These opportunities exist for operating losses, capital losses, unused investment credits, and excess contributions.

TAX AVOIDANCE VERSUS TAX EVASION

Our tax system relies on voluntary compliance by taxpayers. True, the IRS does provide a positive incentive through its audits and the potential of being subject to fines and penalties —over and above the tax owed—for noncompliance. Yet, the system basi-

cally places the task of computing the tax that is due in the hands of the taxpayer. The IRS and those parties involved in the area of taxes (e.g., CPAs, attorneys) stress the need for tax planning (i.e., structuring transactions to minimize the tax burden). Further, there are many areas of the tax code that are subject to differing interpretations by knowledgeable individuals. Taxpayers have every right to use such "gray" areas to their benefit and allow the IRS to pursue any contradictory view that it may adopt. Tax planning and the settlement of doubtful provisions in one's behalf are both examples of legal *tax avoidance*.

On the other hand, *tax evasion* (the outright violation of the law) is *illegal*. Tax evasion can vary from refusing to file a return, to filing a return that is so grossly in error as to constitute fraud, to filing multiple returns (e.g., in order to receive multiple refunds from the government). Tax cases arise from both tax evasion and tax avoidance issues. However, only the former entail potential criminal penalties. Tax avoidance issues (for example, arising when the taxpayer and the IRS disagree on a "gray" area) are commonplace in our complex economic environment. In fact, many knowledgeable individuals feel that businesses engaged in complex transactions are probably not taking advantage of all of the benefits allowed by the Code if their tax returns do not have to be periodically defended against the questioning of the IRS.

TAX RETURNS

The taxpayer's reporting burden is, in part, fixed in that all taxpayers are required to complete a summary form on which their tax is computed. The basic forms for individuals are the 1040 and 1040A (the "short form"). The basic forms for corporations are the 1120 and 1120S (for small business corporations). The summary page of the 1120 is presented in Figure 19-2. Various other forms correspond to other tax entities' status (e.g., partnerships, nonprofit corporations, etc.).

These basic forms also entail a variable reporting requirement that is based on the complexity of the taxpayer's business. For example, line 21 of Form 1120 (see Figure 19-2), instructs the taxpayer to complete Form 4562 *if* any depreciation expense is claimed. Thus, a tax return is a variable length depending upon the taxpayer's individual circumstances. In the more complex tax returns there are literally hundreds of forms and supporting schedules that must be prepared before the taxpayer's taxable income is finally computed (along with the tax liability) on a summary schedule such as that in Figure 19-2.

SOCIOECONOMIC ASPECTS OF TAX REGULATION

This chapter has focused on the "micro" aspects of tax regulation (i.e., how taxes are levied upon individual taxpayers). It is important to understand that there are other "macro" aspects of tax regulation (i.e., how taxes fit into the overall structure of government regulation). Tax regulations have many goals, such as (a) raising of revenue to finance the government (probably the most commonly appreciated aspect), (b)

social control, (c) economic stimulation (or retardation), and (d) political considerations.

The first goal—financing the government—is the one that people primarily, if not exclusively, think of. However, it is important to consider the other goals. They help explain some of the convoluted provisions encountered in the law.

To illustrate the social control aspects of the tax regulations, consider the following:

1. Certain items and activities are regarded as being dangerous to the health and welfare of the general public. Their possession or use is often controlled (i.e., persons that produce or possess such items must file and pay taxes thus making their identity known) by the imposition of taxes. For example, the following items are subject to Federal excise taxes:

   Pistols and revolvers

   Wagering

   Alcoholic beverages

   Tobacco products

   Machine guns

2. Fines and penalties are generally levied (by the courts) for illegal acts or acts that are (at least) not in the public's interest. They are *not* deductible for tax purposes (i.e., they do not reduce the taxpayer's tax liability; he must, therefore, bear their full weight).

3. Expenditures for job training and child care facilities are afforded special tax advantages in order to encourage their incurrence by businesses.

Form 1120

Department of the Treasury
Internal Revenue Service

U.S. Corporation Income Tax Return

For calendar year 1980 or other tax year beginning
.................................., 1980, ending ...., 19......

1980

Check if a—

A. Consolidated return ☐
B. Personal Holding Co. ☐
C. Business Code No. (See page 8 of Instructions)

Use IRS label. Otherwise please print or type.

Name
Number and street
City or town, State, and ZIP code

D. Employer identification number (see Specific Instructions)

E. Date incorporated

F. Total assets (see Specific Instructions)
$

Gross Income	1 (a) Gross receipts or sales $...................... (b) Less returns and allowances $......................... Balance ▶	**1(c)**
	2 Cost of goods sold (Schedule A) and/or operations (attach schedule)	**2**
	3 Gross profit (subtract line 2 from line 1(c))	**3**
	4 Dividends (Schedule C)	**4**
	5 Interest on obligations of the United States and U.S. instrumentalities	**5**
	6 Other interest	**6**
	7 Gross rents	**7**
	8 Gross royalties	**8**
	9 (a) Capital gain net income (attach separate Schedule D)	**9(a)**
	(b) Net gain or (loss) from Form 4797, line 11(a), Part II (attach Form 4797)	**9(b)**
	10 Other income (see instructions—attach schedule)	**10**
	11 TOTAL income—Add lines 3 through 10	**11**

Deductions	12 Compensation of officers (Schedule E)	**12**
	13 (a) Salaries and wages .... 13(b) Less WIN and jobs credit(s) .... Balance ▶	**13(c)**
	14 Repairs (see instructions)	**14**
	15 Bad debts (Schedule F if reserve method is used)	**15**
	16 Rents	**16**
	17 Taxes	**17**
	18 Interest	**18**
	19 Contributions (not over 5% of line 30 adjusted per instructions—attach schedule) . . .	**19**
	20 Amortization (attach schedule)	**20**
	21 Depreciation from Form 4562 (attach Form 4562) ...., less depreciation claimed in Schedule A and elsewhere on return ...., Balance ▶	**21**
	22 Depletion	**22**
	23 Advertising	**23**
	24 Pension, profit-sharing, etc. plans (see instructions)	**24**
	25 Employee benefit programs (see instructions)	**25**
	26 Other deductions (attach schedule)	**26**
	27 TOTAL deductions—Add lines 12 through 26	**27**
	28 Taxable income before net operating loss deduction and special deductions (subtract line 27 from line 11) . .	**28**
	29 Less: (a) Net operating loss deduction (see instructions—attach schedule) . . **29(a)**	
	(b) Special deductions (Schedule I) . . . . **29(b)**	**29**
	30 Taxable income (subtract line 29 from line 28)	**30**

Tax	31 TOTAL TAX (Schedule J)	**31**
	32 Credits: (a) Overpayment from 1979 allowed as a credit . . .		
	(b) 1980 estimated tax payments		
	(c) Less refund of 1980 estimated tax applied for on Form 4466 . ( )		
	(d) Tax deposited: Form 7004.................... Form 7005 (attach).................... Total ▶		
	(e) Credit from regulated investment companies (attach Form 2439)		
	(f) Federal tax on special fuels and oils (attach Form 4136 or 4136–T)		**32**
	33 TAX DUE (subtract line 32 from line 31). See instruction C3 for depositary method of payment .	**33**
	(Check ▶ ☐ if Form 2220 is attached. See instruction D.) ▶ $...	
	34 OVERPAYMENT (subtract line 31 from line 32)	**34**
	35 Enter amount of line 34 you want: Credited to 1981 estimated tax ▶ .... Refunded ▶	**35**

Please Sign Here

Under penalties of perjury, I declare that I have examined this return, including accompanying schedules and statements, and to the best of my knowledge and belief, it is true, correct, and complete. Declaration of preparer (other than taxpayer) is based on all information of which preparer has any knowledge.

▶ ....
   Signature of officer   Date

▶ ....
   Title

Paid Preparer's Use Only

Preparer's signature and date ▶		Check if self-employed ▶ ☐	Preparer's social security no.
Firm's name (or yours, if self-employed) and address ▶		E.I. No. ▶	
		ZIP code ▶	

313–120–1

FIGURE 19-2. IRS Form 1120.

232

4. Education is highly valued by our society. Students are afforded special treatment in income tests that might otherwise prevent them from being claimed as dependents by their parents.

5. Our national dependence on fossil fuels such as petroleum and natural gas is of great concern. Coal, however, is in great supply in the United States. The upshot of this is that boilers fueled by oil or gas are afforded less favorable tax treatment (specifically, they generally do not qualify for the investment credit) than are boilers fueled by coal.

These are but a few of the illustrations of Congress's attempt to move our society in what it deems to be beneficial avenues of activity.

Congress feels that the tax laws are effective devices in either stimulating or retarding the economy. Examples of the former are the allowance of accelerated and bonus first year depreciation and the investment credit. These measures tend to encourage businesses to expand. Examples of the latter (retarding) measures are the windfall profit tax on oil and excess profit taxes that are often resorted to during times of war. Congress can exercise either stimulation or retardation merely by varying the tax rates. For example, in recent years the corporate tax rate has been as high as 22 percent on the first $25,000 of earnings and 48 percent on all earnings over $25,000. Thus, $14,750 more taxes were paid on the first $100,000 of earnings than are presently paid. Currently, the highest marginal rate is 46 percent. The current structure is much more conducive to stimulating business.

Illustrations of the political considerations are rampant in the tax code. Some examples are:

1. Percentage depletion allowances (whereby a set percentage of revenue is allowed as a deduction in arriving at taxable income) for certain selected industries.

2. Special tax exemptions being afforded certain classes of taxpayers (people over 65; the blind).

3. Contributions to war veteran organizations are deductible; contributions to communist organizations are not.

4. Exclusion of up to $100,000 of the gain on the sale of a principal residence by individuals who are 55 years of age or older.

5. Use of the Federal tax to provide a check-off procedure for financing to Federal elections.

6. Note how the noble effort mentioned above, wherein boilers using oil or gas do not qualify for the investment credit, is *somewhat* modified:

> Boilers fueled by oil or gas. Except as indicated in the next paragraph, any boiler that is primarily fueled by petroleum, petroleum products, or natural gas and that is placed in service after September 1978, does not qualify for the investment credit. This rule does not apply to a boiler that was constructed, reconstructed, erected or acquired by a contract that was binding on the taxpayer on October 1, 1978, and at all times thereafter. Nor does the rule apply if the use of coal is prevented by Federal air pollution regulations or by State air pollution regulations in effect on October 1, 1978.
>
> A boiler fueled by oil or gas will not be prevented from qualifying for credit if it is used:

1) In an apartment, hotel, motel, or other residential facility;
2) In a vehicle, aircraft, vessel, or in transportation by pipeline.
3) On a farm for farming purposes;
4) In a shopping center, an office building, a wholesale or retail establishment, or any other facility that is not an integral part of manu- facturing, processing or mining; or
5) In Hawaii.[2]

The tax system that emerges from the interplay of the economic, social, and political forces in our democratic society results in an amalgam that varies from sound economic theory to political expediency.

REFERENCE NOTES

1. The IRS recently issued rules which permit companies to disclose differences between income determined using LIFO and income determined using non-LIFO methods in a supplementary or explanatory fashion (e.g., in footnotes or appendices to the basic financial statements in which LIFO is used).

2. U.S., Internal Revenue Service, *Publication 334: Tax Guide for Small Businesses*, p. 143.

Chapter 20

Small Business Administration

The Small Business Administration (SBA) was established in 1953 as an independent agency to provide a broad range of services to small businesses. The SBA is headed by an Administrator who is appointed by the President, with the approval of the Senate. The SBA is headquartered in Washington, D.C., and has approximately 100 regional, district, and branch offices located throughout the country.

The SBA assists small businesses through a number of programs, such as the following:

1. Financial assistance programs where loans or guarantees of loans are made by the SBA.

2. Bond guarantee programs in which SBA aids small contractors in obtaining bid, performance, and payment bonds which otherwise would not be accessible to them.

3. Management assistance programs in which the SBA attempts to distribute a whole array of resources (training programs, publications, counseling — such as through SCORE, the Service Corps of Retired Executives) to small businesses.

4. Assistance in obtaining Federal contracts under specially designated set-aside awards by the procuring agencies and under regular procurement programs.

The SBA is mainly concerned with accounting matters in its administration of its loan programs. The SBA's loan activity can be classified into two separate categories: individual loan programs and the Small Business Investment Company (SBIC) program. Under individual loan programs, the SBA deals directly with the borrowing small business as creditor (i.e., directly loaning the funds to the small business) or as a guarantor of such loans made by traditional financial institutions to the small business. Under the SBIC program, the SBA licenses and monitors the operations of private companies, the SBICs, who, in turn, finance small business. The SBICs receive financing from the SBA and enjoy a beneficial tax status. The SBIC program is used as a conduit to provide a blend of public and private financing to small businesses.

INDIVIDUAL LOAN PROGRAMS

The SBA has the following individual loan programs in effect:

1. *Regular Business Loans.* This is the largest of the SBA's loan programs with annual activity of over 25,000 loans involving over $3 billion. In over 85 percent of these, the SBA is a guarantor (rather than the lender).

2. *Economic Opportunity Loans.* This program is reserved for economically and/or socially disadvantaged individuals (including racial minorities). Its annual activity is near 3,000 loans involving over $100 million.

3. *Displaced Business Loans.* This program is for firms that are being adversely affected by Federal projects (e.g., construction projects disrupting a business). Its annual activity is about 100 loans involving around $10 million.

4. *State and Local Development Company Loans.* Under these programs, the SBA channels loans through state and local business development organizations. The annual loan activity is about 400 loans involving about $100 million.

5. *Loans to Farmers.* Since 1976, the SBA has been permitted to make bus-

iness and disaster loans to farmers. The annual activity is over 15,000 loans involving nearly $1 billion.

6. *Disaster Loans.* The SBA makes loans for physical (e.g., floods) as well as nonphysical (e.g., closing of nearby military bases) disasters. Annual activity runs to over 60,000 loans involving $1 billion.[1]

As the SBA's name implies, its purpose is to render assistance to *small* businesses. The SBA has a proliferation of definitions of what constitutes a small business. These definitions vary from program to program (e.g., SBA loans versus SBA assistance in obtaining Federal contracts). Within each program, there are differentiations among industries. For example, in the loan program there are a number of industry categories: construction, manufacturing, retail, services, shopping centers, transportation and warehousing, wholesale, mining, and agriculture. Each of these is generally further partitioned. The size tests are then set based upon sales, profits, employees, production capacity, etc.

In order to be eligible for a direct loan from the SBA or for an SBA guarantee of a loan, an entity must establish that it cannot, on its own, obtain private financing. It can establish this by applying for a loan and being turned down by a local bank. (For entities located in larger cities, the entity must have received *two* such rejections.) SBA is *not* in the practice of making loans that are likely to result in a loss. Thus, it requires applicants to go through a rigorous screening process. The SBA will not approve a loan if its interests are not adequately protected so that repayment is likely. Along these lines, the SBA usually insists on security for its loans (e.g., a mortgage on land, buildings, or equipment; a personal guarantee by an owner). Further, the SBA can include restrictive covenants in the loan that limit salaries to officers, withdrawals, or dividends, etc., during the term of the loan.

The SBA requires much the same information from potential borrowers that any commercial lender would require. Among the data required are (a) a current balance sheet, (b) an income statement for the previous full year, and (c) an income statement for the current period ending with the aforementioned balance sheet's date.

The following are some of the guidelines used by the SBA in analyzing potential borrowers' financial statements:

Debt-Net Worth Ratio. There is no rule of thumb as to what constitutes a debt-net worth ratio sufficiently adverse to warrant declination. An acceptable ratio for one type of small business might represent an excessive debt burden for another type of small business. Consideration should be given to the type of business involved, past operating results, and depreciation (giving due regard to replacements that will be required in the future). Debts of a self-liquidating nature (i.e., floor planning and receivable financing) may be excluded from the debt-net worth ratio computation. Debts under complete standby for the term of the SBA loan may be considered as net worth. While the applicant must have a reasonable amount "at stake" in the business, this does not necessarily mean that such amount must be in the form of equity capital. For example, if a principal is pledging outside assets as security for the loan, he is putting them at stake in the business, particularly in cases where the loan authorization requires that an asset be sold and the net proceeds applied to the loan inverse order of maturity

(IOM). Therefore, the applicant's net worth shall be evaluated accordingly. However, if such outside assets can be readily converted into cash for injection into the business and the SBA request reduced accordingly, this shall be done. It must also be recognized that in certain cases, outside assets may have been pledged to secure a loan, and their value included in net worth. Such assets are not a substitute for cash or other operating assets required in the day to day operation of the business, and the loan specialist should make appropriate comment and adjustment in the pro forma balance sheet, removing nonbusiness assets from the net worth. This will result in more realistic balance sheet ratios for analysis purposes.

It must be remembered that this ratio varies considerably from industry to industry, and where disproportion exists, it sometimes can be offset by other favorable factors. However, it is difficult to conceive of a set of circumstances in which an applicant showing insolvency resulting from operating losses could be considered to have a basis for loan approval, unless such losses were beyond the control of management. For example, a fire or robbery loss where insurance coverage was not obtainable; Government regulation (i.e., ban on cyclamates); ingress to applicant's place of business barred for a long period of time during extensive construction—road, sewer, subway, etc.

In cases where a serious deficiency in net worth is apparent, the loan specialist should consider the possibility of referring the applicant to an SBIC. Loan specialists should be familiar with the SBIC's in their territories, just as they are familiar with banks and bank personnel.[2]

The SBA regards itself as a source of last resort for financing. Thus, it prefers loan guarantees to direct loans. Also, it wants potential borrowers to have effectively pursued other sources of potential financing, including *additional* investment by the existing owners. In this regard, the SBA is often interested in the *personal* financial statements of the owners of a business:

> *Review of Personal Financial Statements.* Personal financial statements, preferably on SBA Form 413, are required from proprietors, each partner, each officer, and each stockholder with 20 percent or more ownership. Financial statements are carefully reviewed to ascertain whether any of these persons might have assets which could be used to raise funds in lieu of *part* or *all* of an SBA loan. (An officer having no stock interest in an applicant would not normally be expected to utilize his personal assets.) Where forced sale of assets would result in considerable loss, this would be considered undue hardship. Ordinarily SBA does not insist on forced sale under such circumstances, but would require the orderly liquidation and application of the sale proceeds to the SBA loan in inverse order of maturity. If the financial condition of an individual is such that personal credit might be obtained from private sources it would be expected that he make every attempt to do so. The funds so obtained should be injected into the applicant company either as a loan, under a standby agreement, or as an additional equity investment. SBA does not consider that the desire to protect one's personal estate, nor the fact that income taxes will accrue on the capital gains resulting from the sale of assets, constitutes a hardship. An exception might be made in unusual cases where the individual is of advanced age or preparing to retire from the business because of poor health. Maintenance of reasonable reserves, whether in the corporate name or that of a prin-

cipal, may be justified from a business standpoint since hardship could result from liquidation, as the business itself might suffer.

> If an applicant has assets which are not required in the conduct of its business, and could liquidate these at a price equal to or better than the original cost, it would be considered disposal at a fair price. There might be situations where such assets have become outdated or of no possible future use in the operation of the business; then the liquidation of same at a loss would be preferable to retaining them. This would result in cash which would reduce the amount needed from the Government.[3]

Assuming that a loan (or loan guarantee) is granted, the SBA has some further accounting requirements. The SBA requires *annual* financial statements (balance sheet and income statement) for businesses having SBA loans. Generally, *semiannual* financial statements are required for businesses with loans of over $50,000. Further, *quarterly* (or more frequent) financial statements can be required at the discretion of the SBA. This is usually done in situations involving a high risk, such as loans made in establishing new businesses.

The SBA requires *audited* annual financial statements from recipients of loans of $100,000 and over. The audit must be conducted by an independent qualified public accountant (not necessarily a certified public accountant). For loans of under $100,000, the audit requirement can be waived by the SBA. However, the SBA feels that even for smaller loans, the involvement of " . . . an independent qualified public accountant will prove to be mutually advantageous to SBA and the borrower."[4]

SMALL BUSINESS INVESTMENT COMPANIES

There are two types of SBICs: regular SBICs (numbering about 325) and Section 301 (d) SBICs (numbering about 110). This latter group of SBICs, also known as MESBICs—Minority Enterprise Small Business Investment Companies—are to provide economic assistance to businesses that are owned by socially or economically disadvantaged persons. The regulations governing Section 301 (d) SBICs are substantially the same as for regular SBICs where accounting is concerned.

The SBA serves as a source of funds or "leverage" to the SBICs it licenses. This leverage can be through (a) the SBA's guarantee of the SBIC's debentures, (b) the purchase (by the SBA) of the SBIC's debentures, or (c) the purchase (by the SBA) of the SBIC's preferred stock. The SBIC, in turn, is to provide funds to small business concerns.

The SBA regulates the SBICs in many ways. It specifies the minimum amount of private capital that must be invested in the SBIC ($500,000). It regulates the mix of the SBIC's portfolio of investments in small concerns as to type of investment (loan, stock, guarantee of securities), length of term of loans, degree of operating control exercised by the SBIC over the small concern, arm's length nature of the dealing between the SBIC and the small concern, etc. The SBA's regulations appear to be aimed at the following objectives:

1. Insuring the SBIC is financially sound initially and as it operates.

2. Maximizing the types and terms of funding available for small concerns.

3. Minimizing the SBIC's role in the operating control of the small concern.

4. Insuring that the SBICs do not become holding companies for small concerns.

5. Prohibiting the parties involved in organizing, managing, and controlling the SBIC from using the SBIC as a source of funds.

The SBA's review of the operations of the SBICs is greatly facilitated by the requirement that each SBIC file an annual report (SBA Form 468). This annual report is composed of two sections. The first section—the *Financial Report*—contains the financial statements to be filed by the SBIC and audited by the SBIC's independent accountant. The second section—the *Management Report*—contains more detail about the SBIC than is usually associated with summary financial statements.

There are three documents that are very important to anyone interested in accounting for SBICs. These appear as appendices to Part 107 of Title 13 of the Code of Federal Regulations, which is entitled "Small Business Investment Companies." These documents are:

Appendix	
A	Audit Guide for SBICs
B	Guide for the Preparation of the Annual Report
C	System of Account Classification

Audits of SBICs

The SBA requires that all SBICs have an annual audit by an independent public accountant. The appointment of the independent public accountant is subject to the approval of the SBA. Generally, the auditor must be a certified public accountant. However, there is a "grandfather" provision that a licensed public accountant (who was so licensed as of December 31, 1971) will be eligible to conduct audits of SBICs. If at any time during the audit, the auditor discovers defalcations or other sorts of financial irregularities, he must immediately notify the SBA. Also, the SBIC is required to include in the engagement agreement with the auditor a provision whereby the auditor agrees to make his workpapers available to SBA examiners upon request.

Annual Financial Report

The *financial report* section of the SBIC annual report contains its basic financial statements. SBICs prepare more basic financial statements than do other entities.

Statement of Financial Position. The statement of financial position is presented in reverse order from that usually employed in that the SBIC's loans and investments (usually noncurrent assets) are presented first, followed by current assets and other assets. This reverse ordering is due to the importance of loans and investments as the main operating assets of the SBIC. The liabilities of the SBIC are likewise presented in reverse order with the long-term liabilities being presented first, followed by current liabilities.

Another difference in the statement of financial position is that the SBIC's loans and investments are presented at their *fair value,* as determined by the Board of Directors. This concept of portfolio valuation is discussed later in this chapter. Since the SBICs invest mainly in small, nonpublic companies, the valuation of holdings in these companies is quite subjective. This is embodied in the "fair value" concept.

The SBIC's equivalent of "retained earnings" is "undistributed realized earnings" which is composed of two segments—"Noncash Gain on Sale of Securities" and "Undistributed Net Realized Earnings." This results from the segregation into cash versus noncash categories of earnings recognized on the sale of securities. Thus, in the owner's equity section, in addition to paid-in capital accounts (e.g., capital stock), we find three gradients of accounts: (a) to record valuation increases or decreases in securities held, (b) to record noncash gains on sale of securities, and (c) to record the remaining earnings-related transactions.

In a separate computation appended to the statement of financial position, the SBIC computes the amount of "retained earnings for regulatory purposes." This is equal to the undistributed net realized earnings reduced by any allowance for losses on loans and investments that has been established by the board of directors. Dividends (in cash or stock) are limited to this amount of retained earnings.

Statement of Undistributed Realized Earnings. This statement is roughly the equivalent of the statement of retained earnings for other companies. It differs from such statements in that noncash gains on sales of securities are segregated from other earnings

TABLE 20-1
Form for Statement of Undistributed Realized Earnings

	Noncash Gains		Undistributed Net Realized Earnings		Total
Beginning balance	$ XXX	+	$ XXX	=	$ XXX
Additions:					
Net investment income			XXX	=	XXX
Realized gain (loss) on sale					
of securities	XXX	+	XXX	=	XXX
Adjust:					
Collection of noncash gain	(XXX)	=	XXX		
Deductions:					
Dividends			(XXX)	=	(XXX)
Ending balance	$ XXX		$ XXX		$ XXX

components. Any noncash gains reported in prior years that were collected in the current year would result in a transfer of the noncash gain to undistributed net realized earnings. The basic form of this statement is shown in Table 20-1.

Statement of Operations Realized. This is the SBIC's "realized" earnings statement. It is composed of two basic sections: (a) net investment income that is the result of matching operating revenues (e.g., interest and dividend income) with operating expenses, and (b) realized gain (loss) on sale of securities that is the result of matching on the proceeds from the disposition of a security with the cost of that security.

Statement of Unrealized Gain (Loss) on Securities Held. This "unrealized earnings" statement details the change in the owner's equity account used to accommodate the SBIC's carrying their investments at fair value rather than cost.

Statement of Changes in Financial Position. This is the same statement prepared by all operating entities as a basic financial statement.

Statement of Realized Gain (Loss) on Sale of Securities. This statement presents a more detailed explanation of the results of sales of securities (e.g., by type of security, type of proceeds, etc.) than the summary gain or loss presentation in the Statement of Operations Realized (discussed earlier).

Statement of Commitments and Guarantees. If the SBIC has an outstanding agreement to provide financing or has guaranteed the borrowing for another company, the details are presented in this statement.

Annual Management Report

The *management report* component of the SBIC's annual report contains a great deal of accounting data, much of which ties into the statements presented in the accounting report. The main line of demarcation is that the management report is not covered by the independent auditor's opinion (while the accounting report is so covered). The main parts of the management report are reviewed in the following paragraphs.

In the first portion of the management report, general size and classification information is presented. A review of data compiled as of late 1978 shows that over 95 percent of the SBICs are capitalized with less than $5 million of private funds per SBIC. About 25 percent of all SBICs are affiliated with banks or other financial institutions. For every $1 of private capital invested in SBICs, the obligations to the SBA are approximately $1.25. Some SBICs specialize in their investment policy (e.g., retail grocers, real estate, franchise dealers); however, most of the SBICs have a diversified investment policy.[5] The management of the SBIC is also to prepare a narrative description of the activities of the SBIC for the prior year, highlighting any developments that are not brought out elsewhere in the annual report, and disclosing any significant events expected to occur in the coming year.

In addition, the management report includes detailed schedules of the following:

1. Analysis of Unrealized Gain (Loss) on Securities Held
2. Summary of Portfolio Securities
3. Schedules of:
   Loans
   Debt Securities
   Capital Stock of Small Businesses
   Equity Interest in Unincorporated Small Businesses
   Warrants, Options, etc., in Small Businesses
   Details of Certain Portfolio Securities
   Participation and Joint Financing
4. Receivables from Debtors on Sale of Assets Acquired
5. Assets Acquired in Liquidation of Portfolio Securities
6. Schedule of Operating Concerns Acquired
7. Schedule of Other Securities
8. Cash and Invested Idle Funds
9. Average Cash and Invested Idle Fund (by month)
10. Long-Term Debt
11. Capital Stock of SBIC
12. Options on Capital Stock of SBIC
13. Shareholders, Officers, and Directors of SBIC
14. Actual Loss Experience
15. Management Certification

Many of these detailed schedules reconcile to amounts appearing in the audited financial statements contained in the SBIC's financial report.

System of Accounts

The SBA's Appendix C to 13 CFR 107 (*Rules and Regulations for SBICs, System of Account Classification for SBICs*) presents a very detailed description of the accounting procedures to be followed by SBICs. It gives an account by account analysis. It even goes so far as to illustrate typical entries to the account. For example, the following analysis of Account 450—*Noncash gain on sale of securities*—(an owners' equity account) is given:

This is a credit balance account and represents gains realized on the sale of securities that have not been converted into cash. While considered to be undistributed earnings, amounts in this account will not be available for distribution or capitalized by corporate action. Therefore, such amounts are considered restricted undistributed earnings realized.

Debit

(a) With amounts of cash collected of such non-cash gains previously recognized.

(b) With amount of non-cash gains written off or disposed of otherwise.

Credit

(a) With amounts of non-cash gains when the securities generating such gain are sold.

SBIC Portfolio Valuation

The SBA requires SBICs to value their investments in securities of small businesses at their "fair value." This is done by the SBICs' boards of directors. To assist them in their task, the SBA has developed a *Valuation Guide (SBA Policy and Procedural Release 2006).* The *Valuation Guide* gives rather general instructions on factors that may be considered in arriving at the valuation of the investment in a specific company.

The *Valuation Guide* is quite brief, being only seven pages in length. The main principles are contained under the caption of "Valuation Criteria" where the following concepts are related to the determination of "fair value":

A. Nature of the Business and History of the Enterprise from its Inception.

B. The Economic Outlook in General and the Condition and Outlook of the Specific Industry.

C. Evaluation of the Small Business Concern's Securities and the Financial Condition of the Concern.

D. Earning Capacity of the Small Business Concern.

E. Evaluation of Financial Requirements.

F. Goodwill or Other Tangible Value.

G. Sales of Stock.

H. Market Prices of Stocks of Corporations of Comparable Size and Earnings in the Same or Similar Lines of Business which are Publicly Traded.

This list of factors mirrors the technique of basic financial analysis wherein the analysis begins with the general environment (i.e., economic trends, industry trends) and moves to the specific factors associated with the firm (i.e., financial statement analysis).

Factors "C" and "D" above entail a heavy reliance on the financial statements of the small business concern. These factors are described in the *Valuation Guide* as follows:

Evaluation of the Small Business Concern's Securities and the Financial Condition of the Concern.

To evaluate the financial condition of the small business concern, balance sheets should be obtained, preferably in the form of comparative annual statements for several years immediately preceding the date of appraisal, together with a balance sheet at the end of the month preceding that date, if the concern's accounting will permit. Any balance sheet descriptions that are not self-explanatory should be clarified by supporting detailed schedules. These statements will disclose (1) quick ratio (current assets, omitting inventories and prepaid expenses, to current liabilities); (2) working capital; (3) gross and net book value of principal classes of fixed assets; (4) short-term borrowings; (5) long-term indebtedness; and (6) classes and amounts of capital investment and surplus.

Earning Capacity of the Small Business Concern.

To determine earning capacity, detailed profit and loss statements, and surplus statements should be obtained and considered for several years prior to appraisal date. Such statements should show (1) sales, cost of sales, and gross profit by line of business with selling, general, and administrative expenses similarly presented to the extent that allocations are possible; (2) components of cost of sales, and other significant expenses such as depreciation and depletion, officers' salaries, income taxes and other taxes, interest on each item of long-term debt, nonoperating income and expense, and extraordinary items; (3) net income available for dividends; (4) rates and amounts of dividends paid on each class of stock; (5) remaining amount carried to surplus; and (6) adjustments to, and reconciliation with, surplus as stated on the balance sheet. With profit and loss statements of this character available, the board of directors should be able to separate recurrent from nonrecurrent items of income and expense, to distinguish between operating income and investment income, and to ascertain whether or not any line of business in which the company is engaged is operated consistently at a loss and might be abandoned with benefit to the company. The percentage of earnings retained for business expansion should be noted when dividend-paying capacity is considered. Potential future income is a major factor, and all information concerning past income which will be helpful in predicting the future should be secured. Prior earnings records usually are the

most reliable guide as to future expectancy, but to resort to arbitrary five- or ten-year averages without regard to current trends or future prospects will not produce a realistic valuation. If, for instance, a record of progressively increasing or decreasing net income is found, then greater weight may be accorded the most recent years' profits in estimating earning power. It will be helpful, in judging risk and the extent to which a business is a marginal operation, to consider deductions from income and net income in terms of percentage of sales. Major categories of cost and expense to be so analyzed include the consumption of raw materials and supplies in the case of manufacturers, processors and fabricators; the cost of purchased merchandise in the case of merchants; utility services, insurance; taxes; depletion or depreciation; and interest.[6]

Pragmatic Valuation Procedures

After reviewing the traditional approaches to valuation, the *Valuation Guide* concludes with the following discussion of approaches that are found in practice:

Current Valuation Concepts.

Some valuation techniques use initial cost of an investment and when the portfolio concern's operations begin to decline, there is a write-down by the Venture manager either by a given predetermined percentage or to a measurable liquidating value. Conversely, when a portfolio concern's operations begin to show positive results, write-ups may be used which reflect: a recent public market price (if broadly traded, less a discount for size of a given block of registered stock), a price based on the same value as a recent purchase by an investment group in a private transaction, a price based on a conservative price earnings multiple (if restricted stock or a privately held portfolio concern), or predetermined percentage write-ups based on various stages of the portfolio concern's increasing positive operations. Again, there are many variations to these valuation approaches, but we give the above just to illustrate a few basic techniques currently being utilized.[7]

SBIC Tax Considerations

Congress has seen fit to encourage SBIC activity by offering a mix of tax benefits to both the stockholders of the SBIC and the SBIC itself. The SBIC stockholders are allowed to treat gains on the sale of their stock (in the SBIC) as long-term capital gains (usually taxed at effectively lower rates than ordinary income) and to treat any losses on the sale of their stock as an ordinary loss (which offsets the usually higher-taxed ordinary income). These provisions are designed to encourage investment in SBICs.

The SBICs enjoy a number of tax advantages: They are entitled to exclude from taxable income *all* dividends that they receive from taxable domestic corporations (in which they invest) and they are exempt from taxes on any claimed excess accumulations of earnings.

REFERENCE NOTES

1. U.S., Small Business Administration, *Annual Report FY 1979*, pp. 17–18.

2. U.S., Small Business Administration, *Policies and Procedures for Financing Function*, pp. 68–69.

3. *Ibid.*, pp. 70–70.1.

4. *Ibid.*, p. 83.

5. U.S., Small Business Administration, *Directory of Operating Small Business Investment Corporations*, 1978, pp. 61, 82.

6. U.S., Small Business Administration, *SBA Policy and Procedural Release 2006, Valuation Guide*, 1975, pp. 3–4.

7. *Ibid.*, pp. 6–7.

Chapter 21

Health Care Financing Administration

The Health Care Financing Administration (HCFA) is a unit of the Department of Health and Human Services (HHS). The HCFA was established as a separate unit within HHS in 1977. It is headed by an administrator who is accountable to the Secretary of HHS. The HCFA administers two main programs: *Medicaid* and *Medicare*.

HCFA PROGRAMS

Medicaid

The Medicaid program provides financial assistance to the needy for their health care expenses (e.g., hospital, doctor, and prescription costs). The Medicaid program is administered jointly by the Federal government and the states. In essence, the states set up a Medicaid system as part of their welfare program. To receive Federal funding,

the plan must comply with Federal guidelines (e.g., eligibility). The Federal government partially funds the program and the remainder of funds are contributed by the states and local governmental units (e.g., counties, municipalities, etc.). The Federal contribution varies depending on the affluence of the individual states. In some states only about 50 percent of the Medicaid program is Federally funded. In others, over 75 percent of the program is underwritten by the Federal government. While the majority of costs of Medicaid are borne by the Federal government, it is, in essence, a state-based program in its deployment of benefits.

Medicare

HCFA's Medicare program is a program of health care *insurance*. It covers the medical needs of those who (generally) receive income support under the

Social Security System. Specifically, it covers (a) most people who are 65 years of age or older, (b) many disabled people under 65 years of age who are receiving Social Security payments, and (c) people (of any age) who are need of care for severe kidney failure (i.e., they need dialysis treatment or a kidney transplant). There are two separate parts to the Medicare program. Part A, *Hospital Insurance,* applies to virtually everyone enrolled in the Medicare program. Part A provides coverage of the costs of hospitalization, treatment in a skilled nursing facility, and certain home health services (e.g., visitation by health care specialists such as nurses and therapists) when it is determined that these are medically necessary for the Medicare beneficiary. Part A coverage generally involves no payments by the beneficiaries for the coverage. However, their benefits are subject to stated coinsurance, deductible, and benefit limitations. During an employee's working life, part of his Social Security tax payment (i.e., "FICA" withholding) goes to finance the Medicare Part A hospital insurance program.

Part B of Medicare, *Medical Insurance,* generally provides coverage for those medical costs not covered by Part A, most notably physician's services, diagnostic tests (e.g., X-rays), and therapy (e.g., radium treatments). Part B also provides coverage for certain home health services and services provided by clinics and rehabilitation centers. Part B must be voluntarily subscribed to by the beneficiaries, who pay a stated monthly premium. Part A and Part B are generally well coordinated so that where Part A coverage ends, Part B coverage begins.

The HCFA payments of benefits un-der the two parts of Medicare are quite different. Under Part A, Hospital Insurance, payment is made for the *reasonable costs* of the hospital care. Under Part B, Medical Insurance, payment is made for the *reasonable charge* for the service. As one would expect, the *reasonable cost* concept under Part A is quite rigidly bound by accounting determinations.

HCFA REGULATIONS

The HCFA regulations are contained in Title 42, Parts 400-499, of the Code of Federal Regulations. Part 405 — Federal Health Insurance for the Aged and Disabled — contains the regulations applicable to Medicare. Subpart D (Sections 405.401 - 405.499) — Principles of Reimbursement for Provider Costs and for Services by Hospital-Based Physicians — contains the majority of accounting regulations. There are also some special accounting provisions for Health Maintenance Organizations (HMOs) in Subpart T, Sections 405.2040 through 405.2056.

Under the Part A, Hospital Insurance, program, the provider of health care services (e.g., hospital) either deals directly with the government *or* (as is more common) elects to deal through a fiscal intermediary (such as a proximate Blue Cross-Blue Shield program) which, in turn, deals directly with the government. Regardless of the relationship, the provider is subject to the same principles of cost determination. These principles control the payments by the government to the provider (either directly or through an intermediary). Providers are subject to audit by their intermediary and the

HCFA to insure compliance with these cost principles, as well as other Medicare regulations. Providers are generally reimbursed on a "cost" basis with two noteworthy caveats.

First, under 42 CFR 405.451, providers' reimbursements are to be the lesser of the "reasonable cost" of services rendered to beneficiary or the "customary charges" for such services. The term *reasonable cost* is described as follows [42 CFR 405.451 (c) (3)]:

> Reasonable cost includes all necessary and proper expenses incurred in rendering services, such as administrative costs, maintenance costs, and premium payments for employee health and pension plans. It includes both direct and indirect costs and normal standby costs. . . . The reasonable cost basis of reimbursement contemplates that the providers of services would be reimbursed the actual costs of providing quality care however widely the actual costs may vary from provider to provider and from time to time for the same provider.

The term *customary charges* is defined as " . . . the regular rates for various services which are charged to beneficiaries and other paying patients" [42 CFR 405.452 (d) (4)].

The reasonable cost versus customary charge test is *not* applied on a service by service basis. Rather, the aggregate of the reasonable cost and customary charges of all services rendered to beneficiaries are compared and the lower is reimbursed. If a provider has any reasonable costs disallowed because they exceed the customary charges, the disallowed costs can be carried forward *two* years. If, during this period, customary charges for services to beneficiaries

exceed the provider's reasonable cost, an equivalent amount of these previously disallowed costs can be recouped by the provider.

Second, the providers' costs associated with general routine inpatient services (i.e., excluding specialized services and outpatient services) will not be reimbursed to the extent that they are found to be in excess of those " . . . necessary in the efficient delivery of needed health services" [42 CFR 405.460 (a)]. The following guidelines are given to assist providers in understanding and complying with this concept [42 CFR 405.460 (b)]:

> In establishing limits under this section, the Secretary may classify providers by type of provider (e.g., hospitals, skilled nursing facilities and home health agencies) and by any other factors the Secretary finds appropriate and practical, including:
>
> (i) Type of services furnished;
>
> (ii) Geographical area where services are furnished, allowing for grouping of noncontiguous areas having similar demographic and economic characteristics;
>
> (iii) Size of institution;
>
> (iv) Nature and mix of services furnished;
>
> (v) Type and mix of patients treated.

This criterion is further bounded by a number of exemptions and exceptions whereby it is not to be applied or it is to be applied in a modified form. For example, if the provider is the sole source of health services in an isolated location, the criterion is not applicable [42 CFR 405.460 (e) (1)].

COST DETERMINATION

The determination of a provider's cost to be claimed for reimbursement proceeds in two stages. The first stage is the determination of the provider's allowable total cost. The second stage is the allocation of these costs between Medicare and non-Medicare beneficiaries. In this chapter, the issue of allowability will be addressed first. Then, the issue of allocating the allowable costs will be reviewed.

Allowable Costs

Depreciation. The HCFA cost principles allow depreciation on assets acquired on or after August 1, 1970 on a straight-line or declining balance (not to exceed 150 percent of the straight-line rate) basis. The straight-line basis is normally required, with the declining balance method *only* being used where [42 CFR 405.415 (a) (3) (iii)]:

> . . . the cash flow from depreciation on the total assets of the institution during the reporting period, including straight-line depreciation on the assets in question, is insufficient (assuming funding of available capital not required currently for amortization and assuming reasonable interest income on such funds) to supply the funds required to meet the reasonable principal amortization schedules on the capital debts related to the provider's total depreciable assets. For each depreciable asset for which a provider requests authorization to use a declining balance method for health insurance reimbursement purposes, but not to exceed 150 percent of the straight-line rate, the provider must demonstrate to the intermediary's satisfaction that

the required cash flow need exists. For each depreciable asset where a provider justifies the use of accelerated depreciation, the intermediary must give written approval for the use of a depreciation method other than straight-line before basing any interim payment on this accelerated depreciation or making its reasonable cost determination which includes an allowance for such depreciation.

For assets purchased (or under contract) prior to August 1, 1970, the cost principles generally permit an accelerated method (without the above-cited test to establish the need therefore). If a provider that employs an accelerated method of depreciation pulls out of the Medicare program (or experiences a "substantial" reduction in the Medicare proportion of its allowable costs), the excess of reimbursements using the accelerated method (as compared with the straight-line method) is to be recovered by the government [e.g., through reducing the final payment(s) or future payments to the provider].

Prior to the start of the Medicare program (in the mid-1960s) many providers maintained sparse documentation of their depreciable assets. In many cases, it was not possible to establish their cost, useful life, additions, retirements, betterments, etc. In light of this, the Medicare cost principles permitted a depreciation allowance as a percentage of operating cost. This began as 5 percent in 1966–67 and was reduced by ½ percent each year so that by the mid-1970s, this "grandfather" provision was eliminated. Even while it was in effect, the provider was limited to a ceiling amount of 6 percent of allowable cost (excluding depreciation) for its depreciation *allow-*

ance *plus* the *actual* depreciation computed on assets purchased after 1965.

When a provider enters the Medicare program, with full or partially depreciated assets, it can establish a new useful life for these assets. For example [42 CFR 405.417 (b)]:

> . . . if a 50-year-old building is in use at the time the provider enters into the program, depreciation is allowable on the building even though it has been fully depreciated on the provider's books. Assuming that a reasonable estimate of the asset's continued life is 20 years (70 years from the date of acquisition), the provider may claim depreciation over the next 20 years—if the asset is in use that long—or a total depreciation of as much as twenty-seventieths of the asset's historical cost. If the asset is disposed of before the expiration of its estimated useful life, the depreciation would be adjusted to the actual useful life. Likewise, a provider may not have fully depreciated other assets it is using and finds that it has incorrectly estimated the useful lives of those assets. In such cases, the provider may use the corrected useful lives in determining the amount of depreciation, provided such corrections have been approved by the intermediary.

Gains or losses on the disposition of depreciable assets result in the reduction (for gains) or increases (for losses) in the allowable cost of the provider.

The basic theory behind HCFA's rules on depreciation appears to be one of insuring the *recovery* of the original cost of fixed assets—to the extent allocable to Medicare patients—through the reimbursement by the intermediary (and, thus, HCFA). In this regard, providers include, in their allowable cost, depreciation on assets that were donated to them and/or financed by government funds. All of this points toward the implicit assumption that, in the future, providers will reinvest in new facilities.

Interest. The cost principles allow a provider's "necessary and proper" interest cost. Various guidelines are given for evaluating necessity (e.g., for capital improvements) and/or propriety (such as the arm's length nature of the borrower-lender relationship). Interest expense must be reduced by any interest revenue. However, providers are allowed to "shelter" interest revenue on funded depreciation (i.e., funds, equivalent in amount to the depreciation expense, that are invested). Providers are strongly urged to employ this mechanism to facilitate maintaining their ability to replace (or expand) fixed assets [42 CFR 405.415 (e)]:

> *Funding of depreciation.* Although funding of depreciation is not required, it is strongly recommended that providers use this mechanism as a means of conserving funds for replacement of depreciable assets, and coordinate their planning of capital expenditures with areawide planning activities of community and State agencies. As an incentive for funding, investment income on funded depreciation will not be treated as a reduction of allowable interest expense.

By not offsetting interest revenue on such funds against interest expense—and thus not reducing allowable cost—the cost principles are, again, in support of the ability of providers to recover the initial cost of fixed assets and to maintain these funds for reinvestment in new fixed assets.

Similarly, providers do not have to offset the interest income earned on (a) the investment of funds received as gifts and grants (provided the investment is segregated, not mingled with other funds) and (b) the funds invested in the providers' qualified pension fund.

Bad Debts. Bad debts, charity allowances (for indigence), and courtesy allowances (for staff members, members of the clergy, etc.) are not allowable costs under Medicare. However, HCFA will reimburse the providers for any deductible or coinsurance amounts that are not collectible from Medicare beneficiaries. The HCFA's disallowance of bad debts, charity allowances, and courtesy allowances is based on the proper accounting view of these items as adjustments in revenue rather than expenses [42 CFR 405.420 (c)]:

> Normal accounting treatment: Reduction in revenue. Bad debts, charity, and courtesy allowances represent reductions in revenue. The failure to collect charges for services rendered does not add to the cost of providing the services. Such costs have already been incurred in the production of the services.

Research Costs. This category of costs is one that many individuals might expect to be allowable considering the aim of research is to improve the state of the art of medical care. However, the cost principles state, "Costs incurred for research purposes, over and above usual patient care, are not includible in allowable costs" [42 CFR 405.422 (a)]. The reasons that these costs are disallowed are [42 CFR 405.422 (b) (1)]:

> There are numerous sources of financing for health-related research ac-

tivities. Funds for this purpose are provided under many Federal programs and by other tax-supported agencies. Also, many foundations, voluntary health agencies, and other private organizations, as well as individuals, sponsor or contribute to the support of medical and related research. Funds available from such sources are generally ample to meet basic medical and hospital research needs. A further consideration is that quality review should be assured as a condition of governmental support for research. Provisions for such review would introduce special difficulties in the health insurance programs.

Grants, Gifts, and Income from Endowments. The provider is *not* required to reduce its costs by these sources of revenue in arriving at allowable costs *unless* the donor has designated the funds to be used to support certain provider costs. In this case, the designated costs must be reduced by the designated funds in arriving at the allowable costs.

Value of Services of Nonpaid Workers. Providers are allowed an imputed cost for the value of services performed by certain nonpaid workers. The workers must be performing duties, on a regularly scheduled basis, that are *normally performed by paid employees* in providing normal care or in otherwise operating the facility. This provision would exclude a claim for a cost of services that are *normally* donated by civic or religious organizations (e.g., "Candystripers" who visit with and distribute books and magazines to patients). The following illustration shows how this provision is applied [42 CFR 405.424 (c)]:

The prevailing salary for a lay nurse working in Hospital A is $5,000 for the year. The lay nurse receives no maintenance or special perquisites. A sister working as a nurse engaged in the same activities in the same hospital receives maintenance and special perquisites which cost the hospital $2,000 and are included in the hospital's allowable operating costs. The hospital would then include in its records an additional $3,000 to bring the value of the services rendered to $5,000. The amount of $3,000 would be allowable where the provider assumes obligation for the expense under a written agreement with the sisterhood or other religious order covering payment by the provider for the services.

Purchase Discounts, Allowances, and Refunds. These items are treated as contra-expense items in arriving at allowable cost. It is interesting to note the cognizance of an evolution in accounting treatment and its impact on these regulations [42 CFR 405.425 (d) (1)]:

> In the past, purchase discounts were considered as financial management income. However, modern accounting theory holds that income is not derived from a purchase but rather from a sale or an exchange and that purchase discounts are reductions in the cost of whatever was purchased. The true cost of the goods or services is the net amount actually paid for them. Treating purchase discounts as income would result in an overstatement of costs to the extent of the discount.

Return to Owners. Proprietary providers (i.e., those organized as proprietorships, partnerships, or corporations with the aim of earning a profit) are

allowed a return on their capital. This return on capital is treated as an allowable "cost" by HCFA. The return on capital is computed at 150 percent of the average (computed monthly) rate of interest paid on public debts issued by the Federal Hospital Insurance Trust Fund. The base to which this is applied is (a) the provider's investment in fixed assets (net of depreciation to date) plus (b) its net working capital. The determination of both the net fixed assets and net working capital is bounded by certain rules. For example, any additions to the provider's facilities that were made after 1972 and were *not* approved by the relevant health care planning agency (e.g., a state board set up to eliminate duplication and/or over-expansion of health care facilities) are not to be included in the equity capital of the provider. This penalty for not conforming to state or local coordinating efforts is extended to the depreciation and operating costs of such unapproved facility additions. They are unallowable under 42 CFR 405.435.

Owners' Salary. Proprietary providers are also allowed to claim as an allowable cost the salary paid to the owners of the provider (i.e., the proprietor, partners, or shareholders) if these individuals work for the provider (e.g., participate in the management of the provider). Any salary paid to the owner(s) must meet the test of reasonableness of the amount, in light of the services rendered by the owner(s).

Physicians' Services. While Part A of Medicare generally does not cover the cost of physician services, there are certain types of physician services that *do* enter into the allowable costs of providers under Part A. An allocable portion of the costs of physicians who are on medical school faculties and who, in conjunction therewith, work in hospitals (e.g., supervising interns and residents) is allowable. Likewise, the costs of hospital-based physicians (e.g., radiologists, pathologists) can be reimbursed, in part, under the hospital insurance (Part A) of Medicare, where their work is not rendered to specific patients but rather is related to the general administration or operation of the provider (e.g., administration of a radiology department).

Educational Activities. HCFA allows the inclusion of an "appropriate part" of the cost of approved educational activities. *Approved* generally means that the program must be licensed or accredited by relevant professional organizations. HCFA has put providers on notice that it is going to reevaluate its acceptance of these costs over time [42 CFR 405.421 (c)] :

> *Educational activities.* Many providers engage in educational activities including training programs for nurses, medical students, interns and residents, and various paramedical specialists. These programs contribute to the quality of patient care within an institution and are necessary to meet the community's needs for medical and paramedical personnel. It is recognized that the costs of such educational activities should be borne by the community. However, many communities have not assumed responsibility for financing these programs and it is necessary that support be provided by those purchasing health care. Until communities undertake to bear these costs, the program will participate appropriately

in the support of these activities. Although the intent of the program is to share in the support of educational activities customarily or traditionally carried on by providers in conjunction with their operations, it is not intended that this program should participate in increased costs resulting from redistribution of costs from educational institutions or units to patient care institutions or units.

Cost Finding and Apportionment

Once allowable costs are determined, the next step is to allocate these costs to the provider's various departments. Through interdepartmental allocations, the costs of non-revenue producing departments are allocated to revenue producing departments. This procedure is referred to as *cost finding*. Next, the costs are allocated between Medicare and non-Medicare patients. This is referred to as *cost apportionment*.

HCFA's regulations governing cost finding and cost apportionment have evolved over the life of the Medicare program. When the program was set up in the mid-1960s, it was found that providers' accounting systems varied in their degrees of sophistication. This obviated the imposition of allocation procedures which presumed that a uniform, fairly sophisticated system was possessed by each provider. (We have already seen one accommodation to the lack of uniform sophistication in HCFA's policy on depreciation where, initially, a factor for depreciation was allowed based upon the provider's other operating costs.) Initially, HCFA promulgated regulations that allowed providers to select from among acceptable methods of cost finding and cost apportionment. Later, they were required to follow a given method of cost finding and cost apportionment based upon their size (i.e., hospitals of less than or greater than 100 beds) or classification (e.g., skilled nursing facilities). After July 1, 1979, all providers had to employ fairly sophisticated methods of cost finding and cost apportionment.

Cost Finding. The HCFA requires providers to use, as a minimum, the *step-down* method of interdepartmental allocation. Other more sophisticated methods can be employed [42 CFR 405.453 (d)]:

(1) *Step-down Method.* This method recognizes that services rendered by certain nonrevenue-producing departments or centers are utilized by certain other nonrevenue-producing centers as well as by the revenue-producing centers. All costs of nonrevenue-producing centers are allocated to all centers which they serve, regardless of whether or not these centers produce revenue. The cost of the nonrevenue-producing center serving the greatest number of other centers, while receiving benefits from the least number of centers, is apportioned first. Following the apportionment of the cost of the nonrevenue-producing center, that center will be considered "closed" and no further costs are apportioned to that center. This applies even though it may have received some service from a center whose cost is apportioned later. Generally when two centers render service to an equal number of centers while receiving benefits from an equal number, that center which has the greatest amount of expense should be allocated first.

(2) *Other methods* — (i) *The double-apportionment method.* The double-ap-

portionment method may be used by a provider upon approval of the intermediary. This method also recognizes that the nonrevenue-producing departments or centers render services to other nonrevenue-producing centers as well as to revenue-producing centers. A preliminary allocation of the costs of nonrevenue-producing centers is made. These centers or departments are not "closed" after this preliminary allocation. Instead, they remain "open," accumulating a portion of the costs of all other centers from which services are received. Thus, after the first or preliminary allocation, some costs will remain in each center representing services received from other centers. The first or preliminary allocation is followed by a second or final apportionment of expenses involving the allocation of all costs remaining in the nonrevenue-producing functions directly to revenue-producing centers.

(ii) *More sophisticated methods.* A more sophisticated method designed to allocate costs more accurately may be used by the provider upon approval of the intermediary. However, having elected to use the double-apportionment method, the provider may not thereafter use the step-down method without approval of the intermediary. Written request for the approval must be made on a prospective basis and must be submitted before the end of the fourth month of the prospective reporting period. Likewise, once having elected to use a more sophisticated method, the provider may not thereafter use either the double apportionment or step-down methods without similar request and approval.

Cost Apportionment. After the cost finding procedure has allocated the service departments to the revenue producing departments, the *departmental method* of cost apportionment allocates the cost between Medicare and non-Medicare patients. In order to understand this procedure, it is important to have a grasp of the following definitions [42 CFR 405.452 (d)]:

> *Routine services.* Routine services means the regular room, dietary, and nursing services, minor medical and surgical supplies, and the use of equipment and facilities for which a separate charge is not customarily made.

> *Ancillary services.* Ancillary services or special services are the services for which charges are customarily made in addition to routine services.

> *Charges.* Charges refer to the regular rates for various services which are charged to both beneficiaries and other paying patients who receive the services. Implicit in the use of charges as the basis for apportionment is the objective that charges for services be related to the cost of the service.

The departmental method of cost apportionment is described by HCFA as follows [42 CFR 405.452 (b) (1)]:

> The ratio of beneficiary charges to total patient charges for the services of each ancillary department is applied to the cost of the department; to this is added the cost of routine services for program beneficiaries, determined on the basis of a separate average cost per diem for general routine patient care areas, taking into account, to the extent pertinent, an inpatient routine nursing salary cost differential (see §405.430 for definition and application of this differential), and in hospitals, a separate average cost per diem for each intensive care unit, coronary care unit, and other special care inpatient hospital units.

Table 21-1 [adapted from 42 CFR 405.452 (e) (2) (ii)] illustrates the Departmental Method.

Nursing Salary Differential. HCFA currently allows providers to claim an above-average amount for routine nursing care (included in "general routine patient care" in the above illustration of the departmental method) provided to Medicare patients. The amount is currently 8½ percent above the average cost of routine nursing care. This factor was originally promulgated to compensate providers for what was felt to be increased cost occasioned by their care of the generally elderly Medicare patients. Since 1975, HCFA has been attempting to terminate this differential. However, a suit has been filed by providers to prevent this termination. An injunction has been issued by the court which requires HCFA to continue this differential until the suit is settled.

HEALTH MAINTENANCE ORGANIZATIONS

Health Maintenance Organizations (HMOs) are a class of health care institutions that offer health services to their subscribers on a *prepaid* basis. (Providers are generally compensated *after* the services are rendered.) The HCFA has set up the procedures for paying HMOs for their members, who are covered by Medicare on a prepaid basis. These prepayments are periodically adjusted and there is a final yearly accounting which matches the HMO's total prepayments with the share of its costs allocable to its members who are covered by Medicare.

TABLE 21-1
Departmental Method of Cost Apportionment

| | (1) | (2) | (3) | (4) | Cost Allocable to Medicare Patients |
| | Charges | | Medicare Percent | Total | |
	Medicare Patients	Total	(1) ÷ (2)	Cost	(3) × (4)
Ancillary Departments:					
Operating Room	$ 20,000	$ 70,000	28 4/7%	$77,000	$ 22,000
Delivery Room	—0—	12,000	—0—	30,000	—0—
Pharmacy	20,000	60,000	33 1/3	45,000	15,000
X-Ray	24,000	100,000	24	75,000	18,000
Laboratory	40,000	140,000	28 4/7	98,000	28,000
Others	6,000	30,000	20	25,000	5,000

| | (1) | (2) | (3) | (4) | |
	Total Cost	Total Patient Days	Cost per Day (1) ÷ (2)	Medicare Patient Days	
General Routine Patient Care	$630,000	30,000	$21	8,000	168,000
Special Care Units:					
Coronary Care Unit	20,000	500	40	200	8,000
Intensive Care Unit	108,000	3,000	36	1,000	36,000
TOTAL ALLOCABLE TO MEDICARE PATIENTS					$300,000

The cost principles employed by HMOs are basically the same ones that apply to providers. The enumeration of allowable costs (e.g., depreciation, interest, etc.) is augmented by certain costs that are specific to HMOs (vis-á-vis providers). For example, HMOs have enrollment, membership, and marketing costs (which are allowable). Generally, providers do not encounter the equivalent of these costs. Also, in providing for the health needs of its members, an HMO may find it advantageous or necessary (e.g., in emergencies) to contract with (and *directly* reimburse) providers (e.g., hospitals) for services to its members. This is in contrast to providers (e.g., hospitals) which generally deal individually with

HCFA for reimbursement for services to Medicare patients.

After the allowable costs of an HMO are determined, the cost finding and cost apportionment methods (discussed earlier) are applied to arrive at the costs allocable to members of the HMO covered by Medicare.

Certain HMOs (generally large, well established ones) can elect to be reimbursed on a "risk basis" as opposed to the cost basis discussed above. Risk-basis HMOs agree to be reimbursed based on the degree to which their (a) *adjusted incurred cost* (i.e., adjusted to make its basis consistent with its "target cost") is greater or less than (b) the HCFA's *target cost* (which is formally known as the "adjusted average per capita cost"). The HCFA's target is computed based on a combination of national and regional factors, and factors that are specific to the individual HMO (e.g., age, sex, race, and disability status of its members). If the risk-basis HMO's incurred cost is less than the target, it is said to recognize a savings and the HMO can keep up to half of the savings, not to exceed 10 percent of the target cost. The remainder accrues to HCFA. If the risk-basis HMO's incurred cost is greater than the target, it is said to have incurred a loss, and this loss is fully absorbed by the HMO. A loss in one period can be carried forward (but not back) to offset against savings in future periods.

Chapter 22

Federal Trade Commission

The Federal Trade Commission (FTC) is an independent agency of the Federal government. It was organized in 1915 to carry out the provisions of the Federal Trade Commission Act of 1914. Curently, it administers all or part of over 20 other laws including the Clayton Act, the Trade-Mark Act, the Fair Packaging and Labeling Act, the Truth in Lending Act, the Fair Credit Reporting Act, the Equal Credit Opportunity Act, and the Energy Policy and Conservation Act. The FTC is headed by a five member bipartisan commission. The commissioners are appointed by the President, with the approval of the Senate, to seven year terms. The chairman is designated by the President.

The FTC operates out of its headquarters in Washington, D.C., and 10 regional offices located throughout the country (Atlanta, Boston, Chicago, Cleveland, Dallas, Denver, Los Angeles, New York, San Francisco, and Seattle).

The principal functions of the FTC are:

To promote free and fair competition in interstate commerce through prevention of general trade restraints such as price-fixing agreements, boycotts, illegal combinations of competitors and other unfair methods of competition;

To safeguard the public by preventing the dissemination of false or deceptive advertisements of consumer products generally and food, drug, cosmetics, and therapeutic devices, particularly, as well as other unfair or deceptive practices;

To prevent: discriminations in price; exclusive-dealing and tying arrangements; corporate mergers, acquisitions or joint ventures, when such practices or arrangements may substantially lessen competition or tend toward monopoly; interlocking directorates which may restrain competition; the payment or receipt of illegal brokerage; and discrimination among competing customers in the furnishing of or the payment for services or facilities used to promote the resale of a product;

To bring about truthful labeling of textile and fur products;

To regulate packaging and labeling of certain customer commodities within the purview of the Fair Packaging and Labeling Act so as to prevent consumer deception and to facilitate value comparisons;

To supervise the registration and operation of associations of American exporters engaged in export trade;

To petition for the cancellation of the registration of trademarks which were illegally registered or used for purposes contrary to the intent of the Trade-Mark Act of 1946;

To achieve true credit cost disclosure by consumer creditors (retailers, finance companies, non-Federal credit unions, and other creditors not specifically regulated by another Government agency) as called for in the Truth in Lending Act; to assure a meaningful basis for informed credit decisions; and to regulate the issuance and liability of credit cards so as to prohibit their fraudulent use in interstate or foreign commerce;

To protect consumers against circulation of inaccurate or obsolete credit reports, and to insure that consumer reporting agencies exercise their responsibilities in a manner that is fair and equitable and in conformity with the Fair Credit Reporting Act; and

To gather and make available to the Congress, the President, and the public, factual data concerning economic and business conditions.[1]

Under this last activity, the FTC carries on two programs, through its Division of Financial Statistics, that involve the primary use of accounting data:

The Quarterly Financial Report Program

The Line of Business Program

FTC REGULATIONS

The FTC's regulations are contained in Title 16, Parts 150 to 999 of the Code of Federal Regulations. The two programs that are described in this chapter are not documented in the CFR. Rather, the FTC's regulations are represented by the instructions to entities that are required to participate in the programs.

QUARTERLY FINANCIAL REPORT PROGRAM

The Quarterly Financial Report (QFR) program has been administered by the FTC since 1947. (Up until 1971, the Securities and Exchange Commission was also involved in the program; since 1971, it has been exclusively an FTC program.) Under the QFR program, selected United States companies are required to submit quarterly financial statements (balance sheet and income statement) of their consolidated domestic activity to the FTC within 25 days after the end of the quarter being reported. The schedule shown in Table 22-1 indicates the correspondence between QFR quarters and the reporting periods of various industry groupings.

The FTC's population estimates based upon the companies' filings are published in its *Quarterly Financial Report for Manufacturing, Mining and Trade Corporations*. The data gathered by the FTC are also used by (a) the Department of Commerce in monitoring business profits and macro-economic

TABLE 22-1
Correspondence Between QFR Quarters and Reporting Periods

QFR Quarter	Manufacturing, mining, and wholesale trade	Retail trade
	Coverage is for corporations whose quarter ends in:	
First	Jan., Feb., or March	Feb., March, or April
Second	April, May, or June	May, June, or July
Third	July, Aug., or Sept.	Aug., Sept., or Oct.
Fourth	Oct., Nov., or Dec.	Nov., Dec., or Jan.

statistics (gross national product, national income, etc.), (b) the Federal Reserve Board in evaluating commercial and industrial credit statistics and profitability, (c) the Department of the Treasury in tracking the estimated receipts from the corporate income tax, and (d) various private users who take advantage of the timeliness and extensive detail of the QFR in incorporating its figures in their analytical models of the economy.

There are four basic industry groupings reported in the QFR:

Manufacturing

Mining

Retail trade

Wholesale trade

Manufacturing is further subdivided into the following categories:

Nondurable Manufacturing Corporations:
Food and Kindred Products
Tobacco Manufacturers
Textile Mill Products
Paper and Allied Products
Printing and Publishing
Chemicals and Allied Products
    Industrial chemicals and synthetics
    Drugs

Petroleum and Coal Products
Rubber and Miscellaneous Plastics Products
Other Nondurable Manufacturing Products

Durable Manufacturing Corporations:
Stone, Clay, and Glass Products
Primary Metal Industries
    Iron and steel
    Nonferrous metals
Fabricated Metal Products
Machinery, except Electrical
Electrical and Electronic Equipment
Transportation Equipment
    Motor vehicles and equipment
    Aircraft, guided missiles, and parts
Instruments and Related Products
Other Durable Manufacturing Products

One of the drawbacks to the QFR is that each corporation (and its consolidated subsidiaries) is classified into only one industry group:

HOW COMPANIES ARE CLASSIFIED BY INDUSTRY:

The industry combinations used in the QFR are defined according to the Enterprise Standard Industrial Classification Manual (ESIC), 1974, which in turn is based upon the Standard Industrial Classification Manual (SIC), 1972 . . .

TABLE 22-2
Sample for the First Quarter of 1980

Asset Size	Manufacturing	Mining	Retail	Wholesale	Total
$10 million and over	4,463	281	582	1,178	6,504
Under $10 million	4,659	281	1,945	2,143	9,028
TOTAL	9,122	562	2,527	3,321	15,532
Universe size	260,000	24,000	525,000	185,000	994,000
Sample as % of Universe	3.5%	2.3%	.4%	1.8%	1.6%

Source: U.S., Federal Trade Commission, *Quarterly Financial Report, First Quarter-1980*, p. 17.

Each corporation in the survey is required to provide a breakdown of gross receipts by source industry. These data are analyzed to determine in which industry or industry group the corporation will be classified. A reporting corporation is initially classified into the particular ESIC Division which accounts for more gross receipts than any other ESIC Division. To be in scope for the *QFR*, more gross receipts of the reporting corporation must be accounted for by *either* (not a combination of) ESIC Division B (Mining) or D (Manufacturing) or F (Wholesale Trade) or G (Retail Trade) than by any other ESIC Division.

A corporation assigned to the Manufacturing Division is normally classified further by the two-digit ESIC Major Group which accounts for more gross receipts than any other two-digit Manufacturing Group. In certain cases, the reporting corporation is classified still further into the three-digit ESIC Group which accounts for more gross receipts than any other three-digit ESIC Group within the two-digit ESIC Major Group in which the reporting corporation is classified.

It should be noted that these procedures may lead to a conglomerate corporation being assigned to an industry group from which only a small proportion of its receipts are obtained.

When a corporation is drawn into the sample, its industry classification is determined using the latest information

at hand. Unless it is deleted from the sample in the interim or there is a change in its corporate structure, the corporation remains in the same industry category for eight quarters, at which time its classification is reviewed on the basis of the latest information at hand.

When there is a change in reporting enterprise's corporate structure (e.g., through a major merger), the industry classification is reviewed to take into account the effect of the change.[2]

Sample Selection

The QFR statistics reported by the FTC are projections based upon samples of companies taken from the various industry groupings. The number of companies included in the sample for the first quarter of 1980 is shown in Table 22-2.

The sample sizes result from the stratification of the various industry groupings. The strata containing the larger entities are heavily sampled. For example, virtually all manufacturing companies with total assets over $10 million are included in each quarter's sample. The other strata are randomly sampled with approximately one-eighth of each prior quarter's sample being replaced by new companies. Thus, for these other strata, a company is generally cycled out of the sample after a two year period (i.e., eight quarters) of reporting.

Sample Precision

The QFR reports all of its statistics as point estimates. However, it does give the reader the following guidance on the precision of the estimates:

PRECISION OF THE ESTIMATES: More than 3,000 aggregates or ratios are estimated each quarter. Each estimate has its own standard deviation, which indicates the difference that can be expected due to sampling between the estimate and a comparable total based on a complete canvass by less than one standard deviation approximately 68 times out of 100, by less than two standard deviations approximately 95 times out of 100, and by less than two and one-half standard deviations approximately 99 times out of 100. The sample is designed so that one standard deviation of the estimate for the item, "Income before income taxes and extraordinary items," for all manufacturing corporations amounts to approximately one-half of one percent of that estimated aggregate. For most of the manufacturing industry groups, one standard deviation of the estimate for the same item amounts to less than five percent of the estimated aggregate, while the comparable figure for mining is approximately five percent and for retail trade and wholesale trade approximately nine percent each.[3]

Generally, the QFR is compiled, printed, and ready for mailing within 75 days after the first three quarters and 95 days after the fourth quarter. The QFR consists of approximately 75 pages of schedules that report virtually all of the financial statement information in ab- solute and relative (i.e., ratio or common size) figures for all industry groupings. Also, many changes over time (e.g., percent change in sales compared to the same figure in the prior year) are reported. The QFR also reports the following financial ratios:

(1) *Annual rate of profit on stockholders' equity at end of period* is a ratio obtained by dividing income for the quarter before or after domestic taxes [including branch income (loss) and equity in the earnings of non-consolidated subsidiaries net of Foreign taxes] by stockholders' equity at the end of the quarter; all multiplied by four to put the ratio on annual basis.

(2) *Current assets to current liabilities* is a ratio obtained by dividing total current assets by total current liabilities. It is expressed as the number of times total current assets cover total current liabilities.

(3) *Total cash, U.S. Government and other securities to total current liabilities* is a ratio obtained by dividing total cash, U.S. Government and other securities . . . by total current liabilities. It is expressed as the number of times (usually less than one) that such assets cover total current liabilities.

(4) *Total stockholders' equity to debt* is a ratio obtained by dividing total stockholders' equity by the total of short term loans, current installments on long term debt, and long term debt due in more than one year. It is expressed as the number of times total stockholders' equity covers the total debt as defined above.

(5) *Annual rate of profit on total assets* is a ratio obtained by dividing income, as defined in deriving the rate of profit on stockholders' equity, both before and after taxes, by total assets at the end of the quarter. The result is multiplied by four to put the ratio on an annual basis.[4]

QFR Accounting

The QFR series is based upon the accounting principles and practices that companies employ for general financial reporting purposes (which may and often do differ from many of the practices used to prepare their Federal income tax returns). The QFR has somewhat modified the latitude that companies have where it is necessary to the stability of the QFR series. For example, the FTC has adopted standardized rules as to what units are to be consolidated (or not consolidated) in arriving at the consolidated domestic operations of the entity:

> Beginning with the fourth quarter of 1973, reporting companies were instructed to consolidate the domestic operations of every corporation which is taxable under the U.S. Internal Revenue Code and is owned more than 50% by a reporting corporation and its majority owned subsidiaries. In addition, consolidation is required for every majority owned Domestic International Sales Corporation. Specifically excluded from consolidation are foreign entities, either corporate or non-corporate; foreign branch operations; and domestic corporations primarily engaged in foreign operations. Therefore, subsidiaries that were created in foreign countries or manufacture and/or sell primarily in foreign markets are not consolidated. Corporations that manufacture goods within the U.S. or base their sales activity in the U.S. and export their goods are considered domestic and are consolidated. Also excluded from consolidation are domestic corporations primarily engaged in banking, finance, or insurance (as defined in major groups 60–63 and in group 672 of the Standard Industrial Classification Manual 1972 edition). The accounting treatment for non-consolidated subsidiaries is optional. Companies that record investments in subsidiaries on the equity method report equity in earnings (losses) on the designated line, whereas companies that carry their investment at cost record dividends from subsidiary earnings with other non-operating income at the time of declaration. In both cases, the investment in a subsidiary is classified as a non-current asset. Foreign branch net income (or loss) is included on the line reflecting equity in earnings (loss) of non-consolidated entities, and the equity in foreign branches is reported as an element of non-current assets.[5]

These consolidation practices override those that entities would use for reports prepared in accordance with generally accepted accounting principles for general corporate purposes.

The FTC does *not*, as a general rule, require modifications to companies' applications of generally accepted accounting principles. For example, during the period 1974–75, many U.S. companies changed their method of accounting for inventories to LIFO (last-in, first-out). This change caused a lack of comparability in the QFR series for the quarters during which the change was being made. The FTC conducted a special study (including a survey of over 3,000 companies accounting for 88 percent of the assets in the manufacturing corporation population.[6] Based on this study, the FTC was able to provide an estimate of the degree to which the affected quarters' figures were influenced by the LIFO changes. This would permit users of the series to adjust their own computations involving the QFR data.

LINE OF BUSINESS PROGRAM

The FTC's involvement in the line of business (LB) program was portended by a study that the FTC conducted in 1969. The study, entitled *Economic Report on Corporate Mergers,* reviewed the economic impact of the "conglomerate" merger movement of the 1960s. One of the observations of that study led to the LB program:

> In an economy increasingly dominated by conglomerate enterprises producing a complex array of products and services and operating across many markets, the amount of public information on performance available to the economic system is greatly reduced. The published financial statements of conglomerates are almost universally presented on a highly consolidated basis. Sales and revenue information is generally reported for such broad and diverse aggregates of activity as to provide little or no information with respect to meaningful product or market categories.
>
> In a market economy, heavy reliance is placed on the response of businessmen and investors to profit opportunities. ... Neither of these basic corrective and balancing operations of the marketplace can function in the absence of information.[7]

The study went on to recommend the establishment of such a reporting program.

The LB program began in 1973. From the beginning the program was vehemently opposed by industry and was the subject of lawsuits for over half a decade. Industry claimed that the FTC had no legal right to set up the program. The first published results of the LB program appeared in 1979 (covering the 1973 LB reports). In a study of the LB program, the U.S. General Accounting Office noted that it was unable to support or refute the benefits claimed by the FTC for the program since the program had been held in abeyance by the litigation. Thus, the FTC's list of benefits to be derived from the LB program were not subject to verification. These potential benefits are the program's ability to:

—Enhance the Commission's insight into how well competition is functioning in major industries and permit the Commission to effectively allocate its enforcement resources.

—Contribute to the ongoing program of industry studies in the Commission's Bureau of Economics.

—Provide a data base of unprecedented richness for economists.

—Provide industrial decisionmakers with better data to identify industries in which competitive entry has been insufficient.

—Aid company executives in judging their own performance against industry-wide averages.

—Provide investment analysts and investors with valuable information in selecting investment opportunities.[8]

Presumably, now that the litigation has been settled in the FTC's favor and now that the LB reports have begun to appear, the benefits (or lack thereof) will be subject to verification.

Since the LB program's inception, changes have been made in the reporting requirements and the criteria for selecting companies who are required to participate in the program. The current criteria will be reviewed here.

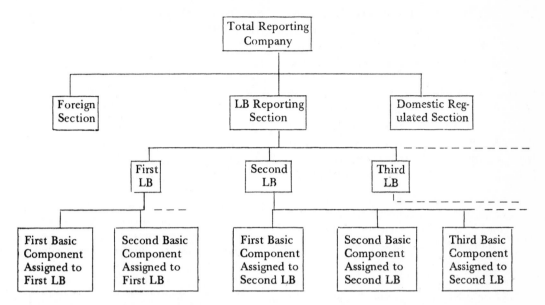

FIGURE 22-1. LB Disaggregation Schematic (*Source:* U.S., FTC, *Form LB Instructions,* p. 5).

Companies Included

The following criteria are the basic rules used to select the companies to be included in the LB program:

A company warrants inclusion in the LB program due to its:

1. Inclusion in the Commission's QFR program, and having assets of more than one billion dollars.

2. Being among the largest 250 firms in terms of domestic manufacturing sales.

3. Being among the largest 1,000 firms in terms of domestic manufacturing sales, and, with respect to some FTC industry category:

   a. being the largest or second largest firm;

   b. being required to insure coverage by at least four firms; or

   c. being required to ensure that reporting firms account for at least twenty percent of sales.[9]

LB Criteria

Companies that are subject to the filing requirement are to complete FTC Form LB. This form, along with its accompanying instructions, contains the LB reporting requirements. Companies have to file this form within 150 days of the end of their fiscal year. The basic reporting framework is shown in Figure 22-1.

All foreign operations and any domestic operations in regulated industries are excluded from the LB reporting requirements. A component of a reporting company is considered to be in a regulated industry if it is "engaged in banking, finance, or insurance or . . . is required to file annual financial statements with the Interstate Commerce Commission, Civil Aeronautics Board, Federal Communications Commission, or Federal Power Commission."[10]

The remainder of the company is referred to as the "LB Reporting Section" and is broken down into individual "lines of business." The following definitions delineate how the concept of the *LB Reporting Section* is developed:

> *LINE OF BUSINESS.* The consolidation of all basic components of the LB Reporting Section which have the same primary activity. . . .

> *BASIC COMPONENTS.* A part of a company which is used in forming lines of business. Some examples are establishments, product lines or groups, organizational units and profit centers.

> *PRIMARY ACTIVITY.* The industry category from the Industry Category List which accounts for the largest percentage of net operating revenues. The term may be used for the whole company or some part of it, e.g., basic component or LB.

> *PRIMARY ACTIVITY CODE.* The FTC code number from the Industry Category List for the industry category associated with the primary activity.[11]

> *ESTABLISHMENT.* A plant or other economic unit, generally at a single physical location, where manufacturing operations or other services are performed.[12]

In short, the *basic components* are the building blocks. The basic component is classified into LBs based upon their primary activity codes. There are 261 LB categories. The primary activity codes were developed from the **ESIC** codes. The degree of refinement in

designating basic components is controlled by the following:

Criteria for Selection of Basic Components

The basic components of the LB Reporting Section must meet two criteria. The first is that the average specialization ratio for the basic components selected must be at least as great as the average establishment specialization ratio. The average establishment specialization ratio is computed by dividing the total operating revenues for all primary products of the establishments by the total operating revenues for primary and secondary products of the establishments. To determine primary and secondary products, the company must analyze each of its establishments separately and segregate its products by FTC industry categories. The products in the industry category accounting for the largest volume of operating revenues of the establishments are the establishment's primary products. All other products are considered secondary. The sum of the primary products for all the company's establishments constitutes the numerator in the average establishment specialization ratio. The denominator, then, is the total operating revenues for all establishments . . .

The average specialization ratio for any proposed set of basic components is computed in the same manner. The operating revenues attributable to the primary products of all the company's basic components divided by the total operating revenues for both primary and secondary products constitutes the average specialization ratio for the basic components . . .

Once a set of basic components has been selected that meets the above criterion, the second criterion must be applied. Each manufacturing line of business with $10 million or more in net operating revenues, as structured by the company from acceptable sets of basic components, must be at least 85% specialized. Again, computing the lines of business specialization ratio is similar to computing the average establishment and basic component specialization ratios. The operating revenues of the FTC industry category accounting for the largest volume of the line of business operating revenues divided by the total operating revenues for the line of business, must be equal to or greater than 85%. For any line of business which does not meet this requirement the company must consider further disaggregation.[13]

These criteria are intended to protect against either too gross or too scrupulous definitions of basic components that might result if individual companies were left to their own devices in disaggregating their company-wide data into lines of business. The FTC's procedures would appear to have been successful in producing relatively "pure" lines of business. In its summary of the 1973 filings of LB reports, the FTC noted that over 90 percent of the industry categories had primary product sales (i.e., sales in that industry category) accounting for over 80 percent of their reported sales.[14]

There are five summary schedules in the LB reporting framework. Generally, each summary schedule is supported by subsidiary schedules. Schedules I and II of Form LB require the reporting entity to classify its operations between the LB Reporting Section and the non-LB Reporting Section areas and to break its LB Reporting Section down into individual lines of business.

LB Reporting

Schedules III (A) and (B) of Form LB require the allocation of the following items to lines of business:

1. Operating Revenues
2. Cost of Operating Revenues
3. Other Expenses—Traceable
4. Other Expenses—Nontraceable
5. Operating Income
6. Assets—Traceable
7. Assets—Nontraceable

Most of these major headings are broken down into subclassifications. For example, "Other Expenses—Nontraceable" consists of: Media Advertising, Other Selling, and General and Administrative expenses.

The FTC's "Traceable—Nontraceable" distinction (items 3, 4, 6, and 7 above) is a bit different from the accountant's usual distinction of "direct-indirect":

> TRACEABLE. Those costs and assets which a company can directly attribute to a line of business or which can be assigned to a line of business by use of a reasonable allocation method developed on the basis of operating level realities.[15]

Thus, the term *traceable* encompasses *all* direct costs as well as those indirect costs that can be allocated on a fairly objective basis.

The following guidelines are given for allocations among lines of business:

> Allocation Procedures
>
> Rigid standards for the distinction between traceable and non-traceable expenses or assets are not proposed here. The same is true for the spreading of

non-traceable expenses or assets across lines of business. The company should use the allocation method for traceable and non-traceable expenses or assets it considers most appropriate; information on these methods should be provided in footnote 1 on Schedule V (A).

For purposes of this report, it would be acceptable (although not required) to utilize the allocation procedures established by the Cost Accounting Standards Board in its Standard 403 on the allocation of home office expenses to segments. Generally, expenses considered under Standard 403 as being allocable on the basis of beneficial or causal relationship between supporting and receiving activities would be included in the traceable category of expenses for the LB Report, while expenses designated as residual in Standard 403 are analogous to the non-traceable category. Similar procedures can be developed for assets.[16]

Special recognition is given to the allocation of research and development expenditures:

All non-contract research and development expense applicable to lines of business in which the LB Reporting Section has operating revenues must be spread among those lines. If R&D applicable to multiple lines of business is conducted in a laboratory serving multiple lines of business, it should be traced or allocated to those lines of business, on the basis of reasonable criteria. Allocation in proportion to operating revenues is acceptable unless some alternative allocation basis seems more appropriate.

If applied R&D performed under contract for the Federal government or other outsiders is unrelated to any of the contractor's existing or contemplated lines of business it should be

reported under LB Category 70.01 "Services". If it is related to existing lines of business of the contractor, then it should be reported under the line of business to which the R&D is most applicable.[17]

Exclusions

The FTC *excludes* the following items from allocation among lines of business:

Exclusions from LB Reporting Section

Several items in the LB Reporting Section are not to be spread across lines of business, but are to be reported in Schedule IV (A) as an adjustment to arrive at the financial information for the LB Reporting Section. They are non-operating income, non-operating expense, interest expense, basic research expense, research and development expense relating to lines of business in which the company has no operating revenues, provision for income taxes, extraordinary items, cumulative effect of accounting changes, and minority interest. Also, long term advances to and investments in the Domestic Regulated and Foreign Sections and other investments accounted for by the equity method are not to be spread across lines of business, but are to be reported in Schedule IV (A) as an adjustment to arrive at the LB Reporting Section.

For purposes of the above paragraph, non-operating income includes such items as equity in net income of the Domestic Regulated and Foreign Sections, equity in net income of other investments accounted for by the equity method, dividends, interest, rent, royalties, etc. Expenses related to corporate headquarters are not to be considered a component of non-operating expenses.[18]

Schedule III (C) requires the expansion of certain information that is presented in Schedules III (A) and (B) for all lines of business:

1. Cost of operating revenues must be broken down as to material, labor, and depreciation, depletion and amortization.

2. Applied research and development must be identified as to its source of financing.

3. The percentage of the ending inventory valued by the various costing methods (LIFO, FIFO, etc.) must be disclosed.

4. The percentage of fixed assets amortized by the various amortization methods (straight-line, sum of years digits, etc.) is required.

5. The percentage of fixed assets acquired within the last 5 years, between 5 and 10 years, etc., is to be disclosed.

6. The use of any or all of the various transfer pricing procedures (market, cost, cost plus, etc.) is to be detailed.

Reconciliation with Published Financial Statements

Schedule IV requires the reporting company to reconcile the figures reported in its LB disclosure with the data appearing in its published financial statements (i.e., Securities and Ex-change Commission Form 10-K, or its annual report to shareholders).

Additional Disclosures

Schedule V, entitled "Footnote Attachment," requires additional disclosures of the following:

1. Bases of allocation of assets and expenses [as made in Schedules III (A) and (B)].

2. Transfers among lines of business.

3. Basic and applied research.

4. Average establishment and basic component specialization ratios.

5. Details of changes in:
   Inventory valuation methods.
   Depreciation methods.
   Transfer pricing methods.

Since the FTC first became concerned with disaggregation of total enterprise data, other bodies, specifically the Securities and Exchange Commission and the Financial Accounting Standards Board (in its Statement No. 14, *Financial Reporting for Segments of Business Enterprises*) have instigated reporting requirements that cause some degree of disaggregation in published financial statements. However, the FTC's LB program remains the most structured and rigorous program, and the only one that uses uniform definitions of segments or lines of business.

REFERENCE NOTES

1. U.S., Office of the Federal Register, *U.S. Government Manual,* 1978/79, p. 548.

2. U.S., Federal Trade Commission, *Quarterly Financial Report, First Quarter—1980,* pp. 5-6.

3. *Ibid.,* p. 8.

4. *Ibid.,* pp. 6-7.

5. *Ibid.,* pp. 4-5.

6. U.S., Federal Trade Commission, *Quarterly Financial Report, Second Quarter—1975,* p. v.

7. U.S., Federal Trade Commission, *Economic Report on Corporate Mergers,* 1969, p. 20.

8. U.S., General Accounting Office, *Audit Report GGD-79-49, B-180229,* p. 3.

9. U.S., Federal Trade Commission, *FTC Line of Business Questions and Answers, No. LB-1 (74),* 1975, pp. 1-2.

10. U.S., Federal Trade Commission, *Glossary of Terms, Form LB,* p. 1.

11. *Ibid.,* pp. 1-3.

12. U.S., Federal Trade Commission, *Statistical Report: Annual Line of Business Report—1973,* p. 65.

13. U.S., Federal Trade Commission, *Form LB Instructions,* p. 6.

14. U.S., Federal Trade Commission, *Statistical Report: Annual Line of Business Report—1973,* p. 15.

15. U.S., Federal Trade Commission, *Glossary of Terms, Form LB,* p. 3.

16. U.S., Federal Trade Commission, *Form LB Instructions,* p. 11.

17. *Ibid.,* p. 10.

18. *Ibid.,* p. 11.

Chapter 23

Federal Election Commission

The Federal Election Commission (FEC) was established in 1974 as an independent agency of the Federal government. The FEC administers the Federal Election Campaign Act (2 USC § 431-455; 26 USC § 9001-9042). This Act, as amended, regulates the activities of candidates and other participants (e.g., independent political committees) in Federal elections. The term *Federal elections* encompasses primary, general, and run-off elections for the U.S. House of Representatives, the U.S. Senate, and the Offices of the President and Vice-President.

The FEC is headed by eight commissioners. Two commissioners are nonvoting ex officio members: the Clerk of the House of Representatives and the Secretary of the Senate. The other six members are appointed by the President, with the approval of the Senate, to six year terms. No more than three of the appointed commissioners can be from the same political party. The Commission elects its own chairman and vice chairman; they cannot be from the same political party.

FEC REGULATIONS

The FEC's regulations are published in Parts 100 through 9038, Chapter I, Title 11 of the Code of Federal Regulations. In addition to these regulations, the FEC has a number of specialized publications that expand on the basic regulations. Some of the more significant ones are:

FEC *Campaign Guides:*

—For State and Subordinate Party Committees

—For Political Committees

—For Congressional Candidates and their Committees

Bookkeeping and Reporting Manual for Candidates and Political Committees

TABLE 23-1
Contribution Limitations

	To each candidate or candidate committee per election	To national party committee per calendar year	To any other political committee per calendar year	Total per calendar year
Individual may give:	$1,000	$20,000	$5,000	$25,000
Multicandidate committee* may give:	$5,000	$15,000	$5,000	No limit
Other political committee may give:	$1,000	$20,000	$5,000	No limit

*A multicandidate committee is a political committee with more than 50 contributors which has been registered for at least 6 months and, with the exception of state party committees, has made contributions to five or more Federal candidates.

Source: *The FEC and the Federal Campaign Financing Law*, p. 4.

Federal Election Campaign Laws (Compiled)

Reports on Financial Activity Series (Summary Reports of Filings of Candidates and Committees)

Advisory Opinion Requests and *Advisory Opinions*

The Record (FEC's monthly newsletter)

FEC ACTIVITIES

The FEC's duties fall in three main areas: (a) enforcement of contribution and expenditure limitations, (b) compilation and disclosure of reports by political candidates and organizations, and (c) control over the public financing of Presidential primary and general elections and the Presidential nominating conventions of national parties. The funds for the Presidential campaign financing activities come from voluntary checkoffs of $1 by individuals on their Federal income tax returns.

Contribution Limitations

The basic limitations on contributions are set out in Table 23-1. These limitations apply to all Federal elections. The table shows that the FEC monitors the contribution activities of *both* individuals and political committees (which provide funds to other political committees or candidates). In addition to these limitations, there are some outright prohibitions against certain types of contributions:

1. Contributions from general funds by national banks, corporations, and labor unions. (Note: These entities may sponsor committees that receive and disburse contributions. These are commonly called "political action committees.")

2. Contributions from foreign nationals who are not permanent residents of the United States.

3. Contributions from individuals who contract with the Federal government.

4. Contributions in *cash* totaling over $100 from any one contributor per election.

5. "Laundered" contributions (i.e., contributions made by B with funds received from A for the intended purpose of B's making the contribution). These are formally known as "contributions in the name of another."

Adequate Records

Much of the FEC's concern in enforcing the law centers on adequate recordkeeping by participants in Federal elections. The basic recordkeeping requirements for contributions and expenditures are contained in 11 CFR 102.9:

Accounting for contributions and expenditures. (2 USC 432 (c)).

The treasurer of a political committee or an agent authorized by the treasurer to receive contributions and make expenditures shall fulfill all recordkeeping duties as set forth at 11 CFR 102.9 (a) through (e):

(a) An account shall be kept by any reasonable accounting procedure of all contributions received by or on behalf of the political committee.

(1) For contributions in excess of $50, such account shall include the name and address of the contributor and the date of receipt and amount of such contribution.

(2) For contributions from any person whose contributions aggregate more than $200 during a calendar year, such account shall include the identification of the person, and the date of receipt and amount of such contribution.

(3) For contributions from a political committee, such account shall include

the identification of the political committee and the date of receipt and amount of such contribution.

(b) (1) An account shall be kept of all disbursements made by or on behalf of the political committee. Such account shall consist of a record of:

(i) the name and address of every person to whom any disbursement is made;

(ii) the date, amount, and purpose of the disbursement; and

(iii) if the disbursement is made for a candidate, the name and office (including State and congressional district, if any) sought by that candidate.

* * *

(c) The treasurer shall preserve all records and accounts required to be kept under 11 CFR 102.9 for 3 years after the report to which such records and accounts relate is filed.

(d) In performing recordkeeping duties, the treasurer or his or her authorized agent shall use his or her best efforts to obtain, maintain and submit the required information and shall keep a complete record of such efforts. If there is a showing that best efforts have been made, any records of a committee shall be deemed to be in compliance with this Act. With regard to the requirements of 11 CFR 102.9 (b) (2) concerning receipts, invoices and cancelled checks, the treasurer will not be deemed to have exercised best efforts to obtain, maintain and submit the records unless he or she has made at least one written effort per transaction to obtain a duplicate copy of the invoice, receipt, or cancelled check.

The FEC has prepared a *Bookkeeping and Reporting Manual for Candidates and Political Committees* which gives candidates and political committees guidance in establishing a sound accounting system for purposes of complying with the law. The *Manual* provides the reader with an understanding of the basic recording and documentation guidelines that the FEC feels are necessary in order to (a) comply with the law, (b) accumulate the necessary data to properly complete the various FEC forms and reports, and (c) provide an audit trail that may be needed in the event of an FEC audit. The *Manual* is written " . . . to be understood and used by persons with a limited bookkeeping background."[1] The FEC encourages individuals and committees subject to the Federal election laws to go beyond the basic system detailed in the *Manual* and to provide for professional bookkeeping and accounting services.

The Federal Election Campaign Act is sympathetic to the accounting (and legal) needs of candidates and committees and *excludes* the following services from its definition of *contribution* and *expenditure* (both of which are subject to various monetary limitations) [2 USC 431 (8) (B) (ix) for contributions and 2 USC 431 (9) (B) (vii) for expenditures] :

> any legal or accounting services rendered to or on behalf of—
>
> (I) any political committee of a political party if the person paying for such services is the regular employer of the person rendering such services and if such services are not attributable to activities which directly further the election of any designated candidate to Federal office; or

> (II) an authorized committee of a candidate or any other political committee, if the person paying for such services is the regular employer of the individual rendering such services and if such services are solely for the purpose of ensuring compliance with this Act. . . .

While they are not counted as contributions or expenditures, the amounts involved do have to be reported to the FEC. The FEC has recommended to Congress that candidates receiving Federal funds in the Presidential primary or general election should be provided with a block grant of a specified amount for purposes of procuring adequate services for complying with the law.[2] This would remove these functions of the campaign from having to compete for the general campaign funds.

The FEC *Manual's* basic recordkeeping provisions are very important to anyone charged with financial responsibility within an entity regulated by the FEC since one of the defenses that can be raised against claims of violations of the law is where [2 USC 432 (h) (2) (i)] :

> . . . the treasurer of a political committee shows that best efforts have been used to obtain, maintain, and submit the information required by this Act for the political committee, any report or any record of such committee shall be considered in compliance with this Act . . .

It would seem that, in most instances, compliance with the *Manual* would be needed to establish a "best efforts" defense.

ALLOCATIONS

While most of the FEC's accounting-related regulations are more procedural (i.e., related to maintenance of adequate records) than analytical (i.e., dealing with the measurement or allocation of transactions), 11 CFR Part 106, entitled "Allocation of Candidate and Committee Activities," does broach some measurement issues. This Part is composed of the following sections:

Expenditures among (or Between) Candidates and Activities

This section of the FEC's regulations gives guidance to political committees that conduct political activities for candidates for both Federal and non-Federal offices. Since the FEC only regulates Federal election activity, there must be an allocation of costs common to both activities [11 CFR 106.1 (e)]:

> Party committees and other political committees which have established Federal campaign committees . . . shall allocate administrative expenses on a reasonable basis between their Federal and non-Federal accounts in proportion to the amount of funds expended on Federal and non-Federal elections, or on another reasonable basis.

A political committee can make an expenditure that benefits more than one candidate. Where Federal candidates are so benefited, there must be an allocation of the expenditure in order to ascertain that no contribution limitations have been violated [11 CFR 106.1]:

> (a) *General Rule:* Expenditures, including independent expenditures, made on behalf of more than one candidate shall be attributed to each candidate in proportion to, and shall be reported to reflect, the benefit reasonably expected to be derived.

> (b) An authorized expenditure made by a candidate or political committee on behalf of another candidate shall be reported as a contribution in-kind (transfer) to the candidate on whose behalf the expenditure was made. . . .

> (c) *Exceptions:*

> (1) Expenditures for rent, personnel, overhead, general administrative, fund-raising, and other day-to-day costs of political committees need not be attributed to individual candidates, unless these expenditures are made on behalf of a clearly identified candidate and the expenditure can be directly attributed to that candidate.

> (2) Expenditures for educational campaign seminars, for training of campaign workers, and for registration or get-out-the-vote drives of committees need not be attributed to individual candidates unless these expenditures are made on behalf of a clearly identified candidate, and the expenditure can be directly attributed to that candidate.

(3) Payments made for the cost of certain voter registration and get-out-the-vote activities conducted by State or local party organizations on behalf of any Presidential or Vice-Presidential candidate(s) are exempt from the definition of a contribution or an expenditure under 11 CFR 100.7 (b) (17) and 100.8 (b) (18). If the State or local party organization includes references to any candidate(s) seeking nomination or election to the House of Representatives or Senate of the United States the portion of the cost of such activities allocable to such candidate(s) shall be considered a contribution to or an expenditure on behalf of such candidate(s), unless such reference is incidental to the overall activity. If such reference is incidental to the overall activity, such costs shall not be considered a contribution to or expenditure on behalf of any candidate(s).

Expenditures among States by Candidates for the Presidential Nomination

Candidates for a party's nomination to run for the office of President can be eligible to receive Federal matching funds (if they qualify, as discussed later in this chapter). If a candidate qualifies, and receives Federal matching funding for his Presidential primary campaign, he must agree to the following [2 USC 441 (b)]:

(1) No candidate for the office of President of the United States who is eligible under section 9003 of title 26 (relating to condition for eligibility for payments) or under section 9033 of title 26 (relating to eligibility for payments) to receive payments from the Secretary of the Treasury may make expenditures in excess of—

(A) $10,000,000, in the case of a campaign for nomination for election to such office *except the aggregate of expenditures under this subparagraph in any one State shall not exceed the greater of 16 cents multiplied by the voting age population of the State (as certified under subsection (e)), or $200,000; or*

(B) $20,000,000, in the case of a campaign for election to such office. [Emphasis added.]

The monetary limitations in 2 USC 441 (b) are adjusted for inflation by increasing them for changes in the Consumer Price Index since 1974. These limits do not apply to (a) amounts expended for legal or accounting services needed to comply with the law (discussed earlier) and (b) amounts up to 20 percent of these limits which can be incurred for fund raising activities over and above these limits.

In order to establish compliance with the law, the expenditures during the primary contest must be allocated among the various states. The FEC's regulations controlling these allocations are [11 CFR 106.2]:

(a) Expenditures made by a candidate's authorized committee(s) which seek to influence the nomination of that candidate for the office of President of the United States with respect to a particular State shall be allocated to that State. This allocation of expenditures shall be reported on FEC Form 3c.

(b) Expenditures for administrative, staff, and overhead costs directly relating to the national campaign headquarters shall be reported but need not be attributed to individual States. Expenditures for staff, media, printing, and other goods and services used in a campaign in a specific State shall be attributed to that State.

(c) An expenditure by a Presidential candidate for use in two or more States, which cannot be attributed in specific amounts to each State, shall be attributed to each State based on the voting age population in each State which can reasonably be expected to be influenced by such expenditure.

(1) Expenditures for publication and distribution of newspaper, magazine, radio, television, and other types of advertisements distributed in more than one State shall be attributed to each State in proportion to the estimated viewing audience or readership of voting age which can reasonably be expected to be influenced by these advertisements.

(2) Expenditures for travel within a State shall be attributed to that State. Expenditures for travel between States need not be attributed to any individual State.

Travel Costs

The FEC has addressed the thorny issue of allocating travel costs (a) between candidates and (b) between campaign versus noncampaign activity. These regulations appear in 11 CFR 106.3. The thrust of these regulations is as follows:

1. When an individual (who is not a candidate) travels on behalf of two or more candidates, the travel costs are to be allocated among the candidates on a reasonable basis.

2. Travel costs of candidates for the Senate or House of Representatives incurred for trips between Washing-

ton, D.C., and the state or district in which the candidate is running for election are not treated as travel costs of the campaign *unless* they are paid by a political committee.

3. Whenever a candidate takes a trip that includes a number of stops, some of which are campaign related, there must be an allocation of the cost of the trip to such activity. Where a stop includes some—but not all—campaign-related activity, it is held to be a campaign-related stop and its costs must be charged to the campaign.

4. Whenever a candidate uses a government conveyance for campaign purposes (e.g., when a President seeking reelection travels on Air Force-1, the aircraft outfitted for Presidential travel), the campaign must recognize a travel cost at a rate that would be charged for comparable commercial conveyance.

Polling Expenses

When a candidate receives and uses the results of a previously unpublished political poll (conducted by others), the candidate will generally have to recognize a contribution by the group that initially conducted or commissioned the poll. The amount of the contribution is a function of two factors. One is the number of participants in the poll [11 CFR 106.4 (e)]:

The amount of a contribution . . . attributable to each candidate-recipient or political committee-recipient shall be—

(1) that share of the overall cost of the poll which is allocable to each candi-

date (including state and local candidates) or political committee, based upon the cost allocation formula of the polling firm from which the results are purchased. Under this method the size of the sample, the number of computer column codes, the extent of computer tabulations, and the extent of written analysis and verbal consultation, if applicable, may be used to determine the shares; or

(2) An amount computed by dividing the overall cost of the poll equally among candidates (including State and local candidates) or political committees receiving the results; or

(3) A proportion of the overall cost of the poll equal to the proportion that the number of question results received by the candidate or political committee bears to the total number of question results received by all candidates (including State and local candidates) and political committees; or

(4) An amount computed by any other method which reasonably reflects the benefit derived.

The other factor is the amount of time that passes between the release of poll results and the time that the particular candidates receive the results of the poll. If over 15 days have passed since the poll results were made known to any other candidate or political committee, the following modification in the cost allocation must be made [11 CFR 106.4 (g)]:

The amount of the contribution and expenditure reported by a candidate or a political committee receiving poll results . . . more than 15 days after receipt of such poll results by the initial recipient(s) shall be—

(1) If the results are received during the period 16 to 60 days following receipt of the initial recipient(s), 50 percent of the amount allocated to an initial recipient of the same results;

(2) If the results are received during the period 61 to 180 days after receipt by the initial recipient(s), 5 percent of the amount allocated to an initial recipient of the same results;

(3) If the results are received more than 180 days after receipt by the initial recipient(s), no amount need be allocated.

Expenses among Candidates

Under the Federal financing of the Presidential (and Vice-Presidential) general election (discussed later in this chapter), candidates receiving Federal funds must agree to limit spending to the funds received. If expenditures are made which benefit both the Presidential (and Vice-Presidential) candidates and other national candidates (e.g., for U.S. Senator or Representative), the following allocation procedure governs in determining the expenses attributable to the Presidential (and Vice-Presidential) candidates [11 CFR 144.2]:

Allocation of Administrative Expenses

If an authorized committee (including the national committee if authorized) of the candidates of a political party for President and Vice President of the United States also incurs expenses to further the election of one or more other individuals to Federal, State, or local elective public office, expenses incurred by such committee which are not specifically to further the election of such other individual or individuals shall be considered as incurred to further the election of such candidates for President and Vice President in proportion to the number of other candidates supported. For example, if an authorized committee supports the Presidential candidate, the Vice-Presidential candidate, 5 congressional candidates, and 9 State candidates, the total number of candidates supported is 16. The amount of overhead and administrative expenses incurred by the authorized committee for the Presidential and Vice-Presidential candidates is 2/16 or 1/8.

PRESIDENTIAL PRIMARY MATCHING FUNDS

The FEC administers the matching funds program of Presidential primary campaigns. During the Presidential primary elections, eligible candidates receive matching payments from the U.S. Treasury for all *qualified* contributions (e.g., maximum of $250 per contributor) submitted to the FEC for matching funds. In order to be eligible for matching funds, the candidate must establish his viability by raising over $5,000 in individual contributions of $250 or less in 20 or more states. Also, the candidate must agree to an overall spending limit of $10 million (adjusted upward for changes in the price level since the passage of the Act, as was discussed earlier).

After the candidate becomes eligible, he must submit the list of contributors, the amounts involved, and the other necessary documentation to the FEC to establish the amount of contributions that he has raised. The FEC audits

this documentation and, if it is found to be in order, the FEC approves the disbursement of the matching funds by the Secretary of the Treasury. In 11 CFR 9036.3, the FEC describes what it considers to be insufficient documentation:

Insufficient Documentation

Contributions which are otherwise matchable may be rejected for matching purposes because of insufficient supporting documentation. These contributions may become matchable if there is a proper resubmission in accordance with § § 132.5 and 132.6. Insufficient documentation includes—

(a) Discrepancies in the written instruments, such as—

(1) Instruments drawn on other than personal accounts of contributors and not signed by the contributing individual;

(2) Signature discrepancies; and

(3) Lack of the contributor's signature, the amount of the contribution, or the listing of the committee or candidate as payee;

(b) Discrepancies between listed contributions and supporting documentation, such as—

(1) The contributor's name is misspelled;

(2) The listed amount requested for matching exceeds the amount contained on the written instrument; and

(3) A written instrument has not been submitted to support a listed contribution;

(c) Discrepancies within or between contribution lists submitted, such as—

(1) the address of the contributor is missing or incomplete, or the contributor's name is alphabetized incorrectly, or more than one contributor is listed per item; and

(2) A discrepancy in aggregation within or between submissions, or a listing of a contributor more than once within the same submission.

If the FEC finds that sufficient documentation exists for some, but not all, of the listed contributions, the candidate can *either* accept the FEC's finding of a lesser amount than submitted *or* resubmit documentation [11 CFR 9036.4 (a)]:

Certification Review and Notice

The Commission will review the submission to determine if the submission meets acceptable standards of good order under 11 CFR 9036.2 and 9036.3. Those submissions not meeting the standard will not be certified, and the candidate will be requested to resubmit the documentation. Submissions of a sufficient size will be reviewed using statistical sampling, and the candidate will be given a reduced amount based on the results of the sample.

Any items that were rejected by the FEC can be resubmitted, with adequate documentation, for matching funds.

As the primary campaign progresses, candidates are required to maintain their viability by receiving adequate support in the various primaries. If a candidate fails to receive 10 percent or more of the votes cast in two successive primary elections in which he was an active participant, he loses his eligibility for matching funds. A candidate can regain this status by receiving 20 percent or more of the votes in a subsequent primary.

If a candidate's campaign is found to have (a) incurred any unqualified campaign expenses (e.g., paid for illegal activities), (b) spent more than the agreed to limit, or (c) have any unspent matching funds after having liquidated the campaign's debts, the FEC must request that the candidate's campaign committee remit the equivalent amount to the U.S. Treasury.

FINANCING PARTY NOMINATING CONVENTIONS

The FEC administers the program which finances the Presidential nominating conventions of major and minor political parties. (A major party is one whose candidate received 25 percent or more of the popular vote in the last Presidential election; a minor party is one whose candidate received between 5 and 25 percent of the popular vote in the last Presidential election.) A major political party is entitled to $3 million for its convention. A minor party is entitled to [11 CFR 9008.3 (B)]:

Subject to the provisions of 11 CFR Part 9008, the national committee of a minor party shall be entitled to payments under 11 CFR 9008.8, with respect to any Presidential nominating convention, in amounts which, in the aggregate, shall not exceed an amount which bears the same ratio to the amount the national committee of a major party is entitled to receive under 11 CFR 9008.4, as the number of popular votes received in the preceding Presidential election by that minor party's Presidential candidate in the preceding Presidential election by all of the major party Presidential candidates.

The entitlements for major and minor parties are adjusted upward for changes in the Consumer Price Index.

The parties are limited to convention expenditures that equal the amount of their entitlement. The parties are required to repay a portion of any entitlement that is received if they (a) spend more than their entitlement, (b) spend funds for anything other than qualified convention expenses, or (c) have a surplus of public funds remaining after the convention's expenses are paid.

GENERAL PRESIDENTIAL ELECTION

The FEC administers the public financing of the Presidential (and Vice-Presidential) general election. Under the provisions of the law, candidates of major parties are entitled to receive $20 million in public funds for financing the Presidential (and Vice-Presidential) general election campaign. The slate of minor parties is entitled to reduced amounts. (All entitlements are adjusted for change in the price level.) Among the conditions that a candidate must agree to comply with in order to receive the public funds are (a) to limit the general election campaign spending to the amount of public funds received, (b) to accept *no* campaign contributions from private sources, and (c) to use the public funds received for the payment of qualified expenses. The candidates must also agree to repayment of some of the funds in the event that they violate the conditions or if there are any funds remaining at the end of the campaign.

During the general election, the national, state, or their subordinate committees are limited by the following guidelines [2 USC 441a (d)]:

> (2) The national committee of a political party may not make any expenditure in connection with the general election campaign of any candidate for President of the United States who is affiliated with such party which exceeds an amount equal to 2 cents multiplied by the voting age population of the United States (as certified under subsection (e) of this section). Any expenditure under this paragraph shall be in addition to any expenditure by a national committee of a political party serving as the principal campaign committee of a candidate for the office of President of the United States.

> (3) The national committee of a political party, or a State committee of a political party, including any subordinate committee of a State committee, may not make any expenditure in connection with the general election campaign of a candidate for Federal office in a State who is affiliated with such party which exceeds—

> (A) in the case of a candidate for election to the office of Senator, or of Representative from a State which is entitled to only one Representative, the greater of—

> (i) 2 cents multiplied by the voting age population of the State (as certified under subsection (e) of this section); or

> (ii) $20,000; and

> (B) in the case of a candidate

for election to the office of Representative, Delegate, or Resident Commissioner of any other state, $10,000.

These limits are adjusted for changes in the Consumer Price Index.

Here one can see the interplay between the allocation rules and the expenditure limitations. For example, when a committee runs an advertising campaign for a slate of candidates for Federal office, the cost of the campaign must be allocated across candidates in order to test compliance with the above quoted limitation.

AUDITS

The FEC's audit rights and responsibilities flow from the following provision in the law [2 USC 435 (b)]:

> *Audits and field investigations.* The Commission may conduct audits and field investigations of any political committee required to file a report under section 434 of this title. All audits and field investigations concerning the verification for, and receipt and use of, any payments received by a candidate or committee under chapter 95 or chapter 96 of title 26 shall be given priority. Prior to conducting any audit under this subsection, the Commission shall perform an internal review of reports filed by selected committees to determine if the reports filed by a particular committee meet the threshold requirements for substantial compliance with the Act. Such thresholds for compliance shall be established by the Commission. The Commission may, upon an affirmative vote of 4 of its members, conduct an audit and field investigation of any committee which does meet the threshold requirements established by the Commission. Such audit shall be commenced within 30

> days of such vote, except that any audit of an authorized committee of a candidate, under the provisions of this subsection, shall be commenced within 6 months of the election for which such committee is authorized.

In carrying out its responsibilities, the FEC requires audits of recipients of public funds for (a) Presidential primaries, (b) Presidential nominating conventions, and (c) the general Presidential election. In addition, the FEC's audit staff conducts audits of a large number of Congressional candidate committees—selected on a random basis—state party committees, multicandidate committees, etc. The FEC's audit staff follows up on referrals from other units within the FEC (e.g., the Office of the General Counsel) when these other units have evidence that certain candidates or committees need to improve their reporting and/or recordkeeping in order to comply with the law.

The FEC's audit process is designed to be helpful to the candidates and committees. The audit staff attempts to elicit voluntary improvements where violations are found. The affected candidate and/or committee(s) are kept informed of the audit's findings. They receive a copy of the audit report. An example of a summary output of the FEC's audit work is its *Report on the Random Audits Conducted by Congressional Elections.* The report was based on 106 audits of Congressional candidates and committees. The following were the most frequently encountered problems:

1. *Inadequate Supporting Documentation for Expenditures* (11 CFR 102.19 (c))

Many committees audited had not obtained and/or kept receipted bills, stating the particulars for expenditures in excess of $100 (or those which aggregated in excess of $100 to the same payee) during the calendar year. Where a receipted bill was not available, the committees had failed to keep, as an alternative, the cancelled check showing payment, together with the bill, the invoice or a contemporaneous memorandum of the transaction supplied by the payee.

2. *Failure to Itemize Contributions and Expenditures* (2 USC 434 (b) (2) & (9))

The committees frequently failed to itemize a series of contributions which, in the aggregate, exceeded $100 in a calendar year from the same contributor or a series of expenditures which, in the aggregate, exceeded $100 to the same person during a calendar year.

3. *Failure to Itemize All Transfers Received Or Made* (2 USC 434 (B) (4))

Committees did not always itemize all transfers, despite instructions on the reporting forms and schedules. Most of the undisclosed transfers were in amounts of $100 or less, suggesting that the committees were unaware of the requirement to itemize any transfer, regardless of amount.

4. *Acceptance of Prohibited Contributions*

A substantial number of committees accepted contributions from corporate and labor sources (2 USC §441b). Committees also accepted contributions in excess of the dollar limitations (2 USC 441a).[3]

All reports filed with FEC and all audit reports produced by the FEC are available to the public.

REFERENCE NOTES

1. U.S., Federal Election Commission, *Bookkeeping and Reporting Manual for Candidates and Political Committees,* 1978, p. i.

2. U.S., Federal Election Commission, *Annual Report—1978,* p. 42.

3. *Ibid.,* p. 20.

Chapter 24

General Accounting Office

This final chapter deals with an agency—the U.S. General Accounting Office (GAO)—that is unique among those discussed in this book for two reasons. First, it is an agency of the legislative branch of the government (as was the Cost Accounting Standards Board, Chapter 17); all other agencies discussed in this book are executive branch agencies. Second, it exercises the majority of its influence on *other* Federal agencies; the other agencies covered in this book primarily affect entities outside of the Federal government.

The GAO was established by the Budget and Accounting Act of 1921. It is one of four agencies that were established to provide assistance to the U.S. Congress. The other agencies are the Congressional Research Service, the Congressional Budget Office, and the Office of Technical Assistance.

The GAO is headed by the Comptroller General of the United States. The Comptroller General is nominated by the President and approved by the Senate. The President is expected to select his nominee from a list of names recommended to him by a commission composed of the Speaker of the House of Representatives, the President *pro tempore* of the Senate, the majority and minority leaders of the House, and the chairmen and ranking minority members of the House Government Operations Committee and the Senate Governmental Affairs Committee. However, the President can nominate someone who is not on the Congress's list if he so desires. A similar procedure is followed for the appointment of a Deputy Comptroller General. Both the Comptroller General and Deputy Comptroller General receive tenures of 15 years without the possibility of reappointment to the office. The length of the term of office and the inability to succeed oneself were intended to insulate the leadership of the GAO from political pressure.

The GAO is headquartered in Washington, D.C., and operates out of 19 regional and international offices. The GAO operates 12 divisions. Its Accounting and Financial Management Division is responsible for the accounting and auditing policy areas that are detailed in this chapter.

GAO DUTIES

When the GAO was initially established, its major duties were derived from functions that were transferred from the Comptroller of the Treasury. These duties were (a) to investigate all matters involving receipts and disbursements of Federal funds, (b) to make recommendations to Congress regarding legislation for fostering economy and efficiency in Federal operations, (c) to conduct studies and render reports at the request of Congress, (d) to render binding decisions on the legality of proposed expenditures by executive agencies, (e) to settle claims made by or made against the United States, and (f) to prescribe accounting procedures for Federal agencies.[1]

Over the years, the GAO's functions have been modified and/or expanded by various laws. The most significant of these are the Government Corporation Control Act of 1945, the Legislative Reorganization Acts of 1946 and 1970, the Accounting and Auditing Act of 1950, the Congressional Budget and Impoundment Control Act of 1974, and the General Accounting Office Acts of 1974 and 1980.

The basic duties with which the GAO was charged when it was established in 1921 continue to the present. This is particularly true of its accounting and auditing duties, which will be reviewed later in this chapter. In addition to its basic historic duties, the GAO has recently been charged (under the Energy Policy and Conservation Act of 1975) with the verification of energy-related information that is accumulated by energy companies and submitted to the Federal government. Another recent addition to its agenda (under the Congressional Budget and Impoundment Act of 1974) is the responsibility for reviewing the executive branch's execution of the Federal budget as enacted into law. Under this law, the GAO is to examine the executive branch's actions in carrying out the programs approved and funded by Congress. When the executive branch is found to have thwarted the intent of Congress by impounding funds, the GAO is authorized to bring suit against the executive branch. (On one occasion the GAO has done so.)

The GAO is often called upon by Congress to take the lead in new initiatives involving accounting. For example, the Comptroller General was named the ex officio chairman of the Cost Accounting Standards Board (Chapter 17) and the Railroad Accounting Principles Board (see the Interstate Commerce Commission, Chapter 5) when they were established by Congress.

ASSISTANCE TO CONGRESS

The GAO's duties are very clearly quite broad. Some of these duties, particularly those that were transferred over from the Comptroller of the Treasury when the GAO was established, are viewed by some as being more appropriately assigned to the executive branch of the government. That is. they deal more with the laws being "faithfully executed" than with the legislative branch's duty to "make the laws." This is one of the reasons that the GAO is sometimes referred to as the "fourth branch of government."[2] However, in its role of providing assistance to the Congress, the GAO is very clearly living up to its function of being a Congressional support agency.

The GAO provides studies of specific issues of relevance to Congress (a) under provisions of specific laws (e.g., as in the case of the *Feasibility Study* conducted under P.L. 90-370 which gave rise to the establishment of the Cost Accounting Standards Board); (b) under requests from committees, subcommittees, or individual members of Congress; and (c) under initiative taken directly by the GAO. Additionally, the GAO can provide staff assistance to Congressional committees. It also works closely with the other Congressional assistance offices to avoid duplication of effort. The GAO is frequently involved in testifying before Congressional committees.

LEGAL SERVICES

The legal work of the GAO generally involves more of an interface with executive agencies than with the Congress. The GAO renders decisions to executive agencies on such matters as the legality of disbursing funds appropriated by Congress for a specific purpose. The GAO also renders decisions involving contracting and procurement actions by executive agencies (e.g., as to the propriety of awarding of a contract to a specific bidder when another unsuccessful bidder

has protested). These legal decisions are binding on the executive agencies. The GAO also renders legal assistance to Congress, as requested.

GAO REGULATIONS

The GAO published its regulations in Chapter I of Title 4 of the Code of Federal Regulations. Chapter II of Title 4 deals with claims collection and is jointly issued by the GAO and the Department of Justice. Most of the GAO's accounting and auditing regulations are issued as separate documents, not as part of the CFR. One area of GAO regulation that affects many of the agencies reviewed in this book and is documented in the CFR is the clearance (by the GAO) of information gathering practices and reports of independent regulatory agencies. This is discussed later in this chapter.

GAO REGULATION OF ACCOUNTING

From its origin in 1921, the GAO has been concerned with the accounting systems of the Federal executive agencies. For the first 30 years of this involvement, the GAO was an active "doer" of the accounting; for the past 30 years the GAO has been a standard-setter and reviewer of the accounting for Federal executive agencies. The GAO has characterized its involvement with the accounting for executive agencies during its initial decades as follows:

> . . . laws relating to GAO placed the Comptroller General in potential oppo-

sition with the Treasury and the Budget Bureau. GAO accounting responsibilities were basically to assure compliance with law; Treasury's were to keep track of appropriations, expenditures, revenues, debt, and the financial condition of the Government; and the Budget Bureau's were to provide information for effective management and appropriation control. Since cooperation between the agencies could not be achieved, GAO built its own detailed accounts of receipts, expenditures, disbursements, and appropriations. Initially, the foundations of the agencies were the same: appropriations and warrants. However, beyond that similarity they were irreconcilable.

The differences between GAO and the executive agencies on accounting matters continued, at times marked by specific controversy, until the late 1930's when one observer noted that decentralization and the lack of uniformity was so pervasive in Government that management had to rely on less formal devices. Administrators relied on "little black books" crammed with statistics about their agency's financial matters that bore little resemblance to what GAO or Treasury prescribed as official agency accounts. . . .

By the late 1930's the state of the art of accounting in the Federal sector had lagged significantly behind the rapid changes in the sizes and types of Government activities and the advancements made in the private sector. Federal sector accounting was preoccupied with the detailed voucher examinations and other detailed verification. Accounting expertise in Government left much to be desired.[3]

Toward the end of this period, the GAO reached its peak number of personnel of about 15,000. (Currently, the GAO has approximately 5,000 employ-

ees.) This was due to the nature of its work—i.e., a detailed checking of individual transactions and accounts. For example, the following presents some of the workload of the GAO:

In 1947 GAO:

—Kept about 414,000 accounts of appropriations, limitations, accountable officers, and others.

—Countersigned or approved about 74,000 warrants or requisitions for disbursing funds.

—Audited 93,000 accountable officers' accounts containing about 42 million vouchers or contracts and about 350 million postal transactions.

—Settled about one and one-half million accountable officers' or postmasters' accounts or claims.

—Reconciled almost one-half billion checks.[4]

This period was, of course, devoid of any electronic data processing assistance. Manually maintained records, adding machines, and large staffs of clerks were the standard tools of the GAO.

Several things came together over the period from 1945 to 1950 to significantly change the approach GAO took to its involvement with the accounting systems of the executive agencies. One was the passage of the Government Corporation Control Act of 1945. This law required the GAO to conduct the equivalent of commercial audits (i.e., corporate financial audits) of government corporations (such as the Tennessee Valley Authority). These audits required the expertise of certified public accountants (whose domain was, and still is, the conduct of such audits for private corporations).

The GAO started hiring more CPAs to enable it to accomplish this task. Next, the GAO, along with the executive branch's Department of Treasury and the Bureau of the Budget (now the Office of Management and Budget) voluntarily established the Joint Accounting Improvement Program (now known as the Joint Financial Management Improvement Program—JFMIP). The objectives of this program were:

1. Government accounting processes would be consolidated and integrated for the benefit of the Government as a whole.

2. Since individual operating agencies are the points where improvements must be made, improvements must be directed toward effective controls and proper records at the agencies.

3. The responsibilities of GAO as an oversight agency would be prescribing accounting systems and making system inspections and comprehensive audits as opposed to keeping records otherwise kept by Treasury, Budget Bureau, or operating agencies.[5]

Finally, the Accounting and Auditing Act of 1950 officially assigned to the executive agencies the responsibility for maintaining accounting systems and to the GAO the responsibility for (a) prescribing the principles and standards to which those systems were to conform, (b) approving individual agencies' systems, and (c) auditing these systems as an agent of the Congress. Thus, over a period of less than 10 years, the GAO's thrust changed from one of accounting for executive agencies to one of setting accounting standards and approving accounting systems for these agencies. These basic functions continue to the present as the GAO"s basis of involvement in accounting for Federal executive agencies.

ACCOUNTING PRINCIPLES AND STANDARDS

The GAO has developed a body of principles and standards to which executive agency accounting systems must conform in order to be approved by the GAO. This body of principles and standards comprises Title 2 of the *General Accounting Office Policy and Procedures Manual for Guidance of Federal Agencies.* In addition to being a component of this larger work, Title 2 is issued as a separate manual under the title of *Accounting Principles and Standards for Federal Agencies.* This manual, which is about 85 pages in length, is composed of three chapters. The first provides an introduction to the legal basis (i.e., the Auditing and Accounting Procedures Act of 1950, as amended) and objectives of the manual. These objectives are:

PURPOSES AND OBJECTIVES OF FEDERAL AGENCY ACCOUNTING

All management officials in Federal agencies share the responsibility for economical attainment of the purposes and objectives of their agencies. The increasing magnitude of Federal expenditures requires that every reasonable means be sought to obtain full value for each taxpayer's dollar spent. Effective accounting can play an important part in the discharge of this responsibility.

Proper accounting for the financial and other resources entrusted to an agency is an inherent responsibility of the managers of that agency.

STANDARDS FOR INTERNAL MANAGEMENT CONTROL

The general objective of an internal management control system of a Federal agency is to provide positive assistance in carrying out all duties and responsibilities as effectively, efficiently, and economically as possible, considering the requirements and restrictions of all applicable laws and regulations.

The more important specific objectives of a satisfactory control system are to:

(1) Promote efficiency and economy of operations.

(2) Restrict obligations and costs, consistent with efficiently and effectively carrying out the purposes for which the agency exists, within the limits of congressional appropriations and other authorizations and restrictions.

(3) Safeguard assets against waste, loss, or improper or unwarranted use.

(4) Insure that all revenues applicable to agency assets or operations are collected or properly accounted for.

(5) Assure the accuracy and reliability of financial, statistical, and other reports.

An accounting system is an integral part of a management control system since the accounting records and related procedures can contribute significantly to attaining the objectives of the control system. For this reason, the following standards for internal management control require consideration in the design of an agency's accounting system.[6]

The second chapter of the manual contains the accounting principles and standards to which agency systems must conform in order to be approved by the GAO. This chapter comprises over half of the manual. The major sections of this chapter are:

Standards for Accounting Systems

The Accrual Basis of Accounting

Fund Control

Account Structure

Assets

Liabilities

Investment of the U.S. Government

Revenues

Costs

Financial Reporting

Treasury Department Central Accounting and Financial Reporting

While most of the titles of these sections are self-explanatory, two require some amplification. *Fund Control* is defined in the manual as follows:

> The term "fund control" refers to management control over the use of fund authorizations to insure that (1) funds are used only for authorized purposes, (2) they are economically and efficiently used, (3) obligations and expenditures do not exceed the amounts authorized, and (4) the obligation or expenditure of amounts authorized is not reserved or otherwise deferred without congressional knowledge and approval. Each accounting system shall incorporate appropriate techniques to assist in achieving fund control.[7]

The "Investment of the U.S. Government" section coincides with the concept of owners' equity for private entities:

> The investment of the United States in the assets of a Federal agency or activity consists of the residual equity of the Government after accounting for all known liabilities and investments or equities of others.

TABLE 24-1
Matrix of Title II Requirements by Basis and Organization

			Number of Requirements		
	LAW	*GAAP*	*GAO Requirements*	*Executive Agency Requirements*	*Total*
Objectives	9	7	8	0	24
Fundamental concepts	4	5	2	2	13
Total theoretical	13	12	10	2	37
Reporting	30	50	34	3	117
Procedures	19	19	45	1	84
Total practical	49	69	79	4	201
Total	62	81	89	6	238

Source: U.S., General Accounting Office, *An Examination of Accounting Principles and Standards for Federal Agencies (Title II)*, 1980, p. 36.

The major elements comprising the investment of the United States are:

Additions to investment:

Congressional appropriations

Borrowings from the U.S. Treasury

Property and services obtained from other Federal agencies without reimbursement

Donations received

Accumulated net income from operations

Reductions of investment:

Funds returned to U.S. Treasury

Property transferred to other Federal agencies without reimbursement

Accumulated net loss from operations

These major elements of the Federal investment shall be separately accounted for and disclosed in financial reports. Major changes for each fiscal period should be summarized in separate financial schedules.[8]

A recent review by the GAO of its principles and standards concluded that they represent an amalgam of requirements that it classified as accounting objectives, fundamental concepts, procedural requirements, and reporting requirements. Further, it concluded that the sources from which these various requirements were derived were: various laws, generally accepted accounting principles, GAO requirements, and executive agency requirements. Table 24-1 presents a cross-tabulation of the requirements found in the GAO's principles and standards by type of requirement and by source. This categorization and cross-tabulation is somewhat subjective. For example, accrual accounting is a requirement both of GAAP *and* P.L. 84-683.

The GAO is currently conducting a thorough reexamination of its accounting principles and standards for Federal executive agencies. This conceptual framework project has a parallel in the private sector in the work of the Financial Accounting Standards Board (FASB). Like the FASB, the GAO is attempting to arrive at an integrated progression from objectives of accounting and reporting, down through guidelines for the establishing of standards, and the actual establishment of those standards. However, unlike the FASB's responsibilities which end with the establishment of *standards*, the GAO's responsibilities continue on to the development of operational criteria (or requirements) for the implementation of those standards in individual accounting systems. Given that the GAO's conceptual framework project is not yet complete, it is too early to speculate on what standards will be in effect in the future, and how they may differ from the existing principles and standards.

The third chapter of the manual deals with the procedures that agencies must follow in having their accounting systems approved by the GAO. There are basically two stages in the approval process: (a) approval of the agency's statement of principles and standards, and (b) approval of the design of the accounting system. Since the law was enacted in 1950 requiring agencies to have their systems approved by the GAO, about 95 percent of the more than 300 accounting systems of executive agencies have been approved at the first stage (i.e., statement of principles and standards). However, only about two-thirds of the accounting systems have received approval of their design. Addi-

tionally, many of the systems that have received prior approval have undergone significant changes so that reapproval will be required.

A number of factors have contributed to the extended period of time that has passed without completion of the approval process. Initially, the GAO had to have a lead time to develop its standards. Subsequently, it has found that it has no effective censures that it can levy against the reluctant agencies other than bringing them to the attention of Congress. It does this annually in a report to Congress (the most recent edition of which is entitled *Status, Progress and Problems in Federal Agency Accounting During Fiscal 1979*).

GAO INVOLVEMENT IN AUDITING

From its inception, the GAO has had a significant role in the audit responsibility of the Federal government. However, this responsibility has undergone significant change over time. Initially, the GAO's concept of auditing entailed reviewing some aspects of virtually all transactions involving the receipt or expenditure of funds by the Federal government. With the duties assigned to it by the Government Corporation Control Act of 1945, the GAO became involved in the conduct of traditional financial audits. Over the years, as its "doing" of the accounting for Federal agencies was converted to a "reviewing" of the systems of these agencies, the GAO found itself more and more adopting the posture of an auditor. In reviewing the GAO's work at the present, it is apparent that the GAO has forged ahead of the area of corporate financial audits (whose prime concern is the fairness of presentation of the financial statements of the audited entity) into such areas as evaluations of efficiency, effectiveness, and program results.

At present, the GAO has certain legislated or contractual audit rights and duties:

1. The GAO is required to periodically audit government corporations and certain other entities (such as various Congressional offices, e.g., finance office, restaurants, etc.).

2. The GAO is to *review* the annual audit reports of Federally-chartered corporations (such as the American Legion) whose reports are submitted to Congress. These audits are conducted by independent certified public accountants (or licensed public accountants).

3. The GAO has audit rights given to it by law and contractual clauses in most major Federal contracts and grants.

4. Based on a legal requirement, a request from Congress, or on its own initiative, the GAO has audit access to virtually all Federal executive agencies.

In some of its audit roles, the GAO operates like an independent auditor on a corporate financial audit. However, the greatest proportion of its audit work carries the GAO into relatively uncharted waters—dealing with questions of program results and cost/benefits.

In addition to the audit work of the GAO, individual Federal agencies have their own audit functions (e.g., internal audits, inspectors general) and audit rights on their own contracts and/or grants. Generally, these examinations also involve objectives other than those usually associated with corporate financial audits.

In the 1960s, the GAO became concerned with the fact that much of this expanded concept of auditing at the Federal level—both by it and by executive agencies—was not buttressed by codified standards. Standards did exist for audit work that was comparable to that conducted by independent certified public accountants. Such standards are codified by the American Institute of Certified Public Accountants (AICPA) in its Statements on Auditing Standards. However, to the extent that the audits with which the GAO was concerned were of a more diverse nature, these standards were not sufficient to cover its work. The GAO proceeded to develop the necessary standards.

In 1972 it published a pamphlet entitled *Standards for Audit of Governmental Organizations, Programs, Activities and Functions.* In this document, the GAO identifies the attributes of an audited entity, any or all of which might be subject to examination in a particular audit:

1. *Financial and compliance*—determines (a) whether financial operations are properly conducted, (b) whether the financial reports of an audited entity are presented fairly, and (c) whether the entity has complied with applicable laws and regulations.

2. *Economy and efficiency*—determines whether the entity is managing or utilizing its resources (personnel, property, space, and so forth) in an economical and efficient manner and the causes of any inefficiencies or uneconomical practices, including inade-

quacies in management information systems, administrative procedures, or organizational structure.

3. *Program results*—determines whether the desired results or benefits are being achieved, whether the objectives established by the legislature or other authorizing body are being met, and whether the agency has considered alternatives which might yield desired results at a lower cost.[9]

Only the first of these attributes is usually associated with corporate financial audits.

The GAO then proceeded to identify standards to be met in conducting such examinations. In the following quotation, the summary standards are presented. The italicized portions highlight where the standards set by the GAO and the AICPA coincide; the remaining portions are occasioned by the expanded notion of "audit" recognized by the GAO:

GENERAL STANDARDS

1. The full scope of an audit of a governmental program, function, activity, or organization should encompass:

    a. An examination of financial transactions, accounts, and reports, including an evaluation of compliance with applicable laws and regulations.

    b. A review of efficiency and economy in the use of resources.

    c. A review to determine whether desired results are effectively achieved.

    In determining the scope for a particular audit, responsible officials should give consideration to the needs of the potential users of the results of that audit.

2. *The auditors assigned to perform the audit must collectively possess adequate professional proficiency for the tasks required.*

3. *In all matters relating to the audit work, the audit organization and the individual auditors shall maintain an independent attitude.*

4. *Due professional care is to be used in conducting the audit and in preparing related reports.*

EXAMINATION AND EVALUATION STANDARDS

1. *Work is to be adequately planned.*

2. *Assistants are to be properly supervised.*

3. A review is to be made of compliance with legal and regulatory requirements.

4. *An evaluation is to be made of the system of internal control to assess the extent it can be relied upon to ensure accurate information,* to ensure compliance with laws and regulations, and to provide for efficient and effective operations.

5. *Sufficient, competent, and relevant evidence is to be obtained to afford a reasonable basis for the auditor's opinions, judgments, conclusions, and recommendations.*

REPORTING STANDARDS

1. Written audit reports are to be submitted to the appropriate officials of the organizations requiring or arranging for the audits. Copies of the reports should be sent to other officials who may be responsible for taking action on audit findings and recommendations and to others responsible or authorized to receive such reports. Unless restricted by law or regulation, copies should also be made available for public inspection.

2. Reports are to be issued on or before the dates specified by law, regulation, or other arrangement and, in any event, as promptly as possible so as to make the information available for timely use by management and by legislative officials.

3. Each report shall:

   a. Be as concise as possible but, at the same time, clear and complete enough to be understood by the users.

   b. Present factual matter accurately, completely, and fairly.

   c. Present findings and conclusions objectively and in language as clear and simple as the subject matter permits.

   d. Include only factual information, findings, and conclusions that are adequately supported by enough evidence in the auditor's working papers to demonstrate or prove, when called upon, the bases for the matters reported and their correctness and reasonableness. Detailed supporting information should be included in the report to the extent necessary to make a convincing presentation.

   e. Include, when possible, the auditor's recommendations for actions to effect improvements in problem areas noted in his audit and to otherwise make improvements in operations. Information on underlying causes of problems reported should be included to assist in implementing or devising corrective actions.

   f. Place primary emphasis on improvement rather than on criticism of the past; critical comments should be presented in balanced perspective, recognizing any unusual diffi-

culties or circumstances faced by the operating officials concerned.

   g. Identify and explain issues and questions needing further study and consideration by the auditor or others.

   h. Include recognition of noteworthy accomplishments, particularly when management improvements in one program or activity may be applicable elsewhere.

   i. Include recognition of the views of responsible officials of the organization, program, function, or activity audited on the auditor's findings, conclusions, and recommendations. Except where the possibility of fraud or other compelling reason may require different treatment, the auditor's tentative findings and conclusions should be reviewed with such officials. When possible, without undue delay, their views should be obtained in writing and objectively considered and presented in preparing the final report.

   j. *Clearly explain the scope and objectives of the audit.*

   k. State whether any significant pertinent information has been omitted because it is deemed privileged or confidential. The nature of such information should be described, and the law or other basis under which it is withheld should be stated.

4. *Each audit report containing financial reports shall:*

   a. *Contain an expression of the auditor's opinion as to whether the information in the financial reports is presented fairly in accordance with generally accepted accounting principles (or with other specified accounting principles applicable to the organization, program function, or activity audited), applied on a basis consistent with that of the preceding reporting period. If the auditor cannot express an opinion, the reasons therefor should be stated in the report.*

b. Contain appropriate supplementary explanatory information about the contents of the financial reports as may be necessary for full and informative disclosure about the financial operations of the organization, program, function, or activity audited. Violations of legal or other regulatory requirements, including instances of noncompliance, and material changes in accounting policies and procedures, along with their effect on the financial reports, shall be explained in the audit report.[10]

Although many portions of the GAO audit standards are not in verbatim conformance with those of the AICPA, they generally can be regarded as logical progressions of the traditional tenets of auditing into the expanded functions faced by the GAO. The GAO standards are explained and amplified in the more than 50 pages of the pamphlet. Since the standards were issued, the GAO has published a series of supplements which serve to illustrate or expand upon the basic standards.

The standards are quite comprehensive, covering, as they do, the three facets of entities or programs that may be examined during audits. However, it is not necessary that every audit encompass all facets. The GAO recognizes that it (or Congress, or an executive agency) can limit the nature of its inquiry to only one facet, in which

case, only the relevant portions of the standard are applicable.

Since the GAO issued these standards, they have become applicable to (a) all audits conducted by the GAO, (b) all audits conducted by or for Federal executive departments (under a directive of the Office of Management and Budget), and (c) all examinations made by inspectors general (required by the Inspector General Act of 1978). Further, any audit required by a Federal agency (that is made by either state or local governmental auditors or independent CPAs) of contractors, grantees, or other organizations receiving Federal funds, must conform to the applicable standards.

The GAO is currently revising its audit standards to accommodate recent changes in the audit environment (e.g., such as innovations in EDP technology) and new programmatic needs of the government (such as provision for detection of fraud and abuse in Federal programs). The revised standards are expected to remain in close conformity with the standards promulgated by the AICPA where there is a common thread of purpose between the two bodies of standards.

REVIEW OF REGULATORY AGENCY REPORTS

Under the Federal Reports Act of 1973, the GAO was assigned the responsibility of reviewing the reporting requirements levied on businesses by independent Federal regulatory agencies. Currently, 13 agencies must clear their reports with the GAO prior to their imposition on the entities subject to

TABLE 24-2
Number of Audit Reports Issued During Fiscal Year 1980

	Addressee				
	Congress	Committee	Member	Agency Officials	TOTAL
Administration of Justice	11	6	3	4	24
Agriculture.	5	8	2	5	20
Automatic Data Processing	4	9	1	2	16
Commerce and Housing Credit.	3	9	2	3	17
Community and Regional Development	11	12	6	6	35
Congressional Information Services. . . .	1	3	–	–	4
Education, Training, Employment & Social Services.	5	9	8	7	29
Energy	38	35	16	15	104
Financial Management & Information Systems	20	15	1	22	58
General Government	29	52	10	24	115
General Purpose Fiscal Assistance.	4	4	1	1	10
General Science, Space Technology. . . .	6	6	–	3	15
Health.	13	16	11	7	47
Impoundment Control Act of 1974 . . .	20	2	–	–	22
Income Security	11	12	8	7	38
International Affairs	25	7	3	8	43
National Defense.	45	67	25	71	208
National Resources & Environment. . . .	15	13	10	14	52
Non-Discrimination & Equal Opportunity	5	–	1	1	7
Procurement Other Than Defense.	2	9	1	7	19
Transportation	15	14	3	12	44
Veterans Benefits and Services	–	4	1	2	7
TOTAL.	288	312	113	221	934

Source: U.S., General Accounting Office, *Annual Report–1980*, p. 91.

their regulation. These include the following agencies that are reviewed in this book:

Agency	Chapter
Interstate Commerce Commission	5
Federal Communications Commission	6
Civil Aeronautics Board	7
Federal Maritime Commission	10
Federal Energy Regulatory Commission	13
Securities and Exchange Commission	18
Federal Trade Commission	22

The reporting requirements of other Federal agencies are subject to the same degree of control by the Office of Management and Budget.

The GAO's regulations covering this function comprise 4 CFR Part 10—Clearance of Proposals by Independent Federal Regulatory Agencies to Conduct or Sponsor the Collection of Information. The GAO's clearance procedure monitors the proposed reporting requirements for (a) duplication of existing reporting required by other agencies,

(b) the reporting burden placed on the prospective respondents, (c) the cost to the Federal government in supporting the program, and (d) the intended use and expected benefits to be derived from the program. If clearance is granted by the GAO, the agency can implement the program. However, the GAO's clearance is given only for a specified period of time. The regulatory agency must then resubmit the program for another review by the GAO.

GAO: PEOPLE AND PRODUCT

The GAO currently has a staff of about 5,000 employees. About 80 percent are professional employees; the remainder are clerical and administrative. About three quarters of the GAO's professional employees are classified as "evaluators." A majority of those in this classification have accounting and auditing backgrounds. Other professional groups represented on the GAO's staff include attorneys, actuaries, engineers, economists, and data processing specialists.[11]

Table 24-2 presents an overview of a recent year's output of GAO reports. Most of these reports are made available to any interested members of the public. Single copies are available at no cost.

In addition to its reports, another "output" of the GAO is its testimony before Congressional committees. In recent years, the GAO has had the Comptroller General or members of its staff testify before Congress approaching 200 times per annum.[12]

REFERENCE NOTES

1. U.S., General Accounting Office, "The General Accounting Office and Its Functions—A Brief Historical Outline," *The GAO Review,* Summer 1971, p. 3.

2. Joseph Pois, *Watchdog on the Potomac: A Study of the Comptroller General of the United States,* (Washington, D.C.: University Press of America, 1979), p. 1.

3. U.S., General Accounting Office, *An Examination of Accounting Principles and Standards for Federal Agencies (Title II),* 1980, pp. 8-9.

4. *Ibid.,* p. 11.

5. *Ibid.,* p. 12.

6. U.S., General Accounting Office, *Accounting Principles and Standards for Federal Agencies,* 1978, pp. 2-4-2-5.

7. *Ibid.,* p. 2-17.

8. *Ibid.*, pp. 2-41-2-42.

9. U.S., General Accounting Office, *Standards for Audit of Governmental Organizations, Programs, Activities and Functions,* 1972, p. 2.

10. *Ibid.*, pp. 6-9.

11. U.S., General Accounting Office, *Annual Report—1980,* p. 24.

12. *Ibid.*, p. 4.

Agency Addresses and Telephone Numbers

This Appendix provides the address and telephone number(s) for the information and/or publication office(s) of the agencies reviewed in this book. Some agencies maintain a single office for information and publications. Others maintain separate offices. Yet others have no central office for publications; the information office can direct callers to the appropriate office for inquiries about access to publications.

CIVIL AERONAUTICS BOARD
1825 Connecticut Avenue, N.W.
Washington, D.C. 20426

Information: 202/673-5990
Publications: 202/673-5174

COST ACCOUNTING
STANDARDS BOARD

Direct inquiries to the U.S. General Accounting Office.

ENERGY INFORMATION
ADMINISTRATION

U.S. Department of Energy
2000 M Street, N.W.
Washington, D.C. 20461
Information: 202/633-8500

FEDERAL COMMUNICATIONS
COMMISSION
1919 M Street, N.W.
Washington, D.C. 20554

Information: 202/632-7260
Publications: 202/632-6427

FEDERAL DEPOSIT INSURANCE
CORPORATION
550 17th Street, N.W.
Washington, D.C. 20429

Information: 202/389-4221

FEDERAL ELECTIONS
COMMISSION
1325 K Street, N.W.
Washington, D.C. 20463

Information and publications:
202/523-4068

FEDERAL ENERGY REGULA-
TORY COMMISSION
825 North Capitol Street, N.E.
Washington, D.C. 20426

Information: 202/357-8055

FEDERAL HOME LOAN BANK
BOARD
1700 G Street, N.W.
Washington, D.C. 20552

Information: 202/377-6677

FEDERAL MARITIME
COMMISSION
1100 L Street, N.W.
Washington, D.C. 20573

Information: 202/523-5707

FEDERAL RAILROAD
ADMINISTRATION
400 7th Street, S.W.
Washington, D.C. 20590

Information and publications:
202/426-0881

FEDERAL RESERVE SYSTEM
20th Street & Constitution Avenue,
N.W.
Washington, D.C. 20551

Information: 202/452-3000
Publications: 202/452-3244

FEDERAL TRADE COMMISSION
Pennsylvania Avenue & 6th Street,
N.W.
Washington, D.C. 20580

Information and publications:
202/523-3598

GENERAL ACCOUNTING
OFFICE
441 G Street, N.W.
Washington, D.C. 20548

Information: 202/275-2812
Publications: 202/275-6241

HEALTH CARE FINANCING
ADMINISTRATION
Department of Health & Human
Services
200 Independence Avenue, S.W.
Washington, D.C. 20201

Information: 202/245-0923

INTERNAL REVENUE SERVICE
1111 Constitution Avenue, N.W.
Washington, D.C. 20224

Information: 202/488-3100
Publications: Contact nearest regional office

INTERSTATE COMMERCE
COMMISSION
12th Street & Constitution Avenue,
N.W.
Washington, D.C. 20423

Information: 202/275-7252
Publications: 202/275-7307

MARITIME ADMINISTRATION
Department of Commerce
Washington, D.C. 20230

Information and publications:
202/377-2746

NATIONAL CREDIT UNION
ADMINISTRATION
1776 G Street, N.W.
Washington, D.C. 20456

Information: 202/357-1050
Publications: 202/357-1000

OFFICE OF THE COMPTROLLER
OF THE CURRENCY
409 L'Enfant Plaza East, S.W.
Washington, D.C. 20219

Information and publications:
202/447-1768

RURAL ELECTRIFICATION
ADMINISTRATION
Department of Agriculture
Washington, D.C. 20250

Information: 202/382-1255

SECURITIES AND EXCHANGE
COMMISSION
500 North Capitol Street
Washington, D.C. 20549

Information: 202/272-2650
Publications: 202/523-3761

SMALL BUSINESS ADMINISTRA-
TION

1441 L Street, N.W.
Washington, D.C. 20416

Information and publications:
202/653-6365

URBAN MASS TRANSPORTATION
ADMINISTRATION
400 7th Street, S.W.
Washington, D.C. 20590

Information: 202/426-4043

U.S. COAST GUARD GREAT
LAKES PILOTAGE
9th District Headquarters
Federal Building
Cleveland, Ohio 44199

Information: 216/522-3950

Appendix B

Selected Bibliography

BANK REGULATION

American Bankers Association. *Guide for Audit and Control in the Smaller Bank*. Washington, D.C.: American Bankers Association, 1972.

American Institute of Certified Public Accountants. *Audits of Banks*. New York: American Institute of Certified Public Accountants, 1969.

Bank Administration Institute. *Bank Administration Manual*. Park Ridge, Ill.: Bank Administration Institute, 1974.

———. *BAI Accounting Bulletins*. Park Ridge, Ill.: Bank Administration Institute, (periodic).

Commerce Clearing House, Inc. *Federal Banking Law Reports*. Chicago: Commerce Clearing House, Inc., (weekly).

Coopers & Lybrand. *The Coopers & Lybrand Banker*. New York: Coopers & Lybrand, (periodic).

Deloitte Haskins & Sells. *Financial Information System for Community Banks*. Chicago: Bank Administration Institute, 1976.

Edwards, Franklin R., ed. *Issues in Financial Regulation*. New York: McGraw-Hill Book Co., 1979.

Ernst & Whinney. *Financial Reporting Trends: Banking*. Cleveland: Ernst & Whinney, (annual).

———. *SEC Reporting Form 10-K: Bank Industry Supplement*. Cleveland: Ernst & Whinney, (annual).

Garcia, F. L. *How to Analyze a Bank Statement*. 6th ed. Boston: Bankers Publishing Company, 1979.

Peat, Marwick, Mitchell & Co. *Principles and Presentation: Banking*. New York: Peat, Marwick, Mitchell & Co., (annual).

Price Waterhouse & Co. *Banking Industry Newsletter.* New York: Price Waterhouse & Co., (periodic).

_____. *Coping with Bank Regulation: A Bankers Guide to Effective Compliance Management.* New York: Price Waterhouse & Co., 1980.

_____. *Survey of Financial Reporting and Accounting Developments in the Banking Industry.* New York: Price Waterhouse & Co., (annual).

Savage, John H. *Bank Audits and Examinations.* 2d ed. Boston: Bankers Publishing Company, 1980.

U.S., General Accounting Office. *Comparing Policies and Procedures of the Three Federal Bank Regulatory Agencies.* Washington, D.C.: General Accounting Office, 1979.

_____. *Highlights of a Study of Federal Supervision of State and National Banks.* Washington, D.C.: General Accounting Office, 1977.

_____. *The Federal Deposit Insurance Corporation's Financial Disclosure Regulations Should Be Improved.* Washington, D.C.: General Accounting Office, 1977.

U.S., Office of the Comptroller of the Currency. *National Bank Surveillance System User's Guide.* Washington, D.C.: Office of the Comptroller of the Currency, 1979.

Wood, Oliver G. *Commercial Banking: Practice and Policy.* New York: D. Van Nostrand Company, 1978.

FEDERAL HOME LOAN BANK BOARD

American Institute of Certified Public Accountants. *Audit and Accounting Guide: Savings and Loan Associations.* New York: American Institute of Certified Public Accountants, 1979.

American Savings & Loan Institute. *Savings and Loan Accounting.* Chicago: American Savings & Loan Institute, 1972.

Coopers & Lybrand. *Savings and Loan Letter.* New York: Coopers & Lybrand, (periodic).

Deloitte Haskins & Sells. *Savings & Loan Associations: Illustrative Disclosures for FHLBB Annual Report.* New York: Deloitte Haskins & Sells, 1977.

Ernst & Whinney. *Financial Reporting Trends: Savings & Loan.* Cleveland: Ernst & Whinney, (annual).

Ketz, J. Edward. *Savings & Loan Accounting.* Chicago: The Institute of Financial Education, 1979.

Peat, Marwick, Mitchell & Co. *Principles and Presentation: Savings and Loan.* New York: Peat, Marwick, Mitchell & Co., (annual).

Price Waterhouse & Co. *Survey of Financial Reporting and Accounting and Federal Taxation Developments in the Savings and Loan Industry.* New York: Price Waterhouse & Co., (annual).

U.S., Federal Home Loan Bank Board. *PA Bulletins,* (periodic).

NATIONAL CREDIT UNION ADMINISTRATION

U.S., National Credit Union Administration. *Accounting Manual for Federal Credit Unions.* Washington, D.C.: National Credit Union Administration, 1975.

————. *Statement of Accounting Principles and Standards for Federal Credit Unions.* Washington, D.C.: National Credit Union Administration, 1974.

————. *Supervisory Committee Manual for Federal Credit Unions.* Washington, D.C.: National Credit Union Administration, 1976.

INTERSTATE COMMERCE COMMISSION

Association of American Railroads. *Railway Accounting Rules.* Washington: Association of American Railroads, 1977.

Ernst & Ernst. *Study of Common Carrier Depreciation Rate Practices and Policies.* Cleveland: Ernst & Ernst, 1977.

Ernst & Whinney. *Financial Reporting Trends: Motor Carrier.* Cleveland: Ernst & Whinney, (annual).

Financial Accounting Standards Board. *Discussion Memorandum: Effect of Rate Regulation on Accounting for Regulated Enterprises.* Stamford, Conn.: Financial Accounting Standards Board, 1979.

National Association of Regulatory Utility Commissioners. *Annual Report on Utility Carrier Regulations.* Washington, D.C.: National Association of Regulatory Utility Commissioners.

————. *Public Utility Depreciation Practices.* Washington, D.C.: National Association of Regulatory Utility Commissioners, 1968.

Price Waterhouse & Co. *Trucking Industry Newsletter.* New York: Price Waterhouse & Co., (periodic).

U.S., General Accounting Office. *Problems in Implementing Regulatory Accounting and Costing Systems for Railroads.* Washington, D.C.: General Accounting Office, 1980.

Wyckhoff, D. Daryl, and Maister, David H. *Motor-Carrier Industry.* Lexington, Mass.: Lexington Books, 1977.

FEDERAL COMMUNICATIONS COMMISSION

Deloitte Haskins & Sells. *Public Utilities: Accounting Practices 1978.* New York: Deloitte Haskins & Sells, 1978.

————. *Public Utilities Manual.* New York: Deloitte Haskins & Sells, 1980.

Financial Accounting Standards Board. *Discussion Memorandum: Effect of Rate Regulation on Accounting for Regulated Enterprises.* Stamford, Conn.: Financial Accounting Standards Board, 1979.

National Association of Regulatory Utility Commissioners. *Annual Report on Utility and Carrier Regulations.* Washington, D.C.: National Association of Regulatory Utility Commissioners.

———. *Public Utility Depreciation Practices.* Washington, D.C.: National Association of Regulatory Utility Commissioners, 1968.

———. *Separations Manual.* Washington, D.C.: National Association of Regulatory Utility Commissioners, 1971.

———. *Uniform System of Accounts—Radio Common Carriers.* Washington, D.C.: National Association of Regulatory Utility Commissioners, 1976.

Suelflow, James E. *Public Utility Accounting: Theory and Application.* East Lansing, Mich.: Michigan State University, 1973.

———, & Pomerantz, Lawrence S. *Allowance for Funds Used During Construction.* East Lansing, Mich.: Michigan State University, 1976.

U.S., General Accounting Office. *Outlook Dim for Revised Accounting System Needed for Changing Telephone Industry.* Washington, D.C.: General Accounting Office, 1979.

———. *Actions Needed to Improve the Federal Communication Commission's Financial Disclosure System.* Washington, D.C.: General Accounting Office, 1976.

CIVIL AERONAUTICS BOARD

Deloitte Haskins & Sells. *Airline Industry: Accounting Practices.* New York: Deloitte Haskins & Sells, (annual).

Douglas, George W., and Miller, James C. *Economic Regulation of Domestic Air Transport: Theory and Practice.* Washington, D.C.: Brookings Institution, 1974.

Financial Accounting Standards Board. *Discussion Memorandum: Effect of Rate Regulation on Accounting for Regulated Enterprises.* Stamford, Conn.: Financial Accounting Standards Board, 1979.

O'Connor, William E. *Introduction to Airline Economics.* New York: Praeger Publishers, 1978.

URBAN MASS TRANSPORTATION ADMINISTRATION

U.S., General Accounting Office. *Analysis of the Allocation Formula for Federal Mass Transit Subsidies.* Washington, D.C.: General Accounting Office, 1979.

U.S., Urban Mass Transportation Administration. *Uniform System of Accounts; Records and Reporting System* (3 volumes). Washington, D.C.: Urban Mass Transportation Administration, 1977.

FEDERAL MARITIME COMMISSION & MARITIME ADMINISTRATION

Cheng, Philip C. *Financial Management in the Shipping Industry.* Centerville, Md.: Cornell Maritime Press, Inc., 1979.

FEDERAL ENERGY REGULATORY COMMISSION

Commerce Clearing House, Inc. *Federal Energy Regulatory Commission Reports.* Chicago: Commerce Clearing House, Inc., (periodic).

Coopers & Lybrand. *Federal Petroleum Regulatory Newsletter.* New York: Coopers & Lybrand, (periodic).

Defliese, Philip L. *Changing Accounting Objectives—What About Utilities.* New York: Coopers & Lybrand, 1972.

Deloitte Haskins & Sells. *Public Utilities: Accounting Practices 1978.* New York: Deloitte Haskins & Sells, 1978.

_____. *Public Utilities Manual.* New York: Deloitte Haskins & Sells, 1980.

Financial Accounting Standards Board. *Discussion Memorandum: Effect of Rate Regulation on Accounting for Regulated Enterprises.* Stamford, Conn.: Financial Accounting Standards Board, 1979.

May, Alan. *The Revised Petroleum Accounting Rules.* New York: Coopers & Lybrand, 1980.

National Association of Regulatory Utility Commissioners. *Annual Report on Utility and Carrier Regulations.* Washington, D.C.: National Association of Regulatory Utility Commissioners.

_____. *Electric Utility Cost Allocation Manual.* Washington, D.C.: National Association of Regulatory Utility Commissioners, 1973.

_____. *Interpretations of Uniform Systems of Accounts for Electric, Gas, and Water Utilities.* Washington, D.C.: National Association of Regulatory Utility Commissioners, 1974.

_____. *Public Utility Depreciation Practices.* Washington, D.C.: National Association of Regulatory Utility Commissioners, 1968.

_____. *Uniform System of Accounts—Electric Classes A and B.* Washington, D.C.: National Association of Regulatory Utility Commissioners, 1976.

————. *Uniform System of Accounts—Electric Classes C and D.* Washington, D.C.: National Association of Regulatory Utilities Commissioners, 1976.

————. *Uniform System of Accounts—Gas, Classes A and B.* Washington, D.C.: National Association of Regulatory Utility Commissioners, 1976.

————. *Uniform System of Accounts—Gas, Classes C and D.* Washington, D.C.: National Association of Regulatory Utility Commissioners, 1973.

Peat Marwick Mitchell & Co. *Principles and Presentation: Oil and Gas.* New York: Peat, Marwick, Mitchell & Co., (annual).

Pomeranz, Felix; Cancellieri, Alfred J.; Stevens, Joseph B.; and Savage, James L. *Auditing in the Public Sector: Efficiency, Economy, and Program Results.* Boston: Warren, Gorham & Lamont, 1976.

Price Waterhouse & Co. *Natural Gas Policy Act of 1978.* New York: Price Waterhouse & Co., 1978.

————. *Public Utilities Update.* New York: Price Waterhouse & Co., (periodic).

————. *Survey of Financial Reporting and Accounting Developments in the Petroleum Industry.* New York: Price Waterhouse & Co., (annual).

————. *Survey of Financial Reporting and Accounting Developments in the Public Utility Industry.* New York: Price Waterhouse & Co., (annual).

Salmonson, Roland F., ed. *Public Utility Accounting: Models, Mergers, and Information Systems.* East Lansing, Mich.: Michigan State University, 1971.

Suelflow, James E. *Public Utility Accounting: Theory and Application.* East Lansing, Mich.: Michigan State University, 1973.

———— and Pomerantz, Lawrence S. *Allowance for Funds Used During Construction: Theory and Application.* East Lansing, Mich.: Michigan State University, 1975.

ENERGY INFORMATION ADMINISTRATION

U.S., Energy Information Administration. *Performance Profiles of Major Energy Producers.* Washington, D.C.: Energy Information Administration, 1977.

RURAL ELECTRIFICATION ADMINISTRATION

U.S., Rural Electrification Administration. *REA Bulletins,* (periodic).

PROCUREMENT AGENCIES

American Institute of Certified Public Accountants. *Audits of Government Contractors.* New York: American Institute of Certified Public Accountants, 1975.

Commerce Clearing House, Inc. *Government Contracts Reports.* Chicago: Commerce Clearing House, Inc., (weekly).

Price Waterhouse & Co. *Accounting for Government Contracts: An Introduction.* New York: Price Waterhouse & Co.

———. *Government Contracts Industry Newsletter.* New York: Price Waterhouse & Co., (periodic).

Tierney, Cornelius E. *Federal Grants-in-Aid: Accounting & Auditing Practices.* New York: American Institute of Certified Public Accountants, 1977.

———. *Governmental Auditing.* Chicago: Commerce Clearing House, Inc., 1979.

Touche Ross & Co. *Basic Cost Accounting Considerations in Government Contracting.* New York: Touche Ross & Co., 1978.

U.S., Department of Defense. *Prime Contract Awards.* Washington, D.C.: Department of Defense, (annual).

U.S., General Services Administration. *Procurement by Civilian Executive Agencies.* Washington, D.C.: General Services Administration, (annual).

Wright, Howard W., and Bedingfield, James P. *Government Contract Accounting.* Washington, D.C.: Federal Publications, Inc., 1979.

COST ACCOUNTING STANDARDS BOARD

Allied Council for Technical Advancement. *Regulation of Accounting and Financial Reporting: A Growth Industry and a Growing Problem for Industry.* Washington, D.C.: Machinery and Allied Products Institute, 1975.

Commerce Clearing House, Inc. *Cost Accounting Standards Guide.* Chicago: Commerce Clearing House, Inc., (monthly).

Deloitte Haskins & Sells. *Cost Accounting Standards Board—Summary of Activities.* New York: Deloitte Haskins & Sells, 1980.

Price Waterhouse & Co. *Cost Accounting Standards.* New York: Price Waterhouse & Co., 1976.

Touche Ross & Co. *Basic Cost Accounting Considerations in Government Contracting.* New York: Touche Ross & Co., 1978.

Wright, Howard W., and Bedingfield, James P. *Government Contract Accounting.* Washington, D.C.: Federal Publications, Inc., 1979.

SECURITIES AND EXCHANGE COMMISSION

Abdel-Khalik, A. Rashad, ed. *Government Regulation of Accounting and Information.* Gainesville, Fla.: University Presses of Florida, 1980.

Allied Council for Technical Advancement. *Regulation of Accounting and Financial Reporting: A Growth Industry and a Growing Problem for Industry.* Washington, D.C.: Machinery and Allied Products Institute, 1975.

Arthur Young & Company. *Foreign Corrupt Practices Act of 1977: Toward Compliance with the Accounting Provisions.* New York: Arthur Young & Company, 1979.

Buckley, John W.; Buckley, Marlene H.; and Plank, Tom M. *SEC Accounting.* New York: John Wiley & Sons, 1980.

Buckley, John W., and Weston, J. Fred, eds. *Regulation and the Accounting Profession.* Belmont, Calif.: Lifetime Learning Publications, 1980.

Carmichael, D. R., and Makela, B., eds. *Corporate Financial Reporting: The Benefits and Problems of Disclosure.* New York: American Institute of Certified Public Accountants, 1976.

Chatov, Robert. *Corporate Financial Reporting: Public or Private Control.* New York: Free Press Division of Macmillan Publishing Co., 1975.

Commerce Clearing House, Inc. *Accounting Series Releases and Staff Accounting Bulletins.* Chicago: Commerce Clearing House, Inc. 1980.

_____. *SEC Accounting Rules.* Chicago: Commerce Clearing House, Inc., (periodic).

Ernst & Whinney. *SEC Reporting Form 10-K.* Cleveland: Ernst & Whinney, (annual).

_____. *SEC Reporting Form 10-K: Bank Industry Supplement.* Cleveland: Ernst & Whinney, (annual).

Hill and Knowlton, Inc. *The SEC, the Securities Markets, and Your Financial Communications.* New York: Hill and Knowlton, Inc., 1979.

Kellogg, Howard L. *Accountants SEC Practice Manual.* Chicago: Commerce Clearing House, Inc., 1971.

Kripke, Homer. *The SEC and Corporate Disclosure: Regulation in Search of a Purpose.* New York: Law & Business, Inc., 1979.

Merino, Barbara D., ed. *The Impact of Regulation upon Accounting Theory.* New York: Academy of Accounting Historians and Vincent C. Ross Institute of Accounting Research, New York University, 1978.

Poloway, Morton, and Charles, Dane. *Accountants SEC Practice Manual.* Chicago: Commerce Clearing House, Inc., (monthly).

Rappaport, Louis H. *SEC Accounting Practice and Procedure.* 3rd ed. New York: Ronald Press Company, 1972.

Skousen, K. Fred. *An Introduction to the SEC.* 2d ed. Cincinnati: South-Western Publishing Co., 1980.

Thomas, Eliot B. *Federal Securities Act Handbook.* Philadelphia: Joint Committee in Continuing Legal Education of the American Law Institute and the American Bar Association, 1969.

Touche Ross & Co. *The Touche Ross Guide to Filing the 1980 10-K under the SEC's Integrated Disclosure System.* Chicago: Commerce Clearing House, Inc., 1980.

————. *The SEC's Integrated Disclosure System.* Chicago: Commerce Clearing House, Inc., 1980.

U.S., Securities Exchange Commission. *Accounting Series Releases.* Washington, D.C.: Securities Exchange Commission, (periodic).

————. *Staff Accounting Bulletins.* Washington, D.C.: Securities Exchange Commission, (periodic).

Weinstein, Stanley. *SEC Compliance.* Englewood Cliffs, N.J.: Prentice-Hall, Inc., 1976.

Wiesen, Jeremy. *Commission on Auditors' Responsibilities No. 2: Securities Acts and Independent Auditors: What Did Congress Intend.* New York: American Institute of Certified Public Accountants, 1978.

INTERNAL REVENUE SERVICE

Allied Council for Technical Advancement. *Regulation of Accounting and Financial Reporting: A Growth Industry and a Growing Problem for Industry.* Washington, D.C.: Machinery and Allied Products Institute, 1975.

Commerce Clearing House, Inc. *U.S. Master Tax Guide.* Chicago: Commerce Clearing House, Inc., (annual)

————. *Federal Tax Guide.* Chicago: Commerce Clearing House, Inc., (weekly).

Prentice-Hall, Inc. *Federal Tax Handbook.* Englewood Cliffs, N.J.: Prentice-Hall, Inc., (annual).

————. *Prentice-Hall Federal Taxes.* Englewood Cliffs, N.J.: Prentice-Hall, Inc., (weekly).

Ture, Norman B., and Sanden, B. Kenneth. *The Effects of Tax Policy on Capital Formation.* New York: Financial Executives Research Foundation, 1977.

SMALL BUSINESS ADMINISTRATION

American Institute of Certified Public Accountants. *Audits of Investment Companies.* New York: American Institute of Certified Public Accountants, 1973.

Deloitte Haskins & Sells. *Small Business Investment Companies: Accounting Practices 1978.* New York: Deloitte Haskins & Sells, 1979.

HEALTH CARE FINANCING ADMINISTRATION

American Institute of Certified Public Accountants. *Hospital Audit Guide.* New York: American Institute of Certified Public Accountants, 1972.
_____. *Medicare Audit Guide.* New York: American Institute of Certified Public Accountants, 1969.
Coopers & Lybrand. *A Layman's Guide to Hospitals I—An Introduction to Health Care Organization, Management and Finance.* New York: Coopers & Lybrand, 1974.
_____. *A Layman's Guide to Hospitals II—An Introduction to Finance and Economics.* New York: Coopers & Lybrand, 1978.
Deloitte Haskins & Sells. *Topics in Health Care Financing: Uniform Reporting.* Germantown, Md.: Aspen Systems Corporation, 1979.
Financial Accounting Standards Board. *Discussion Memorandum: Effect of Rate Regulation on Accounting for Regulated Enterprises.* Stamford, Conn.: Financial Accounting Standards Board, 1979.
Gordon, Richard S. *Health Care Regulation.* New York: McGraw-Hill Book Co., 1979.
Price Waterhouse & Co. *Hospital and Medical Services Industry Newsletter.* New York: Price Waterhouse & Co., (periodic).
_____. *Survey of Financial Reporting and Accounting Developments in the Hospital Industry.* New York: Price Waterhouse & Co., (annual).
Seawell, L. Vann. *Hospital Financial Accounting Theory and Practice.* Chicago: Hospital Financial Management Association, 1975.
_____. *Introduction to Hospital Accounting.* rev. ed. Chicago: Hospital Financial Management Association, 1977.
Silvers, John Byron, and Prahalad, C. K. *Financial Management of Health Institutions.* New York: Spectrum Publications, 1974.
Touche Ross & Co. *Annual Review of Hospital Operations.* New York: Touche Ross & Co., (annual).
U.S., General Accounting Office. *Health Management Organizations Can Help Control Health Care Costs.* Washington, D.C.: General Accounting Office, 1980.
_____. *Rising Hospital Costs Can Be Restrained by Regulating Payments and Improving Management.* Washington, D.C.: General Accounting Office, 1980.

FEDERAL TRADE COMMISSION

Allied Council for Technical Advancement. *Regulation of Accounting and Financial Reporting: A Growth Industry and a Growing Problem for Industry*. Washington, D.C.: Machinery and Allied Products Institute, 1975.

U.S., Federal Trade Commission. *Annual Line of Business Report*. Washington, D.C.: Federal Trade Commission.

————. *Quarterly Financial Report*. Washington, D.C.: Federal Trade Commission.

FEDERAL ELECTION COMMISSION

American Institute of Certified Public Accountants. *Compliance with Federal Election Campaign Requirements*. 2d ed. revised. New York: American Institute of Certified Public Accountants, 1978.

Arthur Andersen & Co. *Audit Criteria for Federal Political Campaigns*. Chicago: Arthur Andersen & Co., 1974.

Commerce Clearing House, Inc. *Federal Election Campaign Financing Guide*. Chicago: Commerce Clearing House, Inc., 1981.

Price Waterhouse & Co. *The New Federal Election Law*. New York: Price Waterhouse & Co.

U.S., Federal Elections Commission. *Bookkeeping and Reporting Manual for Candidates and Political Committees*. Washington, D.C.: Federal Elections Commission, 1978.

GENERAL ACCOUNTING OFFICE

American Institute of Certified Public Accountants. *Auditing Standards Established by the GAO: Their Meaning and Significance*. New York: American Institute of Certified Public Accountants, 1973.

Cancellieri, Alfred, and Enstrom, Darryl. *The Expanded Scope of Governmental Auditing*. New York: Coopers & Lybrand, 1976.

Commerce Clearing House, Inc. *Federal Audit Guides*. Chicago: Commerce Clearing House, Inc., 1981.

Hoffman, Robert D., and Tierney, Cornelius E. *Federal Financial Management: Accounting & Auditing Practices*. New York: American Institute of Certified Public Accountants, 1976.

Kloman, Erasums H. *Cases in Accountability: The Work of the GAO*. Boulder, Colo.: Westview Press, 1979.

Mosher, Frederick C. *The GAO: The Quest for Accountability in American Government*. Boulder, Colo.: Westview Press, 1979.

Pois, Joseph. *Watchdog on the Potomac: A Study of the Comptroller General of the United States*. Washington, D.C.: University Press of America, 1979.

Smith, Darrell H. *The General Accounting Office: Its History, Activities and Organization.* New York: AMS Press, 1974.

Tierney, Cornelius E. *Governmental Auditing.* Chicago: Commerce Clearing House, Inc., 1979.

————. *Federal Grants-in-Aid: Accounting & Auditing Practices.* New York: American Institute of Certified Public Accountants, 1977.

U.S., General Accounting Office. *Accounting Principles and Standards for Federal Agencies.* Washington, D.C.: General Accounting Office, 1978.

————. *An Examination of Accounting Principles and Standards for Federal Agencies (Title II),* 1980.

————. *Frequently Asked Questions about Accrual Accounting in the Federal Government,* 1970.

————. *Guidelines for Financial and Compliance Audits of Federally Assisted Programs,* 1978.

————. *Monthly List of GAO Reports.*

Index

107255